D1208698

THE HANDBOOK OF COLLEGE ATHLETICS AND RECREATION ADMINISTRATION

THE HANDBOOK OF COLLEGE ATHLETICS AND RECREATION ADMINISTRATION

George S. McClellan, Chris King, and
Donald L. Rockey, Jr.

JOSSEY-BASS
A Wiley Imprint
www.josseybass.com

Published by Jossey-Bass
A Wiley Imprint
One Montgomery Street, Suite 1200, San Francisco, CA 94104-4594—www.josseybass.com

Jossey-Bass books and products are available through most bookstores. To contact Jossey-Bass directly call our Customer Care Department within the U.S. at 800-956-7739, outside the U.S. at 317-572-3986, or fax 317-572-4002.

Wiley also publishes its books in a variety of electronic formats and by print-on-demand. Some material included with standard print versions of this book may not be included in e-books or in print-on-demand. If the version of this book that you purchased references media such as CD or DVD that was not included in your purchase, you may download this material at http://booksupport.wiley.com. For more information about Wiley products, visit www.wiley.com.

Library of Congress Cataloging-in-Publication Data

McClellan, George S.

The handbook of college athletics and recreation administration / George S. McClellan, Chris King, Donald L. Rockey, Jr. – First edition.

pages cm. – (The Jossey-Bass higher and adult education series)

Includes bibliographical references and index.

ISBN 978-0-470-87726-5

ISBN 978-1-118-22098-6 (pdf) – ISBN 978-1-118-23474-7 (epub) – ISBN 978-1-118-25935-1 (mobipocket)

1. College sports–United States–Management–Handbooks, manuals, etc. 2. Recreation centers–United States–Management Handbooks, manuals, etc. 3. Sports administration–United States–Handbooks, manuals, etc. 4. College sports–United States–Finance. I. King, Chris, 1972 July 23– II. Rockey, Donald L., Jr., 1969– III. Title.

GV351.M377 2012

796.04′30973–dc23

2012016815

Printed in the United States of America

FIRST EDITION

PB Printing 10 9 8 7 6 5 4 3 2 1

THE JOSSEY-BASS HIGHER AND ADULT EDUCATION SERIES

CONTENTS

FIGURES AND TABLES

Figures

Tables

PREFACE

The *Handbook of College Athletics and Recreation Administration (HCARA)* is intended to serve as an authoritative, comprehensive, practical, and informative resource for undergraduate or graduate students in a formal program of study in intercollegiate athletics and college recreation and for those who are helping prepare those students. *HCARA* is also intended to serve as a resource for professionals changing roles within the field or coming into the field from another career area.

The book is organized in three parts:

1. Foundations
2. Skills
3. Issues

The authors contributing chapters to *HCARA* are among the leading names in intercollegiate athletics and recreation and represent a rich blend of practitioners, scholars, and scholar-practitioners. As a group they draw on their work in a wide variety of institutional settings and professional roles. Both their personal diversity and diversity of theoretical perspectives reflect that of college recreation and athletics.

The chapters in *HCARA* present theories and models of practice, cite classical and contemporary literature for support, and highlight issues in the contemporary professional administration of intercollegiate athletics and recreation. Each chapter includes a list of key points that can serve as either a study guide or executive summary, and case studies are shared throughout Part One and Part Two to provide opportunities to apply the information about professional foundations and skills to professional practice.

In addition to the main themes of the book, a great deal of effort has gone into assuring that the content of *HCARA* addresses both college athletics and recreation in a variety of institutional types, sizes, and athletics associations. The reader will also find that while topics such as ethics, diversity, and the law each have their own chapter, these issues are also woven throughout *HCARA* as essential considerations in all aspects of professional practice.

Audience

HCARA is presented to meet the needs of undergraduate or graduate students in courses or programs on intercollegiate athletics and recreation administration and to faculty members for those courses or programs. It is also intended to serve as a useful professional resource for entry-, mid-, or senior-level professionals in the field. Individuals entering into college recreation or athletics from another area or who are entering a new facet of recreation or athletics should find *HCARA* to be a helpful tool in their transition as well.

ACKNOWLEDGMENTS

The *Handbook of College Athletics and Recreation (HCARA)* represents the collective efforts of a host of people who have contributed in a variety of ways. Each of those contributors has been in turn supported in a variety of ways by their own network of colleagues, friends, and family. We would like to take this opportunity to thank our contributors and their supporters, who provided invaluable support to us throughout our work on this project.

The idea for this handbook originated with Dr. Dudley B. Woodard, Jr., a faculty member in Higher Education at the University of Arizona (U of A) who, in addition to his many other forms of service to that institution, for years served as the Faculty Athletics Representative. Nearing his retirement, Dr. Woodard decided not to pursue the book project. Several years later George McClellan, a doctoral student at U of A and Dr. Woodard's graduate assistant at the time the project was originally discussed, took the idea up again with the editorial staff of Jossey-Bass. Over a decade after the idea was initially proposed it has come to fruition in the form of this book. We are grateful to Dr. Woodard for inspiring this project.

We are particularly grateful to the authors who have contributed or co-contributed chapters to *HCARA*. Our goal was to attract a diverse and talented pool of practitioners and scholars to this project. A review of the experience and reputation of our authors shows them to be just such a group.

We also appreciate the work of our colleagues on the editorial staff at Jossey-Bass. Erin Null, Alison Knowles, and David Brightman make a terrific team, and we are fortunate to have had their advice and counsel throughout our work on *HCARA*.

◆ ◆ ◆

George S. McClellan. Thanks to Chris and Don, my co-editors for this project. Working with them has been educational, enjoyable, and entertaining. What more could one ask for from one's partners? I am also grateful to my colleagues and friends at Indiana University–Purdue University Fort Wayne (IPFW) for their collaboration and encouragement. I especially appreciate the support I receive for my scholarly endeavors from Chancellor Michael Wartell. I am deeply indebted to my friend and mentor Peggy Barr for her advice, cheer, and high standards. Most important, I thank the students I have been fortunate enough to serve throughout my career. They inspire me, particularly the student-athletes whose achievements in the classroom, in the community, and on the field are truly remarkable.

Chris King. I would like to thank my co-editors George and Don for the opportunity to be part of a collaborative effort that has been built upon the contributions of successful educators and practitioners in higher education. I also thank the late Dr. Susan Hofacre, Dr. Dave Synokwa, and Tom Olson, who were great teachers and role models at Robert Morris College (now Robert Morris University). They were vested in my development as an undergraduate student and made sure that I graduated with practical experience in the college sports industry. I am grateful to have worked for, with, and alongside a number of great coaches, colleagues, faculty, and university administrators in my career. I owe a deep debt of gratitude to the staff and coaches at Campbell University, Liberty University, the University of Central Florida, University of Alabama, and currently the University of Texas–Pan American. I would particularly like to thank my athletic director mentors and teachers: Tom Collins, Kim Graham, Steve Sloan, and Mal Moore, who provided me with the necessary skills, guidance, and professional development to become an athletic director. Most important, I would like to thank my wife Alica for her understanding of the time invested in this project, support through the transition to the University of

Texas–Pan American, and the wonderful gift of our first-born child, Kylie Marie.

Donald L. Rockey, Jr. I would like to express my sincerest appreciation to George McClellan, who invited me to work on this project. This is the third project we have worked on together, and each time has been a valuable learning experience. George's guidance and mentoring have been greatly appreciated. I would also like to thank Chris King, who keeps my faculty mentality well grounded and humble. I am grateful to all the faculty members who provided guidance and leadership through my college years. While the list of names is lengthy, I particularly wish to acknowledge Dr. Kim Beason, Dr. Jim Gilbert, Dr. Judith Cole, and Dr. Linda Chitwood. Finally, I would like to thank my wife Christine Rockey for all her support and patience as I worked on this project.

◆ ◆ ◆

The readers will have the ultimate say in whether or not we have achieved our goals for *HCARA*. To whatever extent that is the case, the credit goes to all our contributors and supporters. Wherever there is a sense that the goals have not been fully realized, the responsibility is ours.

THE AUTHORS

Robertha Abney is an associate professor at Slippery Rock University in the Department of Sport Management and previously served as associate athletic director and senior women administrator at that institution. She teaches undergraduate and graduate courses in sport management and ethics, sport communication, and introduction to sport management. Her areas of research include role models and mentoring women in sport (WoMentoring), and the status of minorities and women in leadership roles in sport. Abney has written several chapters in sport management textbooks. She is a board member on the Commission on Sport Management Accreditation and has served on six committees within the National Collegiate Athletic Association. She is a past president of the National Association for Girls and Women in Sport.

Robert J. Barcelona is an assistant professor in the Youth Development Leadership program and the Department of Parks, Recreation, and Tourism Management at Clemson University. He has worked with numerous recreation and sport organizations in both programming and research efforts and is a member of the Society of Park and Recreation Educators' Board of Directors. Barcelona has won teaching excellence awards at both Indiana University and the University of New Hampshire, and he received a special citation award from the New Hampshire Recreation and Parks Association for his work with youth sports and coaching education. His research on sport and recreation management has been published in refereed journals, trade magazines, and textbook chapters. Dr. Barcelona is also co-author, along with Amy Hurd and John Meldrum, of *Leisure Services Management.*

Valerie M. Bonnette is president and founder of Good Sports, Inc., Title IX and Gender Equity Specialists, a consulting firm assisting colleges, universities, and secondary schools in complying with the athletics provisions of Title IX (www.titleixspecialists.com). She is the author of "Title IX and Intercollegiate Athletics: How It All Works—In Plain English," a self-evaluation manual and desk reference for colleges and universities. Prior to founding Good Sports, Inc., in 1994, Bonnette was a senior program analyst for 15 years in the Washington, D.C., headquarters office of the Office for Civil Rights, United States Department of Education. She coauthored OCR's 1990 Title IX Athletics Investigator's Manual, trained OCR attorneys and staff on Title IX athletics policy, and provided technical assistance to educational institutions.

Scott Branvold is a professor of Sport Management and the internship coordinator in the Marketing Department at Robert Morris University. He also serves as the institution's Faculty Athletics Representative. Branvold has 26 years of college teaching experience in sport management programs at both the undergraduate and graduate levels at Robert Morris and the University of Oklahoma. He has taught Sport Marketing, Sport Sociology, Legal Issues in Sport, and other sport management courses. Branvold is the coauthor of *Sports Public Relations: Managing Organizational Communication* (2006) with G. Clayton Stoldt and Stephen Dittmore, and he has published articles in both the *Journal of Sport Management* and the *Sport Marketing Journal.* He has presented papers at various conferences including the North American Society for Sport Management, the Sport Marketing Association, the American Alliance for Health, Physical Education, Recreation, and Dance, and the International Sports Business Conference.

Walter Brock began his duties at Conference USA as assistant director of Sport Services in September 2008. Before joining Conference USA, he was the assistant director of Athletics at the University of New Haven.

Michael L. Buckner is a licensed attorney and private investigator who specializes in advising organizations on athletics compliance, investigation, and ethics issues. Mr. Buckner represents academic institutions before all NCAA committees, including colleges and universities in the enforcement process. As an independent consultant for the NCAA (2006–07), he conducted on-site investigative audits of nontraditional and preparatory schools in the United States and Puerto Rico. He is the author of two books, *Athletics Investigation Handbook: A Guide for Institutions and Involved Parties During the NCAA Enforcement Process* and *The ABCs of Ethics: A Resource for Leaders, Managers, and Professionals.* Mr. Buckner is admitted to practice before the United States Supreme Court, the United States Court of Appeals for the Eleventh Circuit, and all federal and state courts in Florida.

Scott Bukstein is a faculty member at the University of Central Florida (UCF). In addition to teaching undergraduate and graduate sport business and sport law courses, he is the program coordinator of the undergraduate Sport Business Management Program at UCF. Bukstein's research focus is on leadership and diversity issues in sport, the perceptions and academic performance of college student-athletes, and the intersection of sport and the law. He is a former corporate law attorney.

Timothy D. DeSchriver is an associate professor of Sport Management in the Department of Business Administration, Alfred Lerner College of Business and Economics at the University of Delaware. Dr. DeSchriver instructs undergraduate and graduate courses in sport finance, sport economics, and sport marketing. He is the coauthor of *Sport Finance* (1st and 2nd eds.) along with Gil Fried and Steve Shapiro; and has published research articles in journals such as the *Journal of Sport Management, Sport Management Review, Sport Marketing Quarterly,* and the *Eastern Economic Journal.* Dr. DeSchriver serves on the editorial boards of the *Journal of Sport Management,* the *International Journal of Sport Finance,* and *Sport Marketing Quarterly.* He has also made numerous professional presentations at international sport management conferences including presentations in South Korea, Turkey, and Thailand.

John H. Dunkle is the executive director of the Counseling and Psychological Services at Northwestern University. He is a frequent presenter on issues related to addressing the mental health needs of college students. Dunkle's written work includes serving as editor of *Dealing with the Behavioral and Psychological Problems of Students: A Contemporary Update* (New Directions in Student Services no. 128), coauthor of "Helping Students with Health and Wellness Issues," a chapter in the *Handbook for Student Affairs Administration* (3rd ed.), and author or coauthor of numerous other articles.

Joy Gaston Gayles is an associate professor of higher education administration at North Carolina State University. Her research focuses on the college student experience and diversity issues in higher education, most notably for intercollegiate student-athletes. In 2007 she was named an Emerging Scholar for the American College Personnel Association (ACPA).

James E. Greenwell is the executive senior associate director of Athletics for Georgia State Athletics. He formerly served as senior associate director of Athletics for Facilities, Operations and Events at the University of Maryland and as the assistant AD for Facilities and Operations at the University of Central Florida.

Bill Hogan is the director of Athletics at Seattle University. He has served as an NCAA director of Athletics for 30 years, including 10 years at Saint Joseph's College (IN) and the University of San Francisco (USF) for 15 years. He was selected as the NACDA West Regional Athletic Director of the Year and was a tenured associate professor of Business Administration at Saint Joseph's College (IN) while serving as head men's basketball coach and director of athletics. While serving as the director of athletics at USF and Seattle, Hogan also taught undergraduate Business classes in Marketing and Management and Sports Administration.

Mary F. Howard-Hamilton is a professor of Higher Education in the Department of Educational Leadership at Indiana State University. Her areas of research are multicultural identity development and diversity issues in higher education. She has been presented with numerous awards, most notably the University of Iowa Al Hood Outstanding Alumni Award and the Robert Shaffer Award for Excellence as a Graduate Faculty Member.

C. Keith Harrison is an associate professor of Sport Business Management in the College of Business Administration and is also the associate director of the Institute for Diversity and Ethics in Sport at the University of Central Florida. He is also founder and director of the Paul Robeson Research Center for Academic and Athletic Prowess. Harrison has held faculty positions at Washington State University, the University of Michigan, and Arizona State University. He has published numerous peer-review journal articles and book chapters on intercollegiate athletics, diversity in sport, and representations of athletes in mass media.

Carrie A. Jaworski the director of the Division of Primary Care Sports Medicine and Primary Care Sports Medicine Fellowship director. She is an assistant clinical professor in the Department of Family Medicine at the University of Chicago's Pritzker School of Medicine, NorthShore University HealthSystem and serves as a Board of Trustee Member for the American College of Sports Medicine.

Edgar N. Johnson is an associate professor of Sport Management in the Department of Business Administration, Alfred Lerner College of Business and Economics at the University of Delaware. Mr. Johnson was the director of athletics at the University of Delaware for twenty-five years and director of athletics and recreation services for the last eleven years of his administrative career. He has served on the NCAA Transition Management Council and on the NCAA Management Council (1996–2001). He has also served on numerous conference committees in both the America East and Colonial Athletic Association along with holding several conference leadership positions. He instructs courses in Sport Law and Finance at the undergraduate level.

Chris King serves as the director of intercollegiate athletics at the University of Texas–Pan American. He has also worked in intercollegiate athletics at the University of Alabama, University of Central Florida, Liberty University, and Campbell University. King authored a chapter on developing gambling action teams and coauthored (along with Don Rockey) a chapter on sports wagering in *Ahead of the Game: Understanding and Addressing College Gambling*. He also served as a member of the Harvard University Division on Addiction's Task Force on College Gambling Policies.

Heather J. Lawrence is an associate professor of Sports Administration and director of the Professional Master of Sports Administration program at Ohio University. She also holds a visiting professor appointment at Instituto de Empressa Business School in Madrid, Spain. Prior to beginning her academic career, Lawrence worked in various administrative positions within intercollegiate athletics. She is co-editor of *Event Management Blueprint: Creating and Managing Successful Sports Events* and has published in the areas of the student-athlete recruiting experience, luxury suite ownership in professional sport, and sport facility management.

George S. McClellan is the vice-chancellor for student affairs at Indiana University–Purdue University Fort Wayne (IPFW). Before coming to IPFW he was vice-president for student development at Dickinson State University and served students in a variety of roles at the University of Arizona and Northwestern University. He is the author, coauthor, and co-editor of numerous books, book chapters, monographs, and articles related to various topics in student affairs. Most recently McClellan coauthored *Budgets and Financial Management in Higher Education* (2011) with Margaret Barr, co-edited *Ahead of the Game: Understanding and Addressing College Gambling* (2006) with Thomas Hardy and Jim Caswell, co-edited *Serving Native American Students in Higher Education* with MaryJo Tippeconic Fox and Shelly Lowe (2005), and co-edited the *Handbook of Student Affairs Administration* (3rd ed., 2009) with Jeremy Stringer. McClellan was recently honored as a Pillar of the Profession by the National Association of Student Personnel Administrators Foundation.

Colleen A. McGlone is associate professor of Recreation and Sport Management at Coastal Carolina University. Her areas of research involve hazing in collegiate athletics, legal aspects of hazing including institutional liability, and organizational culture and leadership in sport environments. McGlone serves on the board of directors for the National Sport and Recreation Law Association.

Barbara Osborne is an associate professor of Sports Administration at the University of North Carolina. Prior to becoming a faculty member she held a variety of administrative roles in intercollegiate athletics, including service as the senior woman administrator and associate athletics director at Brandeis University. Osborne is the author of numerous chapters and articles legal issues in sports. She is admitted to practice law by both the North Carolina and Massachusetts Bar Associations.

Stephen Rey is the director of intramural-recreational sports and an adjunct faculty member of Kinesiology, Recreation, and Sport at Western Kentucky University (WKU). Prior to arriving at the WKU campus, he served as the associate director of recreational sports and an instructor in the School of Human Performance and Recreation at the University of Southern Mississippi. Rey has 30 years of experience in recreational sports and is a registered collegiate recreational sports professional.

B. David Ridpath is an Assistant Professor of Sport Administration at Ohio University in the College of Business. Ridpath has several years of practical experience in the sports industry and teaches classes in marketing, sponsorship, risk management, sports law, issues in intercollegiate athletics, and other areas. He serves as faculty advisor and associate general manager of the Southern Ohio Copperheads, a summer collegiate wooden bat baseball team that is a main experiential learning laboratory for graduate and undergraduate sports administration and sports management students and is entirely student run. Ridpath previously served at Ohio University as assistant wrestling coach from 1994 to 1995. Prior to returning to Ohio University, Ridpath spent two years directing the graduate sports administration program at Mississippi State University and over a decade working in intercollegiate athletic administration and higher education at Marshall University and Weber State University. He has over 30 national and international refereed presentations and a dozen peer reviewed academic articles in print, three published academic book chapters, and writings and editorials featured in the NCAA News, Sports Business Journal, and Legal Issues in College Athletics.

Donald L. Rockey, Jr. is an associate professor in the Recreation and Sport Management Program at Coastal Carolina University (CCU). For the past 17 years, in addition to teaching recreation courses at CCU, he has taught at the University of Mississippi, Missouri Western State College, Texas State University, and Shepherd College. Rockey has conducted research in college student gambling, fantasy sport participation, and tourism. He has presented 34 papers at national and international conferences and has nine publications in professional journals. Rockey also collaborated with Chris King in writing a chapter entitled "Sport Wagering" for *Ahead of the Game: Understanding and Addressing College Gambling.*

David A. Shor is assistant director for clinical services of the Counseling and Psychological Services at Northwestern University. Dr. Shor also serves as liaison and mental health consultant to Northwestern's Department of Athletics and Recreation.

Jeremy Stringer is founder and director of the master's program in Student Development Administration at Seattle University. He has served as a vice-president for student development, associate provost, dean of students on board the Semester at Sea, chief housing officer, and department chair for several academic programs. Athletics and recreation are two areas that have reported to him during his career. Along with George McClellan he is co-editor of the *Handbook of Student Affairs Administration* (3rd ed.). He was in the inaugural class of the NASPA Faculty Fellows and served as chair of the Faculty Fellows for two years.

David P. Synowka serves as director of Sport Management and professor of Sport Management at Robert Morris University. He has been at Robert Morris University for over 32 years as a part of both the Sport Management and the NCAA Division I Athletics programs. Synowka has also served as a visiting professor and acting chair for the Sports Medicine Education Program at West Chester University and as an assistant professor of sport medicine in the Graduate School of Health and Physical Education at the University of Pittsburgh.

John R. Thelin is University Research Professor at the University of Kentucky. Prior to joining the University of Kentucky in 1996, he was Chancellor Professor at The College of William & Mary in Virginia and professor at Indiana University. He is a member of the NCAA's research advisory board and was an invited speaker at the Knight Commission on the Future of College Sports hearings in 1990 and in 2009. He is the author of *Games Colleges Play* and *A History of American Higher Education*, both published by The Johns Hopkins University Press. An alumnus of Brown University, he concentrated in history, was elected to Phi Beta Kappa, and was a letterman on the varsity wrestling team. In 2006 the Ivy League selected John for its 50th anniversary celebration of outstanding scholar-athletes.

Michael A. Wartell serves as chancellor of Indiana University–Purdue University Fort Wayne (IPFW). Prior to taking on that role in 1994, he was the vice-chancellor for academic affairs. In addition to his service at IPFW, Wartell's academic career includes serving as a faculty member and department chair in chemistry at Metropolitan State College in Denver, dean of the School of Natural Sciences and Mathematics at Slippery Rock University, dean of the College of Letters and Sciences at James Madison University, and provost and vice-president for academic affairs at Humboldt State University. His professional experience also includes being a department manager for Sandia National Laboratories. Wartell is a member of the U.S. Army Science Board and a recipient of the State of Indiana's Sagamore of the Wabash honor.

David F. Wolf has been involved in higher education fundraising and development for more than twelve years. Wolf currently serves as executive director for the Office of Planned and Major Gifts at UCLA. He has previously served as vice-president for advancement at the University of Southern Mississippi, assistant vice-president and director of Athletic Development at the University of Alabama, vice-president for development at Cameron University, and director of Development at the University of Texas at Arlington. Prior to working in university development, Wolf worked in the cable television advertising industry.

THE HANDBOOK OF COLLEGE ATHLETICS AND RECREATION ADMINISTRATION

PART ONE

FOUNDATIONS

Higher education can be a complex and challenging field in which to work, and the administration of college athletics and recreation in higher education is an important role on many college campuses. The complexity, challenge, and importance, coupled with a rapidly and ever-changing environment, requires intercollegiate athletics and recreation professionals to be quick learners and adaptive managers. While theirs is a dynamic arena in which to serve, these administrators can draw from a substantial and stable foundation of history, theory, ethics, law, and governance to inform their practice. Part One focuses on these elements in that foundation.

The first two chapters provide a historical overview. In Chapter One, John Thelin traces intercollegiate athletics from its origins at Harvard to its contemporary expression in the 21st century. Drawing on historical, cultural, and sociological perspectives, he thoughtfully points out how the uniquely American model of intercollegiate athletics emerged and evolved. Donald Rockey and Robert Barcelona provide a similar overview for the history of fitness and recreation in Chapter Two. They clearly describe the origins and development of the various elements of collegiate recreation, including physical education departments, organized recreation programs, open exercise and recreation opportunities, outdoor recreation programs, and wellness education.

In Chapters Three and Four, the authors expertly take abstract constructs and demonstrate to the reader their tangible applications. Mary Howard-Hamilton and Joy Gaston Gayles discuss a variety of bodies and models of theories that inform campus recreation and intercollegiate athletics administration. Issues in campus recreation and intercollegiate ethics are addressed by Michael Buckner within the broad framework of every day ethics.

Legal principles and precedent also provide a foundational framework for the administration of college athletics and recreation. While there is no substitute for sage legal counsel, it is helpful and important for practitioners to have an understanding of the law as it relates to their work. Barbara Osborne offers a thorough and practical discussion of important relevant topics in the law in Chapter Five. Gender equity is a critically important legal topic in intercollegiate athletics and recreation, and Title IX is at the heart of the law in this area. Valerie Bonnette's work in Chapter Six highlights both the letter and spirit of Title IX while also offering useful insights on evaluating and assuring compliance.

Governance is an essential element of the organizational framework in which intercollegiate athletics and campus recreation take place at the institution as well as throughout the nation. In Chapter Seven David Ridpath and Robertha Abney provide a description of the elements of governance from faculty senates to athletics associations.

CHAPTER ONE

COLLEGE ATHLETICS

Continuity and Change Over Four Centuries

John R. Thelin

Intercollegiate athletics at American colleges and universities date back to the 19th century, and they have grown to become an integral part of American society. An "All American" refers to a student-athlete selected as one of the best *collegiate* players in the nation. The award does not extend to a professional athlete in the National Football League, Major League Baseball, or the National Basketball Association. Furthermore, the United States is the only nation that has relied on intercollegiate athletics as a primary source of highly talented athletes to fill Olympic teams in a wide array of sports, as well as to prepare players for professional teams in football, basketball, and baseball. These traditions and practices reinforce the distinct identity of intercollegiate athletics in our American popular culture (Michener, 1976).

This chapter offers an historical narrative of the evolution and growth of college sports as a distinctive, even peculiar, American institution. The chapter addresses four eras in college sports: its 19th-century roots within the American campus; its growth during the first several decades of the 20th century; its prosperity and problems following World War II; and its standing as a high-stakes enterprise on many campuses in the early years of the 21st century.

Origins of College Sports: 19th-Century Roots

Although college sports have a long tradition, their place in higher education was not inevitable. Early faculty resistance to campus sports was born of both religious and educational concerns. To the Protestant denominations who established colonial colleges, the notion of students playing for recreation or enjoyment was antithetical to religious doctrine that emphasized hard work. College presidents, most of whom were also ordained clergy, denounced early student sporting events as frivolous. They argued that if students wanted physical exercise, they could find it by moving rocks and clearing lands on campus (Rudolph, 1962). In addition, any activities outside the established curriculum of the classroom were suspect as not contributing to student learning if not undermining student learning.

Despite faculty objections, students organized their own teams and games with other local college teams. Recognized and sanctioned varsity sports programs were the result of a long campaign by undergraduates to have their athletic contests played between rival colleges be accepted by college administrators as legitimate programs that were part of campus life. The Harvard Athletic Association, founded in 1852, for example, is the oldest formal athletics program in the United States. Old as this is, it lags far behind the founding of Harvard College in 1636.

Another important breakthrough in the early acceptance of intercollegiate athletics came from England, where legend has it that the Duke of Wellington praised the role of school boys playing the game of rugby, exclaiming, "The Battle of Waterloo was won on the playing fields of Eton." Thereafter, playing fields were seen as important preparing grounds for future political and military leaders. Sport competitions between institutions served as tests of the preparation of these leaders. American colleges in the late 19th century relied on the English model of sports and schools to make the case that playing football had educational value for building character and transmitting values (Smith, 1988).

College sports were one of the few activities that were truly intercollegiate, as distinguished from intramural. Starting with boat racing (eventually known as crew and rowing), the two oldest American colleges—Harvard and Yale—entered into spirited regattas that attracted the enthusiastic alumni and students as spectators along the river banks of New England. It also ushered in professionalism and commercialism, as wealthy alumni provided cash incentives to publicize and glorify the competition. Crew was first and foremost but soon was joined by baseball, track and field, rugby, and eventually the rudiments of what we now know as American football (Smith, 1988).

Early 20th Century

The early 20th century saw important developments in intercollegiate athletics. The emergence of football as the major college sport was particularly important. This section discusses football's new prominence, its growth and the consequences of that growth, and the impact it had on the growth of other college sports. It also addresses the nexus between the Olympic movement and college student-athletes.

Football's Rise

By 1880 intercollegiate sports were dominated by what has been called the rise of football (Rudolph, 1962). Originally, the teams were run by and for students. They collected athletics fees from fellow students and arranged for playing fields, practice facilities, and scheduling games against student teams at other colleges. Each season the student who was elected team captain was responsible for organizing practices as well as strategy and decisions during a game. When spectator demand for seating at football games surpassed the size of the campus playing fields, the student teams relocated to large football stadia in such major cities as New York, Philadelphia, Chicago, and Cleveland. Large crowds for games involving Harvard, Princeton, Yale, and Pennsylvania finally helped college football gain revenues from ticket sales (Rudolph, 1962). Later, college football was elevated to a nondenominational religious experience, as pre-game ceremonies included a member of the clergy leading the spectators in prayer (Michener, 1976).

Media Coverage and Popular Interest. College sports also worked into the popular media during this era. Newspapers competed for paying readers. Front page coverage of college football games meant that a new generation of Americans learned how to "read football" according to the new vocabulary of sportswriters (Oriard, 1993). Newspapers devoted coverage for weeks prior to a big game. When printing technology allowed photographs, college football players were featured prominently.

Emergence of the Coach. Changes in media promoted the rise of the great college coach as a national figure. Notre Dame spearheaded this movement, as their successful coach, Knute Rockne, supplemented his on-field coaching duties with endorsements of commercial products, a radio show, a newspaper column, and a lucrative contract as a motivational speaker for the Studebaker Automobile Company whose main factory was nearby in South Bend (Thelin, 1994). Once again there were neither precedents nor restrictions on these enterprises (Smith, 2001).

By 1900 powerful college football teams underwent a change. Control of teams and the game shifted from student players to a new figure—the highly paid coach. At Harvard, for example, in the early 1900s a famous football coach was paid $5,000 per year—second in salary only to the university president and several times more than the highest paid professor earned (Smith, 1988). At the young University of Chicago, founded in 1892, the ambitious president hired a former Yale football star to serve both as football coach and a new position called "athletic director." The coach–athletic director was given tenure as a professor yet was allowed to bypass usual academic budgeting procedures by submitting his financial requests directly to the board of trustees. The University of Chicago Athletics Department became the model of empire building within a campus, as the football coach who also was athletics director was overseer for all sports. The athletics director charged faculty and staff fees to use "his" tennis courts. He developed a recruiting network with high schools across the state by hosting the annual state track and field championships at the University of Chicago stadium. Above all, he successfully courted the industrialists and merchants of the city to be donors and season ticket holders as the university football team came to be the toast of the town (Lester, 1995).

Nationwide and Regional Expansion. College football went from news to publicity with the appearance of Walter Camp's annual selection of the All-American collegiate football squad. Camp, a Yale grad and former football player, used his base in New York City to write a syndicated column, endorse products, and control the All American selection process. Since most of the American population lived on the East Coast, concentrated in the larger cities of New York, Boston, Philadelphia, and Washington, D.C., college football awards had a strong regional bias. In the 1890s and well into the early 1900s Yale was the undisputed long-time football dynamo, followed by Princeton, Harvard, and Pennsylvania. Gradually, the teams from the Midwest at such universities as Chicago and Michigan gained a strong regional following and, grudgingly, some national recognition. The influence of the oldest universities was displayed in the convergence of standardizing football rules and the boom in constructing large football stadia. A number of coaches haggled over the size of the official college football field, some urging it to be a checker board rather than a gridiron. The discussions were moot when in 1904 Harvard built and opened its magnificent Soldiers' Field, a horseshoe shaped stadium whose borders made the Harvard football field narrow. By default, this determined the nationwide dimensions and shape of all college football fields.

An important trend in making intercollegiate sports truly All American was the demographic and geographic spread of top caliber teams. In 1937, *Life* magazine featured a photo essay that proclaimed a new era as college championships moved west—breaking the monopoly of such colleges as Harvard, Princeton, and Yale (Thelin, 1994). Thanks to support from alumni and state legislatures, colleges in California, Washington, Minnesota, Iowa, and Texas now joined the traditional East Coast collegiate powers in gaining national championships and honors. An important, interesting example of this trend is football in the South. Although the southern colleges were latecomers to football, due in part to impoverished state economies, by the late 1920s and 1930s such football teams as Alabama, Georgia, Georgia Tech, Texas Christian University, Southern Methodist University, and North Carolina gained a prominent place in the national rankings compiled by sportswriters and publicized by newspapers nationwide.

Origins of Booster Groups. What had been an informal activity became a renegade pursuit. Eventually presidents, boards, and faculty conceded to student priorities—but in so doing, they attempted to harness varsity sports by placing them under administrative control. Much to the surprise of the presidents, the students' enthusiasm for varsity football found a strong ally among alumni, who had great power as potential donors to their Alma Mater. The result was that at many colleges the sports program veered toward control by an athletics association dominated by recent graduates and alumni donors, with only incidental involvement of the president. College sports were here to stay. The new entity of the athletics association had power to collect revenues, hire and fire coaches, and set budgets and schedules outside the purview of the academic administration.

Origins of the NCAA and Bowls. The spread of college football programs eventually led to concerns about its rules. This involved two areas: first, the rules of the game on the playing field; and, second, the control of athletics program and policies by external bodies. The absence of standardized rules on the field lent itself to injuries and even fatalities. President Theodore Roosevelt, who looked at Sunday newspaper photographs of injured college players and expressed disgust with the brutality, resolved to bring about reform. He invited presidents of numerous universities to the White House to discuss football reforms. This led to the cooperation and creation of what would become the National Collegiate Athletic Association (Lawrence, 1987). The disappointing news was that the presidents of the most prestigious universities—and those with the most powerful football teams. such as Harvard, Yale, and Princeton—chose not to attend. So national regulation was voluntary and, hence, lacked much regulatory power.

Meanwhile, college football's popularity continued spread to colleges large and small across the nation. In metropolitan areas of the West and South, mayors, public audiences, and civic organizations latched on to the trend, as they established elaborate festivals whose parades and celebrations culminated with an end of season bowl game matching two outstanding teams. The original source of this "bowl fever" was the Festival of Roses in Pasadena, California—home of the familiar and still popular "Rose Bowl" game held on New Year's Day. It was no accident that cities in warm weather climates were the host of these New Year's Day college football spectaculars, as their week-long festivities, banquets, and parades attracted tens of thousands guests from college alumni in the cold Midwest. Eventually this practice extended across the nation to the Cotton Bowl in Dallas, the Sugar Bowl in New Orleans, the Orange Bowl in Miami—and even the Bacardi Bowl in warm, albeit distant, Havana, Cuba (Thelin, 1994). University presidents and alumni also capitalized on the events. The message was that intercollegiate football continued to ascend in its widespread appeal to sponsors far beyond the campus. While it may be difficult for readers in the 21st century to imagine, a hundred years ago there were no professional football teams to vie for spectators. College football remained the biggest game in town, whether in New York, Boston, Chicago, or Los Angeles. College football evolved into a source of state pride and for relatively young state universities of the Midwest and the Pacific Coast. Testimony to this state pride and championship football teams was that governors in the Midwest and Pacific Coast regularly attended big games and declared that a victory for the state university was no less than a victory for the entire state (Thelin, 1994).

Regulations and Reforms. The lack of regulation of college sports into the 1920s did not necessarily indicate illegal practices by college coaches, players, and boosters. Rather, it suggested absence of laws rather than disobeying laws (Thelin, 1994). College sports still lacked any strong governing body apart from the voluntary association of conferences. Although the Western Conference, later well known as the Big Ten, provided some measure of faculty oversight to the large universities of the Midwest, it was the exception rather than the rule. Standards for student eligibility to play sports, ground rules for financial aid to student-athletes, and codes of conduct for coaches were either absent or unenforced. Once in a while, as was the case with the Pacific Coast Conference, institutional members became sufficiently upset with the flagrant academic abuses of one member institution that a program might be suspended from conference play. Penalties were rare and conferences had only slight influence on curbing abuses.

One historical example of the lack of regulation, as well as the customs that separate college sports of the 21st century from the teams and programs of the early 20th century, centered on the issue of gambling. Well into the late 1920s neither college coaches nor players considered wagering on college sports to be either wrong or illegal. What was not tolerated as part of the college student-athlete's code was betting that one's own team would *lose* a game. Betting on sports was an accepted American pastime. Only years later would this climate change, with the NCAA penalizing gambling by student-athletes and coaches.

College sports were beyond the control of college and university presidents. Alumni and donors, known as "boosters," were identified as the source of power for expensive programs. Such was the controversial finding of the 1929 report on college sports written by Howard J. Savage for the Carnegie Foundation for the Advancement of Teaching (Thelin, 1994). Newspapers gave front page coverage to the critical and candid report. The Carnegie Foundation report was denounced by numerous university presidents whose teams had been cited for excesses and abuses in their sports programs. The Carnegie Foundation stood by their allegations and countered the disgruntled university presidents by documenting all their claims.

One development in the wake of the 1929 Carnegie Foundation report was the development or refinement of collegiate conferences. This often meant the addition of a new officer—the commissioner, whose duties included oversight of appropriate and ethical practices within the ranks of member institutions. How well this charge was carried out varied greatly from one conference to another. Indeed, what is most interesting about the reform movement starting in the 1930s is that conference commissioners often increased law abiding behavior by declaring certain practices as acceptable. Such was the case with the practice of providing financial support to student-athletes—whether in the form of jobs provided by alumni or direct scholarship awards.

Football's Impact on the Development of Other Sports Teams. Football was king—and its success tended to promote the addition of new varsity sports. Already crew, track and field, and baseball had a vigorous following among students and spectators. These eventually would be joined by minor sports (or Olympic sports) such as swimming, cross country, wrestling, boxing, gymnastics, and some regional sports such as ice hockey, lacrosse, field hockey, or water polo. Opportunistic football coaches persuaded boards of trustees and alumni associations to build new football stadiums that seated from 50,000 to 60,000 by using the argument that robust ticket sales for football would be the golden goose to subsidize all other sports. This movement gained momentum after World War I, as hundreds of colleges and universities nationwide constructed new facilities for football—usually with the designation "Memorial Stadium" to honor alumni and state citizens who had served in the armed forces during World War I (Thelin, 1994).

The array of popular college sports rounded out with a new game—basketball—that was created at the YMCA in Springfield, Massachusetts. The sport's most enthusiastic supporters were in the colleges of the Midwest. The popular appeal of basketball required colleges to add a new kind of facility—the field house or gymnasium that was able to accommodate one to two thousand spectators during the winter season.

Olympics and College Student-Athletes

Although football was the main story in college sports, it was not the only story. Thanks to the revival of the international Olympic Games by France's Baron de Coubertin in 1896, the United States joined with European nations in fielding squads every four years to compete for Olympic medals, especially in track and field. The intercollegiate track teams of the United States were the primary source of the nation's Olympic athletes. And they excelled, bringing home an abundance of gold medals (Smith, 1988). The happy result was a reciprocal effect in which colleges looked forward to grooming future Olympic athletes—and their subsequent success in international Olympic competition inspired a next generation of college student-athletes to train for the Olympics. An excellent example of this development was Jim Thorpe, a Native American from Oklahoma, who ultimately was an All-American football player and outstanding student-athlete in track at the Carlisle School for Indians in Pennsylvania (Jenkins, 2007). Thorpe won numerous gold medals, including the heralded decathlon, in the 1912 Olympics held in Stockholm, Sweden. A few years later, his fame turned to shame, as he was indicted for having accepted summer pay in sandlot baseball. Although this was later found to be a bogus charge, Thorpe had to forfeit his Olympic medals. His story illustrated the perennial conflict of amateurism and professionalism in American collegiate athletics. It also brought attention to the exploitation of student-athletes, especially those who were from modest income background and minority groups.

The ties of American college sports with the Olympics reached great heights and international influence at the 1936 games held in Munich, Germany when Jesse Owens, a student-athlete from Ohio State University, won an unprecedented four gold medals in track and field competition. Owens, an African American, provided real and symbolic American rejection of the Aryan racial superiority that the host nation Germany had proclaimed as part of the politicization of sports by the leader of their Nazi party, Adolf Hitler. Once again, abuses associated with race and class were part of the story along with triumph and celebration. Jesse Owens, for all his collegiate and Olympic accomplishments, was prohibited from living in dormitories or using dining halls on campus because of his race.

Prosperity and Problems After World War II

During World War II most intercollegiate sports programs were suspended. The alternative development was that the armed services leadership was persuaded that having college players who had enlisted in the military play on teams representing naval bases or army forts was good for national morale and also an effective source of preparing future military leaders. Most interesting was the accommodation and encouragement given to the service academies, especially West Point (Kemper, 2009). The official position was that it was in the national interest to allow a college football player who had already graduated and completed varsity eligibility at another college to enroll at West Point and play for the football team. Even though there were no systematic studies to confirm the effectiveness of such provisions and programs, they became fixtures in our national life. When World

War II ended in 1945 the veterans who had played on the powerful military football squads often found a smooth transition into civilian life, including going to college. University presidents and athletics directors recruited the military coaches and their players to enroll and play immediately, often with little concern for the usual protocols of checking school transcripts or passing admissions exams because university officials eagerly sought to assure the personnel necessary for a championship season.

The postwar years of 1945 to 1952 represented the extreme accommodation of college sports (Lawrence, 1987; Kemper, 2009; Thelin, 1994). Once again, the absence of any national requirements on academic standards or limits on athletics expansion opened the floodgates. At many state universities with an enrollment of about 5,000 students, it was not unusual to have more than 300 students report for opening football practice. In the early 1950s, college players who later signed with professional teams in the National Football League discovered that their professional salary was often less than the compensation provided by a college athletics scholarship.

The foremost abuses of unregulated intercollegiate sports after World War II did not involve football. It was the relatively new sport of basketball that ascended most rapidly in its appeal to students, student-athletes, alumni, spectators—and gamblers. The heart of this development was Madison Square Garden in New York City, where each weekend during the winter season, local college teams played a total of five to eight games. Often, the New York area colleges would be joined by visiting opponents who were top teams in other regions and conferences nationwide. The result each week was a large crowd watching a local team play against teams from the Midwest or South, for example, Bradley University or the University of Kentucky. For bookies and bettors, the real game was off the court, as one wagered that a particular college team would *beat the point spread.* For a gambler, the aim was not necessarily to fix a game so that one team was guaranteed to beat another. The scheme was subtle—a college player was bribed merely to miss some shots so that his team would still win—but by fewer points than projected by bookmakers. By 1951 newspaper articles in the popular press combined with charges and indictments by federal officials placed the national spotlight on college players who had cooperated with gamblers in what was known as *point shaving.* These scandals served as a tipping point to force the United States Congress to consider college sports oversight (Thelin, 1994).

Congress itself did not want to take on this responsibility, opting instead to continue a national tradition of minimizing direct federal intervention by relying on voluntary associations as a reliable proxy. This was the successful approach Congress used in calling on regional accreditation agencies to vouch for the good standing of colleges and universities that wished to be eligible to receive federal student financial aid payments from the GI Bill. As for oversight of college sports, the next step then was for a congressional subcommittee to hold hearings and to invite national organizations of academic leaders and university presidents to take on this new, official role. The disappointing result was that arguments and differences within the ranks of college and university presidents derailed the attempt to have the American Council on Education become the intercollegiate sports governing board (Lawrence, 1987; Sperber, 1998). By default, then, Congress asked the National Collegiate Athletic Association (NCAA) to regulate college sports.

The NCAA had a small staff housed in an office suite in Chicago. Heretofore its organizational mission was to sponsor championship events and tournaments in selected sports—a roster that did not include an NCAA championship for the premiere sport, college football. Even the NCAA's championship tournament for basketball was often surpassed in prestige by the National Invitational Tournament (NIT). In the late 1940s proposals to have the NCAA approve and then carry out nationwide standards defining admissions and financial aid terms for varsity student-athletes either were rejected by member institutions or, if passed, were ineffective and short-lived. This changed when the NCAA accepted the congressional offer, and it meant that two disparate and perhaps antagonistic responsibilities—the commercial promotion of college sports championships plus the educational regulation of college sports—now were combined in the same organization.

Rise of the National Collegiate Athletic Association

The energized NCAA, strengthened by its congressional mandate, soon introduced a new level of oversight and regulation to college sports. First, it upheld the decision of the Southeastern Conference to have the University of Kentucky suspend varsity basketball for the 1953–54 season—a penalty imposed on the basis of court cases involving charges of point shaving by Kentucky players. Second, the NCAA established ongoing committees and staff assignments with authority to monitor the conduct of athletics programs at member institutions. During the same years the NCAA asserted involvement and, eventually, primacy in regulating television broadcasts of football games. One reason for the latter initiative was the widespread fear among athletics directors that the popularity and affordability of television would eventually induce potential ticket buyers to stay away from attending college football games, opting instead to watch televised games at home. By the late 1950s the NCAA had put together a format of the "Game of the Week" in a contract with national television networks. The result was that each week, a total of only eight college football games were to be televised. This was broken down to specify four geographic regions within the continental United States, with viewers in each region having access to an early afternoon game and a mid-afternoon game. Individual colleges were prohibited from negotiating their own television arrangements. By 1960 the combination of powers in regulation and in commercial broadcasting had transformed the NCAA into a formidable governing body in college sports nationwide (Lawrence, 1987).

Race and Social Justice

Beneath the surface of the NCAA's consolidation and control of college sports nationwide several issues of social justice showed growing signs of stress and conflict that would increasingly shape the character of college sports for the next half century (see Chapter Seventeen for a discussion of current diversity issues in intercollegiate sports and recreation). In matters of race, college sports in the post-World War II era were characterized by outright racial exclusion and segregation, ranging at best to nominal racial desegregation (Demas, 2010). Many of the New Year's Day bowl games held in the South refused to invite college teams whose rosters included African American players. Major conferences such as the Southeastern Conference, the Southwestern Conference, and the Atlantic Coast Conference were slow to allow racial integration—a reform that in some cases did not take place until the 1970s. A few major universities had embraced genuine racial integration in their intercollegiate squads—foremost exemplified by UCLA. Jackie Robinson gained fame in 1947 for breaking the so-called "color line" of major league baseball. Equally important is that he, along with such fellow students as Woody Strode and Kenny Washington, earlier had been student-athletes at UCLA—with All Star honors in football, basketball, track, and baseball. The 1951 University of San Francisco football team was undefeated and ranked by some sportswriters as the top team in the nation. However, the team voted unanimously to refuse an offer to play in the Sugar Bowl game if—and only if—the USF team did not bring their players who were African American. In college basketball, the National Association of Intercollegiate Athletics (NAIA) was a pioneer in allowing and encouraging historically black colleges and universities to compete against predominantly white colleges in the national championship tournament.

The NAIA was exceptional in its race relations. What one finds is that college coaches either grudgingly allowed or actively recruited an increasing number of African American student-athletes (Oriard, 2009). In some cases, such as at the University of Wyoming, this gain in racial equity had a dysfunction—namely, the isolation of Black student-athletes as second-class citizens within a predominantly white student body. As a result, starting in the late 1960s Black student-athletes nationwide started to assert their requests and demands for full inclusion in the academic and extracurricular life of the campus (Demas, 2010; Michener, 1976; Oriard, 2009). One important facet of this initiative was awareness of the widespread exploitation of Black student-athletes—in which athletics directors, coaches, and even academic deans showed little concern for the undergraduate education and bachelor's degree completion for these recruited student-athletes.

Women and Gender Equity in College Sports

In addition to conflicts and changes over race in college sports, gender became a significant and contentious concern by the late 1970s. The slow but ultimately potent mechanism for this new era and new deal in college sports was the federal 1972 Title IX legislation that prohibited discrimination in educational programs on the basis of race and gender (see Chapter Six for a thorough discussion of Title IX). Although intercollegiate sports was not a primary focus of those who drafted the legislation, by about 1974 there were test cases that gave a preview of how visible and substantive the issue of women as student-athletes would be in the gradual implementation and enforcement of Title IX (Suggs, 2005). Heretofore women did have some organized structures for intercollegiate competition—namely, the Association of Intercollegiate Athletics for Women (AIAW). There was a complete separation of women's varsity programs from those provided for men. This separate-but-unequal funding arrangement on most major college and university campuses started to change—or, at least, was brought into question—in 1978 when the NCAA made a drastic change in its long-time policy of limiting its purview to sports for male student-athletes. The NCAA phased in its sponsorship of championship events for women, with such sports as gymnastics, basketball, track and field, and soccer. By the 1980s membership in the NCAA required a college to adhere to the NCAA's new, increasingly rigorous standards for sponsoring varsity sports for women. Eventually this included criteria to demonstrate good faith efforts that a college was moving toward reasonable if not equal funding for women in terms of grants-in-aid, coaches' salaries, practice facilities, uniforms and equipment, and travel budgets. Compliance was sparse and slow—but these provisions, along with Title IX enforcement and court cases, assured women's varsity sports an enduring place and increasing gains in the intercollegiate athletics arena.

Intercollegiate Athletics: High Stakes in the 21st Century

The heritage of intercollegiate sports in the United States has led to the formalization of a substantial athletics enterprise in the early 21st century in which more than 2,000 degree granting colleges and universities sponsor annual competition for over 400,000 student-athletes. Institutional programs are organized into voluntary conferences and national associations (see Chapter Seven for an in depth discussion regarding the various governing bodies in intercollegiate athletics and campus recreation). In the first decade of the 21st century American colleges were a fertile source of highly talented student-athletes whose contribution to their colleges' championships and publicity often was followed by excellence in international competition such as the Olympic Games or in various professional leagues. The growth of college sports from its founding days to its contemporary construction can be viewed as an outstanding and uniquely American success story, but that success has brought with it significant challenges at the onset of the 21st century.

The increasing specialization and professionalization of intercollegiate athletics has brought unprecedented emphasis to college sports within the American campus—a trend that diffuses to almost all colleges and is not confined just to the NCAA Division I programs. Even academically selective colleges give admissions priority to applicants who offer athletic skills that matched with a college's particular sports priorities (Bowen and Levin, 2003). This, in turn, fosters a sense of entitlement among student-athletes, who often have a college experience apart from most of their fellow classmates. This development raises the question as to whether many of the high-pressure varsity programs have transformed the *student-athlete* into the *athlete-student* (Oriard, 2009).

In a similar vein, colleges and universities eager for winning teams to bolster institutional reputation and alumni donations escalate the stakes by being willing to pay a coach high salaries—usually far beyond the compensation for faculty and in many instances surpassing the salary and benefits of a college or university president—and by building extensive and expensive sports complexes. The Achilles Heel of college sports nationwide in this period of popularity is that, in fact, only a small number of athletics programs were financially self-supporting (Associated Press, 2010). National reports by blue ribbon groups such as the Knight Commission have expressed alarm at the expenses of college sports at all levels—and warned that presidents and academic leaders are having increased problems of maintaining appropriate educational oversight of the intercollegiate athletics programs. This is the critical situation in which college sports found themselves by 2010.

Conclusion

How do historical trends in intercollegiate athletics have consequences for a new generation of students and professionals in higher education and sport administration? One finding that emerges is that the definition of what it means to be a student-athlete has changed dramatically over time. The implication for the present and future is that one needs to revisit this definition to make certain it is both pertinent for contemporary situations and appropriate educationally. This is no easy or obvious task, given the increasingly competitive and commercial character of American society. The dramatic historical changes in diversifying the gender, racial, and ethnic profile of college student-athletes represent a start—but this remains unfinished business. Reconsidering and reforming the profile will require discussion and coordination with numerous campus offices, especially if a college wishes to have its athletes be successful students.

For college and university presidents, rethinking the connections of an intercollegiate sports program to campuswide governance is crucial because recent reports by the Knight Commission on the Future of Intercollegiate Athletics indicate that many presidents, especially at Division I institutions, feel that presidents have lost control of college sports (2011). Governance is closely linked to policies and practices involving budgeting and appropriation of resources. A fundamental question is, "How should a college's athletics policies harmonize with its educational philosophy?" In the area of governance, the recurrent question calling for review is, "How much autonomy and interdependence should college sports have in relation to other parts of a campus?" Perhaps one of the most potentially powerful participants in this issue will be the board of trustees, a group that is relatively silent and invisible in program deliberations.

The most striking characteristic of intercollegiate sports over two centuries is that intercollegiate sports have experienced growth in participation, resources, visibility, and support from campus constituencies and the American public and media. This success has created in the 21st century what may be termed the *paradox of popularity*. Success and even fame have been accompanied by increased scrutiny and accountability to various, often conflicting, audiences and stakeholders. There is little doubt that this will be an important, interesting field in which to work and lead.

Chapter One Key Points

1. Early faculty resistance to campus sports was born of both religious and educational concerns. Despite faculty objections, students organized their own teams and games with other local college teams. American colleges in the late 19th century relied on the English model of sports and schools to make the case that playing football had educational value for building character and transmitting values (Smith, 1988).
2. By 1880 intercollegiate sports were dominated by what has been called the rise of football (Rudolph, 1962). Changes in media promoted the rise of the great college coach as a national figure.
3. An important trend in making intercollegiate sports truly All American was the demographic and geographic spread of top-caliber teams.
4. College sports were beyond the control of college and university presidents. Alumni and donors, known as "boosters," were identified as the source of power for expensive programs. One development in the wake of the 1929 Carnegie Foundation report was the development or refinement of collegiate conferences. Football was king—and its success tended to promote the addition of new varsity sports.
5. The intercollegiate track teams of the United States were the primary source of the nation's Olympic athletes. And they excelled, bringing home an abundance of gold medals (Smith, 1988). The happy result was a reciprocal effect in which colleges looked forward to grooming future Olympic athletes, and their subsequent success in international Olympic competition inspired a next generation of college student-athletes to train for the Olympics.
6. During World War II most intercollegiate sports programs were suspended. The postwar years of 1945 to 1952 represented the extreme

accommodation of college sports (Lawrence, 1987; Kemper, 2009; Thelin, 1994).

7. Congress did not want to take on the responsibility of governing college sports, opting instead to continue a national tradition of minimizing direct federal intervention by relying on voluntary associations as a reliable proxy. By default, then, Congress asked the National Collegiate Athletic Association (NCAA) to regulate college sports. The energized NCAA, strengthened by its congressional mandate, soon introduced a new level of oversight and regulation to college sports.
8. In matters of race, college sports in the post-World War II era were characterized by outright racial exclusion and segregation, ranging at best to nominal racial desegregation (Demas, 2010). In addition to conflicts and changes over race in college sports, gender became a significant and contentious concern by the late 1970s.
9. The growth of college sports from its founding days to its contemporary construction can be viewed as an outstanding and uniquely American success story, but that success has brought with it significant challenges at the onset of the 21st century.
10. Even academically selective colleges give admissions priority to applicants who offer athletic skills that match with a college's particular sports priorities (Bowen and Levin, 2003). This, in turn, fosters a sense of entitlement among student-athletes, who often have a college experience apart from most of their fellow classmates. This development raises the question as to whether many of the high-pressure varsity programs have transformed the *student-athlete* into the *athlete-student* (Oriard, 2009).
11. The Achilles Heel of college sports nationwide in this period of popularity is that, in fact, only a small number of athletics programs were financially self-supporting (Associated Press, 2010). National reports by blue ribbon groups such as the Knight Commission have expressed alarm at the expenses of college sports at all levels—and warned that presidents and academic leaders are having increased problems of maintaining appropriate educational oversight of the intercollegiate athletics programs.
12. The most striking characteristic of intercollegiate sports over two centuries is that they have experienced growth in participation, resources, visibility, and support from campus constituencies and the American public and media. This success has created in the 21st century what may be termed the *paradox of popularity*. Success and even fame have

been accompanied by increased scrutiny and accountability to various, often conflicting, audiences and stakeholders.

References

Associated Press. *NCAA report: Economy cuts into sports.* 2010. Accessed on November 28, 2011 at http://sports.espn.go.com/ncf/news/story?id=5490686.

Bowen, W. G., and Levin, S. A., *Reclaiming the Game: College Sports and Educational Values.* Princeton, N. J.: Princeton University Press, 2003.

Demas, L. *Integrating the Gridiron: Black Civil Rights and American College Football.* New Brunswick, New Jersey and London: The Rutgers University Press, 2010.

Jenkins, S. *The Real All Americans: The Team That Changed a Game, a Nation, a People.* New York: Doubleday, 2007.

Kemper, K. E., *College Football and American Culture in the Cold War Era.* Urbana, IL: University of Illinois Press, 2009.

Knight Commission. *Presidential Control and Leadership.* Miami, FL: Knight Commission, 2011. Accessed April 30, 2011 at http://www.knightcommission.org/index.php?option=com˙content&view=article&id=6&Itemid=75.

Lawrence, P. R. *Unsportsmanlike Conduct: The National Collegiate Athletic Association and the Business of College Football.* New York: Praeger, 1987.

Lester, R. *Stagg's University: The Rise, Decline, and Fall of Big-Time Football at Chicago.* Urbana, IL: University of Illinois Press, 1995.

Michener, J. *Sports in America.* New York: Random House, 1976.

Oriard, M. *Reading Football: How the Popular Press Created an American Spectacle.* Chapel Hill, NC: University of North Carolina Press, 1993.

Oriard, M. *Bowled Over: Big-Time College Football from the Sixties to the BCS Era.* Chapel Hill, NC: University of North Carolina Press, 2009.

Rudolph, F. *The American College and University: A History.* New York: Knopf, 1962.

Smith, R. A. *Sports and Freedom: The Rise of Big-Time College Athletics.* New York: Oxford University Press, 1988.

Smith, R. A. *Play-By-Play: Radio, Television, and Big-Time College Sport.* Baltimore, MD: The Johns Hopkins University Press, 2001.

Sperber, M. *Onward to Victory: The Crises that Shaped College Sports.* New York: Henry Holt, 1998.

Suggs, W. *A Place on the Team: The Triumph and Tragedy of Title* IX. Princeton, NJ: Princeton University Press, 2005.

Thelin, J. *Games Colleges Play: Scandal and Reform in Intercollegiate Athletics.* Baltimore, MD: Johns Hopkins University Press, 1994.

CHAPTER TWO

AN OVERVIEW OF FITNESS AND RECREATION IN COLLEGIATE SETTINGS

Donald L. Rockey, Jr. and Robert J. Barcelona

"Campus recreation is the umbrella term used to describe a myriad of recreation and leisure activity programming on university and college campuses" (Hums and MacLean, 2008, p. 137). These activities include programming in intramurals, clubs, outdoor/adventure, fitness, aquatics, informal recreation, and instructional classes. The purpose of this chapter is to provide the reader with a historical perspective of campus recreation and fitness as it pertains to the American higher education system.

This chapter covers the history and development of campus recreation, as well as the theories that have influenced this development. It identifies common programs in campus recreation and discusses trends in campus recreation and fitness before offering concluding thoughts.

Evolution of Campus Recreation and Fitness

Campus recreation and fitness has gone through an evolution in the American higher educational system. This section discusses how the role and purpose of campus recreation and fitness, as well its components, have changed over time, from its early beginnings as an element of athletics and physical education to its transition to the realm of student affairs.

Early Beginnings of Campus Recreation and Fitness

Recreation on the collegiate campus did not have an auspicious start. The religious beliefs of the early colonists extended into higher education. Included in these religious beliefs was a negative attitude toward recreation and play. Recreation and play led to sin. Hence, they were to be avoided, as should people who sought out recreation and play (Sessoms and Henderson, 1994). Institutions such as Princeton University even enforced penalties on students who played ball in certain areas on campus because these activities were believed to be unbecoming of gentlemen students (Means, 1952).

As America moved toward the Civil War in the 1800s, a change in the views toward recreation and fitness began to develop. Competition among groups on college campuses, as well as between colleges, began to gain momentum. Baseball, rowing, and football owe part of their popularity and growth to the interest of college students in them and students' participation on college campuses. Although the onset of the Civil War slowed the growth of sport on college campuses, it did generate interest in fitness. To meet the need for fit men to fill the military ranks, the University of Minnesota organized a compulsory physical activity program for all men in the freshman class (Burton and Wade, 2003).

After the Civil War, recreation continued to expand its offerings on college campuses. This growth was partly due to the fact that recreational activities such as baseball were encouraged by military leaders during the Civil War (Kirsch, 1998). Intercollegiate games also became more common nationwide. It was also at this time that campus recreation and sport found an unlikely new supporter, the Protestant Church. Leading church figures of the time began to realize that sport and physical activity can build morality and good character (McLean, Hurd, and Rogers, 2008). The movement that evolved from this combination of church and recreation was called the Muscular Lyceum, or Muscular Christianity Movement, and it helped break down some of the stigmas associated with recreation and sport on college campuses.

Despite the growth in interest among students across campuses nationwide in recreation, college administrators still had a negative view of such activities. Many thought recreation on campus had no importance or educational value (Means, 1952). They took the stance that recreation needed to be "either tolerated or restricted" (National Intramural-Recreational Sports Association [NIRSA], 2008, p. 23).

Early forms of campus recreation participation took three primary forms: (1) informal leisure activities that students organized for themselves with little outside assistance, such as hiking, paddling on the lake, or equestrian activities, (2) organized physical activity and instruction programs focused on calisthenics, hygiene, and military training, and (3) semi-organized games and competitions played against fellow college students, local club teams, or students from other universities. During the latter half of the 19th century, there was little or no distinction between student-athletes and the rest of the college population, as most organized sport and athletic activities and contests were run for students by students themselves. However, as time progressed, the semistructured games between students became more organized, as coaching, formalized rule sets, league affiliations, and the growing presence of spectators became the norm.

Much of the early history of intercollegiate athletics competition, football in particular, was marked by open tension between faculty and students, with the former trying to exert pressure to either close down or seriously control what was perceived to be a threat to the culture of higher education. At the same time, instruction in physical activity was being offered for the general campus population, primarily for the purposes of health and exercise (calisthenics), and for military training and physical readiness to fight, especially for men. While watching athletics contests became an increasingly popular activity for college students, they "wanted physical exercise that was more interesting and fun than the rigid calisthenics, marching and drilling, and exercise or gymnastics programs that were favored by campus faculties" (NIRSA, 2008, p. 23).

What most people think of today as recreation—structured and organized leisure-time activities that are freely chosen, focus on broad-based participation, and are primarily intrinsically rewarding—was not necessarily on the minds of early college faculties. It was, however, on the minds of college students at the turn of the 20th century, as large numbers of students who were not on intercollegiate teams were participating informally in sport clubs and in recreational sport activities such as baseball, football, rowing, and running (Lewis, Jones, Lamke, and Dunn, 1998). College faculty and administrators recognized the growing popularity of participating in sport for fun and enjoyment as opposed to competition. This led to the creation of sport programs run by coaches and physical education instructors for students who were not intercollegiate athletes at places such as Cornell University in 1904, and the creation of separate intramural athletics departments at the University of Michigan and Ohio State University in 1913 (Lewis et al., 1998; NIRSA, 2008). It is at this point that the separation between intercollegiate athletics and campus recreation began to formalize.

New Thoughts on Campus Recreation and Fitness

The Great Depression and World War II had a profound impact on the country's views of leisure and recreation and this led to additional changes in the leaderships' views on recreation and fitness on college campuses. Americans began to view recreation as a wise use of leisure time. With approximately one-third of the American population unemployed during the Great Depression, effective use of nonwork time had to be explored. To meet the need to use free or leisure time effectively, many of Franklin D. Roosevelt's New Deal programs involved recreation and sport. Programs such as the Works Progress Administration and the Federal Emergency Relief Administration built recreational and sport facilities and hired leaders in the field of recreation These New Deal programs created the expectation that the provision of recreation was the responsibility of the government on the federal, state, and municipal levels (McLean, Hurd, and Rogers, 2008). With the government providing recreation and sport, college campuses found it harder to justify a lack of support for the recreational needs of their students. Also creating a newfound interest in fitness on college campuses was the finding that nearly half of all draftees for World War II were either rejected or given noncombat positions due to low fitness levels (Rice, Hutchinson, and Lee, 1958). In response to the issue of poor physical health and fitness, after World War II schools at all levels strengthened their programming in physical fitness.

Also after World War II, higher education in America was booming. Many of the former servicemen who returned from Europe were offered opportunities to continue their education with financial assistance from the federal government through the Montgomery GI Bill. These servicemen had grown to expect recreational opportunities be provided to them. Universities had to meet that need. This led to a question coming out of the 1947 American Alliance for Health, Physical Education, and Recreation Conference: Who is responsible for the development of recreational programs in the college setting (NIRSA, 2008)? Should it be physical education departments, athletics departments, or even student affairs? It was not until the late 1950s that this question would finally be answered.

An additional significant event that occurred in the late 1940s was the William Wasson study of black college intramural programs across the

United States, which led to the written report, *A Comparative Study of Intramural Programs in Negro Colleges.* This report in turn resulted in a meeting between twenty-two male and female intramural directors from eleven universities at which the National Intramural Association, which later became known as the National Intramural-Recreational Sport Association, was created (NIRSA, 2008). Since its creation NIRSA has been the leading resource for campus recreation professionals.

Time of Change and Growth in Campus Recreation and Fitness

From the late 1950s to the 2000s, campus recreation and fitness has gone through both change and growth. Students' interest in strictly intramural programming began to wane as they became more interested in noncompetitive activities. Based upon this interest, campus recreation expanded into offering other forms of programming, including instruction, aquatics, wellness, and outdoor and adventure.

Women also were offered more opportunities in campus recreation during the 1970s. At first Title IX, which was passed in 1972, had a negative impact on campus recreation for women in recreation, particularly women's intramural programming. Since it opened up more opportunities for women to compete on the intercollegiate athletics level, fewer participated in intramurals. With the growth of athletics opportunities for women and the acceptance that women can be athletes, more recreational and sport programming evolved out of campus recreation.

In the 1980s and 1990s, campus recreation was looked upon as making significant contributions on college and universities (Barcelona and Ross, 2002). College and university administrators began to see that campus recreation can serve as a means, for example, to recruit and retain students and faculty and can enhance the overall image of the institution. With this recognition, campus recreation and fitness programming saw a significant amount of growth.

Foundations of Campus Recreation

Campus recreation programs tend to focus on participation, that is, providing opportunities for recreation, sport, and fitness participation for the widest range of students regardless of ability. This focus contrasts with that of departments of athletics or physical education, where the emphasis is placed either on competitive sport experiences and elite participation for the former, or basic skill instruction and the professional preparation of physical education teachers for the latter. Historically, campus recreation departments have been associated with departments of athletics or physical education. However, given the growth of campus recreation programs and offerings and the philosophical divide that separates much of campus recreation programming from other organized forms of sport participation at college, campus recreation departments have started to recognize their commonality with other areas of student affairs, including residence life, student union programming, clubs and activities, and fraternities and sororities.

The growing recognition prompted in a report by Bryant, Anderson, and Dunn titled, "Rationale for Independent Administration of Collegiate Recreational Sports Programs" (1994). The report was considered a landmark, in that it argued persuasively for separate administrative support such as facilities, staff, and budget for campus recreation programs. The report advocated for recreational sport programs that focused on "leadership development, appreciation of differences, group development, self-discipline, conflict resolution skills and safety awareness" (Bryant et al., 1994, p. 1). The authors recognized the role that campus recreation programs can play in helping to educate the whole student—a hallmark of student affairs programs and services. The report is still considered to be significant today in terms of articulating a view that campus recreation departments are philosophically and administratively different from their counterparts in athletics and physical education or academic affairs. This reflected a movement that saw 61% of campus recreation departments administratively housed in divisions of student affairs versus the 34% which were administratively housed in athletics or academic programs such as physical education (Bryant, et al., 1994). Today, the number has increased to approximately 75% (Haines, 2007).

It has been suggested by others that the 1994 document was the impetus that began shifting the thinking in campus recreation toward a focus on student learning and development and away from merely providing recreational activities for their own sake (Franklin, 2007). That is not to say that the facilities, programs, and services that campus recreation departments offer to students are not important. On the contrary, proponents of college student learning and development approach believe that "transformative learning always occurs within the active contexts of student lives" (Keeling, 2006, p. vii). To that end, intentionally and purposefully designed campus recreation programs and experiences can provide the platform for student learning and development to take place outside the formal classroom experience.

Theories That Impacted Development of Campus Recreation

In this section some of the major theories that have influenced the development of campus recreation are discussed. These theories include sport theories and recreation-play theories. Additional theories are elaborated in Chapter Three.

Sport Theories

Sport theories help campus recreation administrators understand and explain the significance of the service they offer. Although the theories may seem abstract, they can suggest practical applications to the planning and implementation of campus recreation. Several of these sport theories are of particular importance to the club and intramural sport leader.

Functionalist Theory. The functionalist theory focuses on how sports contribute to the smooth operations of societies, communities, organizations, and groups (Coakley, 2009). Based upon this theory, sport helps to preserve the status quo. Hence, club sport and intramurals maintain values, such as goal achievement and teamwork, which preserve stability and order on a college campus.

Conflict Theory. The conflict theory is based upon the assumption that every society is a system of relationships that are shaped by economic factors. According to this theory, all aspects of social life depend upon economic interests and the people who control the economy (Coakley, 2009). Based upon this theory, social order is achieved through "coercion, exploitation, and manipulation; the distribution of power; and the use of that power to facilitate change" (Franklin and Hardin, 2008, p. 9). Professional and collegiate sports are controlled by leadership that controls the money such as owners and university administrators. The athlete, if he or she wants to participate, must fall into line and follow the rules set up by the financial leadership. Club and intramural sports provide participants the opportunity to increase their control of the situation since profit is not a motive.

In addition, club sports allow the members of the team to share in the decision-making process of how the team's finances will be used.

Critical Theory. Rather than focus on society as a whole in order to understand it, critical theory focuses on the diversity, contradictions, and changes that characterize social life (Coakley, 2009). Critical theory considers sport, not as a simple reflection of society, but as a means by which culture is produced, reproduced, and changed. Critical theory, as applied to club sport and intramurals, emphasizes the need for multiple and diverse forms of sport participation as the needs and interests of the participants change. Club sports and intramurals are easily adaptable to meet the requirements for diversity in sport.

Interactionalist Theory. As humans interact with one another they give meaning to themselves, others, and the world (Franklin and Hardin, 2008). Based upon these meanings they make decisions and take action. This is the premise behind the interactionalist theory. In this context, the meaning and interaction of sport becomes the focus. The interactionalist theory, as applied to club sport and intramurals, emphasizes the athletes as responsible for organizing and controlling their sport.

Play and Recreation Theories

Play theories were originally developed as a means to explain the need for recreation and play but they apply to campus recreation. Several theories of play have had an impact on the development and growth of campus recreation and fitness. Five of the major theories include the surplus energy theory, the compensatory theory, the catharsis theory, the flow theory, and the conflict-enculturation theory.

Surplus-Energy Theory. The surplus-energy theory suggests that recreation provides an outlet to burn energy otherwise not used during daily life (Schiller, 1875; Spencer, 1873). Evidence for this theory can be observed on a college campus in the many recreational activities of students such as playing basketball, running and jogging, and cycling.

Compensatory Theory. Reaney's (1916) and Robinson's (1920) compensatory theory suggests that recreation serves as a substitute outlet for desires and goals when other avenues to accomplish goals are blocked or unfulfilled. Recreation allows an individual to make up for unpleasant experiences such as a poor grade on a test.

Catharsis Theory. The catharsis theory suggests that recreation provides a positive outlet for participants to purge antisocial urges. Recreation is a safety valve that vents excess energies and emotions. Playing an intramural sport, for example, provides such an outlet for these negative emotions.

Flow Theory. Csikszentmihalyi's flow theory (1990) suggests that play and recreation provides an alternate state of consciousness that people seek out to experience. When a person enters "flow" he or she loses all sense of self-consciousness and ego and feels a sense of personal control or power. Many campus recreation experiences are created to try to allow the participant to reach flow by matching skill level with challenge level.

Conflict-Enculturation Theory. The conflict-enculturation theory suggests that recreation offers the participant an opportunity to experience and learn new behaviors in a safe environment (Sutton-Smith, 1997). Based upon this theory, college students are prepared for adulthood and trained in abilities such as cooperation, competition, fair play, and handling emotions through recreational experiences.

Common Program Areas of Campus Recreation

Colleges and universities offer areas of recreational programming that are quite diverse in hopes of covering students' wide range of interests. Here we discuss some of the most common areas of programming that are offered on university campuses. These areas are not discreet, however, and a program or activity may be included in more than one of them.

Aquatics

Many college and universities have one or more swimming pools on campus to cater to students' interest in water-based forms of recreation and fitness. Programming that occurs in this area may include open swim (lap swim), intramurals (water polo), club teams (swim team), instructional classes (swim lessons, scuba), fitness (aqua aerobics), and outdoor recreation (scuba kayak, and canoeing).

Fitness

College students have become more health conscious, so offering fitness programming is an important element of most campus recreation programs. Included in the large on-campus recreation facilities are areas for students to take part in fitness-related activities. Campus recreation departments commonly offer group fitness classes (Zumba, Yoga), personal training, informal training (weight and cardiovascular equipment), intramurals (basketball), and instructional classes to meet the students' needs in this area.

Intramurals

Intramurals are school-based recreational sport pursuits involving some form of competition between one or more participants. The key element of intramural sport is the freedom of choice. Unlike intercollegiate athletics, the participants have a choice in programs in which to participate, the formats, and at what level to compete. Intramural programming is a staple for most campus recreation departments and may range from a fishing tournament to the more traditional flag football and basketball.

Club Sports (Extramurals)

Club sports differ from intramurals in the fact that the club teams or individuals compete against other club teams or individuals not housed on their own college campus. Club sports are similar to intercollegiate athletics except the pressure to win is not as high, and the leadership for the team derives from the team members. Campus recreation departments commonly rely on students to develop ideas for club teams and then support them once interest has been established. Similar to intramurals, club sports may include anything that allows participants to compete against others, such as traditional flag football, baseball, and even the more contemporary extreme sports such as wake boarding.

Outdoor Recreation and Adventure Recreation

Outdoor recreation requires interaction between the individual and an element of nature. Adventure recreation, which is often used interchangeably with outdoor recreation, can include nature-based recreation but it does not have to occur in nature and it has an element of perceived risk involved.

Outdoor recreation and adventure programming includes hiking, backpacking, camping, rock climbing, skiing (alpine and cross-country), scuba, and other nature-based recreation, as well as challenge courses. Some universities such as the University of North Carolina-Chapel Hill, Harvard University, and Prescott College offer incoming freshmen an opportunity to take part in a wilderness-based recreation activity as a means to acclimate the students to college.

Informal

Informal or open recreation programming provides the opportunity for students to participate in recreation activities without requiring leadership or direct planning from the campus recreation department. Often campus recreation departments provide this in the form of having the basketball courts open for students to just show up and play or offering an open weight room where students may work out without any guidance. To further assist and encourage informal recreation, campus recreation departments commonly allow students to check out or rent equipment needed to participate in these activities. Informal recreation allows campus recreation providers opportunities to reach students who do not want their leisure time structured or planned for them.

Instructional Classes

Instructional classes refer to those recreational programs that have the purpose of teaching a new skill or activity to students. These programs are not academic courses. The students have the ability to freely choose to take part in these courses and they do so because they want to learn the related skill or activity. Campus recreation departments may offer instructional programming, for example, in dance (ballroom, Hip Hop, and Salsa), fitness, wilderness first aid, kayaking, scuba, lifeguarding, swimming, and officiating.

Significance and Role of Campus Recreation and Fitness

As mentioned earlier in the chapter, it was not until the 1980s and 1990s that campus recreation was looked upon as making significant contributions at colleges and universities (Barcelona and Ross, 2002). In this section, we discuss these significant contributions.

Retention of Students

Campus recreation and fitness helps retain students. In the current economically challenging environment, student retention is an issue on most college campuses. Research suggests that campus recreation and fitness facilities have a positive impact on student retention and graduation rates (Belch, Gebel, and Mas, 2001; Bryant, Banta, and Bradley, 1995; Haines, 2001; Hall, 2006; Huesman, Brown, Lee, Kellogg, and Radcliffe, 2009; Lindsey and Sessoms, 2006). In addition, Moffitt (2010) found that intramural sport participants were more satisfied with their academic life and campus life.

Recruitment of Students

Campus recreation and fitness provides can also help universities is in the recruitment of students. Research suggests that students view campus recreation as an important element in the decision-making process (Latawsky, Schneider, Pederson, and Palmer, 2003; Zizzi, Ayers, Watson II, and Keeler, 2004). In fact, it was found that 30% of enrollment decisions were influenced by the quality of campus recreation facilities (Bryant, Banta, and Bradley, 1995).

Academic Curriculum Development

With the growth of interest in campus recreation, an area of specialized academic learning and teaching has been born. Colleges and universities view campus recreation as an opportunity for curriculum development. There are approximately 500 colleges and universities that offer recreation programs across the United States (E. Rodgers, personal communication, March 12, 2011). Out of these degree programs, some offer specialization in campus recreation or recreational sport.

Wellness

Wellness is a state of optimal well-being oriented toward maximizing an individual's potential (Patton, 2009, p. 27). Obviously campus recreation departments are focused toward the physical and mental health related benefits derived through their programs and facilities. Campus recreation programming is looked upon as a preventative health resource that will improve the overall wellness of the campus community (Kampf, 2010).

Recreational programs offered at colleges and universities influence lifestyle choices and healthy behavior, including physical activity patterns and involvement in positive social outlets such as intramural sports and instructional classes (American College Health Association, 2002). Research suggests that such lifestyle choices and behaviors started during students' college years are likely to continue into adulthood (Buckworth, 2001). Chapter Eighteen offers an extended discussion on wellness issues in athletics and recreation on campus.

Cocurricular Experiences and Student Development

Campus recreation also provides academic and professional development for students. Students have opportunities to work with campus recreation providers as a means of employment. During this employment, students learn about the field of recreation and fitness. In addition to the learning aspects that come along with employment, campus recreation also provides learning experiences for the participant outside the traditional classroom setting. Many of the learning experiences that occur on the intramural fields or courts or in the out-of-doors are the most memorable of students' college years. Research suggests that the enforcement of good sportsmanship in intramural programs helps clarify student values, thus contributing to the overall development of the student (Rothwell and Theodore, 2006).

Enhancing the University's Image

The programs and facilities offered through campus recreation help create a positive image of a university in the eyes of parents, students, and potential students. As already discussed, well planned and implemented recreational programming and facilities show the university in a positive light and demonstrate a concern for the whole student, not just academics. This goes a long way in providing a connection between the university and the students, as well as social integration.

Trends in Campus Recreation

The field of campus recreation continues to grow and change, as it has since its earliest days. Predicting trends is often an uncertain science. However, evidence supports the following developments as significant and growing priorities for campus recreational sports professionals:

1. Increased diversity in higher education and greater emphasis on meeting diverse needs
2. Continuous building boom of signature campus recreational sports facilities
3. Growth of opportunities for extramural and club sport competitions
4. Enhanced professional development opportunities and growth of the campus recreational sports profession

Each of these trends is discussed below, with particular emphasis on their impact for students and campus recreational sports professionals.

Increased Diversity in Higher Education

Enrollment in degree-granting institutions increased 28% between 1993 and 2007, and recent projections predict continued growth over the next ten years. In particular, enrollment for women, nontraditional aged students, and racial and ethnic minority students is expected to far outpace their demographic counterparts (Hussar and Bailey, 2009).

Increasing diversity has long been celebrated in higher education, as there is a general belief that a more diverse student body enriches the educational experience for all students. In fact, areas such as cultural competency, social responsibility, interdependence, and appreciation of differences have been noted as desired student outcomes that can accrue through purposeful and intentional participation in out-of-class activities (Komives and Schoper, 2006).

Campus recreational sport activities involve large numbers of students. It stands to reason that these programs and facilities can provide opportunities for interacting with and learning from people of different backgrounds and beliefs.

Although past research has shown that participants are likely to be men, traditional aged students, and those who live on campus (Barcelona and Ross, 2002), increasing institutional diversity is influencing the way campus recreational sports departments are doing business. For example, the growing number of women on college campuses has led to the proliferation of women's sport opportunities, both at the varsity and recreational levels. Some successful women's sport clubs have been elevated to varsity status, such as was the case at the University of California-Berkeley, whose women's golf and lacrosse clubs transitioned to varsity athletics programs. In other cases, the contraction of intercollegiate athletics teams has led to increased opportunities for recreational sport club participation for women, such as when the women's varsity crew program was cut at the University of New Hampshire and later reconstituted itself as a successful sport at the club level. Increasing diversity in participation has also created policy issues for campus recreation administrators. Offering unisex bathrooms, family locker rooms, child care, women's-only gym times, universally accessible fitness equipment, and more diverse sport offerings such as cricket, table tennis, wheelchair basketball, and Futsal (indoor, five-a-side soccer) are just snapshots of the changes being implemented based on the growing diversity of college and university recreational sports programs. A more intensive discussion of diversity issues can be found in Chapter Seventeen.

Building Boom Continues

Facilities for recreational sports participation on college campuses have a long history dating back to the early 1900s. In the 1980s as campus recreational sports departments emerged as organizationally separate programs from intercollegiate athletics and academically oriented schools and colleges, the building of new, modern, and separate facilities for student participation in recreational sports proliferated (Blumenthal, 2009). These facilities differed from their earlier ancestors in that they were likely to be dedicated solely to recreational sports participation, were built to accommodate a multitude of recreational and physical fitness activities, generally followed an open architectural design that showcased active participation, and included a range of amenities, including study spaces, lounges, and retail centers.

The building boom of the 1980s and 1990s has continued unabated. According to a report by Kerr-Downs Report (NIRSA, 2002), it was estimated that 200 indoor and 318 outdoor facilities would be built or renovated between 2002 and 2007. A more recent study by the National Intramural-Recreational Sports Association showed that 174 colleges and universities had planned over $8 billion in facility construction, expansion, or renovation through 2013. While the recent economic downturn may have stalled or limited plans for campus building projects, recreational sport facility construction and renovation at many colleges and universities appears to have survived many of these cuts. For example, the 2011 National Intramural-Recreational Sports Association's Outstanding Facilities Awards winners totaled more than $275 million in new facility construction, not including land and design fees, for an average of $39 million per facility (NIRSA, 2011a).

Trends in facility construction have mirrored many of the priorities of student affairs divisions, including focusing on spaces that help to strengthen student community, enhance student learning and development, increase physical activity, and improve health and wellness. The nationwide trend in sustainable and green building initiatives has also been reflected in campus recreation building projects. For example, Portland State University's Academic and Student Recreation Center has achieved a LEED (Leadership in Energy and Environmental Design) green building rating. The mixed use building includes the campus recreation center, outdoor recreation space, general classroom areas, and retail opportunities (Gallagher, 2010). As colleges and universities recognize the importance of campus facilities in attracting and retaining students, and with a renewed emphasis on out-of-class student learning and development opportunities, it is likely that the construction of new and innovative campus recreation facilities will continue into the future.

Growth in Extramural and Intercollegiate Club Sport Opportunities

While high-quality recreation facilities attract students and provide venues for a wide variety of activity participation, intramural sport programs have tended to be the signature programs for campus recreation departments. The term *intramural* literally means "within the walls" and has traditionally focused on competition between individuals and teams from the same university. However, a growing emphasis on extramural and club sport events has provided opportunities for competition between individuals and teams from different colleges and universities.

For example, the National Campus Championship Series (NCCS) presented by the National Intramural-Recreational Sports Association includes events such as the NCCS Regional and National Flag Football Championships, the NCCS National Soccer Championships, the USTA National Campus Championship, and the NCCS Regional and National Basketball Championships. Regional qualifying tournaments are held for certain sports, allowing regional winners to compete in a national championship format. The recent NCCS National Flag Football Championships attracted high-profile national sponsorships, such as Powerade, as well as television coverage by CBS College Sports. Other national championship-type events are provided by American Collegiate Intramural Sports (ACIS), including the ACIS Fitness Championships, which also attracted national level sponsorship and received television coverage on Fox College Sports. A variety of national organizations provide opportunities for intercollegiate sport club competition, including the American Collegiate Hockey Association (ACHA), National Club Volleyball Federation (NCVF), USA Rugby, and US Lacrosse, among others. Extramural and sport club championship events not only provide competitive opportunities for recreational sport athletes—they can also provide economic impact for host communities. For example, a recent study showed that the ACHA Division II National Championships yielded an approximate $2 million in economic impact for the Fort Collins, CO area (Veltri, Miller, and Harris, 2009).

Enhanced Professional Development Opportunities

As the field of campus recreational sports has matured, professional development opportunities have continued to grow and evolve. The field's history is steeped with a desire for greater professionalism. Notable steps along the way included the founding of the National Intramural Association in 1950, the development of the Research Grant Program in 1965, the publication of the *NIRSA* (now *Recreational Sports) Journal* in 1977, the introduction of the Certified Recreational Sports Specialist (CRSS) certification in 1981, the development of the professional *Code of Ethics* in 1984, and the creation of the NIRSA School of Recreational Sport Management in 1989 (NIRSA, 2011b). More recent initiatives include the growing number of institutes and symposiums dedicated to professional training and development offered through the National Intramural-Recreational Sports Association. These opportunities include the Sport Club Symposium, Executive Institute, Sports Facilities Symposium, Outdoor Recreation Symposium, Marketing Symposium, Fitness Institute, and the development of the Research Institute in partnership with Ohio State University.

The continued and growing alignment between campus recreation professionals and student affairs staff is a natural outgrowth of the increasing focus on student learning and development. This alignment has been evident in a number of key partnerships, including the joint work between the National Intramural-Recreational Sports Association and student affairs organizations on the *Learning Reconsidered 2* document, which outlined an agenda for implementing a whole-student approach to learning and education (Keeling, 2006). In addition, NIRSA has adopted the 2007 Council for the Advancement of Standards in Higher Education (CAS), outlining an explicit set of standards that emphasize student learning and development outside the classroom, with a focus on outcomes such as, "effective communication, healthy behavior, enhanced self-esteem, collaboration, appreciating diversity, meaningful interpersonal relationships, satisfying and productive lifestyles, intellectual growth, social responsibility, personal and educational goals, realistic self-appraisal, clarified values, independence, career choices, and spiritual awareness" (Blumenthal, 2009, p. 56). As the field of campus recreational sports moves into the 21st century, the focus for professionals will be on demonstrating how meaningful and healthy recreation activities contribute to the higher education mission through the documentation and assessment of clear learning and student development outcomes.

Trends in Campus Fitness

The trends that are currently occurring in the realm of campus fitness mirror those that are occurring in the overall field of fitness. This section highlights a few of the most prevalent trends.

Technology

The use of technology is having more impact in fitness, as it is in most elements of society today. Campus recreation fitness centers are offering more technological bells and whistles to attract students to participate. Equipments such as treadmills and elliptical trainers have iPod and television interfaces. Some facilities have computer-based workout programs that track the student's workout and document it for future review.

Exergaming, which is a combination of exercise and virtual gaming, is another example of how technology is impacting campus fitness. For instance, Coastal Carolina University and the University of South Florida have exergaming rooms in their fitness centers that allow students the opportunity to exercise while playing video games.

Individualized Training

In addition to the use of technology, other trends have an impact on campus fitness. Individualized training or more personal training opportunities are becoming available to students, faculty, and staff. Many universities now offer personal training for their participants. They are offering this as an opportunity for exercise science students to practice the skills learned in the classroom (with the guidance of a professional) or through hired professionals.

Core Strength Training

Core strength training, which is the training of muscles that support the spine and the pelvis, is another trend in the field of campus fitness. Core strength training attempts to replicate the muscles working in unison rather than in isolation as in traditional strength training. Most universities now offer group fitness classes that focus on core strength training as well as equipment for that purpose.

Fitness Testing

Many universities also now offer fitness testing for the students, faculty, and staff. The testing allows participants to understand baseline fitness levels as well as monitor progress. Testing can range from Body Mass Index and skinfold tests to measuring actual maximum oxygen uptake (V02 max). Again the testing is commonly done through students who are training to work in the exercise science field, by exercise science professionals, or through the use of technology that does the testing without the need of guidance.

Group Fitness Classes

Although it is not a new trend, group fitness classes are still very popular on college campuses. One of the areas that is very popular is the dance-based fitness classes such as Zumba, which is a fusion of Latin and international music with elements of aerobics and fitness that help to tone and sculpt one's body. Yoga is another group fitness class that has found popularity on college campuses and offers participants training in flexibility, core strength, and balance, as well as stress management.

Conclusion

Campus recreation and fitness has come a long way since its early beginnings. Rather than a negative and distracting influence on campus, it is now viewed as a means to help in the development of the student as well as the university. Campus administrators now understand that campus recreation and fitness has not only physical, social, and educational benefits for students but also helps recruit and retain students while enhancing the university's image. The challenge that administrators face is keeping up with trends in recreation and fitness and the interests of students. Joining professional organizations such as NIRSA and having certified staff help keep administrators knowledgeable and better able to meet the needs of students, faculty, and staff.

Chapter Two Key Points

1. Campus recreation includes an array of recreation and leisure activity programming including intramurals, clubs, outdoor/adventure, fitness, aquatics, informal recreation, and instructional classes.
2. The Civil War marked a turning point in the development of recreation programs on campuses as fit men were needed for service during the war and, following their earlier opposition to such activities, churches after the war began to encourage recreation activity as a means to building morality and good character.
3. Early recreation programs were run by students for students as college officials saw such programs as not contributing to student learning and as detrimental to campus culture.
4. Following growth in the popularity of participation in recreation for recreation (as opposed to competition), colleges began to develop recreation programs distinct from intercollegiate athletics programs in the early 20th century.
5. The National Intramural Recreation Sports Association was formed at a meeting in 1950 following the publication of William Wasson's *A Comparative Study of Intramural Programs in Negro Colleges.*
6. The latter half of the 20th century saw a number of important changes in campus recreation programs. These changes include growth in the number of programs as both college enrollments and the number of colleges increased following World War II. There was increasing student interest in noncompetitive recreation opportunities, and the growing diversity of students on campus was reflected in campus recreation programs.
7. The report by Bryant, Anderson, and Dunn (1994), "Rationale for Independent Administration of Collegiate Recreational Sports Programs," capped the decades of growth and change with a clear call for recreation departments as stand-alone administrative entities on college campuses.
8. Theories of sports, play, and recreation inform contemporary professional practice in campus recreation.

9. Campus recreation programs can have a positive impact on student recruitment, retention, learning, and development. They can also have a positive impact on wellness for all members of the campus community, as well as on the image of the institution.

References

American College Health Association. *Healthy Campus 2010: Making It Happen.* Baltimore, MD: American College Health Association, 2002.

Barcelona, R. J., and Ross, C. M. "Participation Patterns in Campus Recreational Sports: An Examination of Quality of Student Effort From 1983 to 1998. *Recreational Sports Journal,* 2002, 26(1), 41–53.

Belch, H., Gebel, M., and Mas, G. "Relationship Between Student Recreation Complex Use, Academic Performance, and Persistence of First Time Freshmen." *NASPA Journal,* 2001, 39, 14–22.

Blumenthal, K. Campus Recreational Sports: Pivotal Players in Student Success. *Planning for Higher Education,* 2009, 37(2), 52–62.

Bryant, J., Anderson, B., and Dunn, J. M. *Rational for Independent Administration of Collegiate Recreational Sports Programs: A Position Paper.* Corvallis, OR: National Intramural-Recreational Sports Association, 1994.

Bryant, J., Banta, T., and Bradley, J. "Assessment Provides Insight into the Impact and Effectiveness of Campus Recreation Programs." *NASPA Journal,* 1995, 32, 153–160.

Buckworth, J. "Exercise Adherence in College Students: Issues and Preliminary Results." *Quest,* 2001, 53, 335–345.

Burton, A. W., and Wade, M. G. History of the University of Minnesota, School of Kinesiology, 2003. Retrieved December 15, 2010 from http://www.education.umn.edu/Kin/school/history.html.

Coakley, J. *Sports in Society: Issues and Controversies* (10th ed.). Boston: McGraw-Hill, 2009.

Csikszentmihalyi, M. *Flow: The psychology of optimal experience.* San Francisco: Jossey-Bass, 1990.

Franklin, D. S. "Student Development and Learning in Campus Recreation: Assessing Recreational Sports Directors' Awareness, Perceived Importance, and Application of and Satisfaction with CAS Standards." Unpublished doctoral dissertation. Ohio University, 2007.

Franklin, D. S., and Hardin, S. E. "Philosophical and Theoretical Foundations of Campus Recreation: Crossroads of Theory." In NIRSA (Ed.), Campus recreation: Essentials for the professional (pp. 3–20). Champaign, IL: Human Kinetics, 2008.

Gallagher, S. "News: Portland State University academic and student recreation center awarded 1st place." Portland State University, 2010. Retrieved on May 23, 2011 at http://www.pdx.edu/registration/news/portland-state-university-academic-and-student-recreation-center-awarded-1st-place/.

Haines, D. J. "Undergraduate Student Health Benefits from University Recreation." *Recreational Sport Journal,* 2001, 25(1), 25–33.

Haines, D. J. *National Intramural-Recreational Sports Association Member Survey Results.* Columbus, OH: National Research Institute for College Recreational Sports and Wellness, The Ohio State University, 2007.

Hall, D. "Participation in a Campus Recreation Program and Its Effect on Student Retention." *Recreational Sports Journal,* 2006, 20, 40–45.

Huesman, R. L., Brown, A. K., Lee, G., Kellogg, J. P., and Radcliffe, P. M. "Gym Bags and Mortarboards: Is Use of Campus Recreation Facilities Related to Student Success?" *NASPA Journal,* 2009, 46(1), 50–71.

Hums, M. A., and MacLean, J. C. *Governance and policy in sport organizations* (2nd ed.). Scottsdale, AZ: Holcomb Hathaway, 2008.

Hussar, W. J., and Bailey, T. M. *Projections of Education Statistics to 2018* (NCES 2009–062). Washington, D.C.: National Center for Education Statistics, Institute of Education Sciences, U.S. Department of Education, 2009.

Kampf, S. "Impact of College Recreation Centers on Enrollment." *Recreational Sports Journal,* 2010, 34, 112–118.

Keeling, R. P. Introduction. In R. P. Keeling (Ed.). *Learning Reconsidered 2: Implementing a Campus-wide Focus on the Student Learning Experience.* 2006. Retrieved from www.acpa.nche.edu/pub/documents/LearningReconsidered2.pdf.

Kirsch, G. B. "Bats, Balls, and Bullets." *Civil War Times Illustrated,* 1998, 37(2), 30–37.

Komives, S. R., and Schoper, S. In R. P. Keeling (Ed.). *Learning Reconsidered 2: Implementing a Campus-wide Focus on the Student Learning Experience.* 2006. Retrieved from www.acpa.nche.edu/pub/documents/LearningReconsidered2.pdf.

Latawsky, N. R., Schneider, R. G., Pederson, P. M., and Palmer, C. J. (2003). "Factors Influencing the College Selection Process of Student-athletes: Are Their Factors Similar to Non-athletes." *College Student Journal,* 2003, 37, 604–610.

Lewis, J. B., Jones, T. R., Lamke, G., and Dunn, J. M. "Recreational Sport: Making the Grade on College Campuses." *Parks and Recreation,* 1998, 33(12), 72–77.

Lindsey, R., and Sessoms, E. "Assessment of a Campus Recreation Program on Student Recruitment, Retention, and Frequency of Participation Across Certain Demographic Variables." *Recreational Sports Journal,* 2006, 30, 30–39.

McLean, D. D., Hurd, A. R., and Rogers, N. B. *Kraus' Recreation and Leisure in Modern Society* (8th ed.). Sudbury, MA: Jones and Bartlett, 2008.

Means, L. E. *The Organization and Administration of Intramural Sports* (2nd ed.). St. Louis, MO: C.V. Mosby, 1952.

Moffitt, J. "Recreating Retention." *Recreational Sports Journal,* 2010, 34, 24–33.

National Intramural-Recreational Sports Association. "2002 Recreational Sports Expenditure Survey." 2002. Accessed on February 28, 2012 at http://www.nirsa.org/Content/NavigationMenu/Individual/Research/Recreational_Sports_Expenditure_Survey.pdf.

National Intramural-Recreational Sports Association. "History and Evolution of Campus Recreation." In NIRSA (Ed.), *Campus Recreation: Essentials for the Professional.* Champaign, IL: Human Kinetics, 2008.

National Intramural-Recreational Sports Association. "NIRSA Outstanding Sports Facilities Awards." 2011a. Accessed on May 23, 2011 at http://www.nirsa.org/Content/NavigationMenu/AboutUs/Awards/OutstandingSportsFacilitiesAward/Oustanding_Sports_F.htm.

National Intramural-Recreational Sports Association. "Timeline." 2011b. Accessed on May 23, 2011 at http://www.nirsa.org/Content/NavigationMenu/AboutUs/History/Timeline/Timeline.htm.

Patton, J. "Healthy Relationship: More Schools Are Realizing That Student Health and Student Recreation Can Be Compatible Cohabitants Under One Campus Wellness Roof." *Athletic Business*, November 2009, 26–31.

Reaney, M. J. "The Psychology of the Organized Group Game." *Psychological Review*, 1916, 4, 76.

Rice, E. A., Hutchinson, J. L., and Lee, M. *A Brief History of Physical Education*. New York: Ronald Press, 1958.

Robinson, E. S. "The Compensatory Function of Make-believe Play." *Psychological Review*, 1920, 27, 429–439

Rothwell, E., and Theodore, P. "Intramurals and College Student Development: The Role of Intramurals on Values Clarification." *Recreational Sports Journal*, 2006, 30, 46–52.

Schiller, F. V. *Essays Esthetical and Philosophical*. London: George Bell, 1875.

Sessoms, H. D., and Henderson, K. A. Introduction to Leisure Services (7th ed.). State College, PA: Venture Publishing, 1994.

Spencer, H. *Principles of Psychology*. New York: Appleton, 1873.

Sutton-Smith, B. *Ambiguity of Play*. Boston: Harvard University Press, 1997.

Veltri, F., Miller, J., and Harris, A. "Club Sport National Tournament: Economic Impact of a Small Event on a Mid-sized Community." *Recreational Sports Journal*, 2009, 33(2), 119–128.

Zizzi, S., Ayers, S., Watson II, J. C., and Keeler, L. A. "Assessing the Impact of New Student Campus Recreation Centers." *NASPA Journal*, 2004, 41(4), 588–630.

CHAPTER THREE

THEORETICAL FOUNDATIONS

Mary F. Howard-Hamilton and Joy Gaston Gayles

Using theory can help in making sense of and responding to important issues that occur on a daily basis. This chapter reviews selected theoretical perspectives that can inform intercollegiate athletics and recreation administration in that effort. The chapter begins by defining what theory is and how it can be used in practice. The balance of the chapter presents key families of theories and how the principles and assumptions of those theories can be applied to college athletics and recreation administration.

Definition of Theory

Before discussing various families of theories and applications for athletics and recreation administration, it is important to define theory. At a basic level, theory is derived from the need for individuals to understand the world and their experiences. Thus, theories often serve as a way to organize a large number of data about a phenomenon. As a result of the need to make sense of experiences in the context of the world around us, people develop *theories in use* (Argyris and Schön, 1974), individually based assumptions and propositions to help explain and interpret what we see and experience on a daily basis. However, we cannot rely solely on informal theories in use because there is no way to know whether our interpretations are accurate. Formal theories, unlike theories in use, have been tested empirically and are considered valid interpretations that explain interrelationships among two or more constructs. As such, formal theories provide a level of confidence in interpretations of and connections between variables or constructs of interest.

There are many definitions of theory in the literature. Kerlinger's (1979) description is one of the most often cited in the research methods literature. Kerlinger defines theory as "a set of interrelated constructs (variables), definitions, and propositions that presents a systematic view of phenomenon by specifying relations among variables with the purpose of explaining natural phenomenon" (p. 64). This definition is popular because it clearly delineates the key components of a theory and how they work together to explain a phenomenon. The systematic aspect of the definition is important because it serves as a bridge that connects two or more constructs together that would otherwise exist at random.

Creswell's (2009) rainbow metaphor offers a helpful illustration of how theories work. Take a moment to envision a rainbow. At opposite ends of the rainbow are two different variables. Theory, represented by the rainbow, is the overarching rationale that ties the two variables together in a meaningful way and explains the interrelationship between them (Creswell, 2009). Without the rainbow, or the overarching rationale, the variables would otherwise remain separate and unrelated. Thinking about theory as a way to explain relationships between variables is a simplified way of defining theory that helps make sense of our experiences and the world around us (Singleton and Straits, 2005). Theory can also outline anticipatory relationships—that is, how constructs are expected to relate to one another—and are usually stated in the form of propositions or hypotheses about the interrelationship between two or more constructs about a phenomenon of interest.

Uses of Theory

In addition to serving as a rationale to explain how constructs are interrelated, theory has several important uses for those who work in college settings. Evans, Forney, Guido-DiBrito, Patton, and Renn (2010) identify four key uses of theory. First, theory can be used to describe what is happening in the environment in terms of attitudes, values, and behaviors of individuals and across various domains. Second, theory can be used to help us make sense of behavior. Third, theory can be used to predict behaviors that might occur given a predetermined set of criteria. Although not many theories actually achieve this purpose, it would be ideal to use theory to predict outcomes of interest based on background characteristics and other attributes of individuals. The fourth use of theory has not yet been actualized, and that is using theory to control outcomes. For example, a well-supported theory might allow college administrators to produce developmental outcomes such as high levels of critical thinking or positive identity formation by controlling various aspects of the college environment to produce these desired outcomes. Most of the theories reviewed in this chapter are highly descriptive and most useful for describing and explaining behavior. More empirical research is needed to test and validate the theories covered here before the last two uses can be realized.

Challenges to Using Theory

Applying theory to practice should play a central role in intercollegiate athletics and recreational administration, yet there can be challenges to doing so. Taking the time to apply theory to everyday practice is time consuming. Practitioners often find that they do not have adequate time to stay up-to-date on the literature and think through situations from a theoretical perspective that need an immediate response. Nonetheless, practitioners should be encouraged explore ways to effectively integrate theory into practice in their work environments and regularly participate in professional development activities to stay current in the field. Discussing ways to integrate theory into practice should be a regular part of staff meetings and training.

Another barrier to using theory is the lack of knowledge about relevant theories. Not all administrators have the same level of education, nor do they all earn their degrees in the same discipline. There may be wide differences between colleagues in terms of theoretical knowledge and breadth that can be applied in practical situations. As a result, administrators must identify resources, such as this text, or perhaps enroll in courses that introduce various theoretical perspectives from a practical standpoint.

In addition, not all administrators on college campuses are supportive of using theory in practice, and there is often debate about which theories are considered relevant or valid. Our view is that theory, although imperfect, should be used when applicable. Campus administrators may find that theories are rarely used in their entirety, but rather in chunks. It may also be helpful to encourage individuals to use theories that make the most sense to them and at least partially explain or describe their own experience. Those who are less supportive of using theory in practice might benefit from professional development opportunities to learn more about various theories and how to apply them in practice.

The misuse of theory poses a serious danger to students as well as administrators. The inappropriate use of theory, such as using theory to place people into boxes or label individuals, should be strongly discouraged (Evans, Forney, and Guido-DiBrito, 1998). It may be tempting to rely on and apply theory in its entirety; however, it may be more appropriate and useful to apply key ideas or perspectives from a theory or multiple theories to interpret or better understand a situation. In sum, gross misuses of theory should be avoided at all cost and the appropriate uses of theory should be a central part of professional training and development for administrators.

Bodies of Theory

Theories can be used to adjust personal perspectives and views on how students act or react to certain situations, observe and understand how the administrative team behaves or interacts with others, and assess how the organizational environment is or is not conducive to human development. As mentioned earlier, many people use a set of concepts daily but are not aware of how the processing of their environment and activities is directly connected to actually making decisions based upon those informal theories (Evans et al., 2010). Having an understanding of a few formal theoretical concepts allows more diverse perspectives to become part of a repertoire and opens up possibilities for innovative solutions to everyday issues.

Developmental Theories

There have been numerous theories and models created over the past seven decades to explain how and why individuals may act or react to other individuals, certain situations, and the environment where they live and work. Understanding the behaviors of an individual using the psychosocial identity developmental theories can be instrumental in gaining more insight about people and what major development tasks they face at various points over their lifetime (Evans et al., 2010). Assessing intellectual or cognitive development can help in understanding how individuals process information and reason about their life experiences. The environment also shapes behavior, habits, and cultures so the ecological theories can explain the adaptation process that occurs within organizations and how that process impacts everyone in the setting (Evans et al., 2010).

Psychosocial Development. Psychosocial theories address the interaction between individual identity and social relationships, and they often focus on human development. The seven-vector model of Chickering and Reisser (1993) is commonly used in higher education. Chickering and Reisser (1993) conceptualized human development as a movement through seven vectors, a variety of complicated tasks and challenges to enhance one's growth and development: (1) developing competence, (2) managing emotions, (3) moving through autonomy toward interdependence, (4) developing mature interpersonal relationships, (5) establishing identity, (6) developing purpose, and (7) developing integrity.

College presents a safe environment for individuals to make progress on these tasks. Although the vectors are not specifically associated with any particular life stage, the general thought is that the first four vectors are resolved during the early college years, and the last three are resolved during the later college years. However, there is some evidence that suggests that individuals grapple with establishing identity and developing purpose earlier in their college experience (Foubert, Nixon, Sisson, and Barne, 2005).

Moral Reasoning. The sensitivity to understand the implications of one's behavior is at the foundation of moral behavior and thought. Kohlberg's (1969) work is one example of a theory on the development of moral reasoning. The steps to gaining a high level of moral judgment are represented as a six-stage process. The six stages of Kohlberg's model are divided into the three levels: preconventional, conventional, and postconventional. The stages describe how individuals reason about moral issues in terms of what is just and the concept of reciprocity or mutual exchange. In the first stage individuals define what is just by obeying rules and regulations to avoid punishment. In the second stage individuals determine what is right or just "by what is fair, and equal exchange, or agreement" (Evans et al., 2010, p. 103). What is just in the third stage involves behaving properly in order to meet the expectations of friends, family, and other close associates. What is just in the fourth stage is defined by societal rules and regulations that are typically obeyed because it is considered morally correct to uphold the law and rules. The final two stages recognize that human rights are tantamount and decisions are made based upon equality and universal principles that sometime supersede law and order.

Intellectual Development. The theorist associated with this concept is William Perry, who researched college students and assessed their mode of thinking and learning (Love and Guthrie, 1999). From his research on college men, Perry developed nine positions of cognitive development which can be capsulated into three broader categories: (1) duality, (2) multiplicity, and (3) relativism. Dualistic thinkers make decisions based upon a right or wrong frame of reference in which there are no gray areas. Multiple realities do not exist, and there is a clear right or wrong answer for every question. Individuals have the capacity to consider and begin to examine multiple points of view in the second area of cognitive development and accept that there may be more than one correct answer, method, or sense-making of a particular situation. Finally, the relativist is constantly thinking, processing, and adapting to new ideas and information because there is a plethora of areas for which there is no concrete answer. Relativistic thinkers are able to use the evidence that they have to date to build an argument to support their position in spite of uncertainty about knowledge. Further, they are able to use these justifications in their decision-making process.

Consider Case Study 1 at the end of the chapter, the athletics academic advisor working with student-athletes with a high grade-point average. The application of intellectual development could provide some intervention tools to work with everyone engaged in perpetuating a "dumb jock" mindset. Danni should acknowledge the higher level of intellectual complexity and curiosity of the student-athletes and have them create a support group. A discussion among them could be the academic image of the student-athlete. Another intervention would be to involve the student-athletes in leadership honor organizations such as Omicron Delta Kappa that would emphasize their intellectual capabilities and athletic skills. The intellectual growth for the student-athletes is critical so they can move from multiplicity to relativism. Stagnation or temporizing in one stage and even regression to a lower stage could occur in the intellectual development of the student-athletes if they continue to meet with a lack of support for their cognitive skills (Love and Guthrie, 1999).

Racial Identity. A multiculturally competent person has the awareness, knowledge, and skills necessary to work effectively with diverse groups. This person is aware that there is diversity everywhere and is apprised of situations in which one may say or do the wrong thing that may hurt someone else. The person also has complete and accurate knowledge about people different from himself or herself that is free of stereotypes and false media representation. The multicultural competent administrators have, in addition, the ability to combine their awareness and knowledge about diverse groups to working effectively with people different from themselves. The culminating task of this theory is using one's awareness, knowledge, and skills to challenge systemic oppression or to be the person who speaks up when there is an issue of discrimination (Howard-Hamilton and Hinton, 2011). Sensitivity to persons from diverse backgrounds is important because of the transitioning of racial and ethnic groups on college campuses.

Observing the dissonance that occurs when majority students become uncomfortable with diverse students was presented in the Howard-Hamilton and Hinton Behavioral Model of Multicultural Competence (Howard-Hamilton, Cuyjet, and Cooper, 2011). It was found that individuals from the dominant group, or European-Americans, struggled with the concept of difference because they had been taught to homogenize themselves, and if asked "who are you" they would answer I am "American" rather than identify by a racial or ethnic group. This discomfort was categorized by five behavioral stages. First, there is discomfort or anxiousness of having to process and discuss issues related to race. Second, there begins to be some desire to explore and the person is curious about the ways in which differences can be an avenue into a new journey about another person's culture. The next step is to embrace one's privileged status so no barriers will exist between the parties attempting to understand each other's point of view and cultural experiences. This allows the individual to communicate from a level of comfort and openness in stage four, knowing that it was a lifetime of indoctrination to conform to society's notions of race. Thus the last stage is embracing a lifetime of diversity development and encounters, and being willing to see differences.

Sociology of Sport Theory

Sport is a sociological manifestation when it is defined or perceived from the lens of those who are the observers, the public (Polite, Waller, Hill, and Norwood, 2009). Furthermore, it is "how dominant ideologies are formed, sport as a social institution, the role of the coach, the athlete, black and white, the fan, the economics of sport and the assessment of the sports creed" (Polite et al., p. 148). Sport is a significant behavioral and motivational tool in our society because it has the covert and overt power to act as "agent for social change" (Polite et al., p. 148) if those who administer the teams and athletes create avenues to make this a reality.

Dr. Harry Edwards is a pivotal scholar in sports sociology. He is a faculty activist who was engaged in sport reform during the 1960s through the mid-1980s. His seminal book, *The Sociology of Sport* (Edwards, 1973), critiqued the role of sport in our society and in particular the role and perceptions of the Black athlete from a political perspective (Polite *et al.*, 2009). Edwards' overall contribution to the developing concept of sociology of sport from a postmodern perspective is that he discussed at great length how sports permeates all structures in society and creates specific images that society internalizes about athletes and athletic ability. This timely and accurate understanding of the impact of sports in our society has become globalized beyond the predictions that Edwards proffered because of our use of technology, the expansion of cable networks dedicated 24/7 to sports, and the dependence on athletics teams to bring revenue into institutions. Using sociological perspectives to understand the influence of society on the decisions that are made by athletics administrators and the trickle-down effect on the staff and student-athletes provides an additional theoretical concept to use when engaged in practice on a day-to-day basis.

Organizational Theory

Administration can be defined as "the arrangement of personnel for facilitating the accomplishment of some agreed upon purpose through the allocation of roles and responsibilities" (Selznick, 2010, p. 3). Both athletics and recreation departments mobilize large numbers of staff, students, and university officials to complete a multiplicity of assigned functions. Given the large tasks at hand for these complex organizations, what type of leadership practices should be in place to achieve the desired goals and outcomes for the administrative unit and all of its stakeholders? Understanding organizational theory allows leaders to successfully implement programs, policies, and procedures in a timely manner because they take the time to observe and implement the correct action by applying the theory to practice. If leaders are "armed with an understanding of organizations and how they work" they can "appreciate the need for good, consistent, integrating decisions" (Hodge, Anthony, and Gales, 2003, p. 23). The understanding of organizational theory can explain what may be confusing or challenging, thus saving time, thought, and energy. An effective organizational theory can also assist in understanding how the environment has a direct impact on the behavior and outcomes of the persons interacting within that unit (Lewin, 1936).

Bolman and Deal (2008) provide leaders with four frames to observe and make sense of their organizations: political, structural, human resource, and symbolic frames. Frames are tools for performing different tasks using a perspective, a set of connected ideas, or a story-line that gives order and meaning to disparate bits of data. The leadership frames are useful for organizational effectiveness because they can be easily translated to most systems. The key is for the leader to adapt and use each frame interchangeably.

When using the *political* frame the metaphor that can be envisioned is the organization as a jungle with a lot of species living in the ecosystem. As the saying goes, in this environment the lion will lie down with the lamb but the lamb will not get very much sleep. Organizations are coalitions of divisions, individuals, and groups, but there may be enduring differences among coalition members. In this organization there may be scarce resources, so the motivation of individuals may be, "what will I get out of this and will there be enough to go around?"

The political frame uses conflict as a central process, with power as a key resource. Often, no amount of data or logic will get people to agree. In order for organizational members to coexist, goals emerge from bargaining along with negotiation among stakeholders. Political people know more about politics than they think they do, and they are uncomfortable with the concepts of politics.

The *structural* frame is the oldest frame rooted in organizational theory (Bolman and Deal, 2008). A metaphor often used to understand how this concept emerged is viewing organizations as factories to maintain efficiency. The overall assumption is that organizations exist to achieve goals. There should be rationality, tasks, goals, and human relations. Differentiation occurs within the organization, and there should be a division of labor. If the organization is to thrive there must be some integration of abilities and skills by pulling every person together around a shared vision. This could be achieved by aligning the structure with situations, goals, technology, and environment.

The *human resource* frame evolved out of the early 20th century and post WWII work environments (Bolman and Deal, 2008). The extended family is a common metaphor for the human resource frame because relationships with each other are important. A cohesive organizational family exists to serve people, and the people need each other. The organization has the team aligned and there are reciprocal benefits between administration and worker. In other words the organization and staff need each other and one or both will fail if the fit is poor.

The final frame is the *symbolic* frame in which the organization is metaphorically viewed as a theater or temple (Bolman and Deal, 2008). "The whole world is a stage," and it is the same with organizations; they play to an audience, and there are messages sent to the audience about the functioning of the unit and its members. Conceptually this frame is more challenging because the organization is trying to reach the correct audience, telling a story that is appropriate for them. Many events and activities are more important for what they express than what they achieve. There are traditions, symbols, history, and rituals that are part of the symbolic nature of an organization. The leader should respect the symbols of the organization and provide rewards or incentives when the team engages in the appropriate theatrics that give the audience the story that has meaning and provides an empowering message.

Leadership Theory

A theoretical framework that can be easily compared to the behaviors, tasks, and traits of a coach, team, and athletics administrators is the Path-Goal Theory (Northouse, 2009). Path-Goal Theory focuses on the importance of leaders as motivators to get individuals, or in this case teams, to achieve specific goals. There is a relationship among the leader's or coach's style, the attributes of the staff or team, and the work environment or athletics venue. The overarching goal of this theory is to motivate those who work for an organization through performance enhancements and to have individuals comfortable with the output of energy for that organization and leader (Northouse, 2009).

The Path-Goal Theory rests upon the importance of having a motivational leader, such as an athletics administrator, who can inspire the organization staff and provide some visualization that an outcome will have long-term benefits because they are exceptionally capable and competent in their performance. When connecting the theory to the practice of leadership in intercollegiate athletics there is a direct relationship because the coach must have the team in harmony to achieve a specific goal, such as a conference championship, and the motivational incentives. The incentives or rewards are given when there is some improvement in the skill set of the subordinate that helps the organization or team meet a goal. An athletic or sport example would be the presentation of a game ball to a player who was inspirational in helping the team win a game or a helmet sticker to a player or players who excelled on and off the field or court. Northouse (2009) states that the primary objectives of the Path-Goal Theory are (1) define goals, (2) clarify a path, (3) remove obstacles, and (4) provide support.

There are four types of leadership behaviors that can be used when attempting to motivate a team toward specific goals (Northouse, 2009).

The first behavior is *participative leadership,* in which there is an invitation to share in the motivational tasks of achieving a goal. The leader is very collaborative and seeks others' opinions so that they can be integrated into the method for achieving the team goals. The team who works with this type of leader becomes internally driven because team members feel personally connected to the decisions being made and have control over their own destiny. The second behavior is *achievement-oriented leadership,* which entails a high standard of excellence and challenging goals, along with the outcome of continuous improvement by the team. In *supportive leadership,* the third behavior, the coach attends to the needs and nurturance of the team. There is an emphasis placed on creating an overall supportive environment with egalitarian policies and procedures so that all voices are heard and respected. The student-athlete who seeks out this type of leadership may have a strong need for affiliation with staff, administrators, coaches, and teammates. The fourth leadership behavior, the *directive leader,* sets specific timelines for the completion of activities and provides thorough and detailed directions. There may be rules, policies, and regulations attached to the tasks that are required so that there can be accuracy and expediency to the completed tasks. The student-athlete who seeks this type of leader has a desire for routines and structure.

Path-Goal Theory is useful in athletics administration because there are a large number of individuals who assist in making the organization effective (Northouse, 2009). The diversity within an athletics administrative organization ranges from the president of the university or college to the student-athlete on the court or field. The range of behaviors that the leader can choose from in this theory can be adapted for any person, group, unit, team, and situation. The leader needs to be comfortable in adapting to multiple situations with the outcome being the creation of an environment that has motivated and goal-oriented members.

Campus Ecology Theory

Campus ecology theories describe the relationship between campus environments and individuals within the environment. More specifically, this framework involves how the physical and social environments affect individuals within college settings and how administrators, faculty, and staff can create conditions that lead to desired behaviors and outcomes of student learning and personal development (Strange and Banning, 2001). In essence, campus ecology theories explore how the environment influences the people within it and, in turn, how people influence their environments.

This framework can be very useful for athletics and recreation administrators in their work with students on the college campus.

Strange and Banning (2001), in their book *Educating by Design: Creating Campus Learning Environments That Work,* discuss four components of campus environments—*physical, human aggregate, organizational,* and *constructed*—and how they can be used by campus administrators to design effective learning environments.

Physical Environment. The *physical environment* consists of both natural and synthetic aspects of the campus environment. Natural aspects of the environment include the climate, geographical location, and weather, whereas synthetic features of the environment are the landscape, architectural design, spatial arrangements, and the layout of campus facilities and buildings. Campus administrators should give attention to the physical aspects of the campus environment because they have the potential to make a strong statement about and a lasting impression of the institution for visitors and prospective students. Further, the physical aspects of the environment send powerful nonverbal messages about what is valued at the institution and the kinds of behaviors that are expected, as well as those deemed unacceptable. Finally, physical aspects of the campus environments function to limit some behaviors but encourage other behaviors. For example, it is common to see large green spaces on campuses lined with cement paths to and from buildings that dictate where people should walk between buildings. The cement paths send a nonverbal message to individuals not to walk on the grass and at the same time encourage individuals to walk along the cement path to arrive at their destination. In reference to the scenario in Case Study 4 at the end of the chapter, Wilson College has designated green space on the south side of campus for students to play intramural sports, which encourages students to spend time outdoors and interact with their peers when not in class or studying. Athletics and recreation administrators can appreciate the usefulness of physical aspects of the campus environment to communicate desired behaviors and send important nonverbal messages to individuals about the importance of goals and values within the unit.

Human Aggregate Environment. The *human aggregate dimension* of campus environments describes the collective characteristics and traits of students and subcultures of students within the campus environment. Some campuses are known by the traits that students exhibit that dominate the campus environment. Wilson College is known for the high percentage of students who participate in intramural sports. It follows that recreation participation is a characteristic that dominates the environment at Wilson College. Similarly, Ivy League institutions are known for having students with high academic ability and are often described by others in this way. The collective characteristics of the environment ultimately have an influence on the extent to which individuals are satisfied with, attracted to, and retained within the environment. A freshman attending Wilson College who enjoys outdoor and recreation activities is likely to be attracted and satisfied at Wilson and also likely to persist through graduation.

The study of students in the aggregate and characteristics of student subcultures within campus environments began as early as the 1950s. Clark and Trow (1966) collected data from students at the University of California Berkley during the 1950s and 1960s—the results of which formed their typology of student subcultures. Clark and Trow's typology of student subcultures is one of the most commonly cited in the literature and continues to be relevant today. Clark and Trow identified two major orientations—the extent to which individuals identify with ideas and the extent to which individuals identify with an institution—that lead to the formation of four dominant subcultures. The academic subculture is characterized by students who identify with intellectual ideas as well as the institution. Students within this subculture are considered to be serious students who work hard, achieve good grades, and relate to faculty very well. Although members of the academic subculture are also interested in the institution, they place a premium on the intellectual life at the institution.

Students who identify with the institution, but not so much with the ideas within the institution are classified as the collegiate subculture. The collegiate subculture, unlike the academic subculture, places a premium on campus social life, extracurricular activities, athletics, and friendships. However, they tend show resistance toward serious intellectual demands of the institution. The vocational subculture is characterized by students who exhibit little identification with either the ideas within the institution or the institution itself. These students enter college with specific goals related to career preparation and training. Vocational students view higher education as a means to upward social mobility. Because vocational students are very career oriented, they often times remain detached from both academic and social life at the institution.

Students who identify with ideas, but not as much with their institution, are characterized as nonconformist. These students value individual style and show concern about their personal identity and self-awareness. As such, they typically perform well in classes of interest to them, but do not put forth much effort in courses that hold no personal value to them.

Further, nonconformists are often characterized by their hostility toward university administration and their lack of interest in the social aspects of college life. However, they tend to be most interested in the cultural and political aspects of the university and the surrounding community.

Since Clark and Trow's (1966) classification of student subcultures, other scholars developed other classifications of student subcultures that in some ways mirror their work and in other ways expand upon it. Similar to Clark and Trow, Horowitz (1986) developed a typology of student subcultures with four dominant groups: outsider, collegiate man, new outsider, and rebel. Astin (1993) used data from the Cooperative Institutional Research Program at UCLA that examines attitudes, expectations, behaviors, and values of incoming freshmen each year to examine student subcultures. Seven student types were derived from the data (as opposed to four), which included scholars, social activists, artists, hedonists, leaders, status strivers, and uncommitted students.

Three constructs are important to understanding dominant subcultures or characteristics in the college environment. *Differentiation* involves the extent to which a particular subculture or type dominates the college environment. Campuses that have a high percentage of students who identify with one type are considered highly differentiated. Undifferentiated environments are more difficult to understand because no one particular subculture dominates the environment, which is instead made up of multiple subcultures. *Consistency* within the environment is defined as how subcultures are related to each other. Highly consistent environments are those with large populations of students who are of similar types. Inconsistent environments consist of divergent student types within the campus environment, a situation that makes it difficult to understand rewards and demands. Finally, *congruency* refers to the extent to which a person's type matches the environmental type.

Organizational Environment. The *organizational component* of campus environments involves the systemic structures within colleges and universities related to goals such as decision making, rewards, regulations and rules, resource allocation, and complexity. Strange and Banning (2001) noted seven organizational structures that influence campus environments. First, organizational *complexity* is described by the level of expertise within various units on campus. Organizations with a high degree of complexity typically have a large percentage of professionally trained individuals with high levels of expertise in a given field.

Second, *centralization* involves how power and decision making is distributed throughout the institution. In highly centralized units, few individuals, usually those at the top of the organization, hold most if not all of the decision-making power within the institution. Within decentralized units, the decision making is dispersed in a much more collaborative manner, with the result that many individuals within the institution hold decision-making power. Case Study 4 involving Wilson College's decision to convert the intramural field to a parking lot is an example of a decision that was made at the top of the organization, thus indicating a centralized institution.

The third component, *formalization*, is associated with the role that rules and regulations play in an organization. Their importance and degree of formality, the process through which they are developed and the ways in which they are enforced, and the extent to which they reflect the needs and interests of the full array of members of the organization all impact on the organizational environment.

Fourth, *stratification* refers to the reward structure within an organization. Institutions with many levels of status and reward systems are considered to be highly stratified. Status levels consist of titles and rank, which are often related to reward structures such as prestige, salary, and other privileges reserved for those higher in rank. Highly stratified environments have the potential to be divisive and foster competition within the environment, which can have negative consequences for productivity and morale.

The fifth organizational structure identified by Strange and Banning (2001) is *production*, which is described as the quality and quantity of products and services within the organization. An organization is often measured by the products it produces and the services it provides. Higher education institutions are measured by product demands such as the labor market outcomes of graduates, amount of grant dollars received, and number of publications per faculty member, to name a few. An efficient organization is one in which the quantity of production is high. However, administrators must be cautious, as increases in production often lead to sacrifices in quality. This trade-off should be heavily considered in terms of how well higher education institutions are meeting their educational goals as outlined in the mission statement.

Sixth, organizational *efficiency* involves getting the most of the products and services provided for the least amount of cost. A highly efficient unit is one in which maximum efficiency can be obtained for the lowest cost possible (without sacrificing quality). One of the difficulties of organizational efficiency cited by Strange and Banning (2001) is that cost reduction is difficult to evaluate and monitor within higher education institutions. Placing a dollar value on some of the more abstract outcomes of higher education institutions, such as number of publications by faculty member or leadership opportunities for students, is not the most effective way of gaining a sense of the institution's efficiency.

Lastly, morale plays an important role in the organizational environment. The greater a member's morale, the more likely it is that the or she will be committed to being an active, contributing, and ongoing member of the organization. The lower the morale, the less likely that person will be engaged, positive, and retained.

Taken together, these seven organizational structures can be used to create academic environments that are either static or dynamic (or somewhere in between). Dynamic environments are those characterized as flexible and adaptable to change. Static environments are characterized as rigid and resistant to change. Further, dynamic environments are characterized by high degrees of complexity and low degrees of centralization, formalization, stratification, and efficiency, and they place a premium on the quality of production in terms of services and outcomes produced. Static environments, in contrast, are characterized by low degrees of complexity and high degrees of centralization, formalization, stratification, and efficiency. In addition, static environments may place too much emphasis of efficiency, which leads to a focus on quantity over quality.

Constructed Environment. The *constructed environment* focuses on the personal views and experiences of people within the campus environment. These subjective views are interpreted as measures of environmental press, social climate, and/or organizational culture. The extent to which people are satisfied, attracted to, and remain stable in an environment is largely based on their perceptions and experiences within that environment. More specifically, environmental press is derived from the collective activities as perceived by individuals within the environment. For example, a high percentage of students on a campus reporting earning a grade point average of 3.0 or better would indicate an academic achievement environmental press at that institution. Eleven types of environmental press have been identified in the literature: aspiration level, intellectual climate, student dignity, academic climate, academic achievement, self-expression, group life, academic organization, social form, play-work, and vocational climate (Pace and Stern, 1958).

Social climate represents another component of constructed environments and has been described as the personality of the environment (Hamrick, Evans, and Schuh, 2002). Based on the work of Moos (1979, 1986) on studying social climates, three general domains can be found within the campus environment—relationships, personal growth and development, and system maintenance and change. The relationship domain represents individuals' involvement and mutual support for one another within the environment—or in essence the interactions between people within the environment. Personal growth and development is described as areas in which individuals change in positive ways in accordance to intended outcomes of the institution. Finally, system maintenance and change involves the capacity for the environment to adapt to change and how the environment functions overall.

The culture of the environment is understood through the perceptions of the people within the environment. Thus, campus culture refers to the "collective, mutually shaping patterns of institutional history, mission, physical settings, norms, traditions, values, practices, beliefs, and assumptions that guide behavior of individuals and groups in an institution of higher education." (Kuh and Hall, 1993, p. 2). More specifically, scholars have recognized four aspects of campus culture—artifacts, perspectives, values, and assumptions (Kuh and Hall, 1993; Strange and Banning, 2001).

- Campus artifacts are physical, verbal, or behavioral aspects of culture that have shared meaning for individuals within the environment. Physical artifacts, for example, can be historical buildings or landmarks that hold significance for members of the campus community; these are usually a part of formal campus tours that highlight places of special meaning. Verbal artifacts include language, sagas, myths, and stories associated with the institution, whereas behavioral artifacts are events or activities that bring individuals together in a meaningful way.
- Campus perspectives represent shared norms and values within the campus environment, which communicate to members of the campus community what is acceptable and what is not acceptable.
- Campus values include espoused and enacted values. Espoused values are those often communicated in the mission statement, in ceremonial speeches, and within the campus catalog. Enacted values are those that guide decision making within the environment on a daily basis.
- Campus assumptions are tacit beliefs that individuals use to understand their role and how to relate to others; these represent perhaps the deepest form of campus culture (Manning, 1993).

Conclusion

Theories help individuals understand and explain phenomena that occur in environments. The theories and examples provided in this chapter are just the tip of the iceberg in terms of frameworks available to effectively lead an administrative area in athletics or recreation at a college or university. The leaders of such units are being challenged in today's higher education environment "with the necessity to retrench, restructure, and streamline organizations (and even change their mission in some cases) in response to these and other perhaps equally powerful environmental forces if they and their organizations are to survive" (Hodge, Anthony, and Gales, 2003, p. 23).

Case Studies

As noted in the chapter, theory can be useful in helping to identify, understand, and address individual and organizational behaviors. As you read through the following case studies, consider which of the theories discussed might be helpful to work through the challenges and opportunities presented and how you might use them.

Case Study #1

Danni is an athletics academic advisor who has been working with student-athletes with grade point averages above 3.5, many of whom feel constantly torn about their passion for sports and commitment to learning in the classroom environment. The student-athletes feel abandoned because most of the administrators they encounter do not ask about their classroom successes. They sense that the support and encouragement is based solely on their athletic prowess. Danni is looking for a way to help high-achieving student-athletes strike a balance between their academic and athletics goals and interests.

Case Study #2

Mikel plays tennis and was a member of the conference championship team last year. The university administrators began trimming the budget and decided that tennis was a program that needed to be eliminated to save and distribute funds to other intercollegiate sports. There was no discussion with the student-athletes about the decision and there was very little or no time at all to transfer to another university because the decision was made very late in the academic year. Mikel is extremely upset but decides to stay because her grades are good enough for an academic scholarship. But what is going to happen to her other teammates? There is no one to talk to because the coaches have all started their job search.

Case Study #3

Jessi is the associate athletics director at a midsized public university. She has numerous duties that keep her involved primarily with the daily administrative functions of the athletics department. She has discovered that most female student-athletes seek her out for counsel, advice, and issues regarding coach versus student-athlete. She is now aware that there needs to be a model of support in the overall environment so that student-athletes can be confident that everyone in the athletics department has the interests, skills, and sensitivity to be of assistance in any circumstance.

Case Study #4

Students at Wilson College take an active role in intramural sports; over 60% of the student body participate in one or more sport. The student body is heavily involved in deciding and planning the wide array of sports that are offered through the intramural program. The program is so popular that most sports often have a wait-list for participation. It has been a long-standing tradition that green space on the south side of campus is designated for outdoor intramural sports. The student body recently learned that their green space for intramural sports will be transformed into a parking garage for the growing population at Wilson College. This will leave students without a place to play outdoor intramural sports. The student body was not consulted about this decision, and students are very upset about this sudden course of action. They have complained to the director of recreation and sports at Wilson College.

Chapter Three Key Points

1. Kerlinger (1979) defines theory as "a set of interrelated constructs (variables), definitions, and propositions that presents a systematic view of phenomenon by specifying relations among variables with the purpose of explaining natural phenomenon" (p. 64).
2. Evans, Forney, Guido-DiBrito, Patton, and Renn (2010) identify four key uses of theory: describe what is happening; help make sense of behavior; predict behaviors that might occur; and control outcomes.
3. There are several major bodies of theory that can be useful in the professional administrative practice of intercollegiate athletics or recreation:

developmental, sociology of sport, organization, leadership, and campus ecology.

4. The broad array of developmental theories includes several types that can be particularly informative: psychosocial development, moral reasoning, intellectual development, and racial identity.
5. *The Sociology of Sport* by Harry Edwards (1973) is considered one of the founding works identifying and describing the relationship between sports and society.
6. Bolman and Deal (2008) identified four frames for understanding organizations: political, structural, human resource, and symbolic. Each of these frames is a tool for performing different tasks using a perspective, a set of connected ideas, or a story line that gives order and meaning to disparate bits of data.
7. Path-Goal Theory (Northouse, 2009) focuses on leaders as motivators and describes four types of behavior that leaders can use to motivate others: participative leadership, achievement-oriented leadership, supportive leadership, and directive leadership.
8. Campus ecology theories explore how the environment influences the people within it and how people in turn influence their environments. Strange and Banning (2001), in their book *Educating by Design: Creating Campus Learning Environments That Work*, discuss four components of campus environments—physical, human aggregate, organizational, and constructed.

References

Astin, A. W. "An Empirical Typology of College Students." *Journal of College Student Development,* 34, 1993, 36–46.

Argyris, C., and Schön, D. *Theory in Practice: Increasing Professional Effectiveness.* San Francisco: Jossey-Bass, 1974.

Bolman, L. G., and Deal, T. E. *Reframing Organizations: Artistry, Choice, and Leadership* (4th ed.). San Francisco: Jossey-Bass, 2008.

Chickering, A. W., and Reisser, L. *Education and Identity* (2nd ed.). San Francisco: Jossey-Bass, 1993.

Clark, B., and Trow, M. "The Organizational Context." In T. Newcomb and E. Wilson (Eds.), *College Peer Groups: Problems and Prospects for Research.* Chicago: Aldine, 1966.

Creswell, J. W. *Research Design: Quantitative, Qualitative, and Mixed Method Approaches* (3rd ed.). Thousand Oaks, CA: Sage, 2009.

Edwards, H. *The Sociology of Sport.* Homewood, IL: Dorsey Press, 1973.

Evans, N. J., Forney, D. S., and Guido-DiBrito, F. M. *Student Development in College: Theory, Research, and Practice.* San Francisco: Jossey-Bass, 1998.

Evans, N. J., Forney, D. S., Guido-DiBrito, F. M., Patton, L. D., and Renn, K. A. *Student Development in College: Theory, Research, and Practice* (2nd ed.). San Francisco: Jossey-Bass, 2010.

Foubert, J. D., Nixon, M. L., Sisson, V. S., and Barne, A. C. (2005). "A Longitudinal Study of Chickering's and Reisser's Vectors: Exploring Gender Differences and Implications for Refining the Theory." *Journal of College Student Development,* 2005, 46 (5), 461–471.

Hamrick, F. A., Evans, N. J., and Schuh, J. H. *Foundations of Student Affairs Practice: How Philosophy, Theory, and Research Strengthen Educational Outcomes.* San Francisco: Jossey-Bass, 2002.

Hodge, B. J., Anthony, W. P., and Gales. L. M. *Organization Theory: A Strategic Approach* (3rd ed.). New York: Prentice Hall, 2003.

Horowitz, H. L. "The 1960s and the Transformation of Campus Cultures." *History of Education Quarterly,* 1986, 26 (1), 1–38.

Howard-Hamilton, M. F., Cuyjet, M. J., and Cooper, D. L. "Understanding Multiculturalism and Multicultural Competence Among College Students." In M. J. Cuyjet, M. F. Howard-Hamilton, and D. L. Cooper (Eds.), *Multiculturalism on Campus: Theory, Models, and Practices for Understanding Diversity and Creating Inclusion.* Sterling, VA: Stylus, 2011.

Howard-Hamilton, M. F., and Hinton, K. G. "Oppression and Its Effect on College Student Identity Development." In M. J. Cuyjet, M. F. Howard-Hamilton, and D. L. Cooper (Eds.), *Multiculturalism on Campus: Theory, Models, and Practices for Understanding Diversity and Creating Inclusion.* Sterling, VA: Stylus, 2011.

Kerlinger, F. N. *Behavioral Research: A Conceptual Approach.* New York: Holt, Rinehart, and Winston, 1979.

Kohlberg, L. "Stage and Sequence: The Cognitive Development Approach to Socialization." In D. A. Goslin (Ed.), *Handbook of Socialization Theory and Research.* Chicago: Rand McNally, 1969.

Kuh, G. D., and Hall, J. E. "Cultural Perspectives in Student Affairs." In G. D. Kuh (Ed.), *Cultural Perspectives in Student Affairs Work.* Washington, D.C.: American College Personnel Association, 1993.

Lewin, K. *Field Theory in the Social Sciences.* New York: Harper and Row, 1936.

Love, P. G., and Guthrie, V. L. *Understanding and Applying Cognitive Development Theory.* New Directions for Student Services, 88. San Francisco: Jossey-Bass, 1999.

Manning, K. "Properties of Institutional Culture." In G. D. Kuh (Ed.), *Cultural Perspectives in Student Affairs Work.* Washington, D.C.: American College Personnel Association, 1993.

Moos, R. H. *Evaluating Educational Environments.* San Francisco: Jossey-Bass, 1979.

Moos, R. H. *The Human Context: Environmental Determinants of Behavior.* Malabar, FL: Krieger, 1986.

Northouse, P. G. *Leadership: Theory and Practice.* Thousand Oaks, CA: Sage, 2009.

Pace, C. R., and Stern, G. C. "An Approach to the Measurement of Psychological Characteristics of College Environments." *Journal of Educational Psychology,* 1958, 49, 269–277.

Polite, F. G., Waller, S. N, Hill, S., and Norwood, D. "Fostering Dr. Harry Edwards' Legacy." *Journal for the Study of Sport and Athletes in Education,* 2009, 3 (2), 143–158.

Selznick, P. "Foundations of the Theory of Organization." In M. C. Bown II, J. E. Lane, and E. M. Zamani-Gallaher (Eds.), *Organization and Governance in Higher Education* (6th ed., pp. 3–12). New York: Pearson Learning Solutions, 2010.

Singleton, R., Jr., and Straits, B. C. *Approaches to Social Research* (4th ed.). New York: Oxford University Press, 2005.

Strange, C. C., and Banning, J. H. *Educating by Design: Creating Campus Learning Environments That Work.* San Francisco: Jossey-Bass, 2001.

CHAPTER FOUR

ETHICS AND PROFESSIONALISM IN COLLEGE ATHLETICS AND RECREATION

Michael L. Buckner

State University was one of several universities recruiting Mack Moon, who was the best high school quarterback in the country. Moon had set several records and won a state championship under his high school football coach George Maize. Maize, a state football coaching legend, has deep relationships with his players. He is known to advise his players concerning their college choices. Rumors surfaced that suggest colleges and universities are bending over backwards trying to woo Moon. However, Todd Little, the State University director of athletics, has vowed to run a clean program and to follow National Collegiate Athletic Association (NCAA) recruiting rules. One month before signing day, Dallas Nate, State University head football coach, entered Little's office. Nate informed Little that the football program extended an offer of employment to Maize. According to Nate, Maize accepted the offer. Nate advised Little that Maize planned to be on campus the next day to be introduced as the new offensive coordinator at State University. Little did not stop the hire or the press conference. On signing day, Moon announced his intent to attend State University. The media and public referred to Moon's signing and Maize's hiring as a "package deal." The NCAA enforcement staff began an investigation into Moon's recruitment by State University.

State University's recruitment of Moon and hiring of Maize is representative of the ethical and professional issues that college athletics and recreation administrators face on a regular basis. [Note: State University is a fictional institution and will be used in the case studies and examples throughout this chapter.] This chapter describes the ethical and professional framework that undergirds college athletics and recreation administrations. College athletics and recreation administrators are expected to embrace a code of ethics and professionalism that serves to guide their professional and personal behavior and decision making. The chapter brings a more practical (rather than theoretical) approach to explaining the differences between legal, ethical, and professional actions and to describing how administrators can apply ethics and professionalism to daily decision making. Further, the chapter provides examples of ethics codes and expectations adopted by national intercollegiate athletics and recreation organizations. The chapter uses scenarios based on actual legal cases, infractions decisions, and media reports to provide a realistic guide on ethics and professionalism.

Law, Ethics, and Professionalism

A college athletics or recreation administrator cannot successfully apply ethics and professionalism in his or her personal life and professional career without a complete understanding of the core concepts: law, ethics, and professionalism. All three are addressed in this section.

Defining Laws, Ethics, and Professionalism

An important first step in addressing any concept is to develop a clear definition for that concept. Definitions for law, ethics, and professionalism follow.

Law. The law describes the body of statutes, regulations, rules, and ordinances prescribed by a controlling authority (for example, government or regulatory organization) that has compulsory legal force (Black, 1994, p. 884). The development of a law involves the cooperation and influence of numerous parties and addresses a diverse set of factors, issues, and concerns. Chapter Five provides an in-depth discussion of the law as it relates to professional practice in intercollegiate athletics and campus recreation.

Ethics and professionalism are occasionally, but never required to be, considered during the formulation of a law. Accordingly, an action may be legal and unethical at the same time. In fact, some groups do not determine what is ethical when determining courses of action—instead most organizations use what is legal as the standard in decision making (Maxwell, 2003, p. 12). For example:

The State University department of recreation organized another season of intramural basketball. The department offered separate leagues for men, women, co-ed, fraternity, and sorority teams. The director of recreation, Sam Snuff, assigned the men's, co-ed, and fraternity basketball games to the indoor courts at the new multi-million dollar student recreation center. The women's and sorority leagues used the indoor courts at the old student recreation center. The State University general counsel's office previously advised Snuff that the recreation department's organization of the intramural leagues did not violate federal law or university policy. Although Snuff's decisions may have been legal, did the recreation department behave unethically when it relegated the women's and sorority intramural leagues to an older facility? Would the most ethically sound organizational methodology involve rotating all of the league games through both facilities?

Ethics. Ethics encompasses the rules or standards of right and wrong that govern the conduct by which people live their lives or make decisions (Buckner, 2010). Further, ethics require a person to act on the commitment to do what is right and to reject wrong conduct (Maxwell, 2003). A person's ethics are based on his or her culture, experiences, values, and beliefs—all of which result in a personal ethical framework. An ethical self-assessment can be used to explore a person's values and beliefs. A self-assessment involves providing answers to two questions: (1) What do you believe in? (2) How would you react if one or all of your beliefs are confronted, challenged or tested? A strong reaction to a belief being tested indicates that it comprises one aspect of your ethical framework. For example:

Bud Roundup, State University head baseball coach, is known at the institution for his high ethical standards. Roundup preaches to his team each year about the importance on being honest and winning with integrity. During the first game of the season, Todd Johnson, a freshman student-athlete, sat in the dugout during the early innings and solved the intricate signs the opposing team used to relay plays and batting instructions to players. Johnson used the newly acquired information to achieve four hits, including a strategically placed triple in the bottom of the ninth inning to win the contest. Did Johnson's behavior violate Roundup's values and beliefs that comprise the coach's ethical framework?

Professionalism. Ethics establishes a baseline of right and wrong behavior while professionalism requires decision making using a higher standard.

Further, in the words of a former Georgia state Supreme Court justice, "professionalism imposes no official sanctions. It offers no official reward. Yet, sanctions and rewards exist unofficially" (Spears, 1990). In other words, an administrator who fails to make the professional decision faces the greater sanction of lost respect. However, a professional action can result in the greater reward of the satisfaction of doing right for right's own sake. For example:

> A lawsuit filed by former head women's basketball coach Mary Stoner against State University illustrated the difference between legal, ethical, and professionalism considerations. In 1999, Stoner began as the head women's basketball coach at State University. Stoner earned $64,000 a year, which was less than half of the salary of Geoff Rover, who was the men's basketball coach. State University justified the salary differences because Rover had thirty-one years coaching experience, had been an assistant on the United States Olympic team, and was named coach of the year on two occasions. However, Stoner had been a head coach for sixteen years, won three national championships at another institution and, during the last two seasons of her contract, compiled a win-loss record of 23–8 and 22–7 (compared with Rover's 19–10 and 24–6 records during the same period). When her initial four-year contract expired, Stoner sought a salary increase to achieve parity with Rover. Instead, State University offered Stoner a three-year contract starting at $88,000 and increasing to $100,000 by the last year. Stoner rejected the offer. State University countered with a one-year contract for $96,000. Stoner declined the offer and left the institution. Stoner subsequently was hired as head basketball women's coach at Global University, which paid her a salary equivalent to that of the head men's basketball coach. State University's decision may have been legal, but was it ethical and professional? Does Global University's decision to provide Stoner with the same salary as the men's coach change the ethical and professional analysis on State University's actions?

The Golden Rule

One way to demonstrate how a college athletics or recreation administrator can use ethics and professionalism in the campus environment is through the application of the Golden Rule. The Golden Rule is a moral value and suggests every person has a right to just treatment, as well as a responsibility to ensure justice for others. Author John C. Maxwell defines the Golden Rule by asking the following question: "How would I like to be treated in this situation?" (2003, p. 21). Maxwell believes the Golden Rule is based on common sense and is "the closest thing to a universal guideline for ethics a person can find" (Maxwell, 2003, pp. 23–24). The application of the Golden Rule can assist decision making and resolve conflicts in administrators' personal lives and professional careers. It appeals to reasonable people, is easily understood, facilitates win-win situations, and can be generalized in a variety of situations of uncertainty.

State University began the planning and design for the new student recreation center. The master plan called for the multi-million dollar facility to contain the latest in technology, as well as academic classrooms. Most important, the center was to feature indoor basketball courts, a track and swimming pool, as well as the largest weight room in the local area. The center was to be funded by the student recreation fee. The State University athletics department had been requesting for several years a new basketball practice facility and a new venue for its women's basketball program. The basketball teams practiced in the old university gymnasium, which was built in the 1960s. Conversely, the recreation department lacked adequate green-space to field several of its intramural events. The only available property was assigned to the athletics department. The director of recreation, Sam Snuff, offered to redesign the new recreation center to provide sufficient locker room space for the varsity basketball teams. In turn, Todd Little, the State University director of athletics, coordinated with the recreation staff to conduct intramural events on unused athletics fields. Did Snuff and Little apply the Golden Rule to solve their mutual problems? Did the administrators act ethically and/or professionally in this instance? What are some ways the Golden Rule could have been applied in this situation?

Gray Areas

A common excuse or refrain for performing a questionable act or decision is to claim it was in the gray area. However, an ethical and professional administrator understands gray areas usually become the justification for what one should not be doing. In fact, successful administrators avoid gray areas through acknowledging the existence of right and wrong so that employees, students, student-athletes, and other campus constituencies know what actions will not be tolerated (Buckner, 2010). For example:

NCAA rules prohibit coaches from observing prospective student-athletes from participating in pick-up games or open gyms during recruiting visits to institutions. During the recruiting visit of three top national recruits, State University head women's volleyball coach Susan Landers transported the recruits to the student recreation center. Landers invited the recruits to play in the scheduled open gym session, which was organized by the recreation department. Any State University student, staff member, or alum was able to participate in the open gym sessions. At Landers' request, several volleyball boosters and alumni were at the open gym to either observe or participate in the games. The boosters and alumni later briefed Landers on their general thoughts on the recruits' athletics ability. Did Landers and State University break NCAA rules? Does a gray area exist in this instance?

Personal and Organizational Ethics

A college athletics or recreation administrator is impacted by two types of ethics during a typical workday: personal and organizational ethics. A thorough understanding of each type is necessary to facilitate decision making within the department that fulfills ethical and professional standards.

Personal ethics consists of each person's ethical framework. In order to determine one's personal ethics, a two-step process is employed. First, using the ethical self-assessment that was described earlier in the chapter, a person determines his or her values. Values are the core beliefs that guide a person's actions. Second, personal ethics are identified through the sum of a person's values.

Organizational ethics describes the ethical framework of entities such as departments, universities, and professional associations. A code of ethics, which is one example of professional ethics, is a formal collection of rules that establish the acceptable standard for actions, decision making, and behavior for a society, organization, or group. Organizational ethics also can be found in written policies, which are guidelines for actions, decision making, and behavior in particular situations.

Overall, an administrator must recognize the effect of personal and organizational ethics on a department's actions, decisions, and behavior. The personal values of every member of the department (including administrators, staff, and students) will interact, and sometimes conflict, with the written codes and policies to produce organizational actions. Thus, the most effective organizations will only hire employees with personal ethics consistent with the department's ethical standards. Departments with a high ethical standard also will use a comprehensive ethics education and training program to ensure the employee's and students' personal ethics do not conflict with the organization's ethics. Without such actions, colleges and universities can be adversely impacted when employees or students with lower ethical standards make decisions that are not only inconsistent with institutional ethical codes, but that also violate criminal statutes or severely harm others.

State University sought a qualified individual to fill the open associate director of recreation position. After a nationwide search, State University selected Dr. Lee Marvin, a former director of recreation at Global University. Marvin is an expert at managing construction projects and increasing student participation in intramural activities. Marvin also is considered a great sport management professor. State University, which was planning the construction of a new student recreation center, realized Marvin's value. However, a background check revealed Marvin resigned from Global University after a story surfaced pertaining to fraudulent practices at another institution. Further, State University learned Marvin developed a reputation of bending the rules if it resulted in successfully reaching a goal. Nevertheless, the State University board of directors approved Marvin's hiring. Do you think Marvin's personal ethics mirror State University's organizational ethics? What do you believe will be the ultimate outcome of Marvin's hiring?

Ethics, Professionalism, and Departmental Success

A college athletics and recreation department is more likely to achieve long-term success if it is guided by solid ethical and professional principles. In fact, a department's ethical and professional values pull people together. Further, a department's reputation is derived from its philosophy, the quality of its customer (i.e., students, stakeholders) service, its community service involvement, and its commitment to moral and environmental issues. Further, a department's approach to moral and ethical issues also is a concern with employees, students, student-athletes, and other campus constituencies. A department's values as expressed in value statements, annual reports, and employers' daily actions can affect how employees, students, student-athletes, and other campus constituencies feel about the athletics and recreation services. Thus, an administrator should assure that their department's commitment to ethical and professional conduct is clearly and publicly articulated and then act in accordance with that commitment in order to help assure departmental success.

Root Causes of Unethical and Unprofessional Behavior

College athletics and recreation departments across the country have experienced behavior that did not meet stated ethical and professional standards. An administrator intent on addressing unethical and unprofessional behavior is obligated to first identify the causes of the conduct. According to a report by ABC News, the root causes for unethical behavior in any organization can include (1) rationalization, (2) bad role models in the organization, (3) peer-pressure, (4) difficulty in defining what is ethical, (5) organizational culture, and (6) pressure from superiors (James, 2002). Once the root causes have been identified, then an administrator can employ solutions to eliminate or minimize the unethical and unprofessional behavior.

Ethical and Professional Solutions

An administrator can utilize strategic and tactical solutions to create an ethical and professional environment and culture in an athletics or recreation department. An ethical and professional department emerges from the successful combination of the following elements: (1) ethical and professional leadership, (2) ethical and professional management, (3) ethical and professional teamwork, and (4) an ethics education and training program.

Ethical and Professional Leadership. An administrator who practices genuine leadership provides support for, and sets, a new direction or vision for a group (Walters, 1987). A leader who abides by ethical principles and standards follows a five-part approach (Caroselli, 2003). First, ethical and professional leaders set the standard for truthfulness in a college athletics or recreation administration. Second, ethical and professional leaders champion the processes of quality throughout an administration. Third, ethical and professional leaders select the best persons to advise them and the best practices to implement in the administration. Fourth, ethical and professional leaders establish strong administrative standards and operational procedures while grooming younger persons for future leadership within and outside the organization. Fifth, ethical and professional leaders step aside when the needs of the administration dictate (and not to feed personal ego or ambition).

Ethical and Professional Management. Management "is the process of coordinating people and other resources to achieve the goals of an organization" (Pride, Hughes, and Kapoor, 2008, p. 167). An administrator who seeks to fulfill the role of an ethical and professional manager will implement the vision of the ethical and professional leader while ensuring adherence to the organizational ethical framework (Caroselli, 2003). This is accomplished in several ways. To begin with, the ethical and professional manager ensures the department develops an extensive code of ethics and conduct. Further, an ethical and professional manager includes ethical guidelines in employee, student, and student-athlete handbooks. Moreover, the ethical and professional manager incorporates real-life case studies into ethics education and training programs. In addition, the ethical and professional manager creates an ethics hotline for anonymous reports. Finally, an ethical and professional manager establishes an ethics committee or appoints a person whom employees, students, student-athletes, and other campus constituencies can approach with ethical dilemmas.

The first two elements, ethical and professional leadership and ethical management, are intertwined. Both must exist to create the top-down administration needed to cultivate ethical and professional behavior.

The combination of ethical and professional leadership and ethical management is the only way an ethical workplace can exist in any organization. An ethical workplace, in turn, creates six general categories of benefits to a department (Caroselli, 2003). First, the department's productivity will increase. Ethical employees, students, student-athletes and other campus constituencies outperform all others. Second, everyone in the department will be held accountable. Employees, students, student-athletes, and other campus constituencies will take responsibility and feel accountable for their personal behavior. Third, communication is enhanced. Employees, students, student-athletes, and other campus constituencies will want to talk about ethical dilemmas as they arise. Fourth, confidentiality is preserved and respected. The department wins when all employees, students, student-athletes, and other campus constituencies know that privacy issues will be respected. Fifth, the department experiences greater stability. Employees, students, student-athletes, and other campus constituencies interact in an ethical atmosphere—turnover and transfer will be minimized. Sixth, the department can rely on more predictable events. The ethical administration is not blindsided by surprises such as lawsuits and regulatory investigations.

Ethical and Professional Teamwork. An ethical and professional leader and manager fosters ethical and professional teamwork through a skillful combination of several tenants (Caroselli, 2003). To begin with, the members of the administration work together under established principles toward a common vision. Also, the department ensures all persons are valued and enthusiasm is cultivated for all individuals. Further, the administration relishes communication. Moreover, the administration's goals are focused on the customer (i.e., students, student-athletes, and other campus constituencies). The administration also fosters stability. In addition, the administration does not tolerate discrimination and prizes loyalty, honesty, integrity, and fairness. Finally, under an ethical team approach, administrators care for others (e.g., gender-equity, healthy work environment, workplace safety), set fair policies (which are administered consistently), and establish an environment where people can succeed and fail.

Ethics Education and Training. An education and training program is an important final element of an ethical and professional college athletics and recreation department. The first step is to understand the distinctions between education and training.

Education is "concerned with increasing the general knowledge and understanding" of the person's environment (Tripathi and Reddy, 2008, p. 195). Further, education is a needs-driven process self-directed by the learner (Sapieha, 2007). The needs for education can be described as an intrinsic need of the learner, who wants to learn for their perspective and expand their knowledge to fulfill an individually-identified need.

State University director of recreation Sam Snuff permits recreation administrators and staff to attend local and regional conferences conducted by recreation industry groups, especially if a session on ethics is on the agenda. Snuff also encourages his staff to publish articles related to ethics and professionalism in recreation industry journals and newsletters. What are other examples of ethics and professional educational activities?

Training is best described as "the act of increasing the knowledge and skill of an employee for doing a particular job" and "is concerned with imparting specific skills for particular purposes" (Tripathi and Reddy, 2008, p. 195). Moreover, training is a needs-driven process that is typically directed by an organization to the learner (Sapieha, 2007).The needs for training can be described as an extrinsic need usually driven by an organization and not by the learner.

Todd Little, the State University director of athletics, has scheduled monthly training workshops on professional development issues for the entire staff. Little brings in speakers from the campus community to address various issues, including ethics and professionalism. What are other examples of ethics and professional training activities?

Education and training programs should target all members of the athletics or recreation community, including, but not limited to, administrators, faculty, staff, students, and other parties who have duties and responsibilities related to the athletics and recreation department's mission. A comprehensive ethics and professionalism education and training program must address all aspects of ethics and professional issues that may affect employees or students. Most important, an administrator produces the most informed and prepared employees and students when education and training components are utilized in a comprehensive program. Generally, college athletics and recreation administrators should be mindful of the following advice when designing an education and training program:

1. Communicate the code of ethics or conduct promulgated by the institution and the athletics/recreation department. This can be accomplished through electronic mail, a manual, a handbook, and workshops.
2. Budget appropriate funds for staff and students to purchase ethically related resources or to attend conferences, seminars, and workshops.
3. Incorporate hands-on, entertaining activities (i.e., role-playing, small-group workshops, small-group exercises, discussions) into training programs.
4. Use, on an occasional basis or when budget permits, speakers external to the athletics or recreation department during training activities. Excellent speakers with far-reaching knowledge can be found on campus or locally. Further, lawyers, consultants, and other professionals provide a unique perspective on ethical and professional issues.
5. Limit the use of videos (or if videos are used, follow up with small-groups exercises or discussions).
6. Ensure the education and training program addresses the ethical tone of administrators. Staff and students will reject any education and training if it is perceived that administrators are not held to the same standard.
7. Schedule ongoing ethics training efforts—ethics should not be a once-in-a-year topic.
8. Address global and international ethics issue in the education and training program. Due to the large numbers of international students enrolled at American institutions, it is incumbent for staff and students to become aware of ethics issues from other nations.
9. Evaluate and seek continuous improvement on the education and training program. Surveys, department-wide discussions, and other feedback should provide athletics and recreation administrators with sufficient data to base program improvements.

Effective ethics and professionalism education and training programs incorporate a variety of delivery devices. These include

1. Manuals and handbooks
2. Books and other publications (purchased by either the department, staff members or students)
3. Workshops and seminars (in-house programs or off-campus events)
4. Newsletters
5. Small-group discussions
6. Videos

7. E-mail and other electronic communication
8. Memoranda and letters
9. Online tools and resources
10. Tests and exams

Industry Ethical Statements and Expectations

National associations, industry groups, and other organizations have published statements and codes on ethical and professional behavior for athletics and recreation administrators. The ethical and professional statements and codes are designed to be useful guides for athletics and recreation professionals during the performance of their daily duties and responsibilities. Further, the statements and codes assist professionals with anticipating and dealing with ethical and professional issues that may arise in their departments. This section includes a sample of ethical and professional statements and codes promulgated by national associations. Naturally, the summary is not all-inclusive and does not include the ethical and professional statements and codes developed by colleges, universities, state organizations, regulatory agencies, and other bodies.

National Collegiate Athletic Association

The National Collegiate Athletic Association (NCAA) is a nonprofit association of colleges and universities committed to supporting academic and athletic opportunities for approximately 400,000 student-athletes at more than 1,000 member institutions (NCAA, 2011). The association's ethics statement is incorporated in Bylaw 10 of the NCAA Manual (NCAA, 2010). Bylaw 10.1 prohibits unethical conduct by a prospective or enrolled student-athlete or a current or former institutional staff member, which includes any individual who performs work for the institution or the athletics department even if he or she does not receive compensation for such work. Some examples of unethical conduct under the bylaw include (1) refusal to furnish information relevant to an investigation of a possible violation of an NCAA regulation, (2) knowing involvement in academic fraud, (3) knowing involvement in offering or providing a prospective or an enrolled student-athlete an improper inducement or extra benefit or improper financial aid, (4) knowing involvement in providing a banned substance or impermissible supplement to student-athletes, (5) fraudulence or misconduct in connection with entrance or placement examinations, and

(6) engaging in any athletics competition under an assumed name or with intent to otherwise deceive.

National Association of Intercollegiate Athletics

The National Association of Intercollegiate Athletics (NAIA) is an association that organizes athletics competition involving 50,000 student-athletes participating at approximately 300 member colleges and universities throughout the United States and Canada (NAIA, 2010). The association's ethical and professional statements and codes are contained in the NAIA Official Handbook and Policy Handbook (NAIA, 2010). Section A in the association's handbook (called the statement of philosophy) declares a member institution shall maintain high ethical standards through commitment to the principle of self-reporting. Further, Section C of the association's handbook comprises its code of ethics. The stated purpose of the code of ethics is to protect and promote the interests of athletics and the coaching profession, clarify and distinguish ethical practices from those which are detrimental and harmful, emphasize the values of athletics in American and Canadian educational institutions, and stress the functional contributions of coaches to their schools and players. The NAIA code defines ethics as the basic principles of right action in that proper ethics in athletics implies a standard of character that affords confidence and trust.

National Junior College Athletic Association (NJCAA)

The NJCAA is an athletics association of community and junior colleges in the United States. The NJCAA provides its members with an ethical framework in several documents. For example, Article III, Section 2.B. of the NJCAA constitution (NJCAA, 2010) states that as a condition of membership, institutions agree to establish and maintain a high standard of ethics and fair play. Article XX of the NJCAA bylaws (NJCAA, 2010) contains a code of conduct for the association-sponsored events, contests, and tournaments. The NJCAA bylaws also contain an extensive coaches' code of ethics.

National Intramural-Recreation Sports Association

The National Intramural-Recreation Sports Association (NIRSA) is the leading resource for professional and student development, education, and research in collegiate recreation sports. The preamble to NIRSA's

Professional Members Code of Ethics (NIRSA, 1984) states "an outstanding characteristic of a profession is that its members are continually striving to improve the quality of life for the population they serve." Further, the preamble advises that in making the choice to affiliate with a professional association, individuals assume the responsibility to conduct themselves in accordance with the ideals and standards set by the organization. The NIRSA code requires members to fulfill numerous obligations, including encourage integrity by avoiding involvement or condoning activities that may degrade the Association, its members, or any affiliate agency; encourage cooperation with other professional associations, educational institutions, and agencies; and practice nondiscrimination on the basis of diversity related to age, disability, ethnicity, gender, national origin, race, religion, and sexual orientation. The NIRSA code also addresses ethical issues relating to employment and providing programs and services.

Applying Ethics and Professionalism

Ethical and professional conduct by athletics and recreation administrators must go beyond a basic knowledge of ethics statements, codes, and principles. Administrators also should be familiar with how to apply ethical and professional standards to the rigors of the typical university workday (with all its crises, decisions, issues, and dilemmas). In other words, an administrator should always translate the theoretical into reality, which ensures that his or her judgment and actions are anchored by ethically and professionally sound standards.

Although the journey to be more ethical and professional is a life journey, every administrator is responsible for creating opportunities for themselves, colleagues, employees, students, and others to increase their proficiency with ethical and professional standards, behavior, and actions. This can be achieved by (1) developing statements or codes of ethics and professionalism through communitywide discussion, reflection, and analysis; (2) making every decision or action within an athletics or recreation department consistent with the developed ethical and professional statements or codes; (3) using ethical and professional principles when developing new leaders and managers (and revitalizing current leaders and managers); (4) operating the athletics or recreation department as an "ethical team"; and (5) ensuring employees and students are educated about the school's ethics and professional codes and statements, as well as trained by using realistic examples of ethical and professionalism behavior.

Finally, an ethical and professional administrator should develop habits and behaviors that include reaching out for advice and consultation from colleagues and experts, acquiring objective information and data, maintaining proper professional relationships with colleagues and students, and eliminating situations that may create (or be perceived as) conflicts. Collectively, the aforementioned practices, skills, and habits will support ethical decision making within an athletics and recreation department and minimize (or, at the very least, reduce the damage stemming from) ethical breaches. Most important, it will assist the athletics and recreation department with mentoring students with a greater sense of ethics and professionalism.

Conclusion

College athletics and recreation administrators, through their unique knowledge and experience, positively affect the lives of students, student-athletes and other members of the university community. Administrators, in carrying out daily duties and responsibilities, should be committed to applying ethical and professional ideals on college campuses, including ensuring their departments practice fairness, beneficence, integrity, compassion, loyalty, trustworthiness, and respect for others. Administrators should pledge to embody the ethical and professional principles in their diverse roles as supervisor, manager, mentor, and teacher.

Understandably, the work of athletics and recreation administrators pose unique and distinct ethical and professional challenges. The special role colleges and universities possess in the lives of students lies at the heart of most of the hurdles an administrator must address on a daily basis. The duty and responsibility of an administrator to uphold the law and follow institutional regulations, while fostering the proper development of students, demands a thorough understanding of ethics and professionalism.

Chapter Four Key Points

1. It is important that administrators in college athletics and recreation understand the concepts of law, ethics, and professionalism.
2. The law describes the body of statutes, regulations, rules, and ordinances prescribed by a controlling authority (for example, government

or regulatory organization) that has compulsory legal force (Black, 1994, p. 884).

3. Ethics encompasses the rules or standards of right and wrong that govern the conduct by which people live their lives or make decisions (Buckner, 2010). A college athletics or recreation administrator is impacted by two types of ethics during a typical workday: personal and organizational ethics.
4. Professionalism is a higher standard than either compliance with law or congruence with ethics.
5. Ethics and professionalism are occasionally, but never required to be, considered during the formulation of a law.
6. An ethical and professional department emerges from the successful combination of the following elements: (1) ethical and professional leadership, (2) ethical management, (3) ethical and professional teamwork, and (4) an ethics education and training program.
7. National associations, industry groups, and other organizations have published statements and codes on ethical and professional behavior for athletics and recreation administrators.
8. Ethical and professional conduct by athletics and recreation administrators must go beyond a basic knowledge of ethics statements, codes, and principles. Administrators also should be familiar with how to apply ethical and professional standards to the rigors of the typical university workday (with the crises, decisions, issues, and dilemmas that comprise it).

References

Black, H. C. *Black's Law Dictionary* (6th ed.). St. Paul, MN: West Publishing, 1994.

Buckner, M. L. *The ABCs of Ethics: A Resource for Leaders, Managers and Professionals.* New York: iUniverse, 2010.

Caroselli, M. *The Business Ethics Activity Book.* New York: HRD Press, 2003.

James, M. S. "Are You Ethical? The Truth Isn't Exactly Clear." [ABCNews.com]. Feb. 21, 2002. Accessed May 14, 2011 at http://abcnews.go.com/US/story?id=89985.

Maxwell, J. C. *There's No Such Thing as "Business" Ethics: There's Only One Rule for Making Decisions.* New York: Time Warner, 2003.

National Association of Intercollegiate Athletics (NAIA). *Membership Services.* Kansas City, MO: National Association of Intercollegiate Athletics, 2010. Accessed April 30, 2011 at http://naia.cstv.com/member-services.

National Collegiate Athletic Association (NCAA). *NCAA Division I Manual.* Indianapolis, IN: National Collegiate Athletic Association, 2010.

National Collegiate Athletic Association (NCAA). *Who We Are*. Indianapolis, IN: National Collegiate Athletic Association, 2011. Accessed April 30, 2011 at http://www.ncaa.org/wps/wcm/connect/public/NCAA/About+the+NCAA/Who+We+Are/.

National Intramural-Recreation Sports Association (NIRSA). *Professional Member's Code of Ethics*. Corvallis, OR: National Intramural-Recreation Sports Association, 1984. Accessed April 30, 2011 at http://www.nirsa.org/Content/NavigationMenu/AboutUs/GoverningDocuments/CodeofEthics/Code˙of˙Ethics.htm.

National Junior Collegiate Athletic Association (NJCAA). *NJCAA Handbook and Casebook*. Colorado Springs, CO: National Junior Collegiate Athletic Association, 2010.

Pride, W. M., Hughes, R. J., and Kapoor, J. R. *Business*. Mason, OH: Cengage Learning, 2008.

Sapieha, S. "Essay on Adult Education for Use by RM Advisory." 2007. Accessed April 30, 2011 at http://www.scribd.com/doc/8767706/Essay-on-Adult-Education.

Spears, J. W. (Ed.) "Interview with Harold G. Clark, Chief Justice, Supreme Court of Georgia". *Decatur-DeKalb Bar Quarterly*, May 24, 1990.

Tripathi, P. C., and Reddy, P. N. *Principles of Management*. New Delhi, India: McGraw-Hill, 2008.

Walters, J. D. *The Art of Leadership*. New York: Barnes and Noble, 1987.

CHAPTER FIVE

LEGAL ISSUES IN INTERCOLLEGIATE SPORTS AND RECREATION

Barbara Osborne

From contracts to wrongful death to free speech to drug testing to age discrimination to trademark licenses to tax, athletics administrators and recreation managers are exposed to legal issues on a daily basis. This chapter introduces the wide range of legal issues that may be encountered within the civil law. In the United States, civil law is a system that delineates rights, governs disputes, and provides remedies for private parties. It includes the written law embodied in the federal and state constitutions, statutes, and codes, as well as precedent established through prior court decisions.

Whereas civil law governs disputes between private parties, including individuals, institutions, or businesses, criminal law establishes a framework for behavior that is prohibited as harmful to society. Crimes are identified as misdemeanors, lesser offenses that generally warrant a fine, or felonies, more serious offenses that may warrant incarceration. Although circumstances may present themselves whereby athletics administrators and recreation managers encounter the criminal justice system, such as the arrest of a student-athlete for drug use or theft of equipment from a facility, these situations should be deferred to appropriate law enforcement officials and are not addressed in this chapter.

Ideally, awareness of legal issues should improve administrative decision making. However, it is important to note this chapter is not intended to provide legal advice, but only serves to provide information that will help practitioners recognize potential legal liability.

Torts

For all athletics administrators and recreation managers, the safety of those around them should always be a primary concern. When someone is harmed in a sport setting, that person may want to be compensated for his or her injuries—these situations fall within tort law. A *tort* is a wrong for which civil law provides a remedy. An unintentional wrongful act falls within the area of negligence, whereas a purposeful act would be categorized as an intentional tort. The individual actor(s), supervisor(s), and even the institution may be liable for damages (Restat. 3d of Torts, 2000).

Safety First—Negligence

Sports and recreation involve many activities that pose a risk of injury to participants and even spectators. Athletics administrators and recreation managers are not ensurers of everyone's safety, and accidents do happen. However, the institution will be liable if the athletics administrator or recreation manager is negligent.

Because negligence is an unintentional tort, it does not matter whether the person responsible intended to cause harm. In order to prove negligence, the plaintiff has the burden of proving four elements: duty, breach, causation, and damage.

Duty stems from the special relationship between the parties. In sport and recreation contexts, coach-athlete, administrator-coach, supervisor-participant, venue manager–spectator are all examples of relationships inherent to the situation. An individual may also assume a duty, for example, by volunteering. Duty may also be mandated by a statute, such as a law requiring a certified athletics trainer to be on site for all contests involving contact sports. It is important to note that a moral obligation does not create a legal duty (Restat. 3d of Torts, 2000).

Breach occurs when one party fails to perform with reasonable care, which is defined as the behavior of a reasonably prudent person in the same or similar circumstance. When the defendant is a professional (such as a coach, personal trainer, or team physician), the standards established by professional organizations or agencies, such as the National Intramural-Recreational Sports Association (NIRSA), National Collegiate Athletic Association (NCAA), or the American College of Sports Medicine (ACSM), will commonly be used to establish reasonableness. If there are no published standards within a profession, the testimony of experts in the field will help determine accepted practices. Breach may be an act of commission (the person did something he or she wasn't supposed to do) or an act of omission (the person didn't do something that he or she should have).

Causation is often described as an artful term, as it is difficult to define. The actual cause of the injury or damage must be directly related to the breach of the standard of care, or minimally a substantial factor in bringing about the damage or injury. Proximate cause is measured by determining whether or not the harm was the reasonable, foreseeable, natural, and continuous consequence of the defendant's act or omission. Cause is sometimes measured by a "but-for" test: but for the act (or omission) of the defendant, the particular harm suffered would never have occurred. If the same harm may have occurred anyway, the element of causation is not proven (Restat. 3d of Torts, 2000).

Damages, actual physical or emotional injury, must also be proven for negligence to exist. Compensable injuries may include economic losses such as medical expenses or lost wages, physical pain and suffering, emotional distress, and temporary or permanent physical impairment whether it is partial or total. Punitive damages are very rarely awarded, as it would not serve public policy to punish people for acts that are unintentional. However, punitive damages may be awarded when the defendant's action is in reckless disregard for the rights or safety of others (Restat. 3d of Torts, 2000).

The case of *Allen v. Rutgers State University* (1987) provides an excellent example of the elements of negligence, particularly the concept of causation. Tom Allen was a student who attended a football game at Rutgers Stadium with his fraternity brothers. They brought a fruit flavored beverage mixed with grain alcohol into the stadium although there was a no alcohol policy. Allen proceeded to consume the beverage and was visibly drunk. The fraternity brothers attempted to gain access to the track around the football field three times during half-time to perform a prank, but were thwarted by security. Allen and his friends then went to the opposite side of the stadium where he vaulted over a four-foot wall—and fell 30 feet onto concrete stairs on the other side, suffering severe and permanent injuries. In analyzing the elements of negligence, it is clear that there is a special relationship between a university and its football fans, and that Rutgers had a duty to provide a safe environment for fans attending the football game. Allen argued that this duty was breached when stadium security allowed him to bring alcohol into the stadium in spite of the no-alcohol policy. However, the jury found that Allen's injuries were proximately caused by his action of vaulting over the wall. Although Allen suffered significant harm, the institution was not liable, as all of the elements of negligence were not proven (failure to prove causation).

Lack of proper supervision is one of the most frequent claims made in negligence cases. The legal standard requires supervisors to take action to prevent reasonably foreseeable injuries; however, it is important to note that supervisors are not ensurers of the safety of all participants. Risk of injury exists in any activity, so the plaintiff has the burden of proving that the negligent behavior of the supervisor was the proximate cause of the injury, or conversely, that proper supervision would have prevented the injury. In high-risk activity situations, supervisors are expected to be in close proximity providing constant and continuous monitoring. The number of supervisors that should be present will depend on the specific circumstances, including the type of activity, age and number of participants, skill level, and the size of the area.

Lawsuits are also brought against supervisors who provide only general supervision, such as the athletics director, recreation director, or president of the college or university. The standard for liability is the same, in that the supervisor would be measured by the reasonably prudent supervisor in the same or similar situation test. Because general supervision does not require constant scrutiny of the activity, an action or omission of the general supervisor, such as failing to hire competent coaches or not scheduling enough lifeguards, must be the proximate cause of the injury.

Transportation is an area that poses high risks, and as such must be monitored carefully. Athletics and recreation programs use a variety of transportation options, both on campus and for off-campus contests and activities. Many institutions may choose to limit their risks by hiring a competent independent contractor, such as a bus company, to provide drivers and transportation. For programs that own busses and passenger vans, vehicle maintenance and documentation as well as driver selection and training is critical. There is also an expectation that all vehicles will carry appropriate emergency equipment. The institution may retain liability for privately owned vehicles that are used for university business as well. Golf carts and utility carts that are often used on-site also pose liability issues, particularly if the institution has not created a safety policy and required driver education prior to use (Am. Jur. 2d, 2011).

Intentional Torts

Intentional torts are deliberate wrongs done to others that cause harm. Public policy requires those who purposefully harm others to have to pay for their actions. The most common intentional torts are assault and battery (not to be confused with the crimes of the same name). *Assault* is the intentional creation of a reasonable apprehension of an imminent and offensive contact without the person's consent. This could be a verbal or physical act, as long as the victim fears that immediate harm could occur. *Battery* is intentional and unpermitted contact with another person that causes harm. Typical occurrences of assault and battery in sports settings include any combination of players, coaches, officials, fans, and crowd management personnel threatening or striking one another. Fortunately for athletics administrators, liability for intentional torts lies most often with the person who caused the harm (the *tortfeasor*). However, the institution may be liable for the intentional torts of its employees committed within the scope of employment (Restat. 3d of Torts, 2000).

The institution may also have liability for assaults and batteries committed by third parties who are invited onto institutional property if the incidents were foreseeable. Foreseeability can be determined by a record of prior similar acts or incidents, the nature of the area where the assault and/or battery occurred, and the type of activity carried on in the area by the institution (*Gragg v. Wichita State University*, 1997). It is important for athletics administrators and facilities management personnel to keep records of violent activities that occur. Care should be taken to assure that areas are properly lit, there is controlled access, and security appropriately patrols (Restat. 3d of Torts, 2000).

Defamation is another intentional tort that is increasingly litigated in the collegiate sports context. Making a false statement to a third party that injures the reputation, esteem, respect, or goodwill of another person is defamation. If the statement is made orally it is slander, whereas libel is comments in writing, photography, or cartoons (Restat. 3d of Torts, 2000). It is important to note that the person making the statement does not have to intend to harm the victim's reputation; the mere act of publishing the false statement is enough to satisfy the intent element.

Contracts

Although safety concerns should always be foremost in the athletics administrator's or recreation manager's mind, contract law is an area that he or she will is likely to encounter on a daily basis. Employment contracts, television contracts, and sponsorships are obvious contract issues. However, processing simple paperwork such as a purchase order for equipment or supplies is actually a contract governed by the Uniform Commercial

Code (UCC). Every intercollegiate athletics event should be officially documented in a contract. Rental of athletics and recreational facilities or use of fields for summer camps must be put into a written contract because they are transactions involving real property. Licensing agreements for the use of trademarks are also contracts, as are seat licenses in stadiums.

A *contract* is a promise, or set of promises, for breach of which the law gives a remedy, or the performance of which the law in some way recognizes as a duty (Garner, 2011). A contract exists when there is offer, acceptance, and consideration. The offer is a conditional promise made by one party (the offeror) to another (the offeree); it is essentially a promise to do something, or refrain from doing something. Acceptance may be voluntary agreement with the terms and conditions of an offer of a promise, or it may be in actually completing the terms of the offer (Restat. 2d of Contracts, 2009). For example, an equipment manager may request two dozen team uniforms with specific numbers screened on them. The equipment supplier promises to provide the uniforms by a specified date. Assuming consideration, this exchange of promises creates a bilateral contract. However, if the equipment supplier simply shipped the completed uniform order, a unilateral contract was formed.

Acceptance must mirror the offer as to the offer's essential terms, otherwise the offeree has created a counter offer. If an offeree is interested in the offer but wishes to change some of the terms or conditions, the offeree has legally rejected the original offer and becomes the offeror for a new promise of terms (Restat. 2d of Contracts, 2009). Thus, a negotiation becomes a continuum of offer–rejection/counteroffer until there is agreement as to the essential terms. It is critically important to understand this cycle of offer and rejection, counteroffer or acceptance, to determine when a contract has been formed. The original offer is assumed to be valid until it is accepted within a time period that was specified in the offer or for a reasonable amount of time, or if it is revoked or withdrawn by the offeror before acceptance, or if it is rejected by the offeree. An offeree who is frustrated by a lack of agreement in negotiations may wish to just give up and accept the original offer—however, the offeree must actually propose the original offer as a new counteroffer because the original offer no longer exists after it was rejected by the first counteroffer (Restat. 2d of Contracts, 2009).

Consideration is the final element of a contract. As a legal concept, consideration is quite vague. *Black's Law Dictionary* defines it as "something of value given in return for a performance or a promise of performance by another for the purpose of forming a contract; a bargained for exchange of value." If both parties are getting something of relatively equal value from the agreement, the element of consideration can be assumed.

The basics of contract law appear to be quite straightforward, but there are a myriad of legal rules that can complicate whether or not the contract is void, voidable, or unenforceable. A contract is void if it produces no legal obligation because its formation or performance is criminal, tortious, or otherwise opposed to public policy (Restat. 2d of Contracts, 2009). For example, if a gambler were to offer a student-athlete a substantial amount of money in a point-fixing scheme and the student-athlete did intentionally influence the play to keep the score within the spread, the elements of a unilateral contract would be satisfied (assuming that the amount offered would be consideration). If the gambler did not pay the student-athlete for the duly performed services, the student-athlete would not have recourse for breach of contract because the purpose of the contract itself was illegal, making the contract void.

A perfectly legal contract can also be voidable if one or more of the parties has the power to elect to avoid the legal relationship created by the contract. The most common situation relates to capacity—if an individual is not able to fully understand the effects of the agreement, either because they are a minor or infirmed, the party that does not have capacity may seek to void the contract. However, if the party without capacity wishes to reap the benefits of the contract, the party with capacity cannot avoid the contract. Contracts that were created through misrepresentation (one party induces the other party to enter into the contract through a false assertion of fact), undue influence (the dominance of one party over a subservient party unfairly persuades that party to enter into an agreement that he or she would not have entered into without the domination), and duress (a threat or wrongful act which coerces a party to enter into a contract that they would not have voluntarily agreed to) are all voidable at the option of the victim (Restat. 2d of Contracts, 2009).

In other situations, a contract may be legally constructed, but the courts will not enforce it because of technicalities such as the Statute of Frauds or the Statute of Limitations. The Statute of Frauds requires some contracts to be in writing, such as contracts involving real property or contracts for services that cannot be performed within one year of the agreement. In order to satisfy the writing requirement of the Statute of Frauds, the writing must contain all the essential terms of the contract and be signed by the party to be charged. Similarly, the parol evidence rule requires that when a written contract is made, all terms that were verbally agreed to must be reflected in the written document in order to be enforceable. The Statute of

Limitations is a legal device used to assure that claims are made in a timely manner. Although the contract might be perfectly valid, if a claim is not properly filed before the deadline specified by the Statute of Limitations, the court will not enforce it (Restat. 2d of Contracts, 2009).

Employment Contracts

Employment contracts appear to generate the most litigation for college athletics and recreation programs, although the overwhelming majority of staff in those areas do not have written contracts and are considered at-will employees. The doctrine of at-will employment allows for either party in the employment relationship to terminate without liability (Restat. 2d of Contracts, 2009). This allows for maximum flexibility for both parties. However, most employees seek some sort of job security, and most supervisors prefer to have stability in the work force in each academic year. This has led to a practice of providing annual letter agreements, which may or may not be considered a contract depending on the language in the letter and state law. At the very least, a letter agreement will specify the amount of compensation to be paid for a specific position for a designated length of time. It may also incorporate by reference other documents such as a faculty or staff handbook, a position announcement or job description, and the employee benefits manual. For all employees of college athletics programs, a statement that the employee is expected to abide by all university, conference, and national governing body (typically the NCAA) rules is also recommended. The letter agreement is typically signed by the supervisor; to assure that the agreement was received and accepted, a signature line with instructions for the employee to sign and return may also be included.

Although the year-to-year letter agreement provides maximum flexibility and minimizes liability, administrators and/or employees may seek to establish a longer term commitment. The beauty of contracts is that they are infinitely flexible—terms can be drafted for almost anything as long as they are perceived as fair, have been agreed to by both parties, and are not illegal. However, this flexibility is also its Achilles Heel, as the interpretation of employee contract terms continues to be a problem area ripe for litigation. The specific language of the contract must be clear and unambiguous so that reasonable people can easily understand their obligations. If a term is vague or uncertain, the courts will interpret it against the drafter, which is the university as the employer (Restat. 2d of Contracts, 2009).

Though employment contracts may vary from a few pages to very detailed and specific agreement of several dozen pages, all employment contracts should contain the following sections: identification of parties, term of employment, job duties or position responsibilities, compensation and benefits, termination for cause, liquidated damages for breach, integration clause, severability clause, jurisdiction clause, signatures of both parties, and the date of agreement. The contract may also include the following optional provisions: bonuses and/or incentives, reassignment clause, noncompete clause, and an alternative dispute resolution clause requiring mediation or arbitration before a lawsuit can be filed for breach of contract.

Although it is preferred that an employment contract be in writing, a person's word can be a legally recognized contract as long as the oral agreement contains the basic components of a contract—offer, acceptance, and consideration (see *Williams v. Board of Regents*, 2008). When there is no written, signed contract, the relationship may be (but is not always) an at-will employment arrangement.

Constitutional Law

Constitutional law is the interpretation of the rights guaranteed by state and federal constitutions. However, these rights and freedoms are only protected from governmental intervention, not intrusion by private parties (with the exception of the Thirteenth Amendment prohibition of slavery). Any governmental entity, such as a state college or university, as well as their employees, is considered a state actor, while private associations such as athletics conferences or the NCAA are not (see *NCAA v. Tarkanian*, 1988). When state action is present, administrators must be mindful they do not violate constitutional rights.

Due Process

Due process is a variety of legal principles and rules utilized to assure that private rights are not violated by government entities. Athletics administrators and recreation managers at public institutions (who are therefore state actors) must be careful to consider due process when creating policies, procedures, and rules. Because they are not governmental entities, private institutions are not required by law to provide due process to students, staff, or faculty. However, private institutions, which typically spell out a set of rights made available to members of their community, must assure that those rights are in fact provided. Public institutions must do what the law says a government body must do with regard to guaranteeing due process; private institutions must do what they say they are going to do.

The Fifth Amendment of the federal constitution protects government deprivation of "life, liberty, or property without due process of law" (U.S. Const. Amend. V). Similarly, the Fourteenth Amendment prohibits states from depriving citizens of the same rights (U.S. Const. Amend. XIV). Generally, the courts do not recognize a right to participate in athletics or recreation programs. However, athletics-related grant-in-aid (scholarship) and employment contracts are recognized as property rights, and at-will employment has been recognized as a liberty interest (Wong, 1994). No matter how much participants might complain that they will die if they cannot play, there is no recognized life interest in playing sports!

There are two types of due process: substantive and procedural. Substantive due process requires rules to be fair and reasonable in content as well as application. There must be a legitimate organizational objective for the rule, and the rule must clearly be related to accomplishing that objective. Procedural due process involves the methods used to enforce the rule: Is there fairness in the process used to determine whether the rule has been violated and is the sanction imposed also fair (Tribe, 2000)?

The amount of due process required depends upon the value of the interest at issue—the more an individual has at stake, the more extensive and formal are the due process requirements. Minimum due process simply requires notice and a hearing: notification of the problem to the individual and a meeting to discuss both sides. On the other end of the scale, full protection of due process requires notice, a hearing before a neutral decision maker, the opportunity to make an oral presentation and to confront and cross examine adverse witnesses, and the right to have an attorney present, the right to receive a copy of the hearing transcript, and a written decision based on the record (Tribe, 2000).

Equal Protection

Equal protection is the constitutional method of checking on the fairness of the application of any law. The theory of equal protection is to prohibit similarly situated people from having different benefits bestowed or burdens imposed upon them unless there is a constitutionally permissible reason. If the group of people affected can be categorized as a suspect category such as race or country of national origin, or if the rule impacts a fundamental right, then the rule must be necessary to achieve a compelling state interest. If the classification is based on sex or gender, the rule must be substantially related to an important state interest. Finally, for all other group classifications, the rule must merely be rationally related to a legitimate state interest (Tribe, 2000).

First Amendment

The First Amendment to the federal Constitution guarantees basic freedoms related to religion, speech, and assembly and to petition the government to remedy grievances. Public institutions (state actors) may not infringe upon the rights of those participating in their programs, unless a constitutionally permissible reason exists for doing so.

Religion. The First Amendment protects two distinct religions freedoms: the establishment clause and the free exercise clause (Tribe, 2000). An athletics or recreation program may violate the establishment clause when it purposefully or inadvertently promotes religion. This may take the form of holding pre-event prayers, decorating to celebrate religious holidays, or sponsoring an event in conjunction with a church service. The law is quite clear that pregame or postgame or event prayers, whether they are led by a representative of the public institution or a volunteer who is not a state actor, are unconstitutional if the participation of objectors is unavoidable (examples would include prayers broadcast over a public address system or said in a confined space such as a locker room). Conversely, a moment of silence, as long as there is no direction or implication that the silence is to be used for prayer, is allowed.

The free exercise clause of the First Amendment prohibits the government from interfering with a person who is practicing his or her reasonably held religious beliefs (Tribe, 2000). A free exercise issue that often comes up in the context of sport and recreation is wearing of religious clothing, such as a yarmulke or hijab, while participating in activities. In general, playing rules should be modified to accommodate such religious-related items provided that it does not create a safety hazard. Supervisors (coaches, principals, athletics directors, recreation managers) and the institution may be liable if they know of constitutional violations of either the establishment clause or the free exercise clause and do not take action to stop it.

Speech. The First Amendment also protects against government interference with speech, which includes nonverbal types of communication and expression. This fundamental right does not allow anyone to say whatever they want at any time or in any place. State actors are allowed to place reasonable restrictions on the time, place, and manner that expression can occur (Tribe, 2000). For example, facility managers can prohibit protestors from bringing signs into an arena during an event (time is during the event, place is the arena, and manner is the signage). However, they cannot prohibit protestors from carrying signs around the perimeter of the facility (assuming that the protestors are not creating a safety hazard). The content of the speech—the message—may not be regulated, except for narrowly tailored exceptions related to obscenity and fighting words. In these situations, the actual message can be restricted if there is a clear and present danger of imminent harm (Tribe, 2000).

The guarantee of freedom of expression does not mean that a person is protected against consequences for any opinions he or she might express. Student-athletes, coaches, and employees have been banned from participation, lost athletics scholarships, or lost their jobs for speaking their mind. If the expressed opinion involves a matter of public concern, then the individual's right to speak is protected. However, if the statements are purely a private matter, for example, an opinion about whether a coach is giving a student-athlete enough playing time, the courts will not protect the speaker from consequences related to private statements (Tribe, 2000).

The use of social media has presented new challenges for athletics administrators and recreation managers related to freedom of expression. Some institutions have created policies that prohibit student-athletes from making posts on social media sites such as Facebook or Twitter. Others have created policies that warn student-athletes (or employees) that their posts may be monitored and that posts that are inappropriate or violate institutional standards of behavior or codes of conduct may result in punishment or loss of privileges. This area of law is so new that there have been very few cases litigated to determine what the protections and restrictions on expression through social media are. Because participation in athletics and recreation programs is a privilege and not a right, it is assumed that policies that restrict use of social media as a manner of expression are constitutional.

Fourth Amendment

The Fourth Amendment in the Bill of Rights protects people from unreasonable searches and seizure of property by state actors (U.S. Const. Amend. IV). Search and seizure issues are generally raised in the context of drug testing. Search must be reasonable upon its inception and in its scope. Implementing a drug testing program in a sport context has been judged reasonable as a means of deterring drug use, protecting the health and safety of student-athletes, and of assuring fair and equitable competition. Reasonable suspicion and warrants are not necessary in random drug testing situations because the participants voluntarily consent to testing. Consent is considered voluntary even if participants are not allowed to participate if they do not complete consent forms, because participation in activities is a privilege and the participant can freely choose not to participate (*University of Colorado v. Derdeyn*, 1993). Although drug testing programs in sport were highly protested when programs were widely instituted in the 1980s, most participants currently accept testing as a condition of participation. Standardized drug testing protocols such as those utilized by the World Anti-Doping Agency (WADA) and the NCAA are recognized as conforming to constitutional standards (although it is important to recognize that neither of these organizations is considered a state actor).

Administrative Law

The legal concepts discussed thus far in this chapter all fall within a civil law framework. However, the United States is a highly regulated society, and the branch of law related to government agencies (both federal and state), as well as the rules, regulations, opinions, and orders of these agencies, is known as administrative law (Garner, 2011). Athletics administrators and recreation managers do not have to be any more concerned than the average citizen about the creation and operation of administrative agencies. However, Congress has delegated regulatory power to administrative agencies for a number of statutes that do impact athletics administrators and recreation managers.

Equal Employment Opportunity Commission

Employment is an area of the law that is highly regulated. The Equal Employment Opportunity Commission (EEOC) is the federal agency responsible for enforcing several statutes that make it illegal to discriminate against job applicants and employees on the basis of race, color, country of national origin, religion, sex, pregnancy, age, disability, or genetic information. All educational institutions are covered by EEOC laws, as well as all recreation programs that are a part of businesses that employ a minimum of 15 people on an annual (rather than seasonal) basis.

Title VII of the Civil Rights Act of 1964 (Title VII) is the broadest of all the laws related to employment. Employers with 15 or more employees that work 20 or more weeks per year, and whose organizations impact interstate commerce, are required to comply with Title VII. Under Title VII, an employer may not discriminate on the basis of race, color, country of national origin, religion, or sex (including pregnancy) in hiring, during employment, or in termination. Athletics administrators and recreation managers must be careful not to limit or classify employees or applicants based on any of the protected categories. For example, if a program was seeking to hire a coach for a girls or women's team, it is illegal to limit the applicant pool to females only (see *Medcalf v. Trustees of University of Pennsylvania.*, 2003). Sexual harassment is considered discrimination based on sex, and is therefore prohibited under Title VII as well. Employers are also expected to make reasonable accommodations for applicants' and employees' sincerely held religious practices. It is also illegal under Title VII to retaliate against an employee who complains about or has filed a charge of discrimination, or has participated in a discrimination investigation or lawsuit.

The Equal Pay Act of 1963 (EPA) protects against discrimination more narrowly, prohibiting employers from engaging in wage discrimination on the basis of sex. The plaintiff/employee has the burden of proving that the employer paid different wages to an employee of the opposite sex for substantially equal work, as measured by equal skill, physical and/or mental effort, and degree of responsibility performed under the same working conditions. The employer then bears the burden of proving that pay differential was justified based on one or more affirmative defenses: seniority, merit, quantity or quality of production, or any factor other than the sex of the employee. Because employers must prove affirmative defenses, it is very important for athletics administrators and recreation managers to provide detailed job descriptions, conduct measurable performance appraisals, and keep accurate records.

The Age Discrimination in Employment Act of 1967 (ADEA) prohibits employers, employment agencies, and labor organizations (such as unions) from discriminating against people who are 40 or older because of age. Older workers face significant disadvantages in the workplace, both in finding and retaining employment. Organizations that employ or represent at least 20 workers for 20 or more weeks per year are required to comply with the statute. It is not illegal to favor an older employee over a younger one, for example because of seniority or experience, but the law prohibits age discrimination in every aspect of employment including hiring, wages, job assignments, training, promotions, layoffs, or termination.

Harassment, words or actions that create a hostile or offensive work environment or result in an adverse employment decision (such as transfer or demotion) because of age, is also prohibited. It is important to note that this legislation does not prohibit employers from utilizing bona fide occupational qualifications that are age based, nor does it prohibit establishing a normal retirement age.

The EEOC is also responsible for regulating and enforcing the employment-related sections of other, broader based statutes. Title I of the Americans with Disabilities Act of 1990 (ADA) prohibits private employers, as well as state and local governments, from discriminating against an otherwise qualified person in any employment-related function because of a physical or mental disability that substantially limits one or more major life activities. A person is considered otherwise qualified if they meet all of the position requirements in spite of the disability. Employers are required to provide reasonable accommodation to otherwise qualified applicants or employees for known physical or mental disabilities, unless providing this accommodation would create an undue burden on the operation of the business. Reasonable accommodations would include job restructuring, providing flexibility in work schedules, acquiring or modifying equipment to accommodate the disability, or providing readers or interpreters. Employers are not required to make accommodations that would fundamentally alter or substantially modify the position. The ADA also prohibits retaliation against applicants or employees who complain about discrimination, have filed a charge of discrimination, or participated in an investigation or lawsuit related to discrimination. Sections 501 and 505 of the Rehabilitation Act of 1973 prohibit the federal government from discriminating against people with disabilities in any of the aforementioned ways.

United States Department of Justice

In addition to the EEOC, the U.S. Department of Justice also has regulatory authority for enforcing the provisions of the Americans with Disabilities Act. Title II of the ADA prohibits state actors or public entities from excluding otherwise qualified individuals with a disability from participating in services, programs, or activities. Title III of the ADA similarly prohibits private actors who own, lease, or operate places of public accommodations from discriminating on the basis of disability in providing goods, services, facilities, privileges, or accommodations. Places of public accommodation may include privately owned recreational facilities, voluntary membership organizations, shopping malls, movie theaters, or stadia. The legislation provides an exception when the disabled individual poses a direct threat to the health or safety of others.

In 2008, the Americans with Disabilities Act Amendments Act (ADAAA) significantly broadened the definitions of disabilities that are covered under the ADA. Previous court rulings had very narrowly limited coverage of the act to those conditions that severely or significantly restricted a major life activity.

United States Department of Education Office for Civil Rights

Another administrative agency that has regulatory responsibility for enforcing legislation that impacts athletics administrators and recreation managers is the U.S. Department of Education Office for Civil Rights (OCR). Similar to the variety of legislation that the EEOC enforces to prohibit discrimination in employment, OCR enforces legislation that prohibits discrimination on the basis of race, color, national origin, sex, disability, and age in educational programs or activities. This includes all state education agencies, elementary and secondary schools, colleges and universities, vocational rehabilitation agencies, libraries, and museums that receive federal funding.

The Office for Civil Rights has jurisdiction for regulation and enforcement of civil rights laws within federally funded educational settings, whether they are public or private. Title VII of the Civil Rights Act of 1964 prohibits discrimination on the basis of race, color, and country of national origin. Title II of the Americans with Disabilities Act of 1990 and Section 504 of the Rehabilitation Act of 1973 prohibit discrimination on the basis of disabilities in school-sponsored programs or activities, requiring these educational institutions to provide recreation and athletics opportunities for disabled students, as well as accommodating the disabled to allow them to participate and compete with their able-bodied peers. The Age Discrimination Act of 1975 prohibits schools from discriminating on the basis of age, requiring schools that receive federal funding to reconsider age requirements and limitations on students based on age.

Title IX of the Education Amendments of 1972 (Title IX) prohibits discrimination on the basis of sex in educational programs or activities. This includes opportunities to participate in recreational, intramural, and varsity athletics (see Chapter Six). Sexual harassment is discrimination based on sex and is therefore also prohibited under Title IX. However, unlike the employer's liability under Title VII, educational institutions are only liable for sexual harassment if they know of the harassment and are deliberately indifferent to it. Title IX also protects educational institutions from discriminating against students who are pregnant. Schools may not institute policies that universally prohibit pregnant students from participating in recreational, intramural, or varsity athletics activities, nor may they take away athletics related grant-in-aid (scholarships) because of pregnancy. In addition, schools may not intimidate, threaten, coerce, or retaliate against anyone who complains about gender discrimination or participates in OCR investigations or litigation. Although gender discrimination claims regarding participation opportunities continue to dominate media attention, the majority of lawsuits filed under Title IX involve sexual harassment and retaliation claims.

United States Treasury Department Internal Revenue Service

In the United States, how you are taxed depends on your tax status; your tax status is determined by the Internal Revenue Service (IRS). All persons, natural or corporate, are required to pay income tax unless it falls within a specific statutory exception. Collegiate athletics and recreation programs are tax exempt as educational institutions. College athletics departments may be tax exempt as educational institutions, or some have been independently structured as 501(c) (3) corporations, which are still tax exempt.

Even if an organization is tax exempt, it is not necessarily tax free. The Unrelated Business Income Tax (UBIT) provision allows the IRS to tax the gross income derived from unrelated trade or business regularly carried on by the organization [I.R.C. §§ 511(a)(1) & (2)]. To determine whether UBIT applies, the IRS first asks whether the primary purpose for the activity is to generate income or profit, or whether the activity is incidental to the solicitation of charitable donations. For example, a recreation program hosting a 5k road race and charging thousands of participants an entry fee may not be taxed as UBIT if the purpose of the event is to raise funding and generate donations. Next, the IRS examines whether frequency and continuity of the activities are regularly carried on in a way similar to commercial activities. Previous litigation has determined that advertising revenue from game programs, television revenue, and ticket sales from athletics events are all incidental (Kaplan, 1980). Finally, the IRS determines whether or not the activity is unrelated to the tax exempt purpose of the organization. As long as the athletics or recreational revenue-generating activity is not in direct competition with private commercial enterprises and the primary purpose is to generate funding that supports the tax exempt educational or recreational purpose of the organization, UBIT will probably not apply.

It is critically important for athletics administrators and recreation managers to be aware of legislation that impacts the sport and recreation industry. Awareness includes understanding the law, and also the various regulations, policy interpretations, and opinions that are released by the regulating agency. As this can become overwhelming for the average administrator, it is important to develop a good working relationship with the legal experts within your organization. Every organization is required to designate an EEOC and Title IX administrator. Tax questions would probably be directed to a chief financial officer, business office, or general counsel.

Intellectual Property

As athletics and recreation programs strive to find additional sources of revenue to support activities, legal issues involving intellectual property have become more frequent. Intellectual property is creative or artistic work that has commercial value and is protected by copyright, patent, or trademark laws. Legal needs in this area relate both to protecting the institution's intellectual property and to acquiring appropriate permission to utilize others' protected property.

Copyright

The Copyright Act of 1976 identifies the legal rights granted to individuals for protection of their creative work. In order to register for copyright protection, the author must prove that it is an original work that exists in a form that can be reproduced. Athletics and recreation programs may produce literary works, pictorial or graphic works, or motion pictures or sound recordings that could have commercial value and should be protected by copyright. Copyright registration is facilitated by the United States Copyright Office, a service unit of the Library of Congress. The owner of a copyright has the exclusive right to reproduce, distribute, and/or display the work as well as license the work to others. Should an athletics or recreation manager wish to use a copyrighted work, such as a book, song, or film, in conjunction with their programming, permission and/or a license must be obtained from the copyright holder prior to use. A common example would be the use of recorded music to entertain the crowd prior to or during an event.

Trademark

The Federal Trademark Act of 1946, commonly known as the Lanham Act, governs registration of trademarks and allowable action to protect against trademark infringement. A trademark is a word, phrase, symbol, or design that is used to identify the source of goods and distinguish them from those produced or sold by others. Institutional names (often referred to as *word marks*), logos, mascots, and even colors may be registered as trademarks. Colleges may establish rights in their marks simply by using the TM designation with the trademark. However, registering trademarks with the United States Patent and Trademark Office of the Department of Commerce allows the mark holder to use the® symbol which lists the marks on the Patent and Trademark Office online databases and provides legal notice as to the ownership and exclusive right to use the mark throughout the United States. Registration is just the first level of enforcement; the institution or program must continue to use the mark and enforce the exclusivity of usage in order to protect the trademark. For example, technology has made it easy to copy a mark, and many high schools, community groups, or programs utilize others' marks without permission. When a trademark holder becomes aware of the unauthorized use of the mark, a letter must be sent to notify the unauthorized user that they do not have permission to use the mark. If the mark holder stops using the mark (even if it is still registered) there is a danger of losing the rights to the mark because of abandonment. If the mark holder is aware of others' unauthorized use of the mark and fails to send cease and desist letters, there is a danger of losing the rights to the mark. Even if the mark holder vigorously enforces their rights to the mark, it is possible that others may be able to use a similar trademark if it is unlikely that consumers would be confused as to the source of the mark. It is unlikely that the use of a black G on a bulldog wearing a red sweater for the Grandview Bulldogs would be mistaken for a product of the University of Georgia. If it seems harsh that a college or university has to enforce their marks against lowly high school or community programs' use, the simple solution is to grant a license to the unauthorized user, now making them an authorized user, for a nominal fee.

Risk Management

This chapter has provided an overview of some of the most common and most important areas of legal concern for athletics administrators and recreation managers. Failure to comply with the law, or adhere to the accepted standards within the profession and industry, will put the sport or recreation organization at risk of liability. The best way to reduce liability is to conduct a systematic analysis of all operations for potential risks, and then to implement a plan to reduce the risks, commonly known as risk management.

A typical risk management process would start with identifying risks related to personnel, activities, facilities, and emergencies. Risks should then be categorized by measuring the frequency of the risk and the severity of the potential harm. Next, a conscious decision should be made whether to avoid, transfer, reduce, or retain each risk. For example, a risk assessment of facilities may note that electrical outlets are not mounted flush with the walls, creating a risk of injury to participants who might run or fall into the walls. The likelihood of injuries occurring may be fairly high, but the type of injury might be fairly minor, such as scratches, small cuts, or bruising. The facility manager should weigh the cost of changing the electrical outlets against the risk of injuries and decide whether to avoid the risk by replacing the outlets, transfer the risk by using a liability waiver, reduce the risk by putting signs or perhaps padding around the outlets, or just retain the risk and do nothing.

A risk management plan, including policies and procedures, should be put into writing that is easily accessible by employees and participants, such as a handbook or on the program website. All supervisors should have risk management orientation when they are hired, and training on an annual basis thereafter. Once the risk management plan is implemented, adherence should be monitored and feedback provided to evaluate its effectiveness.

Some program risks may be reduced through the use of waivers. A waiver is a contract between the sport or recreation program provider and the participant that holds the provider harmless for injuries resulting from ordinary negligence in exchange for the opportunity to participate in the athletics or recreational program. The effectiveness of the waiver will depend upon how well it is written—a waiver is a contract, so all contract law principles apply. Also, contract law is subject to the peculiarities of the law of the state where the program is located. For example, some states will not allow parents to sign away the rights of a child participant, so athletics and recreation programs in those states remain liable for children under the age of 18 who are harmed as a result of negligence even if parents sign a waiver. Ideally, waivers should be reviewed and approved by legal counsel in order to assure that the document is properly identified and constructed and that the document conforms to the requirements of that particular state law (Cotten and Cotten, 2011).

Risk may also be mitigated by the use of informed consent agreements. Informed consent is a tort law principle that shifts liability from the service provider to the participant who knowingly accepts the risk. Informed consent may be oral, as when an instructor tells participants of the various safety rules and dangers of participating, or in a written document. Informed consent is not a contract, so adhering to contract law principles is not necessary. Instead, informed consent provides the participant with important information related to the foreseeable risks associated with the activity, which helps the recreation or athletics administrator prove what the participant knew or should have known relative to an assumption of risk or comparative negligence defense.

Risk may be transferred from the sport or recreational program through the use of insurance. Liability insurance is also based on contract law, whereby the sport or recreation organization pays a premium to an insurance company in exchange for indemnification in the event the organization suffers a loss as a result of legal liability. It is important for athletics administrators and recreation managers to know exactly what coverage institutional insurance provides, as well as limitations on amount of payouts and/or numbers of incidents.

Conclusion

Athletics administrators and recreation managers are not expected to be legal experts. Athletics administrators and recreation managers are encouraged to develop strong relationships with legal counsel so that legal issues that do arise can be properly addressed.

This chapter provided a sampling of the legal issues and risks that most commonly occur in sport and recreation settings. Astute athletics administrators and recreation managers will use this information to spot these legal issues and seek legal advice to best protect their programs and organizations.

Chapter Five Key Points

1. Whereas civil law governs disputes between private parties, including individuals, institutions, or businesses, criminal law establishes a framework for behavior that is prohibited as harmful to society.

2. A *tort* is a wrong for which civil law provides a remedy. An unintentional wrongful act falls within the area of negligence (the four elements of which are duty, breach, causation, and damage); a purposeful act would be categorized as an intentional tort (examples include assault, battery, or defamation). The individual actor(s), supervisor(s), and even the institution may be liable for damages (Restat. 3d of Torts, 2000).
3. A *contract* is a promise, or set of promises, for breach of which the law gives a remedy, or the performance of which the law in some way recognizes as a duty (Garner, 2011). A contract exists when there is offer, acceptance, and consideration.
4. Employment contracts appear to generate the most litigation for college athletics and recreation programs, although the overwhelming majority of staff in those areas does not have written contracts and is considered at-will employees. The doctrine of at-will employment allows for either party in the employment relationship to terminate without liability (Restat. 2d of Contracts, 2009).
5. Constitutional law is the interpretation of the rights guaranteed by state and federal constitutions. However, these rights and freedoms are only protected from governmental intervention, not intrusion by private parties. Any governmental entity, such as a state college or university, as well as their employees, is considered a state actor, while private associations such as private universities or athletics conferences are not.
6. Concepts from constitutional law that are important for college athletics and recreation administrators to understand include due process, equal protection, freedom of speech, and freedom from unreasonable search and seizure.
7. Administrative law relates to government agencies (both federal and state), as well as the rules, regulations, opinions, and orders of such agencies (Garner, 2011). Administrative law addresses discrimination in employment, educational opportunities, or accommodations (including the provisions of the Civil Rights Act, the Americans with Disabilities Act, and the Educational Amendments of 1972), as well as tax regulations such as those relating to tax-exempt status and to unrelated business income.
8. Intellectual property is creative or artistic work that has commercial value and is protected by copyright, patent, or trademark laws. Legal needs in this area relate both to protecting the institution's intellectual property and in acquiring appropriate permission to utilize others' protected property.

9. Failure to comply with the law, or adhere to the accepted standards within the profession and industry, will put the sport or recreation organization at risk of liability. The best way to reduce liability is to conduct a systematic analysis of all operations for potential risks, and then to implement a plan to reduce the risks, commonly known as risk management.

References

American Jurisprudence (2nd ed.). St. Paul, MN: West Publishing, 2011.

Cotten, D. J., and Cotton, M. B. "Liability Waivers 101," 2011. Accessed March 29, 2011 at http://www.sportwaiver.com.

Garner, B. A. *Black's Law Dictionary* (4th ed.). West, 2011.

Kaplan, R. L. "Intercollegiate Athletics and the Unrelated Business Income Tax." *Columbia Law Review*, 1980, 80, 1430–1473.

Restatement of Torts, 3rd, 2000.

Restatement of Torts, 2nd of Contracts, 2009.

Tribe, L. H. *American Constitutional Law* (3rd ed.). New York: Foundation Press, 2000.

Wong, G. M. *Essentials of Amateur Sports Law* (2nd ed.). Westport, CT: Praeger, 1994.

Legal References

Age Discrimination in Employment Act (1967).

Allen v. Rutgers, State University of New Jersey, 107 N.J. 653 (1987).

Americans with Disabilities Act, 42 U.S.C.S. §12101, et seq. (1990).

Americans with Disabilities Act Amendments Act (2008).

Copyright Act of 1976, Pub. L. No. 94–553, Circular 92 (2009).

Equal Pay Act of 1963.

Genetic Information Nondiscrimination Act of 2008.

Internal Revenue Code, I.R.C. §§ 511(a)(1) & (2).

Medcalf v. Trustees of University of Pennsylvania, 71 Fed. Appx. 924 (2003).

Pregnancy Discrimination Act.

Rehabilitation Act, 29 U.S.C.S. §701, et seq. (2011).

Title VII of the Civil Rights Act of 1964.

Trademark Act of 1946, 15 U.S.C. §1051, et seq. (2011).

University of Colorado ex rel. Regents of the University of Colorado v. Derdeyn, 863 P.2d 929 (1993).

U.S. Const. Amend. I.

U.S. Const. Amend. IV.

U.S. Copyright Office (2011). Retrieved on March 29, 2011, from http://www.copyright.gov.

U.S. Department of Justice (2011). Retrieved on March 28, 2011, from http://www.ada.gov.

U.S. Equal Employment Opportunity Commission (2011) Retrieved on March 28, 2011, from http://www.eeoc.gov/eeoc.

U.S. Patent and Trademark Office (2011). Retrieved on March 29, 2011, from http://www.uspto.gov.

CHAPTER SIX

TITLE IX

Valerie M. Bonnette

Title IX of the Education Amendments of 1972 is a federal law that prohibits sex discrimination in any program receiving federal funding, including any higher education institution that accepts federal funding for research or other activities or through receipt of federal financial aid. It was written primarily to end the common practice of excluding women from certain fields of study. Congresswoman Patsy Mink of Hawaii, one of the authors of Title IX, was herself denied entrance into medical school because of her gender. Title IX, named formally in her honor as the Patsy Takemoto Mink Equal Opportunity in Education Act, bans the very discrimination that she experienced.

No doubt, the authors did not anticipate that Title IX would become known mainly for its coverage of athletics programs in education. The controversy over Title IX's application to athletics programs began in the 1970s and continues to the present day. The continuing debate concerns only one component of thirteen program components addressed by the Title IX athletics policies. That one program component addresses the fundamental protection under all civil rights laws—an equal opportunity to participate; in effect, equal access to the education program that is intercollegiate athletics.

This chapter offers information and suggestions regarding Title IX. The chapter opens with a general discussion of the act and its requirements. It next describes the three-part test for compliance regarding access, followed by description of the twelve treatment issues that must also be addressed for compliance. The chapter concludes with recommendations for administrators in intercollegiate athletics and recreation regarding how to assure that the programs and services for which they are responsible are in compliance with the requirements of Title IX.

Title IX Athletics Policy

The Office for Civil Rights (OCR) of the United States Department of Education has nationwide enforcement authority for Title IX. In 1979, OCR adopted the Intercollegiate Athletics Policy Interpretation (Policy Interpretation) to provide a framework for conducting investigations of alleged sex discrimination in athletics programs. The 1979 Policy Interpretation is the major source for athletics program requirements. The policy follows the pattern for civil rights laws in addressing two basic provisions: equal access to the program and equal treatment for those who participate in the program. The provision of equal access is addressed through the much litigated three-part test, while the equal treatment provision is addressed through twelve program issues. Both the test and the issues are addressed in greater detail later in this chapter.

The Policy Interpretation clarifies that intercollegiate, interscholastic, club, and intramural programs are reviewed separately from each other, and that the three-part test and the other twelve Title IX program components apply to all of these athletics programs. Title IX compliance problems have arisen almost exclusively in intercollegiate and interscholastic athletics programs rather than recreation, club, or intramural programs. The policy explanations herein should clarify why.

Evaluating Compliance

Compliance is determined by comparing the benefits for all female student-athletes to those for all male student-athletes, not by simply comparing the benefits for the women's basketball team to those for the men's basketball team. Benefits, such as equipment, practice schedules, and modes of transportation, may differ for women's and men's teams if there is a balance of benefits in the overall program. Different benefits may be based on the nature of sports, coaches' professional decisions (if made to benefit the students), and student-athletes' preferences, and still comply. Generally, the same percentages of male and female student-athletes should be provided equivalent quality and quantity of benefits. However, for some issues, such as providing athletic trainers and medical staff, assignments should be identical for men's and women's teams in the same sports, as needs are based on the nature of the sport. For other issues, benefits are to be equivalently adequate, even if the needs themselves may differ.

Compliance in nearly every Title IX program area is not determined by the dollars spent, but by the tangible benefits that student-athletes receive. The major exception is athletics scholarships, where compliance is based on the dollars awarded. Otherwise, compliance is determined by the quality of equipment, the modes of transportation, the practice schedules, the availability of coaches, the quality of facilities, and not the cost for these benefits. In other words, what is evaluated under Title IX for modes of transportation is whether female and male student-athletes each travel by aircraft a comparable number of times, not the cost of the airfare.

Title IX imposes no requirements for budgeting practices. Title IX simply requires institutions to provide female and male students an equal opportunity to become athletics participants, and then treat those participants equitably. Institutions are not absolved of these requirements if booster clubs or donors choose to donate only to men's teams. Whatever benefits student-athletes receive via donated monies, tangible gifts, guarantees, and endowments are all viewed as benefits provided by the institution.

Usually, when compliance issues arise, it is because women are disadvantaged. To comply, the institution may improve benefits for the women's program, reallocate benefits from the men's program to the women's program, or reduce benefits for the men's program.

Three-Part Test: The Access Issue

Institutions are required to meet one test of the three-part test addressing an equal opportunity for female and male students to become an athletics participant. Administrators may choose which test the institution shall meet, and may change the institution's method of compliance at any time. Compliance is presumed if the institution offers intercollegiate athletics participation opportunities to women and men at rates that are the same or nearly the same as their respective rates of enrollment as full-time undergraduates (test one—proportionality). If students of one sex are underrepresented in the program—meaning their rate of participation is less than their rate of enrollment—administrators have two methods to show that their actions have not caused this underrepresentation: demonstrate a history and continuing practice of program expansion for the underrepresented sex (test two—program expansion); or fully and effectively accommodate the underrepresented sex in the current program (test three—full accommodation). When students of one sex are underrepresented, it is nearly always women, and the explanations herein assume women to be the underrepresented sex and men to be the overrepresented sex, meaning men are participating in athletics at a rate that exceeds their rate of enrollment.

Test One—Proportionality

Test one requires participation to be proportionate to the full-time undergraduate enrollment at the institution; in effect, if women are 52% of the full-time undergraduates, then women should be 52% or nearly 52% of the intercollegiate athletics participants. OCR issued a 1996 Policy Clarification adopting a complicated formula for determining whether participation is substantially proportional to enrollment. As a practical guide—but not a legal standard—in complying with this formula, institutions with 300 or fewer participants might aim for rates of participation to be within three percentage points of enrollment rates, or between 49% and 55% women's participation for 52% women's enrollment. Programs with more than 300 participants should narrow the gap to less than three percentage points, while the largest of programs (500 student-athletes or more) should consider narrowing the gap to two percentage points. From there, participation may be easily adjusted to meet any legal standards imposed by OCR or the courts. Studies by the Government Accountability Office (GAO, 1996, 2000), the investigative agency for the United States Congress, have shown that approximately 27% of institutions choose test one for compliance.

Test Two—Program Expansion

Test two requires the institution to demonstrate a history and continuing practice of program expansion for the underrepresented sex; in effect, adding women's opportunities to accommodate their developing interests and abilities. There are no standards for the number of opportunities added or time frames for implementing the additions. OCR determines compliance on a case-by-case basis. For example, an institution that dropped women's field hockey in the 1980s and added women's soccer in the 1990s has not expanded its women's program; merely, the opportunities lost were replaced. Adding opportunities on existing women's teams can be program expansion; however, the added opportunities must be student-athletes who receive coaching and practice, not hand out equipment. Test two was a simple compliance method for most institutions in the 1970s and early 1980s as they added women's teams. One report (GAO, 2000) suggests that only 6% of institutions choose test two—program expansion.

Test Three—Full Accommodation

Test three requires an institution to offer every intercollegiate athletics program for the underrepresented sex for which there is sufficient interest and ability to field a team and sufficient competition for that intercollegiate athletics program in the institution's normal competitive region. All three factors of sufficient interest, ability, and competition must be met before an institution is obligated to offer an intercollegiate athletics program under test three. For example, perhaps the women's rugby club is highly competitive and requests intercollegiate status. Currently, intercollegiate competition is insufficient to compel the addition of a women's intercollegiate rugby team to meet test three. The GAO (2000) indicates that two-thirds of institutions choose test three—full accommodation for compliance.

The three-part test has been the source of contentious litigation in eight of the twelve United States Circuit Courts that review education matters. Generally, these lawsuits were filed because institutions dropped intercollegiate teams. The female plaintiffs have won nearly every lawsuit they filed when their team was discontinued. As of 2010, the male plaintiffs have lost every lawsuit filed when a men's team was discontinued because men were overrepresented in each of the programs.

Steps for Compliance

There are a number of basic steps that administrators may follow for achieving compliance with the three-part test. These include

- Identify the full-time undergraduate enrollment by sex.
- Identify the number of female and male participants on each intercollegiate athletics program (count an individual student-athlete for each program on which she or he participates and who is on the squad list as

of the first date of competition, practicing with the program, and receiving coaching).

- Calculate enrollment and participation rates and compare men's and women's rates of enrollment to their respective rates of participation in intercollegiate athletics.
- Determine whether students of one sex are participating at a rate that is three percentage points or more below their rate of enrollment as full-time undergraduates (use two percentage points for a program with 500 student-athletes or more).
- If students of one sex are underrepresented, identify if there are any intercollegiate athletics programs not currently offered to that sex for which there is sufficient competition at an appropriate level in the institution's normal competitive region.
- If competition is sufficient, then determine if there is enough interest to form an intercollegiate athletics program (this involves a judgment, but participation in on-campus programs such as club sports, intramurals, recreation, and elective physical education courses should be reviewed along with participation in feeder programs, such as high schools and community program participation in areas where coaches normally recruit; these factors, combined with the results of any survey or other assessment, are reviewed to determine interest in sports not currently offered).

For example, consider the case study of the University of South Somewhere (USS). Women are underrepresented in intercollegiate athletics. The only sport program not currently offered for which there is sufficient competition in USS's normal competitive region is lacrosse. An institution's normal competitive region includes areas in which conference members are located and the geographic region in which the institution normally competes. The women's lacrosse club wants intercollegiate status, and there are 250 high schools offering girls' lacrosse in regions where coaches normally recruit. The evidence suggests that test three is not met because there is sufficient interest, ability, and competition for a women's lacrosse team, which is not currently offered. The institution does not meet test one—proportionality because women are significantly underrepresented in the program. No women's intercollegiate athletics programs have been added for several years, so the institution is not meeting test two—program expansion. The institution's compliance options are (1) add women's lacrosse, which would achieve compliance with test three—full accommodation, even if with the addition of lacrosse, women remain underrepresented in intercollegiate athletics; or (2) add other women's teams, which might achieve compliance with test two—program expansion; or (3) adjust current participation by adding walk-ons to women's teams and cutting walk-ons to men's teams to achieve participation proportionate to enrollment and compliance with test one—proportionality. This last approach, commonly referred to as *roster management* by athletics professionals, may achieve compliance without the expense of adding a women's team and the challenges of discontinuing a men's team.

Recreation Programs. Compliance concerns for the three-part test are rare for club, intramurals, and recreation programs. Teams in these programs tend to be self-generated by the students, assuming they operate within basic guidelines established by the institution. When club teams or activities are discontinued, it is often due to lack of interest, which is an acceptable reason for discontinuing a club team under Title IX. Assuming the institution allows students to begin their own club, intramural, and recreation teams and activities and continue them as students' interests warrant, then the institution meets test three—full accommodation for each program, regardless of rates of participation.

Twelve Treatment Issues

The 1979 Policy Interpretation outlines factors for review in twelve program components addressing treatment of students who have become participants in the intercollegiate athletics program. These twelve treatment issues are addressed in order of the importance of the benefit and likelihood for compliance concerns.

Athletics Scholarships

OCR has refined the Title IX requirements for athletics scholarships from the 1975 Title IX regulation (which implements the 1972 statute) to the 1979 Policy Interpretation to its 1998 policy guidance. The 1998 guidance states that compliance is presumed if scholarship dollars are awarded to women and men at rates within one percentage point of their rates of participation. Noncompliance is presumed if differences exceed one percentage point and are not justified by nondiscriminatory criteria, such as the difference between in-state and out-of-state tuition. Although OCR does not state this explicitly in its policy documents, summer term and fifth year aid should be reviewed separately from each other and separately from regular year aid because not all student-athletes want or need summer term or fifth year aid.

Intercollegiate Programs. To analyze scholarship awards, administrators should

- Count an individual student-athlete one time only programwide, regardless of the number of teams on which he or she participates.
- Identify women's and men's rates of participation (often different from the rates of participation for the three-part test).
- Identify athletics grant-in-aid dollars awarded during the regular academic year and determine the proportion awarded to women and men.
- Identify whether rates of participation and rates of scholarship awards are within one percentage point.
- Conduct the same analysis for summer term and fifth year aid; if grant-in-aid is awarded to all who need it during the summer term, and separately, fifth year, then compliance is achieved even if awards are significantly disproportionate; and if grant-in-aid must be limited, then awards should be within one percentage point of participation.

Administrators' compliance options include adjusting participation rates, adjusting the dollars awarded, or adjusting both participation and awards to achieve rates of awards within one percentage point of rates of participation.

Recreation Programs. Athletics grants-in-aid are rarely awarded to student-athletes in club, intramural, and recreation programs. Occasionally, an institution or boosters may fund scholarships for club student-athletes. The same Title IX policies apply. For example, if male club student-athletes receive athletics scholarships, then female club student-athletes should receive athletics scholarships, and the dollars awarded should be within one percentage point of men's and women's rates of participation in the club sports program. The same steps outlined above for intercollegiate programs should be employed to review athletics scholarships awarded at the club level.

Coaching

Coaches are an integral element of any intercollegiate athletic program and of some campus recreation programs. Coaches should be equally available and qualified programwide.

Intercollegiate Programs. There are no required standards for providing coaches who are equally available and equally qualified programwide. An easy compliance method is to provide women's and men's teams in the same sport with the same number of coaches for the same percentage of time (for example, full-time, half-time, quarter-time, etc.); for dissimilar sports, provide the number of coaches appropriate to the size of the team and nature of the sport. Otherwise, offsetting assignments are permitted; for example, men's basketball has three coaches and women's basketball has two coaches, which is offset by the assignment of three coaches to the women's soccer team and two coaches for men's soccer. Qualifications (success, years of experience) should be comparable in the overall women's and men's programs.

Recreation Programs. Institutions rarely hire coaches for club, intramural, or recreation programs. Occasionally, club team members may pay fees for a coaching stipend. The institution has no obligation to offset this coaching arrangement, as the individual student-athletes pay for this themselves. However, if donors pay a stipend for a club team's coach, then the institution is responsible for ensuring equivalent coaching availability in the overall club sports program. Similarly, if the institution pays stipends for student employees or graduate assistants, and their duties include coaching, then the institution is responsible for ensuring that the student and graduate assistant coaches are assigned equitably to men's and women's teams.

Recruitment

The recruitment of student-athletes involves three Title IX factors: the opportunity for coaches to recruit, which includes the same considerations as coaching availability; equivalent adequate financial resources; and equitable treatment of prospective student-athletes. A common compliance problem concerns financial resources. Per OCR policy, expenditures should be proportionate to women's and men's rates of participation unless there are appropriate justifications for disproportionate dollars, such as the number of students who graduated in a particular year.

Intercollegiate Programs. Administrators should

- Determine whether recruitment funds are adequate, and if not, the amount needed and the specific purpose (for example, travel to a national tournament).
- Identify whether total recruitment expenditures are proportionate to women's and men's rates of participation.
- If these rates differ by more than five percentage points, and recruitment needs that would justify disproportionate dollars are not significantly different, then increase funding for women's teams (assuming women are disadvantaged), reallocate funds from the men's program to the women's program, or reduce funding to the men's program to ensure equivalently adequate resources.

Recreation Programs. Institutions rarely budget recruitment dollars for club, intramural, or recreation teams or activities. Recruitment funding provided to any of these programs should be proportionate to the rates of men's and women's participation in each program.

Locker Rooms, Practice and Competitive Facilities

The basic compliance goal is to have roughly proportionate numbers of female and male student-athletes to be provided facilities of equivalent quality and availability.

Intercollegiate Programs. Institutions should

- Evaluate the quality and adequacy of each practice and competitive facility, focusing on those facilities used only by teams for one sex (often the baseball and softball fields, the football team's facilities, wrestling and gymnastics practice facilities, or the soccer field and pool or natatorium if only women's and not men's soccer and swimming are offered, or vice versa).
- Determine if a facility has two or more features (for example, scoreboard, fencing, playing surface, lighting) that are missing or of lesser quality.
- Implement remedies if this disadvantage is not balanced elsewhere.

Locker rooms are distinguished by whether teams have exclusive use of the respective rooms; the location in relation to practice and competitive facilities, training, weight, and equipment rooms; and the overall quality in regard to room size (adequate for the number of student-athletes using the room at one time), locker size and quality, and amenities such as carpet, lighting, team meeting or lounge areas with television, video, and/or computer equipment, and special features such as adjoining training room or laundry facilities. Overall, locker room availability and quality should be comparable for equivalent proportions of female and male student-athletes. Reassigning locker rooms is often an easy method for achieving compliance.

Recreation Programs. Often, recreation and intercollegiate teams do not use the same facilities. For those facilities used solely for intramurals or recreation, institutions should follow the same steps as suggested for intercollegiate athletics facilities.

When recreation and intercollegiate athletics use the same facilities, the common concerns are overuse and scheduling issues. If overuse compromises the quality of an intercollegiate team's facility, determine whether this disadvantages students of one sex. If some club teams use the higher-quality intercollegiate facilities, determine whether this provides an advantage to one gender in the overall club sports program. Conduct the same review for the intramurals program and the recreation program.

Locker rooms are rarely assigned exclusively to club and recreation teams. Often, recreation programs use the same locker rooms as are provided for physical education programs for the general student body. If club and recreation teams or the general student body also use the locker rooms assigned to intercollegiate teams, this can be a compliance concern if affecting more women's than men's teams, or vice versa. Again, reassigning locker rooms is often an easy compliance solution.

Scheduling of Games and Practice Times

The number of contests should be the same for women's and men's teams in the same sport and the same percentage of maximum allowable contests for women's and men's teams in dissimilar sports. Game times should be equally desirable in the overall program. Practice times should be equally convenient and sufficient, and preseason and postseason opportunities should be equivalent.

Intercollegiate Programs. Administrators should

- Identify the number of preseason and regular season contests scheduled by each team, including those contests exempted under athletics association rules.
- Identify whether men's and women's teams schedule the same number of contests in the same sports and equivalent percentages of the maximum allowable contests for dissimilar sports.
- Determine whether teams' practice times are sufficient and convenient.
- Adjust scheduling for practice times and games as necessary if differences are not offsetting programwide.

Recreation Programs. The same Title IX policies apply, including for preseason and postseason opportunities. For example, if a men's intramural league schedules a championship tournament, the same opportunity should be provided for women's intramural teams. If a club team has an opportunity to compete in regional or national competition, then that opportunity should be available for both women's and men's club teams.

Travel and Per Diem Allowances

The Title IX factors reviewed include modes of transportation, housing and dining benefits during travel, and special travel, such as trips to Hawaii, Alaska, or Europe. One compliance target for modes of transportation is for women's and men's teams to use the same modes for the same proportion of trips, although distance and travel squad size are acceptable justifications for differences. The number of student-athletes assigned per hotel room often determines whether housing during travel is equitable. Providing the same per diem to all student-athletes is a simple compliance approach for dining benefits. The length of stay and opportunities for special travel should be comparable programwide.

Intercollegiate Programs. Administrators should

- Identify the total number of trips by men's teams, and calculate the percentage of those trips where men's teams used charter aircraft, commercial aircraft, charter buses, school-bus quality buses, and vans.
- Conduct the same calculations for the women's program and compare the percentages to the men's program (for example, men's teams used commercial aircraft for 27% of their trips compared to 29% of all trips

by women's teams; benefits are comparable, as the differences are not significant).

- Determine whether there are acceptable justifications for differences (for example, distance traveled, number of travel squad student-athletes).
- Make adjustments as necessary to achieve a balance.
- Identify the number of student-athletes assigned per hotel room and resolve differences.
- Determine whether dining during travel is satisfactory, and resolve any imbalances.
- Resolve any concerns or affect a balance regarding length of stay.
- Schedule the same number of special travel opportunities for the men's and women's programs or provide offsetting benefits over a generation of students (four years).

Recreation Programs. Travel and per diem benefits are rarely provided for intramural and recreation programs. Some club teams may use institution vans, and may even receive hotel and meal benefits. Applying the same policy for all club teams for travel and per diem allowances should achieve compliance. The same analyses outlined for intercollegiate programs apply to club sports programs should significant travel and per diem benefits be provided by the institution or donors.

Medical and Training Facilities and Services

The assignment of doctors, certified staff trainers, certified graduate student trainers, and noncertified student trainers to home and away events and practices should be identical for women's and men's intercollegiate athletics programs in the same sports, and as appropriate to the nature of the sport for men's and women's athletics programs in dissimilar sports. Certified staff trainers are assumed to be more qualified and provide greater consistency in services than certified graduate student trainers. The quality of weight rooms and training rooms should be equivalently adequate, and the scheduling for these facilities should be equivalently convenient and sufficient for women's and men's intercollegiate athletics programs. Insurance coverage should be nondiscriminatory.

Intercollegiate Programs. Administrators should

- Compare the assignments of athletics trainers and medical staff for home and away events and practices for all teams.

- Identify and resolve differences for women's and men's intercollegiate athletics programs in the same sport, and review whether assignments for dissimilar sports are appropriate.
- Determine whether teams' schedules in the weight rooms and training rooms are sufficient and convenient; if there is more than one weight room, and the weight rooms are of different quality (for example, better or more appropriate equipment, or the room size has greater adequacy for the number of student-athletes using the room at one time), determine whether student-athletes of one sex are assigned more often to the higher-quality weight room; conduct the same evaluation for training rooms if there is more than one.
- Resolve any imbalances identified.
- Identify whether insurance specifically for athletics has gender-specific exclusions, and if so, revise the policy.

Recreation Programs. Usually, institutions do not assign athletic trainers or medical staff to recreation program events. The exception may be for a club team in a specific sport, such as ice hockey. Some institutions may require the club to pay for an athletic trainer's services. Establishing and implementing a consistent policy based on the nature of the sport should achieve compliance. Similarly, implementing a consistent policy for the use of weight rooms and training rooms by club, intramurals, and/or recreation activities should achieve compliance.

Equipment and Supplies

Proportionate numbers of female and male student-athletes should be provided equipment and supplies of the same quality. For example, the football and men's basketball teams represent 40% of the male student-athletes and are provided the highest quality equipment in the men's program. The institution offsets this by providing five of its women's teams that comprise 40% of the female participants with equipment of equivalent quality. The amount and maintenance of equipment (availability of student managers, laundry services, storage convenience and sufficiency) should be comparable for women's and men's teams programwide.

Intercollegiate Programs. Administrators should

- Rate the quality of their teams' game uniforms, practice uniforms, sport-specific equipment, and general equipment.

- Determine whether the amount of equipment is satisfactory.
- Determine whether their teams' equipment storage and maintenance, including the assignment of student and professional equipment management staff, are satisfactory.
- Implement changes as necessary to balance benefits.

Recreation Programs. Some institutions provide nominal funds for equipment in club programs, or basic sport-specific equipment for intramural and recreation programs. Implementing the same policies for women's and men's club teams should comply with Title IX.

Publicity

A simple compliance approach for publicity for intercollegiate athletics programs is to provide benefits and services to the same number of women's and men's teams or, for example, for more women's teams if there are more women's than men's teams offered in the program. These benefits and services include the availability of sports information personnel at home and away events; publications (media guides, game programs, schedule cards, posters, newspaper ads, press releases, website service); and marketing and promotions. Providing sports information staff, marketing personnel, and publications for club, intramural, and recreation teams and activities is unusual. The same policies apply should an institution provide such benefits for any of these programs.

Housing and Dining Facilities and Services

Housing and dining during the regular year and at term breaks should be comparable. Training table meals, and pregame and postgame meals should be equally available.

Intercollegiate Programs. Administrators should

- List any housing or dining concerns for the regular academic year and at term breaks.
- Identify any different housing benefits for women's and men's teams.

Recreation Programs. Usually, students in club, intramural, and recreation programs receive the same housing and dining benefits provided to the general student body rather than the special benefits provided to intercollegiate student-athletes. The same Title IX policies apply should special benefits be provided in the club, intramural, or recreation programs.

Tutoring

Tutors should be equally available and qualified programwide.

Intercollegiate Programs. The Title IX athletics provisions cover only those tutoring programs offered separately to student-athletes. If provided, determine concerns for tutor availability or quality and resolve any differences suggesting imbalances between the women's and men's programs.

Recreation Programs. Usually, club, intramural, and recreation program students have access to the same tutoring programs available to the entire student body, which are not reviewed under the Title IX athletics provisions.

Support Services

Administrative and clerical support should be equivalently adequate based on team needs. Office space and equipment should be comparable overall.

Intercollegiate Programs. Administrators should

- Determine the number of hours of clerical and administrative support provided per week to each team.
- Resolve significant imbalances, which may involve reassigning clerical staff or hiring students to support the professional staff.
- Review office space for overall quality, and the availability of computer and video equipment.
- Calculate the percentage of women's and men's coaches who have private offices.
- Determine whether differences are justified by a particular coach's seniority, unique position, or full-time versus part-time status.
- Reassign office space to resolve clear differences in the proportions of women's and men's coaches who have private office space or other concerns for office quality and equipment.

Recreation Programs. The same policies apply. However, club, intramural, and recreation teams rarely have coaches who receive these benefits.

The Compliance Picture

A difference in benefits between women's and men's intercollegiate athletics programs is not a compliance problem until it creates a disadvantage on the basis of sex, labeled by OCR as a disparity. The higher the percentage of student-athletes affected, the more serious the compliance problem. The more important the benefit (for example, scholarships versus practice uniforms), the more serious the compliance concern when disparities occur.

Failure to comply for either the three-part test or scholarships is likely to violate Title IX. Failure to comply with any of the other eleven areas is likely to be a disparity, not a violation, unless the problems are egregious. However, disparities in the other eleven areas are reviewed collectively to determine whether they create a pattern and practice of discrimination, which may be interpreted by OCR as a violation.

A violation of Title IX, and institution officials' continued refusal to correct the violation, is the point at which OCR may opt to use its main enforcement weapon—termination of federal funds to the institution. Many institutions, even when avoiding a major compliance concern under the three-part test or scholarships, have a series of minor disparities that may be viewed as a pattern and practice of discrimination. Consequently, administrators should address any concerns identified to limit the institution's liability under Title IX.

Low-Cost Solutions for Achieving Compliance

Administrators may consider a variety of options for resolving compliance problems. Several low-cost options are discussed next.

Tier the Program. Most institutions tier their intercollegiate athletics programs informally by providing certain programs with higher-quality benefits than other programs. Administrators should ensure that the same proportion of male and female student-athletes are in each tier. For example, the football and men's basketball teams comprise 40% of the male student-athletes and receive the best benefits in the men's program. If five women's teams comprise 40% of the female student-athletes, those five teams may be provided benefits at the same level as football and men's basketball to achieve compliance. Ensure, however, that athletics scholarships are awarded at rates within one percentage point of rates of participation, regardless of which teams are in which tier.

Roster Management. Adjusting participation may allow institutions to maintain their current sports offerings and comply with test one—proportionality by adding or eliminating opportunities on existing teams. This approach is controversial, but it has been accepted by OCR and the courts (*Neal v. Board of Trustees of California State Universities,* 1999). Test one may be the only compliance method possible for the institution that discontinues teams, or for the institution that should add women's teams to meet test two or test three, but cannot do so at this time.

Reassign Facilities. Reassigning practice facilities, competitive facilities, and locker rooms is a no-cost solution to addressing common compliance problems; similarly, training rooms, weight rooms, and equipment rooms may be reassigned or shared to eliminate compliance concerns. Again, assignments may be alternated annually to achieve compliance.

Reassign Coaches. A common compliance problem is the availability of fewer coaches or the assignment of more part-time coaches in the women's program. Ideally, administrators would hire additional coaches for women's teams or offer full-time status to employees who are part-time. If financial considerations preclude this, then coaches may be reassigned from the men's program to the women's program (assuming greater coaching availability in the men's program), or coaches may assume dual coaching assignments. For example, men's soccer has three coaches, while women's soccer has only two. The men's coach who works primarily with the goalkeepers might coach the goalkeepers for both the women's and men's soccer teams.

Conclusion

Title IX allows administrators to make choices about their institutions' intercollegiate athletics and recreation programs. Nevertheless, contentious litigation regarding Title IX may persist, particularly if the economy forces institutions to consider scaling back their athletics programs.

The three-part test has been a source of contention since the first court rulings confirmed its interpretation in the early 1990s. Ultimately, the continuing controversy is about whether female and male students shall be provided an equal opportunity to participate. As noted by the Eighth Circuit court in *Chalenor et al. v. University of North Dakota,* no court has ever held the three-part test to be invalid, and Congress has not changed the three-part test despite its guiding OCR's enforcement for what now exceeds three decades.

In May 2002, the National Collegiate Athletic Association celebrated Title IX's 30th anniversary at its annual seminar by inviting Patsy Mink to be the featured speaker. Speaking only four months before her death, Congresswoman Mink spoke eloquently of Title IX's effect on American society. She predicted that Title IX would continue to serve into the future in spite of the allegations and disputes that had arisen time and again, "the little fusses" as she called them. As the 40th anniversary of Title IX approaches, Patsy Mink's legacy continues to withstand the little fusses.

Chapter Six Key Points

1. Title IX of the Education Amendments of 1972 is a federal law that prohibits sex discrimination in any program receiving federal funding, including any higher education institution that accepts federal funding for research or other activities or through receipt of federal financial aid.
2. The Office for Civil Rights (OCR) of the United States Department of Education has nationwide enforcement authority for Title IX.
3. Institutional compliance with Title IX is determined by comparing the benefits for all female student-athletes to those for all male student-athletes.
4. Compliance in nearly every Title IX program area is not determined by the dollars spent, but by the tangible benefits that student-athletes receive. The major exception is athletics scholarships, where compliance is based on the dollars awarded.
5. Compliance takes two forms: access to opportunities to participate and treatment of participants.
6. There are three tests related to the access requirement of Title IX: proportionality, program expansion, and full accommodation. Institutions are required to meet one test of the three-part test addressing an equal opportunity for female and male students to become an athletics participant.

7. There are twelve areas of assessment related to the treatment requirement of Title IX. The twelve include athletics scholarships, coaching, recruitment, locker rooms and practice and competition facilities, scheduling, travel and per diem allowance, medical and training facilities and services, equipment and supplies, publicity, housing and dining facilities and services, tutoring, and support services.

References

Chalenor et al. v. University of North Dakota, 291 F.3d 1042 (8th Cir. 2002).

Government Accountability Office. *Intercollegiate Athletics, Status of Efforts to Promote Gender Equity* (GAO/HEHS-97–10). Washington DC: Government Accountability Office, 1996.

Government Accountability Office. *Gender Equity, Men's and Women's Participation in Higher Education* (GAO-01–128). Washington DC: Government Accountability Office, 2000.

National Collegiate Athletics Association. "Remarks of Congresswoman Patsy T. Mink of Hawaii." *NCAA Title IX Seminar,* May 9, 2002, Crystal City, Virginia.

Neal v. Board of Trustees of California State Universities, 198 F.3d 763 (9th Cir. 1999).

Office of Civil Rights. "Intercollegiate Athletics Policy Interpretation." *Federal Register,* 1979, 44(23), 71413–71423.

Office of Civil Rights. *Clarification of Intercollegiate Athletics Policy Guidance: The Three-Part Test.* Washington DC: Office of Civil Rights, 1996.

Office of Civil Rights. "Dear Colleague" letter to Bowling Green State University. Washington DC: Office of Civil Rights, 1998.

Title IX of the Education Amendments of 1972, 20 U.S.C. § 1681 et. seq., Public Law 92–318.

CHAPTER SEVEN

GOVERNANCE OF INTERCOLLEGIATE ATHLETICS AND RECREATION

B. David Ridpath and Robertha Abney

According to Hums and McLean (2009), *governance* means authority or the exercise thereof. The participation of thousands if not millions of people in intercollegiate athletics and campus recreation necessitates effective governance to protect the participants and the enterprise itself. This chapter offers an overview of the system of governance in intercollegiate athletics and recreation. It begins with discussion of governance in intercollegiate athletics administration and then moves to governance in campus recreation. Topics addressed include administrative structures, governing bodies, and professional organizations that drive governance.

Governance in Intercollegiate Athletics

The myriad institutions that participate in collegiate athletics vary by type, size, and mission. Nonetheless, the governance structures that shape athletics across the range of institutions are similar.

Typical Structures of Intercollegiate Athletics Departments—Public and Private

The need to govern intercollegiate athletics programs effectively is crucial as an athletics program is often a main window through which the institution is viewed. To maintain a positive image, the university athletics administration staff works hard to maintain the institutional control of their athletics programs. Institutional control is defined by the National Collegiate Athletic Association (NCAA, 2011, p. 3) as "efforts institutions make to comply with NCAA legislation and to detect and investigate violations that do occur." Based upon the guidelines set forth by the NCAA, the member institutions are required to maintain appropriate levels of institutional control.

A challenge to institutional control can be the need of athletics programs to win and to be profitable. Some university administrators believe that successful athletics programs can generate additional revenue and marketing potential for the institution at large (Gerdy, 2006; Suggs, 2003). With these beliefs, there is little doubt that college athletics is big business, particularly on the Bowl Championship Series (BCS) level.

Governing a multimillion dollar enterprise can be complex, but it is often grounded in a typical business model. A simple way to look at intercollegiate athletics programs is to view them as business operations. At universities with large National Collegiate Athletic Association (NCAA) Division I athletics programs, there are many forces at work, such as sponsorship and television money, that make intercollegiate athletics big business. However, even smaller athletics departments are managed in a similar fashion albeit on a much smaller scale.

It is common for athletics programs in higher education to be organized into two primary areas: internal operations and external operations. Both are addressed in this section.

Internal Operations. Internal divisions (or internal operations) are defined as those functions that deal with the inside functions of a department or business—commonly called operations management. A great deal of focus in operations management is on efficiency and effectiveness of processes. Therefore, operations management often includes substantial measurement and analysis of internal processes. Internal operations in intercollegiate athletics may include (but need not be limited to) the following:

- Academic support systems
- Business and finance

- Clerical and administrative support
- Computing
- Equipment room (accessories, apparel, uniforms, and equipment)
- Facility and event management
- Food service
- Human resource management
- Regulatory compliance/legal
- Sports medicine/athletics training operations
- Strength and conditioning
- Ticketing box office operations and revenue control
- Video services

External Operations. External operations can be defined in simple terms as interacting with business and functional environments that traditionally take place away from the organization, but are still essential components of an organization. Since intercollegiate athletics depends on revenue from outside sources such as ticket sales, sponsorship agreements, special events, and private donations, external operations is viewed as a vital entity of an athletics department. Typical functions of external operations in intercollegiate athletics, but not an inclusive list, are

- Broadcast operations (TV, radio, Internet)
- Corporate sponsorships
- Development/fundraising
- Licensing
- Marketing and promotions
- Merchandising
- Media/public relations
- Special events
- Sports properties rights holders (includes outsourced sponsorship operations)
- Ticket office-external functions with development, marketing, and special events

Supervisory Positions Within a Typical Intercollegiate Athletics Department

Most athletics departments are structured in a similar manner, with the top tier of leadership being the director of athletics (AD). Internal and external departments are headed by associate or assistant athletic directors, and they are supported by assistant athletics or program directors who lead each component. The AD acts as the chief executive officer and focuses primarily on strategic decisions, planning, and revenue generation, while the associates and assistants oversee the department on a day-to-day basis. The NCAA also mandates that member institutions have a senior woman administrator (SWA) position reserved for the highest ranking female in the department. Specific roles for the SWA vary widely among institutions.

As noted earlier, the titles and exact responsibilities of administrators in intercollegiate athletics may vary from institution to institution. Figure 7.1 shows the organizational structure of a typical department.

University Administration in Intercollegiate Athletics Governance

As noted earlier, intercollegiate athletics play a vital role in a university community. Hence, institutional governance extends beyond the department to include a variety of other entities.

Governing Boards. University governing boards, often called trustees, governors, regents, or visitors, play an important role in setting policy and aligning intercollegiate athletics with the educational mission of the institution at large. The overall mission of these oversight boards is to ensure accountability and adherence to the mission of the institution.

According to the *Revised Statement on Board Responsibilities for Intercollegiate Athletics* by the Association of Governing Board (AGB, 2007), AGB recognizes that intercollegiate athletics can attract, generate, or lose large sums of money and often is the institution's most visible component. This compels institutional leaders to pay close attention. Consequently, boards should exercise appropriate oversight while avoiding micromanagement and viewing athletics with a dispassionate perspective. Central to board oversight is to call for the athletics departments to embody the proper tone, direction, and values consistent with the academic mission of the institution (AGB, 2007). The university president reports to the board and serves at their pleasure.

President or Chancellor. In the eyes of both intercollegiate athletics associations and institutional governing boards, the university president or chancellor has primary responsibility for the conduct of the intercollegiate athletics program. The president or chancellor typically plays an important role in the recruitment and selection of the AD whether that individual will report directly to them or not. Chapter Sixteen offers one chancellor's insights on their role related to intercollegiate athletics.

FIGURE 7.1. DEPARTMENT OF INTERCOLLEGIATE ATHLETICS ORGANIZATIONAL CHART

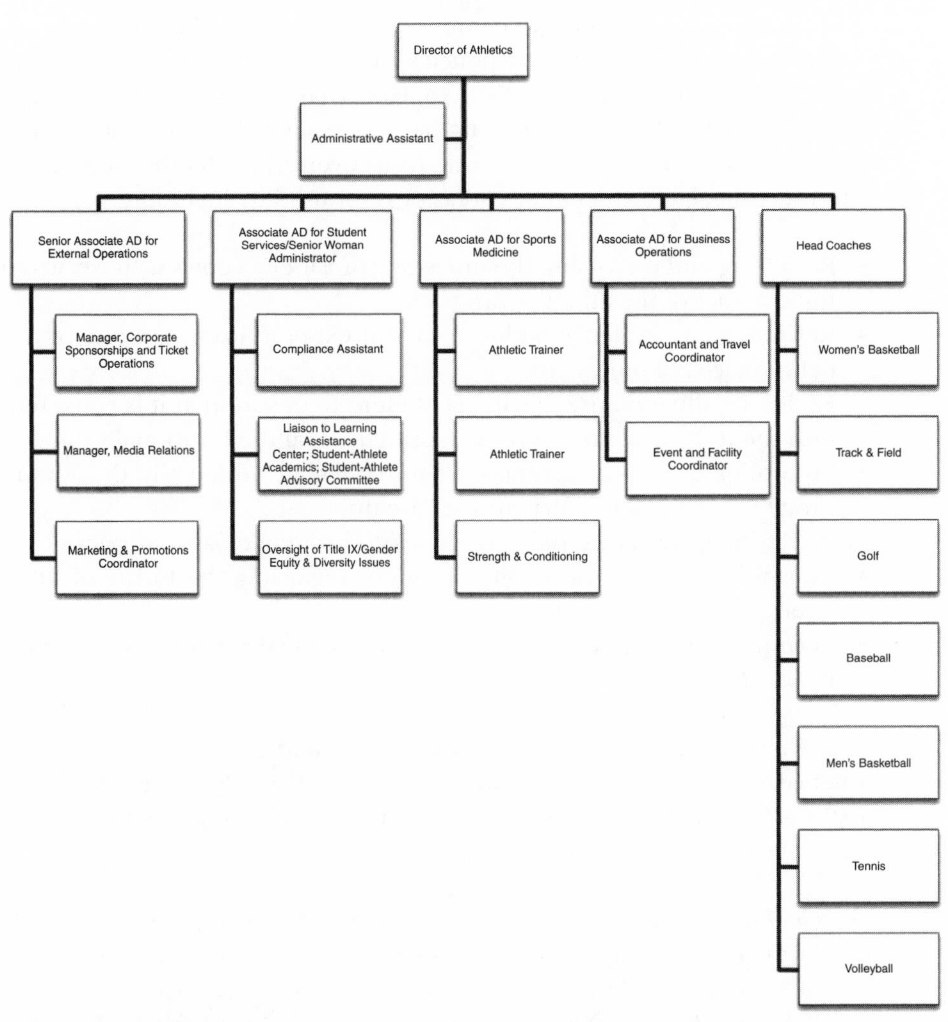

Source: University of Texas Pan American, 2011.

Athletics Committee. Universities often have committees that assist in maintaining institutional control, although such committees are not required by the NCAA or any other governing body. The make-up of most committees is broad and diverse; members range from faculty to administrative staff to athletics staff to students to community members.

The role of this committee varies by institution. Sometimes these committees exist as oversight boards for athletics department decisions, and in most cases they serve in more of an advisory capacity.

The intent of an oversight committee is to scrutinize budgets, approve hires, and approve and enforce policies and procedures. According to Rutgers University Policy number 50.1.14, Governance of Intercollegiate Athletics (April 15, 2010), the athletic board's responsibility falls under the direction of the board of governors. In its oversight role, the Committee on Intercollegiate Athletics has areas of responsibility including

- Reviewing and endorsing the university president's goals with regard to the conduct of the athletics program.
- Reviewing the athletics budgets, capital expenditures, and any future debt-service commitments.
- Reviewing the athletics mission statement to ensure that it is consistent with the university's mission, core principles, and educational values.
- Promoting the full integration of intercollegiate athletics in the administrative and academic structure of the university.
- Reviewing governance policies related to intercollegiate athletics.
- Consulting with the university president regarding the hiring of high-level athletics personnel.
- Recommending approval of contracts over $300,000 (Rutgers University Policy, 2010).

Whereas Rutgers' committee appears to wield great authority and influence, Ohio University's committee serves in primarily an advisory, informational capacity with the director of athletics governing the direction of most of the proceedings:

> General policies concerning athletics at Ohio University are determined by the President and Board of Trustees in consultation with the Director of Athletics. The Intercollegiate Athletics Committee assists the President, Provost, Director of Athletics, and the NCAA Faculty Athletics Representatives in the interpretation and implementation of athletics policies. The ICA is an advisory group reporting to the President; it works closely with the Director of Athletics and the Athletic Department. On an on-going basis, most of the Committee's work will be in direct consultation with the Director of Athletics and other staff in the Athletics Department. As a means of keeping the President informed, minutes of meetings will be sent to the President on a regular basis. (Ohio University, 2011)

In their advisory form, athletics committees do many things. These include

- Review of gender equity plans
- Strategic planning efforts
- Self-study reviews
- Periodic review of governance policies relating to such issues as student-athlete eligibility processes, disciplinary practices, and student absences from campus for athletics participation
- Representation on search committees for head coaches and senior staff
- Response to requests from the president and/or director of athletics as needed

Faculty Athletics Representative. Unlike an athletics committee, the position of faculty athletics representative (FAR) is a requirement of membership in the major governing associations for intercollegiate athletics. The NCAA's Faculty Athletics Representatives Association (FARA) has attempted to standardize the job description and duties of the FAR. According to FARA: "A FAR is a member of the faculty at an NCAA-member institution. He or she has been designated by the university or college to serve as a liaison between the institution and the athletics department, and also as a representative of the institution in conference and NCAA affairs. Each institution determines the role of the FAR at that particular university or college" (Faculty Athletics Representatives Association, 2007). According to one of FARA's Guiding Principles, the role of the FAR is "to ensure that the academic institution establishes and maintains the appropriate balance between academics and intercollegiate athletics." In addition, the FAR usually serves as the chair or as a permanent member, by position, of the intercollegiate athletics committee. The National Association of Intercollegiate Athletics (NAIA) and National Junior College Athletic Association (NJCAA) define the role and responsibilities of a FAR in very similar terms.

State Legislatures. State legislatures play an important role in the governance of public higher education. This role includes both regulatory and financial authority. Many states restrict public or instructional funds from being used for athletics purposes. Although state legislative officials are elected to serve districts, they are often loyal to particular higher education institutions in their state. Their support and involvement can be both helpful and challenging.

Intercollegiate Athletics Conferences

Intercollegiate athletics has come a long way from the days when students ran their own practices, devised their own training programs, and scheduled their own contests. (See Chapter One for a thorough discussion of the field's historical development). The nature of intercollegiate athletics quickly changed from being social occasions to becoming highly competitive events. By 1905 football competitions had become so intense that some people advocated reform or elimination of the sport. One way of implementing reform was to establish conferences and associations to govern intercollegiate athletics (Staurowsky and Abney, 2007).

Intercollegiate athletics conferences exist to organize and promote athletics competition between schools. Conferences are usually regionally based and include institutions of similar size and mission. For example the Mid-American Conference (MAC), whose members are similar in size and mission, is made up primarily of regionally based institutions, most within 500 miles of each other. However, conference realignments sometimes reflect less sensitivity to similarity and proximity of members. Conference USA is made up of dissimilar institutions, some of which are close to 2,000 miles apart. Many variables drive the make-up of an athletics conference, and there is no real one-size-fits-all.

Conferences conduct championships in sports sponsored by member institutions to determine participants in national level competitions and negotiate television contracts that benefit member institutions. Many conferences provide postgraduate scholarships and awards to recognize outstanding student-athletes for their academic and athletic efforts.

Intercollegiate athletics conferences also set academic eligibility standards. As a practical matter, conference standards tend to be equal to or more restrictive than association standards.

Governance of a conference varies, but it mostly grounded in institutional presidential authority, with significant participation of committees. The ADs, SWAs, and FARs at member institutions are also active participants in the business of the conference. Internally, a conference office is usually led by a commissioner, appointed by institutional presidents. Additional staff may include associate and assistant commissioners. Their roles often include monitoring member institution compliance, managing media relations, including television, marketing the conference, overseeing conference operations, managing the conference finances, serving on national governing association committees, and managing community relations

National Governing Intercollegiate Associations

According to Macmillan (2010), a governing body is an official organization that is responsible for making and enforcing rules and regulations. University athletics competition provides many governing bodies that serve that purpose but differ in organizational structure.

The primary governing bodies of intercollegiate sport in the United States are the National Collegiate Athletic Association, the National Association of Intercollegiate Athletics, and the National Junior College Athletic Association. Two other groups, the National Small College Athletic Association and the National Christian College Athletic Association, also serve member institutions in higher education.

National Collegiate Athletic Association. The NCAA is the largest and most influential college sport governing body in the United States. It is a voluntary association of colleges and universities, run by a president and staffed by several hundred employees. Its membership includes more than 1,200 four-year colleges and universities, conferences, and sport organizations (Staurowsky and Abney, 2010). Although the structure of many athletics departments is similar regardless of governing body authority in intercollegiate athletics, the NCAA is the most prominent.

NCAA rules and regulations focus on amateurism, recruiting, eligibility, playing and practice seasons, athletically related financial aid, championships, and enforcement (2010–2011 NCAA Division I Manual, 2010). Membership is separated into three competitive divisions known as Divisions I, II, and III. Football playing institutions in Division I, formerly referred to as Division I-A and I-AA subdivisions are now referred to as the Football Bowl Subdivision (FBS) and the Football Championship Subdivision (FCS). The main criteria used to establish an institution's divisional classification are size, number of sports offered, financial base and sport-sponsorship minimums, focus of programming, football and basketball scheduling requirements, and availability of athletics grants-in-aid (Staurowsky and Abney, 2010).

The NCAA Division I governance structure consists of four major levels: a board of directors (BOD), a leadership council, a legislative council, and cabinets (2010–2011 NCAA Division I Manual, 2010, p. 28). The board of directors consists of 18 presidents and CEOs from various conferences. Within the board's membership there must be at least one ethnic minority, and one female president. According to NCAA Bylaw 4.5.1, the leadership and legislative councils should be diverse and consist of thirty-one athletics administrators such as faculty athletics representatives and institutional administrators who have other significant duties regarding intercollegiate athletics. The leadership and legislative councils report to the board of directors and the cabinets/committees report to the councils.

Although Divisions II and III governance structures are similar to Division I, there are several differences. The primary governance and policy making body is the presidents council (PC). The presidents council consists of one president or chancellor per region for every twenty-two institutions in that region. Two at-large positions are available to enhance efforts to achieve diversity of representation and to accommodate independent institutions (2009–2010 Division II Manual, 2010, p. 21).

The Division II Management Council is comprises one administrator or representative from each of the Division II multisport voting conferences, one administrator or representative of independent institutions, and two at-large positions. The members shall include at least four directors of athletics, four senior women administrators, four faculty athletics representatives, and one conference administrator (2009–2010 Division II Manual, 2010, p. 22).

The Division III Management Council has to include nineteen presidents and chancellors, faculty athletics representatives, directors of athletics, senior woman administrators, conference representatives and student-athletes. The member composition must include at least nine directors of athletics or senior woman administrators, two institutional presidents or chancellors, two faculty athletics representatives, three members of an ethnic minority, eight men, and eight women (2009–2010 Division III Manual, 2010, p. 22; Covell and Barr, 2010, p. 43).

National Association of Intercollegiate Athletics. Membership in the NAIA is open to four-year and upper-level two-year colleges and universities in the United States and Canada. Established in 1940, it is composed of nearly 300 member institutions that range from public to private character-driven intercollegiate athletics. The NAIA governs its business through councils and committees. Policies are developed through councils consisting of campus administrators and faculty members. The purpose of the committees is to implement the policies established by the councils. Administrators and coaches make up the committees, councils, and associations within the twenty-five NAIA conferences (NAIA Legislative Services, 2011).

National Junior College Athletic Association. In 1938, the National Junior College Athletic Association (NJCAA) became the only national governing body of intercollegiate athletics for two-year colleges, and its current membership of 525 institutions is second in number only to the NCAA (NJCAA, 2012). The NJCAA has affiliations with several other governing bodies such as the NAIA and NCAA to work on common interests such as academic eligibility, transfer regulations, and professional sports interests (*Today's NJCAA,* 2011).

Governance in Campus Recreation

Campus recreation is designed to meet the fitness and leisure needs of members of the campus community and their dependents as well as, at least at some institutions, members of the local community. The programs have expanded into new areas to meet the needs of this diverse set of service constituents. Expanding on traditional intramural offerings, programs developed and evolved to include sport clubs, instructional programs, informal recreation, aquatics, fitness, wellness, outdoor recreation, family and youth programs, summer camps, and special events. Whereas intercollegiate athletics has a relatively uniform set of governance structures extending from department level to national level, governance in campus recreation beyond the level of the institution varies by program emphasis.

Typical Structures of Campus Recreation—Public and Private

The structure of recreation departments is typically compartmentalized into several operational and management areas. The following major areas are most common within department structures:

- Intramural sport
- Extramural sport
- Sport camps
- Outdoor adventure
- Sport clubs
- Fitness activities
- Special events
- Wellness programming
- Aquatics
- Dance
- Martial arts
- Family recreation

- Informal recreation
- Adapted recreational sports (recreation opportunities for varying abilities)
- Facility operations (Hums and MacLean, 2009)

Whereas intercollegiate athletics departments are often organized by whether their services are directed internally or externally, campus recreation departments are more commonly organized by program function. The structures of recreation departments tend to be more horizontal than vertical. Figure 7.2 shows the organizational structure for the Office of Recreation at Slippery Rock University and is illustrative of a typical recreation department.

Supervisory Positions Within a Recreation Department

The administration of a recreation department is a complex activity. It is typically undertaken with a department team that includes professional staff and student paraprofessionals.

The head of the department usually carries the title of director. The director typically reports to the director of athletics, vice-president of student affairs, or vice-president of business affairs depending on where recreation falls in the university structure. The director provides oversight for all departmental activities, sets policies, and manages departmental finances (including fundraising and friend making).

The actual development and delivery of programming is led by other professional staff members, as well as student paraprofessionals. Students will help run the respective areas through advisory boards and committees, but a professional staff will manage the department.

Sports Clubs. Sports clubs are somewhat of a hybrid in campus recreation in that they have characteristics of a recreation program, a student organization, and an athletics team. A sport club is a group of individuals who join together voluntarily, in a more or less formal organization, for the purpose of competing against other clubs (Byl, 2002), particularly clubs from other institutions, in a particular sport. Sport clubs in educational institutions are typically student initiated, developed, governed, and operated, and are largely self-financed.

Clubs elect officers from their membership to manage the operations, programs, activities, and events. Most clubs elect at least five of the following officer positions: president, vice-president, treasurer, secretary,

FIGURE 7.2. OFFICE OF CAMPUS RECREATION ORGANIZATIONAL STRUCTURE

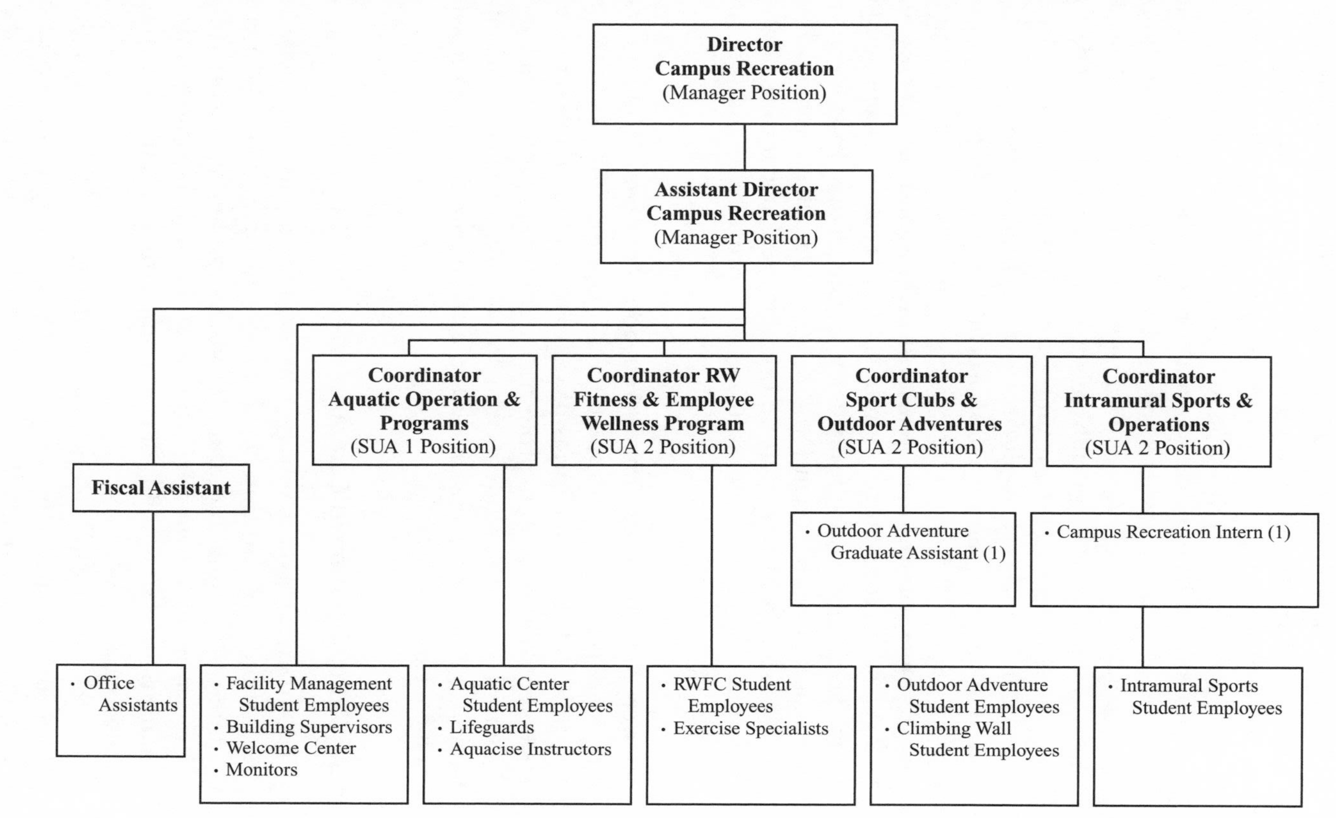

Source: Slippery Rock University, 2009.

fundraising chair, safety officer and/or risk manager. Each position is held by students attending the college or university. Club officer positions and duties vary at different institutions.

Universities support clubs by providing administrators for assistance and guidance with clubs' organization and administration, Club sport administrators primarily act in an advisory capacity. They provide support in various areas such as scheduling, budgets, fundraising, and equipment inventory and storage. A faculty member or university employee may also serve as an advisor. Most clubs select an advisor each year. The role of the advisor is to sign-off on any university request made by the club. Advisors are contacted when disciplinary or recognition matters arise.

Funding mechanisms for sport clubs may vary from institution to institution. Sources of support include self-generated funds, institutional support, student activity fees, sponsorships, gifts, and commercial funds. The two most common forms of funding for sport clubs are dues and fundraising. The majority of universities with club sports provide some form of annual funding for them (NIRSA, 2008). The development of a funding system should involve club representatives. Their involvement can help motivate the club to follow policies and procedures and to ensure funding allocations are based on club needs.

Intramurals and Other Campus Recreation Programs. While sport clubs are commonly administered by students who are members of the club, intramurals and the other forms of campus recreation are planned and implemented by recreation professionals. Although professionals oversee the campus recreation, students who are the primary clients of campus recreation, ought to have a significant role in the governance of those programs on college campuses.

University Administration in Campus Recreation Governance

The governance of campus recreation departments varies from institution to institution. Recreation departments sometimes stand alone as their own administrative unit and, in other instances, they are incorporated into a larger campus athletics department. Sometimes they can be under the administrative responsibility of institutional student affairs or business affairs divisions.

Recreation departments often make use of an advisory council to inform their services and program. The advisory council consists of faculty, staff, and students. The council informs the director of the kinds of activities and events members of the campus community most appreciate. They help organize and implement many specific events and leagues. One way recreation programs involve students is having them participate in campus recreation councils or advisory boards. These councils include a group of students who help with the leadership and implementation of programs. Students' roles may include advising on the administration of programming, participating in the budgeting process and assigning financial priorities, and organizing forums and other feedback opportunities for students. Student volunteers are particularly beneficial to a campus recreation program. They can assist with the administration, promotion, and officiating of the program. They are great resources in any institution's recreation program.

National Governing and Certifying Bodies in Campus Recreation

As noted earlier, the governance of campus recreation programs beyond the institutional level is more diffuse than is the case in intercollegiate athletics. This section provides an overview of the variety of governing and certifying bodies in campus recreation.

National Intramural-Recreational Sports Association. NIRSA was established for professionals working in college and university intramural sports programs. However, today it is committed to promoting quality recreational sports programs in the areas of intramurals, aquatics, extramural sports, wellness and fitness, informal recreation, instructional programs, outdoor recreation, sport clubs, and student leadership and development. NIRSA is the primary generalist association for professional administrators in campus recreation.

At the time this chapter is being developed NIRSA is undergoing a governance transition process.. The components of the potential governance model are board, network, and assembly.

In 2012 when the governance transition is completed, the NIRSA Board of Directors (BOD) will be a seven-person board of three officers in the presidential track (president, president designee, and president elect), three at-large directors, and a board-elected annual director.

The Member Network will include six (6) regional representatives from each region, six (6) regional student leaders from each region, the national student leader and the past presidents representative. The Member Network will focus on networking, professional development; representation, and growing future leaders.

Sports clubs have a national governing body that works in partnership with regional and local leagues. Sport clubs must also abide by the rules and regulations of their governing body. These national governing bodies (NGB) provide standards of competition, safety guidelines, and may provide access to liability or other insurance in their specific sport. Table 7.1 gives a listing of governing bodies and web addresses for club sports.

Other NGBs (Fitness, Aquatics, Outdoors). Professional organizations and governing bodies in campus recreation offer the assistance, guidance, and networking opportunities to administrators working in the field. Some of the main organizations serving campus recreation administrators are discussed in the following section.

Fitness. There are numerous organizations that are available to administrators working in fitness. For example, many of the specific forms of exercise such as Zumba and Pilates have their own associations and certifying organizations. This section focuses on several of the organizations that serve the broadest base of users. Readers who are interested in more specific forms of exercise can refer to the different organizations to find more information.

The largest organization in the realm of health, fitness, and exercise is the American College of Sports Medicine (ACSM). The ACSM's mission is to "promote and integrate scientific research, education, and practical applications of sports medicine and exercise science to maintain and enhance physical performance, fitness, health, and quality of life" (ACSM, 2012). Through research, the ACSM has developed standards that are followed by many professionals in the fitness field and govern exercise and fitness testing, prescription, and training.

In addition to the ACSM, there are other organizations that focus on fitness and exercise training that would be relevant to campus fitness programming. The National Strength and Conditioning Association (NSCA) is an international association that supports and disseminates research-based knowledge and its practical application to improve athletic performance and fitness. Another organization that focuses on fitness is the American Council on Exercise (ACE). ACE's is "committed to enriching quality of life through safe and effective exercise and physical activity" (ACE, 2012). One final organization is the Aerobics and Fitness Association of America (AFAA), which delivers comprehensive cognitive and practical education for fitness professionals. The education is grounded in industry research, using both traditional and innovative modalities (AFAA, 2011).

TABLE 7.1. SPORT CLUB NATIONAL GOVERNING BODIES

Sport	National Governing Body	Web Address
Badminton	USA Badminton	http://www.usabadminton.org/
Baseball	USA Baseball	http://web.usabaseball.com/index.jsp
Bowling	USA Bowling	http://www.bowl.com/bowl/usa
Cheerleading	American Association of Cheerleading Coaches and Advisors (AACCA)	http://ww.aacca.org
Climbing	USA Climbing	http://www.usaclimbing.net/home.cfm
Crew	USA Rowing	http://rowing.teamusa.org/
Cycling	USA Cycling	http://www.usacycling.org/
Dance	USA Dance	http://usadance.org/
Dodgeball	USA Dodgeball	http://www.dodgeballusa.com
Equestrian	Intercollegiate Horse Show Association	http://www.ihsainc.com/
Field hockey	National Field Hockey League	http://nationalfieldhockeyleague.com/
Golf (men's)	Central New York Collegiate Golf League	http://www.cnycglonline.com/
Handball	USA Handball	http://www.ushandball.org/
Ice hockey	American Collegiate Hockey Association	http://www.achahockey.org
Judo	USA Judo	http://www.usjudo.org
Lacrosse (men's)	American Collegiate Hockey Association	http://www.lacrosse.org
Lacrosse (women's)	Women's Division Intercollegiate Athletics – US Lacrosse	http://www.uslacrosse.org/

(*Continued*)

TABLE 7.1. (*Continued*)

Sport	National Governing Body	Web Address
Nordic ski	US Collegiate Ski & Snowboard Association	http://www.uscsa.com/
Paintball	National Collegiate Paintball Association	http://www.college-paintball.com
Roller hockey	National Collegiate Roller Hockey Association	http://www.usahockey.com/
Men's and women's rugby	USA Rugby	http://www.usarugby.org
Sailing	US Sailing	http://www.ussailing.org
Ski racing	US Collegiate Ski & Snowboard Association	http://www.uscsa.com/
Ski	US Ski Association	http://www.ussa.org
Snowboard	USA Snowboarding Association	http://www.usasa.org/
Men's and women's soccer	US Soccer	http://ussoccer.com/
Softball	National Club Softball Association	http://www.clubsoftball.org/
Synchronized swimming	United States Synchronized Swimming	http://www.usasynchro.org/
Surf	National Scholastic Surfing Assoc.	http://www.nssa.org/
Table tennis	USA Table Tennis	http://www.usatt.org/index.shtml
Taekwondo	USA Taekwondo	http://usa-taekwondo.us/
Tennis	United State Tennis Association (USTA)	http://www.usta.com/
Men's and women's ultimate	Ultimate Players Association	http://www.upa.org/
Men's & women's volleyball	USA Volleyball	http://www.usavolleyball.org/
Waterpolo	Collegiate Water Polo Association	http://www.collegiatewaterpolo.com
Water ski	National College Water Ski Association	http://www.ncwsa.com/index.php
Wrestling	USA Wrestling	http://www.themat.com/

Aquatics. Aquatics is a complex element of campus recreation that has several agencies that professionals look to for governance. Governance in aquatics often takes on three forms: operations, fitness, and safety/emergency training. The agencies discussed in the following section are some of the most recognized in aquatics.

The *operation* of water-based facilities is an important realm of the overall aquatics profession. The operations of aquatic facilities include such concepts as pool water chemistry, management, safety, and risk. The agencies that provide governance in this include state health departments, the National Swimming Pool Foundation (NSPF), and the National Recreation and Parks Association (NRPA).

The federal and state governments also take some role in the governance of aquatics operations. This role often takes the form of legislation that is created to maintain safe swimming environments. One important piece of federal legislation that has had an impact on the aquatics field is the Virginia Graeme Baker Pool and Spa Safety Act. An important element of this act is that it requires that each public pool and spa with a single main drain (other than an unblockable drain) must also be equipped with a device or system designed to prevent entrapment. In addition, the state health departments for all 50 states set rules and regulations for public pools and aquatic areas. These rules and regulations vary from state to state but they do have some commonalities such as employment of a certified pool operator, maintenance of pool chemicals, requirements for lifeguards, and requirements of signage. As an administrator in campus recreation, one needs to be knowledgeable on the federal and state requirements for pool operations.

Through their educational programming, the NSPF attempts to increase interest in aquatics, as well as providing safer aquatic facilities. The NSPF offers a Certified Pool/Spa Operators® certification, which has been delivered to more pool operators than any other aquatic training program since 1972 (NSPF, 2010).

While the National Recreation and Parks Association (NRPA) is the largest advocacy organization for the advancement of public parks and recreation, it also provides governance in the operations of aquatic facilities. The NRPA offers training programs in pool and spa operation and the Aquatic Facility Operators (AFO) certification.

As discussed previously, many of the different exercise and fitness specialty areas have governing agencies and provide certifications. The realm of aquatics also includes a *fitness* emphasis area that has agencies that govern the field. Some of these agencies include the Aquatics Exercise

Association and WaterART Fitness International. The Aquatics Exercise Association offers a certification for individuals to teach aquatic fitness classes to the general population. WaterART offers 13 different certifications that are aquatic based. These certifications include a variety of areas ranging from the general WaterART Instructor Certification to the more specific WaterART Arthritis Instructor Certification.

Obviously with the risks associated with pools and other water-based facilities, *safety/emergency training* is an important element of aquatics. Although there are many agencies and organizations that provide governance in this realm, space requirements make it only practical to discuss a few of the most recognized ones that impact campus recreation.

Two widely recognized providers of aquatic safety and emergency training are the American Red Cross and Jeff Ellis and Associates (JEA). The ARC is one of the largest organizations in the teaching of swimming and water safety. In addition to the courses that teach swimming techniques and water safety, the ARC trains and certifies lifeguards. JEA also takes the lead in lifeguard and aquatic emergency procedure training. JEA broke into aquatic safety in 1980 when they developed the National Pool and Waterpark Lifeguard Training course. While the course's original focus was on waterparks, since there were no guidelines for safety at these facilities, it is now used by many aquatic program providers including campus recreation. In addition to lifeguard training, JEA also offers training in comprehensive aquatic risk management which includes lifeguard training as well as training in cardiopulmonary resuscitation, first aid, automated external defibrillator, and emergency oxygen.

Outdoor/Adventure. Outdoor and adventure activities are similar to fitness in that every specialty area has some form of governing agency or agencies. Since this campus recreation is so broad, an all-inclusive list of outdoor and adventure governing agencies is not possible within the confines of this chapter. But this section does discuss some of the most recognized agencies and organizations that broadly serve outdoor recreation.

The Association of Outdoor Recreation and Education (AORE) is a professional organization that disseminates information about outdoor recreation and education to practitioners while promoting the environment. While the organization focuses on all providers of outdoor recreation, it pays particular attention to outdoor recreation and education programs on college and university campuses. Although AORE does not provide any certifications, it is a leader in the general field of outdoor recreation.

The Association of Experiential Education (AEE) is another professional organization whose purpose is to advocate the benefits of experiential education. Outdoor and adventure recreation are modes of experiential education. The significance of the AEE is that it is an effort to raise the quality of experiential education through an accreditation program. Colleges and universities can become accredited in experiential education. Harvard University's First Year Experience and the University of North Carolina's Wilderness Adventures for First Year Students are just two examples of accredited programs that involve campus recreation (AEE, 2012).

The mission of the National Outdoor Leadership School (NOLS) is to "is to be the leading source and teacher of wilderness skills and leadership that serve people and the environment" (NOLS, 2012). One of the areas that the NOLS provides governance and offers certification opportunity in outdoor recreation and leadership is in wilderness medicine. The NOLS offers certifications in wilderness first aid, wilderness first responder, and wilderness emergency medical technician.

The Leave No Trace Center for Outdoor Ethics (LNT) teaches the responsible enjoyment and stewardship of the outdoors. The LNT provides education for interacting with outdoor spaces and resources to minimize the human impact. While it provides educational programming, it does not certify its participants.

The Wilderness Medical Associates (WMA) provides specialized training and leadership in emergency first aid for outdoor situations. Similar to the opportunities for certification offered by the NOLS, an individual can get certified in wilderness first responder, wilderness advanced first aid, and wilderness emergency medical technician.

Table 7.2 provides an extensive, though not all inclusive, list of governing and certifying agencies that serve professions in the field of campus recreation.

Conclusion

Over the years, intercollegiate athletics and campus recreation have evolved from completely student-run programs to highly complex programs. Intercollegiate athletics and campus recreation are valued components of the higher education environment. These programs, and the professionals who administer them, are essential to students' overall collegiate education and experience and are regulated by national systems of governing bodies. Practitioners and future administrators in sports and recreation

TABLE 7.2. ORGANIZATIONS AND CERTIFICATIONS IN CAMPUS RECREATION AND FITNESS

Organization	Campus Recreation Area	Certification(s)	URL
Aerobics & Fitness Association of America	Fitness	Personal Training Group Exercise Kickboxing Step Telexercise® Resistance Training	http://www.afaa.com/
American College of Sports Medicine	Fitness	Group Exercise Instructor Personal Trainer℠ Health Fitness Specialist	http://www.acsm.org/
American Council on Exercise	Fitness	Personal Training Group Fitness Instructor Lifestyle and Weight Management Coach Advanced Health and Fitness Specialist	http://www.acefitness.org
American Red Cross	Aquatics, Safety	Lifeguard Water Safety Instructor	http://www.redcross.org
Aquatic Exercise Association	Aquatics, Fitness	Aquatic Fitness Professional	http://www.aeawave.com
Association for Experiential Education*	Outdoor/Adventure	N/A	http://www.aee.org
Association of Outdoor Recreation and Education	Outdoor/Adventure	N/A	http://www.aore.org/
Jeff Ellis and Associates	Aquatics, Safety	National Pool and Waterpark Safety Lifeguarding Comprehensive Aquatic Risk Management	http://www.jellis.com

Leave No Trace	Outdoor/Adventure	N/A	http://www.lnt.org
National Intramural-Recreational Sports Association	General-Intramurals, Club	Registered Collegiate Recreational Sport Professional	http://www.nirsa.org
National Outdoor Leadership School	Outdoor/Adventure	Wilderness First Aid Wilderness EMT Wilderness First Responder	http://www.nols.edu
National Recreation & Parks Association	Aquatics, General	Aquatic Facility Operator	http://www.nrpa.org
National Strength & Conditioning Association	Fitness	Personal Trainer®	http://www.nsca-lift.org/
National Swimming Pool Foundation	Aquatics, Operations	Certified Pool/Spa Operator®	http://www.nspf.com
Pilates Method Alliance	Fitness	PMA Certified Teacher	http://www.pilatesmethodalliance.org/
Spinning	Fitness	Spinning® Instructor	http://www.spinning.com/
Student Affairs Administrators in Higher Education	General	N/A	http://www.naspa.org/
WaterART Fitness International	Aquatics, Fitness	WaterART Instructor	http://www.waterart.org
Wilderness Medical Associates	Outdoor/Adventure	Wilderness First Aid Wilderness Advanced First Aid Wilderness First Responders	http://www.wildmed.com/
YogaFit®	Fitness	Yoga Fitness Instructor	http://www.yogafit.com/

*AEE has an accreditation process for college programs interested in offering experiential adventure programming.

administration must be familiar with and understand the importance of the various organizations with which they will work and interact in the workforce.

Chapter Seven Key Points

1. It is common for athletics programs in higher education to be organized into two primary areas: internal operations and external operations. Internal divisions (or internal operations) are defined as those functions that deal with the inside functions of a department or business—commonly called operations management. External operations can be defined in simple terms as interacting with business and functional environments that traditionally take place away from the organization, but are still essential components of an organization.
2. Most athletics departments are structured in a similar manner with the top tier of leadership being the director of athletics. Internal and external departments are headed by associate or assistant athletic directors, and they are supported by assistant athletics or program directors who lead each component. The NCAA also mandates that member institutions have a senior woman administrator position reserved for the highest ranking female in the department.
3. Governing boards, presidents or chancellors, athletics committees, and faculty athletics representatives are all elements of institutional governance of intercollegiate athletics programs. State legislatures may play a governance role at public universities.
4. Intercollegiate athletics conferences exist to organize and promote athletics competition between schools. Conferences are usually regionally based and include institutions of similar size and mission.
5. The primary national governing bodies of intercollegiate sport in the United States are the National Collegiate Athletic Association, the National Association of Intercollegiate Athletics, and the National Junior College Athletic Association.
6. Whereas intercollegiate athletics departments are often organized by whether their services are directed internally or externally, campus recreation departments are more commonly organized by program function.
7. The head of a recreation department usually carries the title of director. The actual development and delivery of programming is led by other professional staff members, as well as student paraprofessionals.

8. Recreation departments sometimes stand alone as their own administrative unit and, in other instances, they are incorporated into a larger campus athletics department. Sometimes they can be under the administrative responsibility of institutional student affairs or business affairs divisions.
9. Whereas intercollegiate athletics has a relatively uniform set of governance structures extending from department level to national level, governance in campus recreation beyond the level of the institution varies by program emphasis.
10. The National Intramural-Recreational Sports Association (NIRSA) is committed to promoting quality recreational sports programs in the areas of intramurals, aquatics, extramural sports, wellness and fitness, informal recreation, instructional programs, outdoor recreation, sport clubs, and student leadership and development.

References

Aerobics and Fitness Association of America. "About AFAA." 2011. Accessed on February 29, 2012 at http://www.afaa.com/about˙afaa.htm.

AGB Statement on Board Responsibilities for Intercollegiate Athletics, 2007. Retrieved March 1, 2011 from http://www.agb.org/news/2010–08/agb-statement-board-responsibilities-intercollegiate/athletics

American College of Sports Medicine. "About ACSM." 2012. Accessed on February 29, 2012 at http://www.acsm.org/about-acsm/who-we-are.

American Council on Exercise. "About Us." 2012. Accessed on February 29, 2012 at http://www.acefitness.org/aboutace/default.aspx.

Association for Experiential Education. Accredited Programs, 2012. Retrieved on May 18, 2011 from http://www.aee.org/accreditation/programs.

Byl, J. *Intramural Recreation: Step-by-step Guide to Creating an Effective Program.* Champaign, IL: Human Kinetics, 2002.

Covell, D., and Barr, B. A. *Managing Intercollegiate Athletics.* Scottsdale: Holcomb Hathaway, 2010.

Faculty Athletics Representatives Association. "What Is a Faculty Athletics Representative." 2007. Accessed on February 29, 2012 at http://www.farawebsite.org/whatis.asp.

Gerdy, J. *Air Ball: American Education's Failed Experiment with Elite Athletics.* Oxford: University of Mississippi Press, 2006.

Hums, M. A., and MacLean, J. C. *Governance and Policy in Sport Organizations.* Scottsdale: Holcomb Hathaway, 2009.

Macmillan. *Macmillian Dictionary,* 2010. Retrieved November 20, 2010, from www.macmilliondictionary.com.

National Association of Intercollegiate Athletics Legislative Services, "Governance." 2011. Retrieved March 4, 2011 from http://www.naia.org/ViewArticle.dbml?DB_OEM_ID=27900&ATCLID.=205364900.

National Intramural-Recreation Sports Association (NIRSA). *Campus Recreation: Essential for the Professional*. Champaign: Human Kinetics, 2008.

National Junior College Athletic Association. "About." 2012. Retrieved October 25, 2012, from http://www.njcaa.org/todaysNJCAA.cfm?category=about§ion=National%20Office&articleid=7251.

National Swimming Pool Foundation. *What Is the National Certified Pool/Spa Operator® Certification Program*, 2010. Retrieved May 10, 2011 from http://www.nspf.com/en/cpo.aspx.

2010–2011 NCAA Division I Manual. Indianapolis, IN: National Collegiate Athletic Association, 2010.

2009–2010 NCAA Division II Manual. Indianapolis, IN: National Collegiate Athletic Association, 2010.

2009–2010 NCAA Division III Manual. Indianapolis, IN: National Collegiate Athletic Association, 2010.

National Collegiate Athletics Association. "Charging." 2011. Retrieved February 29, 2012 from http://www.ncaa.org/wps/wcm/connect/public/NCAA/Enforcement/Process/Charging.

National Outdoor Leadership School. "Mission and Values." 2012. Accessed on February 29, 2012 at http://www.nols.edu/about/values.shtml.

Ohio State University, 2010. Retrieved December 10, 2010, from: http://recsports.osu.edu/posts/documents/sport-club-manual-2010–2011.pdf.

Ohio University. Ohio University: Faculty Senate: Standing Committees: ICA Committee page, 2011. Retrieved March 1, 2011 from http://www.ohio.edu/facultysenate/standingcomm/ICA-Committee-page.cfm.

Rutgers University Policy number 50.1.14 Governance of Intercollegiate Athletics, 2010, April 15. Retrieved March 1, 2011 from http://policies.rutgers.edu/PDF/Section50/50.1.14-current.pdf.

Staurowsky, E. J., and Abney, R. "Intercollegiate Athletics." In J. B. Parks, J. Quarterman, and L. Thibault (Eds.), *Contemporary Sport Management* (3rd ed., pp. 67–96). Champaign, IL: Human Kinetics, 2007.

Staurowsky, E. J., and Abney, R. "Intercollegiate Athletics." In P. Pedersen, J. B. Parks, B.R.K. Zanger, and J. Quarterman (Eds.), *Contemporary Sport Management* (4th ed., pp. 142–163). Champaign, IL: Human Kinetics, 2010.

Suggs, W. "Sports as the University's 'Front Porch'? The Public Is Skeptical." May 2, 2003. Retrieved January, 3 2011 from http://chronicle.com/article/Sports-as-the-University-s/11599.

Today's NJCAA, 2011. Retrieved March 2, 2011 from http://www.njcaa.org/todaysNJCAA.cfm.

WaterART Fitness International Inc. "Types of Programs, " 2011. Retrieved on May 10, 2011 from http://www.waterart.org/show_info.php?page_id=125&cPath=125.

PART ONE CASE STUDIES

The following case studies draw on the information shared in Section One (particularly Chapters Five through Seven). They are intended to provide the opportunity to connect the content to professional practice.

Case Study #1

After an off-season workout, which Big Private University's head men's basketball coach and his staff supervised, a men's basketball student-athlete collapsed and died. The autopsy showed that he had a genetic trait that predisposed him to vascular distress during periods of physical stress and contributed to his death. Less than a year after their son's passing, the parents filed a wrongful death suit against the university's board of trustees and the university, alleging that the university was negligent in its treatment of the men's basketball student-athlete.

1. What legal concepts are involved in this case?
2. For whom would you decide and why if you were the judge hearing this suit?

Case Study #2

Big Private University is facing a financial bind in athletics department due to budget restrictions. As a result, it planned to eliminate funding for four sports from the department of athletics: women's water polo, women's gymnastics, men's golf, and men's water polo. The university announced that these teams could continue to play at club level, but that it would withdraw the financial support of varsity team status. As a result of these cuts, the school would realize $1,250,000 savings per year.

While these cuts would affect the women's sports budget much more drastically than the men's, the ratio of female to male varsity sports participants would remain about the same: approximately 42% female participants versus 58% male. However, these varsity sports proportions did not reflect the student body ratio at the university: women comprised 52% of the total student body, while men totaled 48%.

The university offered 11 varsity women's teams and 12 men's teams. Historically, the university had offered 10 women's sports between the years 1990 and 2002 but had made *only one* addition to women's varsity teams since that time.

1. What legal concepts are involved in this case?
2. How would you handle this situation based upon the concepts discussed in this section?

Case Study #3

Big Private University recently named a new president and new athletics director. The university has also added several new sports in recent years, with men's and women's hockey being the latest additions. All the changes have prompted consideration of the future direction of the athletics program.

The new president and athletics director are the two major decision makers for the direction of the athletics department and met to consider the future of the department. One of the topics of discussion was how well the university fit into their current conference and into Division I in general. The conference currently has 12 members located primarily in the New York–New Jersey–Connecticut corridor with the exception of three universities, including your university. The conference sponsors 23 sports (10 for men, 13 for women) and not all members participate in each. The conference also has affiliate members in some sports. Your university competes in 20 of the 23 conference sports offered and also has men's and women's hockey and women's rowing.

One issue that has been raised is the extensive travel required by the university's student-athletes. With the exception of the other two institutions located in Pennsylvania, all other conference members are at least 400 miles from your university. This results in travel time that is much higher than that of other conference members, which creates long bus trips for student-athletes and more missed class time than is desirable.

The president of your university has asked for your recommendation as athletics director.

1. Who will you consult in developing your recommendation?
2. What considerations will factor into your recommendation?

PART TWO

SKILLS

Part Two offers information, insights, and practical advice on the effective administration of intercollegiate athletics and recreation programs. This work requires a broad and sophisticated set of skills. The chapters in Part Two focus on skills related to the management of resources, events, and relationships.

Like most program areas in higher education, the greatest resource of a campus intercollegiate athletics or recreation department is its people. In Chapter Eight, Colleen McGlone and Stephen Rey discuss management, leadership, and supervision as frameworks for administering human resources. The coauthors address the various types of staff that commonly make up an intercollegiate athletics or recreation department on a college campus. McGlone and Rey connect the administration of human resources to institutional mission and review the processes related to recruiting, training, and retaining talented student paraprofessionals and other staff.

Fiscal resources are also important to intercollegiate athletics and recreation programs. Timothy DeSchriver and Edgar Johnson provide an overview of budgets and budget management in Chapter Nine. They identify common budget types and approaches to budget development. They also describe various sources of revenue and categories of expenses. In addition, they discuss the critically important process of budget management.

In Chapter Ten, James Greenwell focuses on facilities, the third principle resource at the disposal of intercollegiate athletics and recreation administrators. He guides readers through the planning and management of facilities. In doing so, he emphasizes the importance of planning and offers insights into strategies for success and common pitfalls for those responsible for athletics or recreation facilities on college campuses.

Events are a major enterprise for intercollegiate athletics and recreation departments on college campuses. In Chapter Eleven, Heather Lawrence points out that events may include programs sponsored by the department such as intercollegiate games, intramural championships, or a series of personal fitness classes, and it may also include programs sponsored by others but hosted by the department such as athletics conference championships, concerts, or charity gatherings. The role of the event manager and the processes of planning and managing events are described in the chapter.

The first in a set of three chapters that focus on relationships and intercollegiate athletics and recreations, David Wolf offers a review of managing fundraising and friend-making in Chapter Twelve. The various types of fundraising efforts are identified followed by an insider's view of the art and science of fundraising as well as the unique nature of raising funds and making friends in college athletics and recreation.

In Chapter Thirteen, Scott Branvold addresses management of the relationship between a college athletics or recreation department with the public through marketing and media relations. He begins by sharing a definition of marketing and then moves into strategic and tactical dimensions of marketing. He then offers a discussion of managing public relations, including managing relationships with the media.

Jeremy Stringer and Bill Hogan focus on the management of interpersonal relationships and campus politics in Chapter Fourteen. They examine relationships with individuals and groups, as well as the political nature of interactions within the campus community and with those outside the community. They also include a thoughtful discussion of the nature of conflict in relationships, and conclude with an interesting case study.

Part Two concludes with Chapter Fifteen. In it George McClellan presents the arguments for the inclusion of an active, comprehensive, and ongoing assessment and evaluation program as critical to the success of an intercollegiate athletics or campus recreation department. McClellan presents plain-spoken and practical information and advice on the purposes, types, and methods of assessment, as well as on how to make use of the data gathered through assessment in evaluation and telling the story of a department's success.

Professional administrators in intercollegiate athletics and recreation draw upon the foundations of their profession as outlined in Part One to provide a broad framework for their exercise of the skills described in Part Two. The administration of resources, events, and relationships in the field are all shaped by its history, ethics, applicable law, and governance.

CHAPTER EIGHT

MANAGING, LEADING, AND SUPERVISING STUDENT EMPLOYEES AND STAFF

Colleen A. McGlone and Stephen Rey

Sport and recreation professionals in college settings are continually required to adapt to new conditions as they face new challenges every day. This chapter focuses specifically on the sport and recreation employee and volunteer and on the fundamental concepts that sport and recreation professionals will need to understand in guiding them as members of a staff. In doing so, the chapter first describes the frameworks of managing, leading, and supervising and then provides a brief discussion of styles of management, leadership, and supervision. Next, the chapter addresses mission statements and their importance. It then addresses types of staff positions and recruiting, selecting, orienting, supporting, and retaining student employees and staff before moving on to concluding thoughts.

Concepts Involved in Working with Staff and Volunteers

College athletics and recreation are labor-intensive endeavors. It takes many employees and volunteers to successfully plan and implement the events and programs. There are three common frameworks related to working with employees and volunteers: management, leadership, and supervision. Although administrators may use different language for these three concepts, they are wise to be familiar with each of them. All three are addressed in this chapter.

Management

Management is a term that is commonly associated with utilization of resources, and a manager is someone responsible for meeting the needs and organizational objectives through effective use of resources. Typically the resources available include information, finances, and the most important resource of all—people. This section focuses on the management of people.

Human resources are managers' most important assets. Human resources management focuses not only on recruiting, hiring, training, and supervising these important assets and the creation of policies and procedures to govern their behavior, but also on developing the organization's culture. If management does not treat their employees and volunteers well, through, for example, staff development opportunities and shared decision making, it will have a negative effect on the organizational goals and the overall working environment (Gupta, 2005). This can have a long-lasting effect for the department.

Leadership

Whereas management may be understood as concentrating on the utilization of resources, leadership can be understood as focusing on development of engagement in ideas or purposes. Good management is the optimization of resource utilization in pursuing organizational goals. Good leadership is pursuing those goals through involving and engaging employees and volunteers in decision-making. According to Bennis and Goldsmith (1997), leaders who can lead with vision, empathy, consistency and integrity can typically maintain the respect of followers.

One simple approach to leading is to create a sense of ownership. This is often easier said than done, as it requires that all employees buy into the programs, services, and facilities, as well as be able to have a voice in making improvements. Therefore, the leader must be open to suggestions and realize that there are different ways to achieve the same goal.

It is also important that a program or department leader understand that there are leaders within the staff. The leader should identify these individuals and ensure their involvement by providing them with the opportunity to develop and administer programs.

Supervision

As noted earlier, management is about resources, and leadership is about ideas or purpose. Supervision, however, is about tasks and responsibilities. Supervision at its core involves monitoring and evaluating department staff and relies on policies and procedures as the yardsticks against which to measure staff performance. Good supervision is assuring congruity between institutional policies and performance standards with staff behaviors.

The establishment of basic understanding regarding rules, regulations, and performance expectations typically comes from an orientation and training process. This process ordinarily starts with an initial orientation session, which can be scheduled as needed or at predetermined times throughout the year depending on the needs of the department. Orientation should be mandatory for all staff members and volunteers and the itinerary should include such topics as introductions of the professional staff and staff responsibilities, a review of all department policies and procedures, and the department's emergency action plan. Good orientation sessions tend to reduce employee turnover and to help increase morale, thus leading to more positive outlooks among new employees (Kacmar et. al, 2006). After the initial orientation it may be a good idea to have the staff, including students and interns who are working in the department, sign a document indicating attendance of the orientation session and an understanding of the policies and procedures of the department.

Supervisors are responsible for enforcing the policies and procedures set forth for the department and must be prepared to address instances in which staff fall short of the required behavior. One way to be prepared is to establish additional policy and procedures for dealing with these issues. An example of the use of policy and procedures to handle discipline is a progressive approach (sometimes called a three strikes policy). The first time there is a problem the supervisor sits down with the staff member and discusses what took place and how to prevent it from occurring in the future. The supervisor should keep notes from the conversation including the date and time it takes place. Should the behavior reoccur, the supervisor should again meet with the staff member to address the problem. It should be noted that this is the second conversation with the staff person regarding the particular shortcoming. Explain once again to the staff member why the policy or procedure is in place, how it will be administered, and future expectations regarding the deviation from the expectations. This conversation should result in a formal written reprimand that references the earlier conversation as well as this second offence, a specific plan for corrective action, a date for a follow-up meeting to discuss progress, and the potential consequences for the staff member of failure to make appropriate and consistent improvement in performance. Should there be a third instance of poor performance, the supervisor will need to either decide to take additional corrective steps appropriate to the specific circumstances or to move to terminate the employment of the staff member.

In all cases of discipline, an appeal process must be in place to administer this policy. It is important to consult with the human resources department when designing any type of monitoring system in order to assure that both the disciplinary process and decision are consistent with institutional policy and applicable law.

Mission

Regardless of whether the framework for guiding staff is one of management, leadership, or supervision, the institutional and departmental mission statements will be important documents. A mission statement articulates the purpose and broad goals of an organization, and it provides a unifying structure for all activities, programs, and services of that organization. One of the responsibilities of the head of a campus athletics or recreation program is assuring that staff members, including student staff, have a clear understanding of the institutional and departmental mission statements and how their work will support the goals outlined in those documents.

Mission statements articulate what an organization strives to be. To reach these goals requires that the culture within an organization is strong and has shared beliefs, values, and assumptions (Schein, 1996). It has been stated that there may be no more important responsibility than the management of culture (Schein, 1985). An example of shared culture would include when a team exhibits the shared value of the name on the front of a uniform is more important than the name on the back. In other words, the organization or team goals come before that of the individual. If this is the case the group would exhibit the shared value of being team-oriented.

Techniques of Management, Leadership, and Supervision

The literature is replete with taxonomies and theories of management, leadership, and supervision. Space constraints prohibit this chapter from offering a thorough discussion of that material. Rather, this section presents a few formal models as well as informal models of techniques for effective management, leadership, and supervision. Those interested in more extensive reading in this area are encouraged to review the Appendix for a list of suggested additional resources.

Management by Objective and Management by Walking Around

Two techniques frequently cited in today's organizational literature include management by objective (MBO) and management by walking around (MBWA). The management by objective philosophy embraces a process in which managers and teams jointly set objectives, set times to evaluate their progress toward those objectives, and then managers provide rewards for meeting those objectives (Drucker, 1954). Management by walking around involves the manager actively observing what is taking place in the areas and units they manage. This can mean taking the time to just wander around and watch the daily operations and having informal discussions or setting aside time to go out and actively engage with employees in their work space. This allows for free flow of information and managers and employees alike can discuss issues and solve problems in a less formal manner (Peters and Austin, 1985). MBO and MBWA are not mutually exclusive techniques. In fact, they may be particularly effective when employed together.

Philosophy of Success

MBO and MBWA are two examples of formal techniques for pursuing success in an intercollegiate athletics or recreation department. However, success can be achieved in many ways. Three simple but very important words that can lead to success in the workplace and in life are preparation, organization, and work.

Preparation. Successful unit heads find a way to always be prepared. In order to prepare when embarking on administering a program, providing a service, or managing a facility one must anticipate and be able to answer several questions. "Are the financial resources in place? Is the number of staff adequate to meet the needs of the program? Is the equipment available for the program? Will the facility accommodate the activity?" Part of preparation is knowing that everything might not go as expected and being ready for the unknown.

Organization. Just because a unit head feels prepared for a program, service, or facility does not guarantee success. He or she must have a list of goals and objectives that will assist in completing the task at hand and assemble goals and objectives into an orderly, structured, and functional group. Goal setting in an organization tends to lead to more motivated employees and higher levels of organizational success. Goals typically challenge and energize employees to work harder in order to achieve success (Latham, 2004). It has also been proposed that when people feel as though they can meet the goals, they tend to be more motivated to go through the desired actions necessary to finish the task at hand (Steel and Konig, 2006).

Work. When it comes to work, it is important to remember that the unit head is only as successful as the workforce. He or she should be surrounded with those who are not afraid to work and are dedicated to accomplishing the task at hand in a successful manner. Department heads are a key element in the work environment and often set the tone for the unit or group. Those who have the ability to relate and show they care about their employees tend to have work teams that perform at high levels (Balkudi and Harrison, 2006).

Know Your Role. Lastly, according to Mintzberg (1973), there are 10 roles that a manager frequently acts out. They include being a leader, liaison, figurehead, monitor, disseminator, spokesperson, entrepreneur, distributor, resource allocator, and negotiator. Every manager will find themselves playing many of these roles every day. These roles require that managers understand and develop their own interpersonal skills, informational skills, and decision-making skills.

Although there may be no perfect formula for being an effective manager, leader, or supervisor, there are some shared traits and skills that research has identified that are used by successful unit heads. These include sound judgment, technical skills, conceptual skills, decision-making ability, flexibility, communication skills, political skills, integrity, leadership ability, and education (Alsop, 2007; Katz, 1974).

Types of Staff

Human resources can make or break a department. To that end, understanding the various roles of the staff is important. Sport and recreation organizations on college campuses have similar staffing needs. Typically both types of organizations rely upon a variety of employment positions and staffing levels to meet their mission. These include full-time employees, part-time employees, student employees, interns, volunteers, and contracted employees. This section focuses on these different types of staff.

Full-Time Employees

The Department of Labor does not define the difference between what constitutes full-time employment and part-time employment (U.S. Department of Labor, 2011). Instead the department leaves that up to each organization and to state guidelines. While there are no legal federal guidelines that regulate full-time employment, the institution or state that you work for typically delineates the policy and requirements of when an employee should be considered full-time. Full-time employment generally consists of an employee working 40 hours per week. However, in some cases, the number of hours worked could be 30 hours depending on the state regulations of where one is employed.

The title *full-time* also typically indicates that some sort of benefit package will be included in the employment contract; for example, health insurance, paid vacation, or sick leave and enrollment in a retirement savings plan. While this is frequently the case, there is no requirement that a full-time employee or organization has to offer these extra benefits.

Part-Time Employees

When staff is hired, they are frequently hired as part-time employees. Since full-time employees often are hired with benefits that require more resources and increased budgets, it is challenging to hire many full-time employees. Part-time employment has many pros and cons. Part-time work allows for a greater workforce than hiring all full-time employees. There are many times when help is needed at peak times and requires a lot of staff, but these peak hours may be as little as eight hours a week. Part-time employees can accomplish the job and do not come with the compensation issues of full-time employees. In addition, many individuals prefer part-time work because it offers an opportunity to be involved or a chance to earn income without compromising other endeavors. Furthermore, part-time employment allows individuals to gain work experience in an area in order to determine whether it as a viable career option.

Students

Often sport and recreation organizations will utilize the services of student employees. This can be a very good option to increase levels of manpower without having to add full or part-time staff. The use of students often creates situations in which both the organization and the student benefit. For example, the unit itself benefits from the additional workforce, as well as the budgetary benefit where fringe benefits do not have to be paid (sick leave, vacation, benefits). In addition, student employees often know many of the people who will use the facility and are cheerful and engaging when assisting them with their needs. Students benefit by learning more about career options and by gaining experience. They also benefit by earning income while gaining experience in a familiar organization where they typically have a vested interest.

In working with student employees, it is important to remember that when using them to carry out duties that may otherwise be assigned to a full-time staff member, these employees do not have the same experience level or knowledge level that full-time or other paid employees might have (Kathman and Kathman, 2000). Also remember that student employees usually are only allowed to work between one and twenty hours a week based on the institution's rules. This may limit their overall commitment to their job, as a majority of their time and interests may not revolve around work. Student employees often have high turnover rates depending on the institution and the student's educational progress. This means that training and orientation may need to take place for students on a more frequent basis.

Interns

The use of interns is also a way to help staff the unit. Utilizing students can be beneficial for both the organization and the student. In most cases students who apply have an active interest in working in the field that they want to pursue. Similar to student employees, interns are often energetic and eager to get involved and help. Interns are typically people who are interested in the area of recreation and sport management and are trying to gain experience. However, they may not fully understand or have the complete skill set to do all of the tasks at hand. They, like student workers and volunteers, will need to be trained in the areas they will be assigned to work. When using interns, it is important that they receive an education while they work. This may not be formal education, but they need to gain experience and should be assigned work tasks that help them meet their goals and that add to their educational foundation. Interns should be asked to do more than basic tasks and given an explanation of why each task is important. Internships, in most cases, cover an extended period in which the student may gain experiences in all program areas of the department. The intern's supervisor should manage his or her schedule effectively by scheduling assignments with the various professional staff in the department.

Volunteers

Department heads in intercollegiate athletics and recreation sometimes need to augment their workforce with volunteers. While a volunteer willingly takes on a task or duty with no expectation of monetary benefits, it is important to understand that people volunteer for a variety of reasons including supporting the event or cause, wanting to give back to the organization, or wanting to learn more about the organization or event itself.

In many cases activities, programs, or services may not be possible without volunteers. Volunteers should be treated in a professional manner and care taken to assure that their needs as a volunteer are met. Some keys to successfully engaging volunteers include ensuring that the individuals are not overscheduled or assigned so many hours that they will become exhausted or feel abused. When possible food and beverage should be provided and breaks should be worked into the schedule. In addition, it is always a nice touch to recognize the efforts of volunteers in some manner (Gladden, McDonald, and Barr, 2009).

Volunteers require training and in some cases may need certifications depending on what their assigned responsibilities. Also in some situations, especially when working with children, elderly, and people with disabilities, volunteers will need to be screened. Volunteers should be supervised similarly to other employees, but may need even closer attention due to their lack of familiarity with various aspects of the organization.

Contracted Services

In some cases, unit heads in intercollegiate athletics and recreation need to hire specialized services through a contractual agreement. Examples of these types of specialized services include, but are not limited to, concessions, officials, technology service, maintenance, security, and medical personnel. In most cases these contracted services will be set up as an independent contractor arrangement.

Independent contractors are people or businesses that provide products or services to another person or business based on the terms of a contract. Although employees of the independent contractor are not employees of the institution, the services contract should specify expectations regarding their behavior while performing services in the name of the university.

Recruiting, Selecting, and Retaining Staff

Human resource management ties directly back into organizational mission and strategic management (Kang, Morris, and Snell, 2007). Managing, leading, and supervising staff involves several important basic processes. These include recruiting, selecting, and retaining employees. This section of the chapter describes each of these processes.

Recruiting

Recruiting is the process of marketing a job opening in order to attract qualified candidates to apply for the position. Each organization will differ in its recruitment policies and procedures; however, the following general observations apply in most cases.

When considering recruiting staff, getting an early start is optimal. Once a department head determines which job(s) need to be filled, he or she will decide whether to recruit internally or externally. No matter which recruiting option one takes, a written announcement should be developed. This should be prepared based on the job description and skills needed. Be careful not to write the description or announcement so broad that more people who are not qualified apply than those who are qualified. Yet being too specific may result in not getting any applicants or interest at all. A good job description or announcement will contain the essential skills needed and the minimum qualifications for the position(s) to be filled. For a position requiring training or additional certifications, the requirements should be stated in the posting.

The success of any search to fill a staff position relies heavily on the extent to which the pool of candidates meets the needs of the search. When a department goes into a search without a particular person in mind, every effort should be made to reach out to qualified potential candidates.

This includes the formal announcements and postings, but it also includes word of mouth contacts through professional networks. Sometimes a department may feel that posting a position is a waste of time because they know who they want to hire. In addition to meeting the legal requirements for an open search, a department is well advised to keep open to the possibility that a candidate may emerge from a pool who is more perfect than the one they had in mind going into the process.

Selecting

Depending on the size and scope of the organization, the selection process may be simple or complex. In any case, selection of staff may involve one or more of the following components: (1) having the applicant fill out an application, including various background information on previous employment and references, 2) conducting an interview or interviews (either in person or on the phone), (3) performing a background investigation (this is particularly important when working with children, elderly, or people with disabilities), and, in some situations, (4) having the applicant perform or display the necessary skills by completing some type of performance test. These methods typically result in finding an employee who displays the capabilities required for the positions (Lyons, 2000).

There have been many news stories involving résumés of potential employees containing false information. It is estimated that 52% employees lied on their résumés and admitted that they would do it again (Christensen, 2007). Intercollegiate athletics and recreation are not immune from these incidents. It is important to make sure all information is verified prior to hiring an individual to work with your organization. It is considered best practice to include reference checking on candidates prior to executing the final hiring process.

Background checks are a common feature of the hiring process, especially in sport and recreation organizations. These checks need to go beyond just checking for violence and/or potential for child abuse. They also need to bring to light any other legal background that may serve as a notice of not only past behaviors but potentially future risks regarding felony and drug charges and convictions. No matter what type a job a person is being hired to do, the department making the hire has a duty to protect its participants and needs to be aware if any concerns exist.

Compensation consists of the total wages and benefits provided to employees for their services. Both wages and benefits are addressed, at least in general terms, in position postings. The specifics of compensation may be best discussed only with finalists in any search and may or may not be negotiable, depending on available resources and institutional practice and polices. Compensation often plays a key role in the ability to retain employees (Carlson, Upton, and Seaman, 2007).

Retaining

All unit heads should strive to retain their good employees if for no other reason than it is expensive and time consuming to find replacements (Kacmar et al., 2006). A key to retention is to ensure that the staff feel valued as members of the department. This can be documented and expressed in several ways, both formally and informally.

Evaluations. Performance evaluations provide a formal opportunity to express appreciation for the contributions of a staff member to the unit. All staff in campus sport and recreation programs should be evaluated based on overall performance established from the job description. Evaluations should always take place in a private area and be performed in a nonthreatening way (Kraus and Curtis, 2000). Time should be set aside to discuss the areas of performance that may need improvement, as well as strengths in performance. Performance appraisals are a systematic process to evaluate the overall strengths and weakness regarding how an employee executes the duties and requirements required in the assigned position. The appraisal will document behavior and provide support or rationale for actions taken by an employer, both positive and negative, including recording of due process. To reduce the chance or appearance of discrimination, evaluations should not be affected or contain comments regarding race, ethnicity, gender, age, religion, or sexual orientation. Occasionally evaluations result in discrimination claims because of information detailing poor or unsatisfactory performance or a real or perceived distortion of behavior. To reduce these claims, it may be a good practice to ensure that employee records are kept up-to-date, including both positive and negative documentation. Remember, if it was not written, it was not done!

When evaluations and performance appraisals are completed, they sometimes lead to an employee filing a grievance or ultimately to termination of employment. Grievance and discipline procedures should be written and made available to employees. Every employee should be made aware of what steps need to be taken if a grievance is to be filed.

There is no reason to complete an evaluation on the staff member, however, if a review is not going to be conducted with the individual and feedback provided to improve work performance. This should be ongoing and not only when presenting the evaluation to the staff member. The employee should not be caught off guard with what is being presented during the evaluation. Throughout employment, the supervisor should provide ongoing constructive criticism to the individual as well as how his or her work assignment may be improved. At the end of the evaluation period, the supervisor evaluates the individual based on the performance after each feedback period.

Professional Development. Another way to show value and support of the staff is to offer professional development opportunities. This may include paying for certifications, professional travel, or memberships for professional development. Webinars, teleconferences, and other computer-mediated programs are a cost-effective approach to professional development in an era when resources are scarce and expenditures subject to a greater degree of public scrutiny.

Awards. Another key aspect in retention is to recognize the exceptional work through the use of recognition and awards. Awards may be given to the Employee of the Week, Employee of the Month, or Employee of the Year for each program area. An award for the Most Outstanding Employee of the department may also be offered. To be eligible for this award an individual should have received an Employee of the Year award for the program area. Awards may also be given for volunteerism, service, special projects, and campus involvement.

Scholarships. Another way to retain students as employees is by offering scholarships or providing graduate assistantships. Scholarship programs may be set up to honor the accomplishments of students in the work place, classroom, and for university and community involvement. Scholarship support for regular staff is typically addressed in the institution's benefits package, but there may be instances in which (with institutional authorization) support is provided for a staff member beyond the benefit package in pursuing additional education.

Celebrations. Celebratory events are another way to show support for the staff that may aid in employee retention. Examples of such events include conducting an end-of-year banquet or potluck dinner. Another option to consider is developing staff retreats. Retreats can be quite effective if they are organized and have a definitive purpose.

Incentives. Incentive programs are usually developed to reward the performance of the staff. These incentives may be either monetary rewards or gifts (T-shirts, warm-up suits, etc.). Incentive programs should have guidelines that must be met by the employee. Years of service and individual evaluations should be used when developing an incentive program.

Conclusion

Much of what has been shared in this chapter about the management, leadership, and supervision of students and other staff has drawn upon a practical or scholarly framework. In this concluding section, we offer the following set of recommendations drawn from a more personal perspective:

- Create an environment for success.
- Be a mentor and teacher for the next generation of leaders and help them be successful.
- Stress the importance of balance and family, and support staff in attending to both.
- Serve as a source of support in difficult times and of celebration in good times.
- Be present. Visit staff on a daily basis and ask them what can be done to help them to achieve their goals.
- Be prepared for staff members to move on to new positions. As they succeed and grow they will look to advance professionally. Let them know that assisting them with advancement is important.

Finally, as discussed in this chapter, the management, supervision, and leadership of students and staff is arguably the most important role of an administrative profession in intercollegiate athletics and campus recreation. As such, it should be the focus of continuous self-assessment and reflection on the part of the administrative professional and should also be informed by a thorough process of evaluation by superiors, peers, and subordinates.

Chapter Eight Key Points

1. College athletics and recreation are labor-intensive endeavors. There are three common frameworks related to working with employees and volunteers: management, leadership, and supervision.

2. *Management* is a term that is commonly associated with utilization of resources, and a manager is someone responsible for meeting the needs and organizational objectives through effective use of resources.
3. *Leadership* can be understood as focusing on development of engagement in ideas or purposes.
4. *Supervision* at its core involves monitoring and evaluating department staff and relies on policies and procedures as the yardsticks against which to measure staff performance.
5. One of the responsibilities of the head of a campus athletics or recreation program is assuring that staff members, including student staff, have a clear understanding of the institutional and departmental mission statements and how their work will support the goals outlined in those documents.
6. Intercollegiate athletics and campus recreation programs rely upon a variety of employment positions and staffing levels to meet their mission. These include full-time employees, part-time employees, student employees, interns, volunteers, and contracted employees.
7. Recruiting, selecting, and retaining staff are important processes in management, leadership, and supervision.

References

Alsop, R. "How Stanford is Grooming Next Business Leaders." *Wall Street Journal*, May 29, 2007. Accessed on May 21, 2011 at http://online.wsj.com/article/SB118038943812516395.html.

Balkudi, P., and Harrison, D. "Ties, Leaders and Time in Teams: Strong Inference About Network Structure's Effects on Team Validity and Performance." *Academy of Management Journal*, 2006, 49, 49–68.

Bennis. W., and Goldsmith, J. *Learning to Lead*. Reading, MA: Perseus Books, 1997.

Christensen, G. J. "Resume and Application Fraud." In Career Directors International *2006–2007 Research Study Career Industry Megatrends: What You and Your Clients Need to Know*. 2007. Accessed on October 18, 2011 at http://www.careerdirectors.com/members/docs/CDI˙Mega˙Trends.pdf.

Carlson, D., Upton, N., and Seaman, S. "The Impact of Human Resource Practices and Compensation Design on Performance: An Analysis of Family-Owned SMEs." *Journal of Small Business Management*, 2007, 44, 531–543.

Drucker, P. *The Practice of Management*. New York: Harper, 1954.

Gladden, J., McDonald, M., and Barr, C. "Event Management." In L. P. Masteralexis, C. A. Barr, and M. A. Hums (Eds.), *Principles and Practice of Sport Management* (3rd ed.). Sudbury, Massachusetts Jones and Bartlett Publishers, 2009.

Gupta, A. "Leadership in a Fast Paced World: An interview with Ken Blanchard." *Mid-American Journal of Business*, 2005, 20, 7–11.

Kang, S, Morris, S., and Snell, S. "Relational Archetypes, Organizational Learning, and Value Creation: Extending the Human Resource Architecture." *Academy of Management Review,* 2007, 32, 236–256.

Kathman, J., and Kathman, M. "Training Student Employees for Quality Service." *Journal of Academic Librarianship,* 2000, 26(3), 176–189.

Katz, R. "Skills of an Effective Administrator." *Harvard Business Review.* September/October, 1974, 90–102.

Kacmar, K, Andrews, D. Van Rooy, R., Steilberg, R., and Cerrone, S. "Sure Everyone Can Be Replaced, But at What Cost? Turnover as a Predictor of Unit-Level Performance." *Academy of Management Journal,* 2006, 49, 133–144.

Krauss, R. G., and Curtis, J. E. *Creative Management in Recreation, Parks, and Leisure Services.* New York: McGraw-Hill, 2000.

Latham, E. P. "The Motivational Benefits of Goal Setting." *Academy of Management Executives,* 2004, 18, 126–129.

Lyons, K. "Personal Investment as a Predicator of Camp Counselor Job Performance." *Journal of Park and Recreation Administration,* 2000, 18(2), 21–36.

Mintzberg, H. *The Nature of Managerial Work.* New York: Harper and Row, 1973.

Peters, T., and Austin, N. *A Passion for Excellence: The Leadership Difference.* New York: Random House, 1985.

Schein, E. H. *Organizational Culture and Leadership.* San Francisco: Jossey-Bass, 1985.

Schein, E. H. "Culture: The Missing Concept in Organization Studies." *Administrative Science Quarterly,* 1996, 41, 229–240.

Steel, P., and Konig, C. (2006). "Integrating Theories of Motivations." *Academy of Management Review,* 2006, 31, 889–913.

U.S. Department of Labor. "Work Hours." Accessed May 21, 2011 at http://www.dol.gov/dol/topic/workhours/full-time.htm

CHAPTER NINE

FINANCIAL MANAGEMENT AND BUDGETING

Timothy D. DeSchriver and Edgar N. Johnson

Financial management is critical to the successful operation of a college athletics or recreation department. It is defined as the process of implementing and managing financial control systems, collecting and analyzing financial data, and making sound financial decisions based on these analyses (Brown, Rascher, Nagel, and McEvoy, 2010).

The purpose of this chapter is to provide an overview of financial management for intercollegiate athletics and recreation departments. The chapter opens with a discussion of several popular types of budgets and approaches to budgeting. Next, it addresses the sources of income and expense for athletics and recreation programs. It then discusses budget development and management. Lastly, the conclusion highlights several important current financial issues faced by administrators in collegiate athletics and recreation.

The chapter makes use of informative examples throughout. These examples are drawn solely from National Collegiate Athletic Association (NCAA) member institutions because such information for institutional members of other athletics associations is not readily available.

Types of Budgets and Approaches to Budgeting

A primary component of financial management for an athletics or recreation department is the development and management of its budget. A budget is a financial plan that projects expected income and expenses for an organization (Fried, Shapiro, and DeSchriver, 2008). Budgets are a key aspect of the management process and should be closely aligned to an organization's mission and goals. Budgets are also a tool for implementing an organization's strategic plan.

For major Division I intercollegiate athletics programs, the annual budget can be quite substantial. For example, both the University of Texas and Ohio State University have annual operating budgets in excess of $110 million (U.S. Department of Education, 2010). These funds are spent in areas such as salaries, grants-in-aid (athletics scholarships), equipment, and team travel in order for these athletics programs to achieve their organizational goals.

There are several different types of budgets and approaches to budgeting. This chapter addresses a number of them. For a more complete review of budgets and budgeting, one may wish to read *Budget and Financial Management in Higher Education* (Barr and McClellan, 2011).

Types of Budgets

There are two primary types of financial budgets that are prevalent within college athletics and recreation programs. The first of these is the operating budget, which is what most people think of when they think of a budget. An operating budget reflects income from all sources and expenses in all categories as they relate to operations of the organization (Barr and McClellan, 2011).

An operating budget provides good-faith predictions of future sources of income, along with the size of these future income streams (Brown et al., 2010). For example, a recreation director may include within his or her operating budget the expected future cash flow from fees collected for fitness and exercise classes. Operating budgets also include estimates on future levels of expense in areas such as salaries and wages, utilities, equipment, travel, meals, and athletics grants-in-aid.

Based on these predictions of income and expense, the manager can determine the breakeven level and projected net income. Most athletics or recreation departments do not generate enough revenue to cover their expenses, thus the operating budget allows them to estimate the amount of funds that may be necessary from revenue sources outside the department such as student fees and institutional support.

The second type of budget is a capital budget. These budgets project the sources and uses of funding for capital projects. Capital projects last more than one year, the usual length of operating budgets, and usually involve the construction and renovation of physical spaces or the purchase of major pieces of equipment (Fried et al., 2008). For example, a capital budget is developed if an institution is building a new student recreation center or renovating a football stadium. These projects take several years to plan and construct, and, as part of this process, a capital budget is developed to estimate the project's cost, the sources of funding and their associated cost, and the expected future revenue streams. If an institution has several different projects from which to select, such as either a new student recreation center or the renovation of a football stadium, capital budgeting can also play an important role in ranking the projects to determine which one should be undertaken.

Approaches to Budgeting

There are a number of commonly used methods for the development and preparation of financial budgets of which three will be discussed in this section. The first is *zero-based budgeting* (ZBB). ZBB is a method for preparing operating and cash flow budgets. With ZBB, one starts with no assumptions, in other words there are no previously accepted levels of income or expense. Past levels of income and expense are important, but they are not taken as given. Each activity that the organization engages in must be justified, and activities are ranked based on importance to the organization. For example, if a recreation department has an annual budget of $5 million, under ZBB each department or program that wishes to receive a portion of those funds must request the amount of funds it would like and provide justification for their funding needs (Brown et al., 2010).

In practical terms, an athletics department that engages in ZBB may require the coach of each team to submit an annual budget request. As part of the ZBB process, the coach may be asked to rank each spending category in order of importance and develop a cost estimate for each line item. The athletics director or financial manager analyzes the budget request to determine which areas are to be funded. Funds are then allocated to those spending areas that are deemed acceptable and appropriate. Given that

ZBB starts with the assumption that all areas of spending must be justified, it can be quite time-consuming and cumbersome.

As an alternative, many athletics and recreation departments engage in *incremental budgeting*. Under incremental budgeting, past levels of expense and income are assumed to continue into the next budget year. Thus, the director of each program or sports team must justify only increases (or, in lean times, decreases) to the previous year's budget.

There are several advantages to incremental budgeting. It is a consistent and rather simplistic form of budgeting. Managers have a fairly accurate estimate of their budget allocations from year to year, and this allows them to easily develop future budgets. Also, a relatively small amount of staff time is necessary for the preparation and implementation of incremental budgets. Also, interprogram conflicts are usually avoided, as each unit is treated fairly similarly from a financial standpoint.

There are, however, several obvious disadvantages. Incremental budgeting encourages programs to spend their full budget to ensure that they receive an equal or higher budget allocation in future years. This may lead to financial inefficiency as programs spend money simply to ensure that they receive the funds in the next fiscal year. Incremental budgeting may also fail to account for changing circumstances such as economic downturns or changes in programmatic priorities. Incremental budgeting also lessens the incentives to both directly reduce costs and develop new initiatives that will reduce costs in the future.

Many athletics and recreation departments engage in a combination of zero-based budgeting and incremental budgeting. Given the time-consuming nature of ZBB, an department may engage in this budgeting process once every three to five years. In the interim, the department will rely on incremental budgeting to complete their annual budgets.

Another budgeting approach that has gained attention within higher education is *cost-center budgeting*, also referred to as *responsibility-based budgeting* (RBB). Within RBB, each university unit is responsible for generating enough revenue to cover expenses, in other words each unit is its own autonomous operation. While RBB may be effective for auxiliary units, it is somewhat difficult to implement for academic, student-supported, and athletics or recreation units that, under even the best of circumstances, do not have the ability to generate adequate revenues to cover expenses (Barr and McClellan, 2011). For an athletics or recreation unit, some level of pre-arranged funding is usually supplied by the university administration. However, once that amount is established, the department is required to generate enough revenue to balance their budget.

An important aspect of RBB is that it decentralizes budgetary decision making. Unit directors such as academic deans and directors of athletics or recreation are given authority over their budgets as opposed to other approaches where financial power is centralized with the central administration. The decentralization of budgetary authority under RBB can lead to greater departmental flexibility to deal with the changing landscape of athletics and recreation along with providing a financial incentive for their efficient management (Stocum and Rooney, 1997). Under RBB, if an athletics or recreation program generates an annual positive net income, it is usually permitted to carry these funds forward to the next fiscal year. However, a disadvantage of RBB may be that each university unit, such as the athletics department, has an incentive to act in their own best interest as opposed to the benefit of the overall university. This may lead to conflicts and conflicting goals across university units.

Income and Expenses in Intercollegiate Athletics

Each sport program will have an individual annual budget. In addition, different units such as marketing, media relations, student-athlete academic support, and athletics training will have unique budgets. It is the job of the athletics or recreation director to work with their staff to develop and implement budgets that will allow each unit to operate at peak efficiency. Within an athletics or recreation program's budget, the sources of income and expense may differ somewhat based on the affiliation of the overall institution.

Sources of Revenue for Intercollegiate Athletics Programs

The following section addresses the primary revenue sources for an intercollegiate athletics program. These sources may differ for several reasons, including whether the institution is public versus private and the affiliation or division of the athletics program (National Association of Intercollegiate Athletics [NAIA], National Junior College Athletic Association [NJCAA], NCAA Division I, II, or III).

State and Public Funding. Many states have laws, regulations, or policies that specifically preclude or severely limit the use of state funding for support of intercollegiate athletics. Meanwhile, some states permit the use of state funding for support of student activities and recreation only. In states where it is permissible for intercollegiate athletics programs to receive state funding, there may be restrictions on how that support is allocated and spent. Typical uses of state funding include athletics grants-in-aid (scholarships) and academic support for student-athletes. Some state legislatures may support capital projects for athletics when the project also has an academic or wider educational use. An example would be the expansion of an athletics facility such as a football stadium. Within the expansion, the institution may include physical space for offices and classrooms for an academic unit such as a kinesiology and physical education department. Generally though, direct state funding for support of intercollegiate athletics is precluded by the majority of states. Obviously, this source of funding is not available for private institutions.

Ticket Sales. Ticket income is an important and growing revenue source for many intercollegiate athletics programs. For NCAA Division I Football Bowl Subdivision (FBS) institutions, ticket income represents as much as 30% of athletically generated income. Ticket income for Division I Football Championship Subdivision (FCS) institutions is 17% of athletically generated income. It is 7% of generated income for Division II, and 2% of generated income for Division III (Fulks, 2009). *Athletics generated revenue* is revenue that is generated by the athletics program and excludes institutional and state support.

The primary sources of ticket income are sports that have potentially large spectator demand and a tradition of spectator support such as football and men's basketball. For some institutions, sports such as women's basketball, baseball, soccer, volleyball, ice hockey, or lacrosse have potential for fan interest and revenue. Other sports may also generate modest ticket income to help an athletics program's bottom line, but those sports will probably be more regional or local in scope. In such cases, an administrator must balance the cost of collecting admission fees versus the income potential of fans attending games that have only a modest following.

In an effort to maximize revenue for both ticket sales and development (see Chapter Twelve for a full discussion of fundraising and friendmaking), many NCAA Division I institutions have started to link the best seats in their facilities, such as luxury boxes, club seating, box seats, and 50-yard line seats, to a mandated minimum annual seat donation. Donation-based seating plans work well when stadiums and arenas are sold-out or nearly sold-out for most home games and the institutional fan base strongly supports the athletics teams. However, institutions operating with partially filled stadiums on game day may face a more challenging environment when linking seat availability to athletics donations. It should also be noted that under the IRS tax codes put into effect in 1988, only 80% of an athletics donation is tax deductible if it is tied to a benefit like better seat location or parking. This may discourage some from making donations to athletics departments. As an example, for a patron to get season ticket club seats between the 35 yard lines at Ohio State football games a donation of $3,500 per seat per year is required (Ohio Stadium Club Seating Program, 2011). Most institutions are not this expensive, but it is a function of market forces and the competitiveness of the football program that enable this level of mandatory donation in order to gain access to premium seats. In another example, Penn State University charges $600 per seat per year for similar seating for football (Juliano, 2009).

Fundraising and Development. Fundraising and development represents the second largest source of income to the athletics program after ticket sales for FBS institutions where cash contributions represent 25% of athletics-generated revenue, and 20% of total athletics revenue. For FCS institutions, cash contributions are 27% of athletics-generated revenue but are only 8% of athletics total revenue (Fulks, 2009). The reason for this difference is because FCS institutions, in contrast to FBS members, require a significantly larger amount of direct and indirect institutional financial support in order to balance their budgets. For FCS institutions, cash contributions represent the fifth largest source of athletics-generated revenue. It is exceeded by ticket sales, NCAA and conference distributions, sponsorships, and guarantees (Fulks, 2009).

Associations and Conferences. Funding from associations and conferences is becoming a more important source of revenue for many institutions. The Men's NCAA Division I Basketball Championship's lucrative television package has continued to increase in size. In April, 2010, the NCAA signed a new 14-year television broadcast deal with CBS Sports and Turner Broadcasting for $10.8 billion. These funds are the primary source for the financial distributions that the NCAA gives back to its member institutions. Over 90% of the NCAA's total annual revenue of $710 million is generated by the Division I Men's Basketball Championship, better known as March Madness ("Revised Budget for Fiscal Year Ended August 31, 2011," 2011). Funds are redistributed back to the conferences and individual member institutions through a number of NCAA programs.

Associations and conferences use specified formulas to determine the distribution of revenues to member institutions, but the specific formulas vary. Some associations and conferences and may use a relatively simple equitable shares approach in which every member institution receives the same funding. Others use formulas with variables that include characteristics of the institution's student body and its intercollegiate athletics program.

University Subsidies. According to the *2004–2009 NCAA Report of Revenues and Expenses for Division I Intercollegiate Athletics Programs* (Fulks, 2009), university subsidies or direct university support for public FBS institutions' athletics programs represented only 8% of total athletics revenue. For private FBS institutions, university subsidies were 21% of total athletics revenue. The university subsidy is revenue to the institution from tuition, endowments, or other non-athletics sources that the university's president or board of trustees provides to the athletics program to help offset athletics operational expenses and potential budget shortfalls. According to the *Report*, many major FBS programs would not operate effectively if it were not for the large university subsidies that they receive annually. Some of the subsidies are in excess of $10 million (Fulks, 2009).

In the FCS division, where ticket revenue is significantly less, university subsidies along with direct and indirect university support accounts for 32% of total athletics revenues for public institutions. This amount increases to 57% for private FCS institutions (Fulks, 2009). Direct support is revenue given to the athletics budget from other university revenue sources, tuition or the university endowment for example; indirect support is expenses that the university assumes and does not charge back to the athletics program such as the payment of utility, custodial, or grounds and maintenance costs. These expenses are often assumed for other academic or auxiliary units across the university.

Direct and indirect university support for all athletics programs is a significant and necessary component of its budget. At many universities, faculty are concerned about such support and have asked that university subsidies to athletics be reduced or eliminated. However, proponents of such funding cite that such subsidies are no different than the support given to academic departments such as theater, music, and biology. If athletics is considered a part of the institution's educational enterprise and there is no other way for an athletics program to meet its financial obligations, it is difficult to envision a time when university subsidies will be eliminated or drastically reduced.

Student Fees. A student fee is an additional expense charged by the university to students beyond tuition, room, board, and books for specified services or programs. Examples of student fees include an equipment fee for a course, a technology fee to support campus information technology infrastructure, or an activities fee to support programming for students. Some student fees are either mandatory or optional. Mandatory fees are those charged to all students. Both the technology fee and activities fee are commonly mandatory fees. Optional fees are those charged only to the users of a service or program. Course equipment fees or parking fees are examples of optional fees. Student fees may be charged to undergraduate students, graduate and professional students, or to all students.

Often, institutions will have multiple fees and will choose to bundle fees for public relations reasons. For example, an institution may have an athletics fee, a recreation fee, and a student center fee. The institution may elect to bundle these fees together under the title of an activity fee or student fee or some other designation. In such cases, the funds are usually allotted to each area according to a predetermined formula.

Student fees in support of intercollegiate athletics are a growing source of funding on many college campuses. According to *USA Today's* analysis of NCAA Division I financial documents, "students were charged more than $795 million to support sports programs at 222 Division I public schools during the 2008–09 school year" (Berkowitz, 2010). According to the Fulks (2009), student fees represented 6% of total athletics revenue in FBS institutions and 16% of total athletics revenue for all FCS institutions. However, for public-only FCS institutions student fees represented 28% of total athletics revenues.

Corporate Partnerships and Advertising. Corporate partnerships and advertising represent a modest form of athletics-generated revenue for both FBS and FCS institutions. According to Fulks (2009), corporate partnerships and advertising represent 8% and 9% of athletics revenue for the respective subdivisions. While this does not seem like a significant amount of revenue, it can have a profound effect on the bottom line of an athletic department's budget. In addition, corporate partnerships and advertising involve the business community in the athletics program and through cross promotional activities help raise the public's awareness of both the athletics program and the corporate partner. Through corporate partnerships, businesses have the ability to reach a large number of potential customer groups. For example, corporations want to have access to the young adults who constitute the student body so that they can advertise and sell their products to this market segment.

Contracts with soft drink companies for concession rights and advertising support or with sport drink companies for team consumption and advertising support are both examples of these types of arrangements. At some universities, when corporate partnerships involve financial institutions, the banks want to add value to the partnership by also having exclusive vending rights to the campus's ATMs, student debit cards, and alumni affinity cards. Universities are willing to bundle these rights and offer exclusivity if the revenue for the bundled partnerships makes financial sense. When banks compete for naming rights for stadiums or arenas, they will almost always insist on having a value-added component that goes beyond signage. An example of this is the University of Minnesota's (U of M) TCF Bank Stadium. In 2010, TCF Bank agreed on a 25 year, $35 million deal with the U of M for the naming rights to their new football stadium. As part of the deal, TCF Bank acquired the right to offer U of M branded debit affinity cards and to place TCF Bank ATM kiosks across campus. This deal provided TCF Bank with the opportunity to increase their business and also provided the U of M with a substantial revenue stream (Steinbach, 2006).

Additional Revenue Sources. Additional revenue sources for athletics programs include concessions, merchandise, parking, sport camps and facility rental fees. The biggest down time for an athletics program is the summer months. Generating revenue during this time by utilizing facilities that would normally be dormant is a bonus for athletics programs. Sport camps managed and operated by the athletics programs' coaches provide additional income for the coach but also provide additional income for the athletics program.

Holding nonathletic events in athletics facilities is another source of additional revenue. Renting arenas for concerts, trade shows, and high school graduations can fill facilities and generate needed income for the athletics program. However, an intercollegiate athletics program should always be aware that its primary constituents are student-athletes and the campus community. Renting athletics facilities in order to host outside events should be secondary to the primary mission of operating an athletics program and supporting the needs of teams, student-athletes, the general student body, faculty, and staff. With that said, as the financial environment becomes more difficult on many college campuses, the rental of facilities to outside groups has grown in volume due to its ability to generate new revenue.

Other revenue sources for many intercollegiate athletic programs include concessions, merchandise, and parking. Together, they account for 2% to 3% of athletics-generated revenue at Division I Institutions (Fulks, 2009). While it is only a small component of athletics generated revenue; parking, concessions, and merchandise can have a significant impact on the fan experience at games. Many times, where one parks for a football game is more important than where one sits during the game. Fans are willing to pay for the convenience of being close to the stadium or having access to tailgating and party areas. Many institutions have realized this and instituted a variety of parking options for games with VIP parking adjacent to or near the stadium coming with a premium price.

With respect to concessions and merchandising, institutions often outsource these operations to outside service providers. In some cases, the concessions are handled by the same company that provides the food for the campus dining halls. In order to have the greatest opportunity for income potential from concessions, ideally athletics programs should retain the right to independently bid concessions at their facilities rather than have them bundled as a part of the food service contract for servicing dining halls or the campus student center. An athletics program's typical share of concession revenues is between 15–25% of total sales. Some institutions may receive more or less, depending on sales volume and the specifics of the concessions contract.

Merchandising, like concessions, may be outsourced. It is not uncommon for merchandising to be handled by the vendor that operates the campus bookstore. In most cases, the athletics program will receive a commission on all sales at athletics events similar to the amounts received from food concessions, approximately 15–25%.

These alternative sources of income are relatively small when compared to the revenue generated by other areas of the intercollegiate athletics enterprise. However, the activities serve the important purpose of engaging the public and having them involved in the university and the athletics program. Hence, the public relations benefit of these additional sources of revenue cannot be overlooked. Having young campers, competitors, and their parents visit the campus and the athletics facilities is a strong recruiting tool. Meanwhile, a fan's experience at a sporting event can be greatly affected by the quality of parking, concessions, and merchandise.

Variances in Importance. The sources of revenue for intercollegiate athletics programs are fairly common across universities, but the importance of any particular source of revenue to a program's budget may vary based

TABLE 9.1. SOURCE OF REVENUE FOR NCAA INTERCOLLEGIATE ATHLETICS PROGRAMS

	Division		
Source	I-FBS (2009)	I-FCS (2009)	II (2003)
Ticket Sales	24%	5	5
NCAA and Conference Distributions	16	4	0
Guarantees and Options	2	3	1
Development and Fundraising	20	8	8
Concessions/Programs/Novelties	3	1	1
Broadcasting Rights	3	0	0
Sponsorship and Advertising	7	2	1
Institutional and Government Support	14	56	62
Student Fees	6	16	15
All Other	5	5	7

Adapted from Fulks, 2004; Fulks, 2009.

on institutional characteristics. An athletics program within a public institution may have the ability to rely on appropriations from their state legislature or other public funds. Conversely, a program based in a private institution would not have access to such funding sources and would need to rely more on other funding such as private donations.

The size of the overall institution may also greatly affect the sources and levels of funding. For example, one popular source of funding for recreation programs are student fees. This source can be very high, in the tens of millions of dollars, at large institutions such as Arizona State University or the University of Central Florida with enrollments in excess of 50,000 students. Meanwhile, student fees may generate much less revenue for the athletics departments at institutions with much smaller enrollments.

For NCAA member institutions, the amount of revenues and expenses varies greatly due to a program's level of competition. There are three primary levels of NCAA competition: Divisions I, II, and III; Division I is separated into two subdivisions based on football. Table 9.1 gives a breakdown of the sources of revenue for NCAA members competing in Divisions I and II.

Sources of Expense for Intercollegiate Athletics Programs

As is the case with sources of revenue, the various expenses for intercollegiate athletics are fairly common across all programs. The variations that

TABLE 9.2. SOURCE OF EXPENSE FOR NCAA INTERCOLLEGIATE ATHLETICS PROGRAMS

	Division		
Source	**I-FBS (2009)**	**I-FCS (2009)**	**II (2003)**
Grants-in-aid	15%	25%	31%
Guarantees and options	3	1	0
Salaries and benefits	33	32	39
Team travel	7	8	9
Recruiting	2	2	2
Equipment, uniforms, supplies	3	3	6
Development and fundraising	3	2	1
Game expenses	4	2	1
Facility maintenance and rental	13	6	n/a
All other	17	19	11

Adapted from Fulks, 2009.

occur are in the proportion of expenses by category, and these variations are a function of institutional characteristics (see Table 9.2). This section offers an overview of common expense categories in college athletics programs.

Salaries and Benefits. Salaries and benefits are a market-driven budget item. Nowhere is this more the case than it is for coaches (and to a lesser extent, athletic directors). Salaries for all coaches, but especially for Division I football and basketball coaches, have risen dramatically in the past few years. Salaries and benefits for coaches and athletics administrators comprise 33% of overall athletics expenditures at FBS institutions (Fulks, 2009).

USA Today reported that 57 of the 120 Division I FBS head football coaches had total compensation packages exceeding $1 million. Six coaches had total compensation packages of over $3 million, and two had salaries over $4 million ("Compensation for Division I Men's Basketball Coaches," 2010). This occurred even though only 14 Division I FBS athletics programs reported net positive revenues for 2009 (Fulks, 2009). A similar study of salaries for the teams that made the 2010 Men's NCAA Basketball Tournament found that 33 of the 65 head coaches had salaries exceeding $1 million ("Compensation . . . ," 2010).

Total compensation packages for coaches may include a base salary along with non-university compensation from sources such as apparel or footware contracts, sports camps, coach's shows, public appearances, and bonuses based on athletics and academic sport program performance criteria. Such compensation levels are now the industry standard for Division I head football and basketball coaches. They often make the head coach the highest paid employee in the university, and it is common for Division I football and men's basketball coaches to earn a larger salary than the university president.

Whereas pressure from salaries has a disproportional impact on certain types of athletics programs, staff benefits are an area in which all athletics programs and their institutions have seen considerable increases in recent years. In particular, the costs of providing health care benefits to staff continue to rise dramatically.

Grants-in-Aid. The cost of athletics grants-in-aid is determined by the university central administration. A full grant-in-aid consists of tuition, room, board, and books. The athletics department decides on the number of grants-in-aid that will be allocated for each sport. The athletics association or governing body for the membership sets the maximum number of grants-in-aid that can be provided in each sport based on the division level of the institution.

Other Areas of Spending. Other areas of spending for intercollegiate athletics programs include student-athlete recruitment, facility maintenance and repair, game management, team travel, equipment, supplies, uniforms, and promotion and marketing These areas combined account for approximately 20–30% of costs for most athletics programs (Fulks, 2009).

For the most part, there is little flexibility in some of these areas. For example, with respect to game management, spending on areas such as security, referees and officials, and utilities is set and can be only slightly altered. While budgetary changes can be made in areas such as recruiting and team travel, the failure to properly invest in these areas may lead to a decrease in on-field success and a poor experience for the student-athletes. Title IX obligations can also play an important part in directing expenses in some of these other areas of spending.

Finally, the quality of athletics facilities is an area of importance to many prospective coaches and student-athletes. The failure to adequately invest in the construction, renovation, and maintenance of athletics facilities such as stadiums, arenas, practice facilities, and locker rooms can quickly place an athletics program at a competitive disadvantage over its rival institutions.

Income and Expenses in Campus Recreation

Having discussed income and expenses for intercollegiate athletics, this section of the chapter will offer similar information as it relates to campus recreation. There are some areas of commonality, but there are also important differences.

Sources of Revenue

Student activity fees are an important source of funding for recreation and intramural programs. Yet even at universities where these fees are mandatory, they often do not cover the full cost of these programs. When there are funding shortfalls, recreation programs have moved to charging additional user fees for intramurals, club, and fitness participation. For intramural programs these added charges may be in the form of a fee for participating teams or individuals. Fitness programs may charge those who enroll in fitness classes such as aerobics, dance, yoga, and weight training. These added fees help cover direct program costs.

When space and enrollment allow, recreation and fitness programs have been opening their doors to alumni and community memberships. Doing so provides both a financial and a public relations benefit for the university and the recreation program.

University recreation and fitness programs have used two additional revenue vehicles to supplement funding. The first of these is corporate sponsorships where an entire program or part of it is sponsored by a corporate entity. One example would be Nike intramural flag football league. Nike gets a presence at the site and on officials' shirts, pinnies, and championship shirts, plaques, or trophies. In addition, advertising space may be sold in your facility to corporations who want to get their product in front of students or other users.

Sources of Expense

Recreation, intramural, and club sport programs are participant-based programs. As such, potential revenue sources will not be the same as they are for athletics programs, which are heavily spectator-based and may also attract corporate sponsorship and advertising. However, expenses for recreation and intramural programs are similar to athletics in at least three leading categories of expenses:

- Salaries and benefits
- Facility maintenance and utility costs
- Equipment costs

These three areas account for the primary expenses in any recreation and intramural program. The highest cost in the operation of recreation, intramurals, and fitness is in the area of salaries and benefits. There are many different types of staff members within a recreation program. These may include full-time and part-time employees, graduate student assistants, and undergraduate student workers. Recreation management must balance the cost of this staff with the need to provide a safe, healthy, and enjoyable experience to its users, who include students, staff, and faculty.

Facility maintenance, utility, and equipment costs represent the bulk of programmatic expenses, after recreation staff salaries and benefits. Intramural programs are actively operating for as much as eight to ten hours a day on many campuses, while fitness programs may operate 16 to 20 hours per day. With such extensive usage, it is obvious that the cost of operation and the wear and tear on facilities and equipment will be continual and extensive. Due to the extensive and continual use of the facilities and equipment, ongoing and deferred maintenance programs, as well as equipment inspection and equipment replacement cycles, will be more frequent in recreation and intramural programs.

Additional expense items may include extramural competitions for club and intramural sports. Club sports have traditionally traveled off-campus for competition, but extramural competition as a part of a comprehensive intramural program is becoming a growing phenomenon. Intramural program directors are cooperating with each other and arranging competitions between their students in a variety of team sports. The participant benefit is easily apparent, but these activities are an additional expense for intramural programs.

Although the cost per participant is well below that of intercollegiate athletics, recreation and intramural programs play an important role in campus and student life and require a budget comparable to its importance and programmatic size. These expenses go hand-in-hand with the operation of a comprehensive recreation, intramural and club sport, and fitness program.

Budget Development and Management

There are several keys to developing accurate and effective budgets. First, budgeting should be considered a process that involves many different stakeholders. When developing a budget, an athletic director, for example, should include important staff members such as coaches, senior and middle-level administrators, and department heads in areas such as athletics training, facilities, media relations, and marketing in the decision-making process. Second, it must also be emphasized that budgeting is a continual and ongoing process throughout the fiscal year. Once a budget is completed, it must then be enacted and monitored. If circumstances change during the year, budgets may need to be reexamined to determine whether changes are necessary. Failure to continually monitor budgets may result in gross overspending, possible financial fraud and the misappropriation of funds, or financial distress for the organization.

To develop an accurate and effective budget, a great deal of financial information about the organization must be collected and utilized. Historical data may be the single most important aspect in the budget development process. These data may include past budgets, other financial documents such as cash flow statements, balance sheets, expense reports, employee salary and benefits information, and job descriptions.

Lastly, in the budget development process, one must consider all factors that may affect the finances of the organization in the future. For example, an athletics director must analyze and estimate the future cost of expense items such airline travel, equipment, hotels, staff salaries, and tuition when developing a budget. Although it is extremely difficult for a manager to estimate these future costs with perfection, by using historical data and knowledge about future events he or she should be able to develop a budget that financially prepares the organization for the future. For example, many athletics directors were forced to greatly adjust their budgets in 2008 after the downturn in the U.S. economy. While virtually no one could foresee the depth of the 2008–2009 recession, an insightful athletics director who developed a budget with the possibility of an economic downturn in mind would have weathered the financial storm much more effectively than peers at other institutions.

One last budget management process that must be addressed is midyear budget adjustments, which are sometimes referred to as reallocations. Circumstances may dictate that a budget be revisited within a fiscal year. For example, due to a sudden increase in fuel prices, the cost of team travel may rise significantly. Realistically, an athletics department cannot decide to play fewer away games in the middle of a season if the cost of travel increases because the athletics program has already signed legal contracts to play these games. Therefore, it may be necessary to reallocate funds toward team travel and away from other areas, such as equipment purchasing or cell phone service. In another example, perhaps one sports team has an unexpected level of success that leads to higher attendance and an increase in ticket sales revenue. An athletics director may reward that team by taking the additional revenue and allowing the coach to spend more in areas such as student-athlete recruitment or team meals.

Conclusion

This chapter has focused on budget and budget management in intercollegiate athletics and recreation. In addition to ongoing responsibilities for the financial integrity of their programs, athletics and recreation directors face a myriad of future financial challenges. Many campuses are in need of substantial capital investment in facilities, field space, and equipment. How will these capital projects be funded? One option is to rely on debt that will be repaid by future revenues or donations; another option for public institutions is to seek state support. Regardless of the funding source, many universities must invest millions of dollars in their recreation facilities and programs to attract the top prospective students.

All intercollegiate athletics and recreation programs face the financial challenges of being in compliance with Title IX. Administrators must analyze the gender-equity implications that occur with the allocation of funds. Failure to comply with Title IX can result in the university spending substantial resources on litigation and legal services. In addition, administrators have a moral obligation to comply with the spirit of Title IX.

For major NCAA Division I institutions, costs in areas such as coaching salaries and capital improvements are spiraling upward. Athletics administrators must decide whether they will continue to pay competitive salaries for football and basketball coaches in an effort to obtain the top talent. Failure to do so may affect the quality of these programs and the corresponding revenue.

Another issue facing athletics programs is the so-called "facilities arms race." To be competitive, many schools have invested, or need to invest, hundreds of millions of dollars in stadiums and arenas. Many critics of intercollegiate athletics oppose these investments and have cited the need for these funds to be used in other areas of the university such as research laboratories and classrooms. However, as with coaching salaries, failure to invest in these athletics facilities may leave the athletics program at a competitive disadvantage that may have an adverse effect on revenue generation.

In closing, it is an exciting time for intercollegiate athletics and recreation on most college and university campuses. These units play an important role in the quality of the student experience and in the marketing and publicizing of most universities, regardless of their size or association affiliation. For an athletics or recreation director to be professionally successful, he or she must have a thorough understanding of the financial and budgetary issues that are faced. In the future, one would expect to see more administrators in college athletics and recreation who have a background in finance and budgeting, along with a strong understanding of the collegiate landscape.

Chapter Nine Key Points

1. Financial management is the process of implementing and managing financial control systems, collecting and analyzing financial data, and making sound financial decisions based on these analyses (Brown, Rascher, Nagel, and McEvoy, 2010).
2. A budget is a financial plan that projects expected income and expenses for an organization (Fried, Shapiro, and DeSchriver, 2008).
3. There are two primary types of financial budgets that are prevalent within college athletics and recreation programs: operating and capital. An operating budget reflects income from all sources and expenses in all categories as they relate to operations of the organization (Barr and McClellan, 2011). Capital budgets project the sources and uses of funding for capital projects (usually the construction or renovation of physical spaces or the purchase of major pieces of equipment).
4. Common approaches to budgeting include zero-based budgeting, incremental budgeting, and cost-center budgeting.
5. The basic elements of a budget are income and expenses.
6. Major sources of income for athletics programs include state and public funding, ticket sales, fundraising and development, conferences and

associations, university subsidies, student fees, and corporate partnerships and advertising. Salaries and benefits and grants-in-aid are common categories of significant expense.

7. Major sources of income for recreation programs include student fees, membership or user fees, and corporate partnerships and advertising. Salaries and benefits, facility costs, and equipment are common categories of significant expense.
8. Developing budgets should be an inclusive process, and managing budgets should be an ongoing one.

References

Barr, M. J., and McClellan, G. S. *Budgets and Financial Management in Higher Education.* San Francisco: Jossey-Bass, 2011.

Berkowitz, S., Upton, J., McCarthy, M., and Gilliam, J. "How Student Fees Boost College Sports Amid Rising Budgets." *USA Today,* September 22, 2010. Retrieved December 15, 2010 at http://usatoday.com/sports/college/2010–09–21-student-fees-boost-college-sports˙N.htm.

Brown, M. T., Rascher, D. A., Nagel, M. S., and McEvoy, C. D. *Financial Management in the Sport Industry.* Holcomb Hathaway Publishers, Scottsdale, AZ, 2010.

"Compensation for Division I Men's Basketball Coaches." *USA Today,* 2010. Accessed December 20, 2010 at http://i.usatoday.net/sports/graphics/basketball˙contracts/2010/flash.swf.

Fried, G., Shapiro, S. J., and DeSchriver, T. D. *Sport Finance* (2nd ed.). Champaign, IL: Human Kinetics Publishing, 2008.

Fulks, D. L. *2004–2009 NCAA Revenues and Expenses of Division I Intercollegiate Athletics Programs.* Indianapolis, IN: National Collegiate Athletic Association, 2009.

Fulks, D. L. *2002–2003 NCAA Revenues and Expenses of Division I and II Intercollegiate Athletics Programs.* Indianapolis, IN: National Collegiate Athletic Association, 2004.

Juliano, J. "Penn State to Announce New Seat-Pricing Plan." *Philadelphia Inquirer,* November 18, 2009. Retrieved December 3, 2010 at http://www.philly.com/inquirer/sports/20091118˙Penn˙State˙to˙announce˙new-seat-pricing˙plan.html on December 3, 2010.

"Ohio Stadium Club Seating Program." Ohio State University, 2011. Accessed May 14, 2011 at http://www.ohiostatebuckeyes.com/ViewArticle.dbml?SPSID=90798&SPID=10402&DB˙OEM˙ID=17300&ATCLID=925254.

"Revised Budget for Fiscal Year Ended August 31, 2011." National Collegiate Athletic Association, 2011. Accessed May 14, 2011 at http://www.ncaa.org/wps/wcm/connect/6d3874004e51aadc96e0d622cf56f2f3/2009–10+Budget+Breakdown˙ALL.pdf?MOD=AJPERES&CACHEID=6d3874004e51aadc96e0d622cf56f2f3.

Steinbach, P. "New Details Surface About Minnesota's $35 Million Naming Rights Deal." *Athletic Business,* October 1, 2006. Accessed May 14, 2011 at http://athleticbusiness.com/articles/article.aspx?articleid=1286&l;zoneid=34.

Stocum, D. L., and Rooney, P. M. "Responding to Resource Constraints: A Departmentally Based System or Responsibility Centered Management." *Change*, 1997, 29(5).

U.S. Department of Education. *The Equity in Athletics Data Cutting Tool.* Washington, DC: U.S. Department of Education, 2010. Accessed December 15, 2010 at http://ope.ed.gov/athletics.

CHAPTER TEN

PLANNING AND MANAGING FACILITIES

James E. Greenwell

Facilities are often the defining characteristics of prestigious collegiate athletics and recreation programs at colleges and universities across the country. One aspect of what many refer to as the arms race in college athletics is the investment of millions of dollars to continuously upgrade facilities in order to keep up with the competition. The same rings true for recreation, as universities find themselves competing for the interest of students to boost enrollment, whether that boost is in the quantity or quality of their students, or both.

In college athletics, nothing demonstrates a program's commitment to their future more than their facilities and their plans to improve their facilities. A college athletics program's facility situation is often a very important factor in the recruitment process for potential student-athletes as well as coaches. This is not just limited to the facilities used for competition. Ancillary facilities, such as weight rooms, sports medicine areas, academic centers, and student-athlete lounges have also become important to the prospective student-athlete. It is not unheard of in today's world of college sports for the wealthiest programs to include hot tubs, luxurious lounges, and big-screen televisions in their facilities.

In recreation, the buzz words seem to be *variety* and *options*. The model for older facilities provided students with a weight room, basketball court, and racquetball courts—spaces suitable for traditional activities. Modern facilities include spaces for traditional activities, but also offer spaces for a wide variety of contemporary programming, including yoga, swimming, and dance. It is not uncommon to see modern recreation facilities outfitted with climbing walls and ropes courses as well. Facility planners really do try to have something for everyone, since colleges are typically trying to recruit a diverse student population.

In this chapter, the planning and management of collegiate athletics and recreation facilities is closely examined. In addition to process, this chapter discusses current trends and problem-solving methods that may be used as a planning tool or to augment planning tools already in place. By the end of the chapter, the reader will be familiar with facility planning, development, and management for collegiate athletics and recreation.

Planning Facilities

Planning, which can be defined as preparing a sequence of actions to achieve a specific goal, is one of the most important project management techniques. If done effectively, it can reduce much of the necessary time and effort of achieving the goal. Improper or inadequate planning all too easily and too often leads a manager to spending too much time on deciding what to do next or taking too many unnecessary, unfocused, and inefficient steps.

A plan is like a map. When following a plan, one can always see how much progress toward the projected goal has been made and how far there still is to go. Knowing where one wants to go and where one is currently is essential for making good decisions on where to go or what to do next. Planning is important in guiding progress from step to step, but it is also crucial for meeting needs during each action step related to time, funding, or other resources. With careful planning, it is easy to see whether, at some point, the project is likely to face a problem. It is much easier to adjust the plan to avoid or lessen a coming crisis rather than to deal with the crisis when it comes unexpectedly.

Facility Master Planning Process

A facility master plan is a strategic document that provides a framework for the orderly physical facility growth of an organization. Developing a long range facility master plan is the key to successful facility development. This process requires careful thought and consideration. Master planners must avoid making decisions in a vacuum.

The master planning process may begin without any consultants involved. One way of starting this effort is to appoint an internal master planning committee. This committee is charged to conduct an assessment of the current facility inventory available to their organization. The master planning committee would then compare the current facility inventory with the goals set forth in their strategic plan and gain an understanding of whether or not the current inventory of facilities can help facilitate the goals. If the facilities cannot do that, it is important that the gaps are identified and solutions created by way of new construction, renovations, or a combination thereof; this, in effect, is the initial master plan.

Facility Program Statement

The facility program statement provides everyone involved with the facility planning process a clear list of space needs for a facility project (Price, 2009). The facility program statement is a jumping off point, if one will, for the design concept for the facility project. Although the typical facility program statement is pretty thorough, part of the design team's responsibilities is to validate the program. During the program validation, the design team will ask questions that reveal and confirm the volume, size, and unique characteristics for space needs. For instance, if a standard exists for office size for administrative positions, this is where that standard needs to be discussed.

Another important factor is the space adjacency requirements. Space adjacency refers to the relationship between spaces and those who will occupy the spaces and how to ensure that all can work together efficiently. Whether the project is a renovation, new construction, or master plan, the facility program statement is a critical component of the planning.

New Construction, Renovation, or Combination

During the planning process, a thorough assessment of current facility inventory is crucial. The assessment will play a key role in helping to determine what projects will be required to meet the programmatic needs. Projects may include construction of a new facility, renovation of an existing facility, or a combination thereof.

While financial factors often determine which delivery method will be planned, there are other considerations. If an existing facility is not meeting programmatic requirements, a renovation may be used. There are circumstances in which renovation projects may not be cost effective, due to a number of reasons, including hazardous material abatement, structural integrity, and land constraints. However, one may also need to consider the historical value of an existing facility or the process required to demolish an existing facility. If the historical value makes up for the difference in project costs or if the process required approving demolition is too lengthy or risky, a renovation project may be the solution.

This is a particularly important part in the urban campus planning process. Urban planning can be much more complicated because of the greater possibility that land for building facilities will be unavailable, or what little land is available may be priced at a premium. In addition, there is a high probability in an urban setting that a project, whether it is new construction or a renovation, will impact facilities adjacent to the project. These considerations must be taken into account in planning project logistics. Urban projects are much more likely to require extensive permitting processes for logistics, utility work, and other site considerations.

Choosing the Right Design Team

The first step in organizing an effective design team is to appoint an internal project planning committee. This committee may be made up of membership that is specific to the key stakeholders. For instance, there are typically team members from the athletics or recreation department, which constitutes the end user, as well as some representation from the campus facilities department or design and construction department, or both. This team of individuals is who the contractors or design or construction teams would refer to as "the owner." The design team is composed of the project planning committee and the architectural and engineering (A&E) services acquired. Both the project planning committee and the A&E services will likely bring subject matter experts into the project planning process as needed. These experts may be coaches, facility managers, or other staff. An easy example to refer to is building a field, whether it is for recreation use, or athletic use, or both. The project planning committee will rely on involvement from the turf management professionals employed by the university. Also, the A&E services will involve an in-house or contracted turf management expert to assist in making sure the project is designed to meet the needs as set forth by the program.

There are many other consultants available for projects. These include those that specialize in lighting, seating, furniture, finishes, performance surfaces, equipment, solar studies, audio/visual, landscaping and many other disciplines.

Leadership in Energy and Environmental Design

Another area that requires special assistance in project planning that has gained traction in recent years is for sustainability. *Sustainability* really means the capacity to endure. When using this term in the sense of building or renovating facilities, it refers to the practice of designing projects that are environmentally friendly. Architects and engineers approach this with the concepts of leadership in energy and environmental design (LEED) at their disposal. These design considerations may be as simple as designing an energy efficient building, recycling waste on the project, or building green roofs. There are many LEED considerations that might be adopted for a project; however, the project budget often determines how many of these concepts become part of the actual project design.

Common Errors in Facility Planning

Anyone who has been involved in facility planning and development understands that errors are common during the planning and development process. While the primary goal of the project is to deliver a facility that meets the goals set forth by the planning committee, it is also important to minimize mistakes, as they typically result in added expense. Table 10.1 notes some common errors in athletics and recreation projects.

What facility considerations are included in facility projects may determine how the facility needs to be managed moving forward. Regardless of what happens in the facility planning process, management of facilities requires as much careful planning as the process to develop them.

Managing Facilities

Managing facilities is an important function for any business. Facilities impact an organization's productivity, efficiency and health, and welfare. The consequences of poorly managed facilities may be catastrophic. The following ten disciplines are essential to consider when building a plan to manage facilities:

- Planning and organization
- Policies and procedures
- Staffing
- Scheduling

TABLE 10.1. COMMON ERRORS IN FACILITY PLANNING PROCESS

1. Failure to provide adequate storage spaces
2. Failure to provide adequate and appropriate accommodations for people with disabilities throughout the facility
3. Failure to provide adequate janitorial spaces
4. Failure to observe desirable current professional standards
5. Failure to build facility large enough to accommodate future uses
6. Failure to provide adequate locker and dressing areas for both male and female users
7. Failure to construct shower, toilet, and dressing rooms with sufficient floor slope and properly located drains
8. Failure to provide doorways, hallways, or ramps so that equipment may be moved easily
9. Failure to provide for multiple uses
10. Failure to plan for adequate parking for the facility
11. Failure to plan for adequate space for concessions and merchandising
12. Failure to plan for adequate supervision of the various activity spaces within the facility
13. Failure to plan for potential delivery pitfalls (i.e., permitting, inspections and weather delays)
14. Failure to provide for adequate lobby space for spectators
15. Failure to provide for an adequate space for the media to observe activities as well as to interview performers
16. Failure to provide for adequate ticket sales areas
17. Failure to provide adequate space for a loading dock and parking for tractor trailers and buses
18. Failure to provide adequate numbers of restroom facilities for female spectators
19. Failure to provide adequate security and access control into the facility and within the facility
20. Failure to provide adequate separation between activities (buffer or safety zones) in a multipurpose space
21. Failure to provide padding on walls close to activity area, padding and/or covers for short fences, on goal posts, and around trees
22. Failure to plan for the next 50 years
23. Failure to plan for maintenance of the facility
24. Failure to provide an adequate financial plan for the project
25. Failure to plan to plan

- Revenue generation
- Risk management
- Alcohol management
- Emergency management
- Facility maintenance
- Custodial and landscape services

Planning and Organization

Just as planning is needed for development of facilities, it is just as critical in the management of facilities. Whether the facility is new or an existing facility, it is important to take an organized approach to managing all facility processes. While an organization's strategic plan will set the direction of the work, managing facilities must take into account every aspect of the use of the facility and every possible scenario that may be presented to the building's operations, including normal everyday use, special events, inclement weather, crime, terrorist acts, power outages, and other area events in order to give the facility users the best chance for a positive experience.

Policies and Procedures

One of the courses of action mentioned earlier is the development of policies and procedures for managing facilities. Most successful organizations use policies and procedures to guide their business practices. Facility management policies are used to manage risk, events, daily use, crisis management, emergency management and all business conducted for the facility by those employed by the university. Policies and procedures also help facility managers create an environment of accountability for their employees and users. While the reasons for employee accountability are obvious, users must be held accountable for their membership agreement, damage to the facility as a result of their use, adherence to rules and regulations prescribed by local authorities, and any other applicable policies.

Staffing

Staffing is essential to managing a facility. An insufficient staffing model may lead to poor operations, lack of customer satisfaction, and ineffective maintenance practices. When building a staffing model all of the operations that may be held in the facility must be clearly identified. A dynamic management team is essential to implement everything needed to manage a facility. Depending on the program elements, the management team must hire qualified personnel for business, planning, maintenance, custodial support, clerical support, and security. There are often needs that require considerations for staffing, either internal or contracted, for audio/visual support, information technology support, and contract administration. See Chapter Eight for an extensive discussion of managing staff.

Scheduling

Effective scheduling is a distinguishing characteristic of a successful facility management operation. Facility scheduling is a layered issue that requires careful thought and collaboration. The facility schedule must meet the needs of the users. For instance, for an athletics facility, the manager must determine when the building must be open to accommodate practices, workouts, academic support, meetings, competitions, special events, and maintenance. A typical facility management approach will establish day-to-day hours, or normal business hours, and then extend those hours when required to do so for events that are scheduled outside of the normal business hours.

Recreation facilities are less likely to require extended hours, however, their normal business hours may present the operation with a longer work day. For instance, the scheduling considerations for a recreation facility will be based on student, faculty, and staff needs, as well as programmatic needs for the broad range of recreation offerings as outlined in the program statement. In a modern campus setting, where classes are offered to a wide variety of students, the recreation center hours may begin as early as 7:00 A.M. and remain open until midnight to accommodate the users.

Scheduling facilities in a campus environment must be a community effort, whether the facility is used by the athletics or recreation departments. Campus facilities typically have a civic responsibility to support the campus needs in addition to the specific needs of the operator and the users. There are typically many other facilities on a campus hosting activities; therefore, a campuswide scheduling effort is essential for the overall success of a facility. Facility managers may encounter very embarrassing and cumbersome problems when they host events that conflict with those being held in adjacent facilities. The traffic and parking issues may result in an overall poor experience for those attending; thus, it is crucial to make sure the lines of communication are open with other facility managers in a campus environment. It is also good to establish a campus committee for scheduling events, if one does not exist, to give anyone who may host events the ability to maximize the success of the event through collaboration.

Revenue Generation

Revenue generation is part of most facility business models. This has become particularly important these days with the tough economic times. Facility managers are being pressed to reduce costs and increase revenues as a means of survival (Barr and McClellan, 2011). There are many components to revenue generation, including booking revenue-generating events, hosting camps and clinics, and managing retail operations, food and beverage services, equipment rental, and memberships and sponsorships.

From an athletics standpoint, revenue generation is a departmental wide function rather than a facility specific effort. For the purposes of this chapter, athletics facility specific revenue opportunities will be discussed.

Booking special events is a challenge in modern athletics facilities, particularly if adequate practice facilities are not readily available. The demands that intercollegiate athletics places on facilities to be available for practices, workouts, and competitions are great. When there is room for a special event, it is important that the act is carefully considered to maximize the potential revenue for the event without compromising the university's goals. There are many ways to approach hosting a special event. The easiest approach is to offer the venue as is, with essential staff, under a flat rate for rental. Any expenses incurred beyond the basic rental agreement will be included in the contract. This puts the burden of planning, promoting, and staffing the entire event on the promoter or event organizers. Alternatively, if substantial ticket sales are projected, the contract may be structured to ensure the facility a percentage of those sales. Other sources of revenue from special events include merchandise sales, food and beverage service, and parking. Again, the most profitable situation for the venue is to be flexible to structure the deal that guarantees the best revenue possibility and minimize financial risk.

Athletics facilities also drive revenue from the competitions hosted within them. For instance, a basketball arena will have revenues available from ticket sales, annual giving related to premium ticket sales, suites, merchandise sales, food and beverage service, and parking.

It is also important to secure sponsorship dollars through signage inventory and premium seating packages. There are many ways to group these packages together to provide sponsorships with a great fulfillment experience. Typically, the inventory will include a combination of courtside advertising signs, banners, message board signs, in-game video spots, and announcements. These items go along with premium seating or hospitality to round out the fulfillment for a sponsor. In most cases, sponsors also group their sponsorship package, a portion of it being cash and a portion being trade of some sort of valuable service or product.

In recreation facilities, memberships are often a large part of the revenue. A community recreation facility will likely have their business model largely based on membership revenue. In a campus environment, student fees are usually a large funding source for the recreation facility; therefore, no financial exchange takes place between the student user and the facility, although a membership is maintained. A campus recreation facility may target faculty, staff, and alumni for memberships, and this is also a good way to provide for social interaction among students, faculty, staff and alumni.

Recreation facilities also conduct special events, although they may be more inclined to host community recreation activities as special events. Another popular special event may be an intramural tournament. Recreation facilities are also equipped to host camps and clinics for a variety of sports, depending on the compatibility of the facility. Many recreation facilities offer users a variety of food and beverage selections that produce revenue as well. These selections are often healthier choices to stay in line with the general theme of the facility. There is still quite a lucrative market for healthy foods and beverages. Recreation facilities also rent equipment in many cases. Whether the equipment is to be used in the commission of the activity on site or off site, this may be a way to generate additional revenue. For instance, equipment such as towels, yoga mats, sports equipment, or camping gear may be rented.

Camps and clinics are a good source of revenue for athletics or recreation facilities during what is generally known to be slower scheduling periods. Specifically, during the summer months, many athletics coaches like to offer summer camps as a means to generate additional income and give youth sports participants an opportunity to see campus facilities. While camps and clinics do not yield a financial windfall, they may provide athletics and recreation facilities with a steady source of revenue during the summer months. In addition to using the facilities, campers will also need to be fed and, in some cases, housed for their camps.

Risk Management in Facility Management

Risk management requires facility managers to identify, assess, and prioritize exposure for their organization. As the assessment of potential risk develops, it is important to develop and implement risk management policies and procedures. The risk may be theft or vandalism of property, personal injury in the facility, or some catastrophic event outside the facility that threatens the lives of those inside. In some cases, preventive measures can be implemented to minimize risk. For instance, systems to secure equipment, cameras, and thorough physical checks are likely to prevent most cases of theft. When the circumstances are completely out of the manager's hands, such as inclement weather, every effort must be made to implement a crisis management and emergency management plan to ensure the safety of everyone in the facility. Having effective response plans in place will minimize the risk and exposure an organization has, but not avoid the risk it altogether.

Alcohol Management

Alcohol management has become an important strategy for athletics facilities. Although collegiate athletics facilities are not permitted to serve alcohol for public consumption for NCAA Championship events, many institutions are serving alcohol to boost revenues during regular season events. Also, tailgating is a time honored tradition for many outdoor venues, especially football stadiums. Campuses often have policies against public consumption of alcohol but relax these rules to allow for tailgating. While it is nearly impossible to properly manage alcohol use in a tailgating environment, it is essential for facility managers to reduce exposure to risk by having mechanisms in place to monitor alcohol sales and consumption in facilities. There are many models to learn from for monitoring alcohol at athletics events. Professional venues seem to be doing well in establishing best practices. A facility manager would be best prepared by looking at what professional venues do and work closely with their law enforcement agency and their alcohol vender to develop an aggressive approach to monitoring the sale and consumption of alcohol.

Underage consumption is a particularly common problem in college campuses. Forming a partnership with the campus Dean of Students Office is a powerful tool in dealing with student violations of alcohol policies. The consequences are usually fair and swift when the Dean of Students Office is involved. At the end of the day, the facility manager must use every resource available to reduce the risk involved with alcohol sales and use.

Emergency Management

An effective emergency management plan requires careful collaboration with local law enforcement and emergency management personnel. Regardless of the emergency, the key to a successful response is to secure the ability for selected leadership to gather and understand clearly what resources they have access to. A facility manager would be smart to invite local first responders to their facility for tours as often as possible. Having first responders familiar with the facility is critical to a speedy response. It is important to work with local law enforcement and emergency management personnel to identify a communications protocol, medical support, law enforcement support, and information management.

The communications protocol established must secure clear communications between all critical personnel. It is also important to identify primary and secondary locations for headquarters, where face-to-face communication can take place among the leadership team. Lastly, it is important to establish how decision making will be conducted. With several organizations having much to risk under these circumstances, it is vital that an appropriate decision-making process be established and that those decisions can be made by well-informed individuals.

Medical support is crucial in emergency management. Again, it is invaluable to allow first responders access to the facility so they are familiar. It is also important to establish predetermined locations for triage and airlift operations. Local medical response professionals appreciate it when facility managers show the initiative to work with them to establish these protocols in advance.

Law enforcement support is important in dealing with any threat. In cases where there is an act of violence, such as a crime or terrorism, law enforcement officials will coordinate their resources to deal with the threat appropriately. A facility manager should provide assistance with those efforts only when asked to do so. When it comes to matters involving law enforcement and emergency response, local authorities must handle those situations carefully, and they are typically not shy about asking for whatever they need to deal with the threat. Once the threat has been resolved, law enforcement officials will work closely with the facility manager to determine when it is safe to return the facility.

Information management during an emergency is an important function of the leadership element. Universities employ public information officers, and the individual in this capacity will normally be the voice of the emergency response. Information officers from the law enforcement agency and leadership from the facility will coordinate the information efforts appropriately. It is very important to keep the media informed. Once media personnel begin to show up to cover the story, it is crucial to inform them when and where press conferences will be conducted and when and where essential personnel will be made available to answer questions.

Long-term viability as a facility operation may be enhanced with a continuity of operations plan. Continuity of operations is an organization's plan to secure vital data backup at a remote site and also provide their staff with a remote site to work from in the case of a catastrophic event. This plan enables the operation to continue working during the disaster. This practice also enhances the facility's ability to recover quicker from the catastrophic event. Please note that it is obviously not feasible for an athletics or recreation facility to function in a manner that supports their core mission during these times. The continuity of operations plan merely enables the staff to work efficiently, in a remote location away from danger to recover quickly and this plan also ensures only a minimal loss in data, if any at all. The data may include membership information, scheduling information, financials, and other business information.

Plans of any sort are best seen as evolving rather than static frameworks, and this is certainly true for emergency management plans. Practice drills help prepare facilities staff for emergencies, and they also provide the opportunity to evaluate the plan—identify both its strengths and challenges. Responding to the discovery of these strengths and weaknesses is one reason for facilities staff to make adjustments in their emergency plan. Other reasons for such updates include changes in features of the facility, changes in mission or audiences served, or changes in applicable insurance requirements or law.

Facility Maintenance

Building an effective maintenance plan is one of the most important functions a facility manager has. An effective maintenance plan should have preventive maintenance, repairs, and deferred maintenance (McClellan and Barr, 2000). All maintenance activities should be documented in order to understand the costs involved; the frequency in which maintenance is needed and preventive maintenance schedules only work if they are documented properly.

A *preventive maintenance* plan is when work is conducted on a schedule before the need has become critical. An example is servicing an emergency generator. The idea of an emergency generator is to be certain it works when a facility loses power. The emergency generator provides enough power for emergency lighting to work and ensure safe egress from the facility. A facility manger jeopardizes the ability to have the function of the emergency generator if it is not properly maintained. Other examples of preventive maintenance are when public access areas are repainted or carpet is replaced periodically. These activities are scheduled to take place in order to keep a high-standard image in these areas, not when the carpet is tattered and falling apart.

Repairs are conducted when something is broken in the facility; for instance, when light bulbs go out, ceiling tiles break, water fountains malfunction, or toilets to do not work properly. These items are typically reported through a work order process that begins a file for the work. The file is closed when the repair is completed and all associated costs, including labor and parts, are recorded. Facility managers must use the information obtained in the records of preventive maintenance and repairs to accurately build their maintenance budget.

Deferred maintenance refers to the practice of opting out of immediate action on a maintenance concern. A deferred maintenance list often contains projects that are needed but lack the funding mechanism to make the repair in a timely manner. It is important to have strict guidelines for deferred maintenance projects. For instance, ensure there is a maximum time limit for maintenance projects to remain on the deferred list. This will help avoid long term neglect that may lead to more serious problems. If proper maintenance is not conducted for facilities, they will crumble beneath the users' feet. As a general rule, deferred maintenance should be avoided because it can put people and facilities at risk.

Custodial and Landscape Services

Custodial services and landscape services are also vital components to a maintenance plan. Although many believe these services only add aesthetics value to a facility, they often have a health and welfare impact. If custodial staff does not clean or if they improperly clean a facility, they may aid in the spread of bacteria and sickness. Also, poorly kept grounds may contribute to an infestation of rodents, insects, or other wildlife that carry disease.

Conclusion

Facility planning and management is one of the most dynamic professional specializations in the broad field of intercollegiate athletics and recreation management. As this chapter demonstrates, professionals in facility management have a wide variety of responsibilities requiring an equally broad knowledge and skill set.

The common theme in nearly every section of this chapter is planning. Being a good facility manager requires planning. From the first moment a facility concept is an idea to the moment the doors are opened, the layers of planning required are substantial. If the planning process is not conducted thoroughly during any step of the facility planning or management process, the consequences are potentially catastrophic. Obviously there are checks and balances during the facility development process that will not allow an unsafe building to be built; however, a safe building does little good if the proper emergency management procedures are not developed and implemented. With customer satisfaction never being more important than now because of the competitive market, it is critical that facility managers develop and manage facilities through proper planning.

Chapter Ten Key Points

1. Facilities are often the defining characteristics of prestigious collegiate athletics and recreation programs at colleges and universities across the country.
2. Planning, which can be defined as preparing a sequence of actions to achieve a specific goal, is one of the most important project management techniques. Projects may include construction of a new facility, renovation of an existing facility, or a combination thereof.
3. A facility master plan is a strategic document that provides a framework for the orderly physical facility growth of an organization, and the facility program statement provides everyone involved with the facility planning process with a clear list of space needs for a facility project (Price, 2009).
4. Planning and organization, policies and procedures, staffing, scheduling, revenue generation, risk management, alcohol management, emergency management, facility maintenance, and custodial and landscape services are all important considerations in facilities management.
5. Facility management policies are used to manage risk, events, daily use, crisis management, emergency management, and all business conducted for the facility by those employed by the university. Policies and procedures also help facility managers create an environment of accountability for their employees and users.
6. Scheduling facilities in a campus environment must be a community effort, whether the facility is used by the athletics or recreation departments.
7. There are many components to revenue generation, including booking revenue-generating events, hosting camps and clinics, and managing retail operations, food and beverage service, equipment rental, and memberships and sponsorships.

8. Building an effective maintenance plan is one of the most important functions a facility manager has. An effective maintenance plan should include preventive maintenance, repairs, and deferred maintenance (McClellan and Barr, 2000).

References

Barr, M. J., and McClellan, G. S. *Budgets and Financial Management in Higher Education.* San Francisco: Jossey-Bass, 2011.

McClellan, G. S., and Barr, M. J. "Planning, Managing, and Financing Facilities and Services." In M. J. Barr and M. K. Desler (Eds.), *The Handbook of Student Affairs Administration* (2nd ed.), pp. 197–215. San Francisco: Jossey-Bass, 2000.

Price, J. "Facilities Planning and Development." In G. S. McClellan and J. Stringer (Eds.), *The Handbook of Student Affairs Administration* (3rd ed.). San Francisco: Jossey-Bass, 2009.

CHAPTER ELEVEN

MANAGING EVENTS

Heather J. Lawrence

Intercollegiate athletics and recreation events in colleges and universities can take many forms, including competitive intercollegiate athletics, intramurals, student organization fundraising tournaments, and special events such as midnight madness and spring football games. Events serve a variety of purposes within higher education, but one of the main themes is that events bring people together who share a common interest. Intercollegiate athletics and recreation managers can achieve a range of organizational goals through the successful execution of events. However, putting on successful events requires a strategic approach with substantial time and effort involved in all phases of the planning process. This chapter serves to describe the variety of sport and recreation events that occur on college and university campuses, discuss the purpose of such events, provide information on the role of the event manager, and offer a sequential guide to planning and organizing events.

Types of Events

Intercollegiate athletics and recreation events can be categorized into two main types: non–revenue driven and revenue driven. Non–revenue driven events encompass the bulk of sport and recreation events on a college campus, including intramurals, club sports, and many regular season intercollegiate athletics events. Although it is certainly possible to realize financial gain from these events through entry fees, concessions, or tickets, revenue is not a central focus to their operations. Conversely, revenue driven events are easy to spot because the operational focus is centered on generating revenue. Ticket sales, sponsorships, concessions, merchandise, and even television are common revenue streams for these events. The participants are still a critical element, but the experience of the spectator is a central focal point to event organizers. There must be a high level of interest in the participants and the outcome for an event to make a substantial amount of money. This interest might stem from a rivalry, an exceptional level of talent, a well-known participant, or it might just be that that sport is traditionally an event that spectators enjoy. Major intercollegiate athletics events fall into this category, such as conference and national tournaments, but even regular season football or basketball games at major institutions are revenue driven. Having a good understanding of the purpose of the event will help clarify whether the event is non–revenue or revenue driven.

The purpose of the event will determine much of the planning process. Is the purpose of a three-on-three basketball tournament to make money for a student organization? If so, the event organizers must consider how to best reach potential participants as well as how to strategically price the entry fee to attract a large number of teams. Is the purpose of hosting a National Collegiate Athletic Association (NCAA) Volleyball Regional to give the home team a competitive advantage in advancing to the NCAA Championship? If so, then attracting as many home fans as possible and creating a great atmosphere might be the most important aspect to event planning. Is the purpose of a golf scramble to expose members of the community to a renovated and updated campus golf course? If so, then attracting participants from the surrounding campus community and making their playing experience the best it can possibly be is critical. Common purposes of creating or hosting events in a college and university include:

- Following mandates by intercollegiate athletics rules and regulations
- Generating revenue
- Providing participation opportunities for students
- Fundraising for charity
- Aligning with the mission of the university, a student organization, or other campus organization
- Providing a competitive advantage by playing on the home court or field

- Highlighting the campus, organization, sport facility, or participants
- Enabling people to try a new activity
- Bringing people together for a common activity or cause

These examples provide a glimpse into the variety of purposes an event might have in sport and recreation on a college campus. The essential concept is that the event organizers identify the purpose of the event first and then set goals and objectives that align with the overall purpose.

The Event Manager

Event management merges together many skill sets possessed by sport and recreation professionals to produce an event. Marketing, sales, budgeting, ticketing, contract management, facility operations, parking management, customer service, risk management, and staffing are all important when planning sport and recreation events. In addition to the task-oriented skill sets an event manager must possess, an understanding of how to lead and manage people, how to effectively communicate with diverse groups, and how to navigate campus politics is important. This all must be done while also being organized and flexible. Someone working exclusively on planning a large event might be dressed in a business suit at an 8:00 A.M. sponsor meeting, in khaki pants and a polo shirt crawling around under tables ensuring there are enough power outlets at 10:00 A.M., and then back in a business suit at noon for a lunch meeting with the college or university communications department to establish an event-marketing strategy. Because of the variety associated with managing events, it is an exciting profession in which no two days are exactly the same.

The Event Management Process

When someone is asked to manage or create an event, it can seem like a daunting challenge. However, the creation of an event can be broken down into three distinct and manageable phases: event conceptualization, event development, and event execution (Lawrence and Wells, 2009). Using a phased process will help event managers ensure that the major event components have been taken into consideration from start to finish.

Event Conceptualization

Event conceptualization is the first phase of the process. During this phase, the idea of the event and its purpose are tested and the infrastructure to support the event is put into place. Before any real planning can take place, the event manager must evaluate whether a rights holder owns the event, there is a bid process to host the event, and a sanction is needed.

Rights Holders. Most established events have a rights holder, which is defined as "organizations or businesses that control and own the rights to an event" (Lawrence, Yiamouyiannis, and Wells, 2009, p. 7). In a college or university setting, the institution might be the rights holder. If the event is being brought in from elsewhere, another entity is probably the rights holder. For example, the Warrior Dash is a relatively new event that combines running and an obstacle course (climbing walls, running through mud, and climbing steep hills). The event is organized and owned by Red Frog Events Production, and a student group could not host a Warrior Dash without working with Red Frog Events Production. As the rights holder, it is likely that Red Frog Events Production would set the rules, the course, and the fees; limit the types of merchandise for sale; and generate much of the revenue.

Sometimes the rights holder is also a specific sport governing body. Governing bodies set rules, establish championships, certify officials, and provide structure to sports and their associated events. The National Football League (NFL), the Amateur Athletic Union, Inc. (AAU), and USA Track and Field are all governing bodies, and thus rights holders, with very different missions. Whether the rights holder is a business, a broad-reaching youth governing body, a collegiate governing body, or a professional sport governing body—event managers must be aware of who the rights holder of the event is early in the planning process. A rights holder will not be involved if a new event is being created, thus allowing event managers much more flexibility and freedom in planning as well as the ability to retain more revenue.

Bidding. Rights holders often use a bid process to ensure that the best site is chosen for their premier events. Major events, such as a national collegiate championship, will probably require a competitive bid process. From the perspective of the rights holder, a bid system helps compare possible host sites on key criteria related to the integrity of the event, the experience for the athletes, and potential revenue generation. From the perspective of the bidding site, the process requires the potential host to examine the key components of hosting the event and weigh the costs, benefits, and challenges associated with bidding and hosting. Not all events with a rights holder require a bid. Sometimes all that is needed is for the event managers to contact the rights holder and request permission to host an event using the established rules and guidelines of the rights holder.

Sanctions. Another consideration is the sanctioning of the event. Whether there is a bid process or not, many rights holders require their events to be sanctioned. It is commonly accepted an event sanction is the approval from the rights holder to the event host to hold the event. There is usually a cost associated with the sanction, but a sanction allows the host to call the event "officially sanctioned," qualifies an event for inclusion in a larger tournament or competition system, or both. For example, anyone can create and host a soccer tournament on a college campus. However, for the soccer tournament to be a qualifier for the National Campus Championship Series (NCCS), the tournament must be recognized by the National Intramural—Recreation Sports Association (NIRSA) as a Regional Qualifying Tournament and sanctioned. This sanction allows for the NIRSA name to be used in the tournament title, recognizes the tournament as a qualifier, requires that all the NIRSA rules will be followed, and provides that the qualifying teams will advance to the NCCS National Soccer Championships. Other aspects to a sanction sometimes include insurance for the participating athletes, as well as the event organizers, standards for measuring the length of courses (i.e., cycling, swimming, running), and standards for the education of game officials. Once the event organizers understand who the rights holder is, whether there is a bid process to host the event, and if a sanction is needed, they can move on to examining the feasibility of the event.

Feasibility. The feasibility process ensures that if the event occurs it will meet the purpose, goals, and objectives of the organization. Examining the needs of the event should be done early to ensure that everything that is needed is available to run the event. Specifically, the following areas (depending upon the purpose of the event) should be evaluated:

- Institutional support (financial, human, and general)
- Needs and availability of facilities and equipment
- Agreements, permissions, or contracts needed
- Spectator and participant interest

- Competing events in the area
- Needs and availability of lodging
- Needs and availability of transportation
- Needs and availability of staffing
- Media interest
- Sponsor interest
- Security needs

Once these areas are evaluated, a decision can be made whether or not to move forward with the event. If it is decided to proceed with the event, the next step is to put infrastructure in place to support the rest of the planning process. Each institution has its own policies and procedures associated with the use of facilities, so event managers must conduct their own research to ensure that appropriate protocols are followed for their campus. This includes agreements and permissions between college or university departments, as well as contracts with outside organizations or people. For example, some institutions will allow any group associated with the college or university to use an area in the campus recreation center for no charge. Other institutions charge a fee, require a contract, and might even charge for use of equipment.

At this point in the planning process, thinking ahead and identifying event details that might become challenges later in planning can help to avoid problems further down the road. Something as seemingly insignificant as logo use could become a problem without proper planning. The uninformed event manager can run into big problems later if research is not conducted during this phase. The use of an institutional or athletics department logo to market the event might be allowable on one campus or for certain types of events but in other situations it might not be permissible. What would happen if a student organization printed 1,000 T-shirts with the university logo for a 5K fun run and did not have permission to use the logo? The group could lose $5,000 or more on one mistake.

By the end of the conceptualization phase, the event should have a facility secured, internal university agreements and external contracts should be executed, and the event manager should have an understanding of the tasks that lie ahead in the development stage.

Event Development

Once the conceptualization phase is completed and a decision has been made to move forward with the event, it is time to really get to work. During event development, the financial planning, marketing and sponsorship, ticketing and participant registration, and risk assessment takes place. For some event managers, this is a time in which they will need to rely on others with specific expertise to ensure comprehensive planning in each area. Delegating some of these tasks or having someone else double check the work will make certain that each aspect of development meets the needs of the event. For most events, a general checklist leading up to the event day (see Table 11.1) will help manage tasks. This list should indicate each major task, the person responsible, the goal date of completion, and the actual date of completion.

Budget. The event budget can be as simple or complex as the event itself. In higher education, event managers might find that the institution has certain guidelines and protocols for the development and management of the budget. First and foremost during financial planning is making sure that institutional policy is followed. If no guidance is provided by the institution, then a simple financial spreadsheet can meet the needs of the most event managers.

Event managers should start with a projected budget in which anticipated expected revenues and expenses are accounted for. A final budget with actual revenues and expenses will not be complete until after the event concludes, but a projected budget will allow the event manager to manage the budget throughout the process and adjust as necessary. Although all events will have different needs, Table 11.2 provides of the most common revenue and expense items associated with hosting events.

Many items show up on both the revenue and expense list because there is a cost associated with the item, yet there is also revenue potential. For example, food and supplies need to be purchased to provide concession items, but there is also expected revenue through the sale of concessions. It is clear that there are limited ways to generate revenue, yet almost unlimited ways to spend money.

While establishing the budget, event managers need to be aware of cash flow. For many events, revenues are not realized until the event day (such as event day ticket sales). In these cases, managing cash flow can be challenging. What can an event manager of a 5K race do when the event needs to purchase $1,000 in awards but is waiting for walk-up registrations for the majority of the revenue? In this case, if the event manager was aware of the need for $1,000 early in planning, maybe a cash sponsor could provide an early payment to cover the cost of awards. As this example demonstrates, the management of the budget can make or break the event. If

TABLE 11.1. GENERAL EVENT MANAGEMENT PLANNING LIST

Task	Person Responsible	Due Date	Complete
Bid submission			
Sanction event			
Reserve facility/facility contract			
Reserve equipment/order equipment			
Explore available institutional support (financial/in-kind)			
Secure event day staff			
Secure event day medical			
Secure event day security			
Establish parking plan/cost			
Secure officials			
Event/liability insurance			
Develop budget			
Produce marketing materials			
Create/purchase advertising			
Print tickets			
Develop website			
Develop participant registration system (technology, payment processing, waivers)			
Activate participant registration system			
Secure sponsors			
Fulfill sponsorships			
Order merchandise			
Order concessions product			
Order participant gifts			
Order awards			
Block hotel rooms			
Reserve transportation			
Order signage			
Plan ancillary event(s)			
Order office supplies			
Purchase staff/officials hospitality food/drink/decorations			
Purchase participant hospitality food/drink/decorations			
Prepare event day documents (timeline, checklists, fast facts, credentials)			
Physical set-up of all spaces (signage, parking, locker rooms, courses/courts/fields, hospitality, media)			
Test all equipment			
Pre-event staff meeting			
Prepare event day book (fast facts, timeline, checklists, phone lists, rule books, memos, contracts)			
Event wrap-up (debrief meeting, event file, incident reports, payroll, sponsor reports, thank you notes, pay bills, ticket/registration reports, final budget)			

Adapted from Miller, 2009.

TABLE 11.2. A GUIDE TO COMMON EVENT REVENUE AND EXPENSE ITEMS

Revenue Items	Expense Items
Participant registration/entry fees	Event bid fee
Ticket sales	Event sanction
Sponsorships	Staffing (event day and planning time)
Concessions	Medical support (EMTs/ambulance/ athletic trainers)
Merchandise	Facility rental
Parking	Equipment rental/purchase
Commission from hotels/rental car	Event/liability insurance
Television rights	Marketing materials
Ancillary events	Advertising
Grants, donations, institutional support	Ticket printing
	Credit card processing fees (ticketing)
	Website development/maintenance
	Sponsorship fulfillment
	Concessions purchases
	Merchandise purchases
	Participant gifts
	Awards
	Staff/officials hospitality
	Participant hospitality and/or banquet
	Transportation
	Lodging
	Communications equipment
	Event day signage
	Ancillary events
	Television broadcasting
	Office supplies
	Contingency (unplanned expenses)

Adapted from Wells, 2009.

awards are promised to the 5K participants, the awards better be there on race day! It is up to the event manager to predict, keep track of, manage, adjust, and finally to reconcile the budget.

Marketing. Marketing and sponsorship (discussed in the next section) are critical to the success of most events, and entire books are written on these topics. For the purposes of this chapter, some key points that event managers should consider are highlighted. Marketing an event can range from simple flyers posted around campus to in-depth multiyear marketing plans. Most events fall somewhere in between these two extremes, and the budget often dictates how much marketing is done for the event. The type of event marketing depends on the audience the event manager is trying to reach. Traditional forms have been tested over time for a variety of events and can be effective. Traditional marketing includes advertising in newspapers, on radio, on the Internet, on television, and through direct mailing campaigns. Some of these avenues can be expensive but they might not be the most effective for those in a college setting.

Promotions, publicity campaigns, guerilla marketing, and social media are all areas of which contemporary event managers should be aware. Promotional campaigns consist of special discounts and give-aways and are often tied into some form of traditional advertising. For example, an athletics department might purchase radio advertisements the day of each home match for the season. The radio station then gives away free tickets to the event on the day of each match. This type of arrangement combines advertising and additional event promotion and is a win-win for both the radio station (listeners might tune in for the possibility of winning tickets) and the event (additional publicity).

The term *publicity* is used when an event generates news coverage. Publicity is free for the event and can be a terrific way to get the word out to a wide audience. In cases when a star student-athlete is participating in the event, the event manager might arrange a press conference, resulting in articles about the participant and event. An event does not have to have a big-name player to capitalize on publicity, events that benefit charities or have human interest stories associated with them can also generate publicity.

Guerilla marketing (also called grassroots marketing) is when the marketing efforts are focused on a local and personal level of getting the word out. It can be very effective on a college or university campus, and common techniques include posting and handing out flyers, chalking sidewalks, and painting a graffiti wall (when allowed). This type of marketing reaches college or university students where they are and helps connect them to the event. Social media accomplishes some of the same things as guerilla marketing, except that technology is the medium used. It is no secret that Facebook, Twitter, Foursquare, and other developing social sites can help in marketing events. Social media allow event managers to make large groups of people aware of events quickly and for very little cost. Creating the appropriate marketing mix of the various strategies is up to the event manager and will be driven by the goals, objectives, and budget of the event.

Sponsorship. Along with marketing, sponsorship can vary greatly from one event to the next. Sport and recreation event managers have a few advantages over other marketers because many businesses want to be associated with the healthy active lifestyle promoted by these types of events. There are two basic types of sponsorships: cash and in-kind. Cash sponsorships provide the event money to help with operations. Conversely, in-kind sponsorships provide a good or service to the event resulting in less overall cost to the event.

Rarely will a company become aware of an event and seek to sponsor it. Instead, the event manager will have to research potential sponsors and then sell each sponsor on why they should partner with the event. Generally, companies want to associate with an event either to make the participants and fans more aware of their service or product or to increase the sales of the service or product. It is up to the event manager to figure out which category the potential sponsor falls into and then to create a sponsorship that meets the needs of the company. If a student group was looking to host a student bench-press competition, they might start researching potential sponsors that might want to increase awareness of their business among weight-lifting students. As such, local sporting good stores, health food stores, nutritional supplement companies, weight loss companies, and fitness centers could all be considered potential sponsors. Then, knowing that the event needs prizes for the winners, the event manager might seek out a cash sponsorship from a nutritional supplement company so that medals can be purchased. In-kind gift-cards from the sporting goods store could be used as additional prizes. The event might also invite all the sponsors to display (and even sell) their products during the event. Sponsorship can become much more complex than this, but the basic premise remains the same—event managers must match the needs of the sponsor with the needs of the event.

Participant Registration and Ticketing. Most events need to register participants, sell tickets, or both. Participant registration can be done through a third-party service, by setting up an online registration system, by allowing on-site registration, or through a combination of registration options. For events with a small number of entries, it may be feasible for the event managers to handle the registration and save money by avoiding a third-party vendor. For larger events, a third-party vendor might prove to be useful and cost effective. There are some commonalities among many online third-party vendors; most allow all types of sport and recreation events to set up accounts and registration processes on their website and then the website takes a fee from each registration to support the use of their service. They also allow the event to take credit card payments, provide a framework in which to set up registration forms, and offer tools for downloading registrations. During registration, participants will pay the entry fee, as well as provide personal information, and may also sign an informed consent form (sometimes referred to as a waiver form).

Allowing participants to register before the day of the event via an online form or in person will help the event manager plan for how many participants to expect. On-site registration helps increase participation of those who were unsure whether they wanted to participate, those who might have been waiting to see what the weather was like, and those who did not know about the event earlier. A combination early and on-site registration process is very common for events such as road races and cycling races.

Ticketed events require more planning than events without ticketing. Establishing ticket prices, seating arrangements, the ticket design, the sales process, and staffing of ticket sales all take time and cost money. Sometimes, the institution or athletics department might have a ticketing office for some venues that can help with ticketing. Other times, the event manager might have to start from scratch to establish everything related to ticketing. Once there is a charge for admission to an event, more event staff is inherently needed. There must be a physical boundary between those who paid and those who have not paid and that boundary must be managed. It might seem as though a building provides an easy boundary, but even indoor events require staffing; every door needs to be staffed to ensure those inside do not allow entry to others who have not paid. If there is reserved seating or different price points in the seating area, there must be a system in place to ensure people sit in their ticketed seat. Since many events rely on the registration and ticketing revenue to support costs, proper planning and attention to detail is needed throughout the process.

Risk Assessment. The assessment and management of risk can be a major undertaking for an event. In fact, entire college or university courses and text books are dedicated to this subject. Major events require safety and security planning that involves local police, fire, and even Department of Homeland Security officials. However, for most campus intercollegiate athletics and recreation events, a few simple guidelines can prepare event managers to conduct a risk assessment that will meet their needs. (Osborne offers a discussion of risk management strategies in Chapter Five.) In addition, the legal or general counsel office can provide guidance to event organizers if questions arise.

With all aspects of event development, there are a lot of important decisions event managers have to make. Attention to detail is critical in the development phase because it leads into the quality of event execution.

Event Execution

The execution of the event begins with the physical preparations (i.e., signage printed, facility set-up, welcoming participants) and does not conclude until the last bill is paid, the final thank you note is written, and assessment of the event occurs. Execution includes event day resources, staffing, event operations, crowd management, and event wrap-up. Many event managers find these responsibilities are the most fun because it is when all the hard work in preparing pays off by seeing the event become a reality.

Event Day Resources. Event day resources such as checklists, time lines, phone lists, event day information sheets, and diagrams can be very helpful to a busy event manager. The general checklist (Table 11.1) that was established during the event development phase helps event managers ensure the major tasks have been accomplished. However, a more detailed checklist with times of each activity noted should be created for the event day. This helps everyone involved understand the sequence of activities.

A phone list is an essential piece of event day communications. Ideally, all event staff will have access to two-way radios for communications as well—but cell phone communication is still necessary even with radios because occasionally a private conversation between two staff members is necessary. The event manager should also have a phone list of vendors, police, physical plant maintenance staff, and other essential personnel available at all times.

Event day information sheets (sometimes called fast facts) should be provided to all event staff and offer the basic information to help them answer frequently asked questions that participants and spectators might have. At a minimum, event day information sheets should include the basic event schedule, venue entrance locations, ticketing and will-call locations, registration locations, first aid locations, lost and found information, media information, staff and volunteer check-in location, and contact information for the event manager.

Finally, a diagram might or might not be necessary for the event. Diagrams are extremely useful when the venue is nontraditional, such as a city park and streets for a road race. The diagram depicts the location of everything from the start and finish lines to the on-site registration tables to the medial support areas, and can then be given to all parties to enable their own set-up on the event day. All of these resources will assist the event manager stay organized and make the event a success.

Staffing. Ensuring there is an adequate number of qualified staff also falls under the role of event manager. Any event that utilizes volunteers or paid staff will need to carefully follow human resource procedures established by the institution. Often, the human resources department can be a tremendous help to the event manager by ensuring that all legal procedures are followed in the interviewing, hiring, and payment of event staff.

Many campus events rely heavily on volunteers to staff events. Whether it is a student group earning community service hours or sport management students gaining practical experience, securing enough volunteers is an important element of event management. Event managers can also seek volunteers and staff from off-campus community groups to help manage their events. Local church groups, nursing homes, veterans associations, and even Boy Scout troops might all be interested in volunteering. In return, the event manager might be able to provide the group a small donation, a percentage of revenue earned (very common in concessions), public recognition, or a gift provided by an event sponsor.

All staff, whether volunteer or paid, must be educated about their position at the event. Training can range from a pre-event meeting about their duties, where they receive the event information sheet, to more intensive training depending on the needs of the event. For example, a volunteer staffing a water station at a charity cycling event needs substantially less training than paid event staff ushering a sold-out college football game.

Operations. The event manager becomes a true jack of all trades at this point in the management process. Whether a reporter does not know where the media hospitality is or there is a problem at a concession stand, the event manager must be prepared to handle it all. Although it would be impossible to predict every occurrence during an event, there are some measures that can be taken to be as prepared as possible to handle the unexpected.

One of the core responsibilities of event management is to ensure the facility is ready to go and in top condition for the event. For some event managers, that may mean working with local authorities on closing streets at the appropriate time for a running event and for others it may mean making sure the intramural soccer fields are cut, lined, and the goals set-up. After the event, the facility usually needs to be returned to pre-event condition, so the event manager needs to plan for break-down tasks as well. For example, if sideline benches and concession tables are borrowed from the student recreation center for a flag football tournament, then those items must be returned after the event is over.

Parking for participants and spectators is also part of the event. Adequate parking should be available and for on-campus events this can sometimes pose a challenge. Most colleges or universities require parking permits, so the event manager needs to work with the campus parking authorities to guarantee that there is event-day parking available. In some cases, the event might actually be able to charge a fee for parking to generate additional revenue.

There are a variety of additional operational issues depending on the event size and type. The following areas require consideration for some events:

- Participant check-in
- Game-day ticket sales and will-call
- Concessions operations
- Merchandise operations
- Sponsor, participant, media, VIP, officials hospitality
- Staff and volunteer check-in
- Press box operations
- Awards ceremonies
- Officials' dressing rooms
- Security checks
- Tailgating
- In-game promotions
- Field maintenance (i.e., baseball field maintenance between innings)
- Inclement weather procedures
- Coordination of medical support (i.e., emergency medical technicians or ambulances on site)
- Trash and recycling removal

The larger and more complex the event, the more likely it is that some or all of the above areas need attention. The basics are the same whether the event is a recreational basketball championship game or the NCAA Final Four Championship game, but the integrated pieces of the event increase based on size, perceived importance, amount of money involved, and number of spectators and participants.

Crowd Management. Managing the crowd is easier for small events than it is for large events, but the basic principles of crowd management apply no matter what size the event. First, the event manager should establish a facility set-up that is conducive to easy event flow. Event flow refers to how spectators and participants move from one area to the next. If parking is 2 miles away from the venue or if restrooms are hard for spectators to find, that is not good flow. Conversely, if spectators are able to move quickly and easily through the process of entering the parking lot, parking, walking to the ticket sales area, purchasing a ticket, entering the venue, visiting merchandise and concession stands, finding their seat, leaving their seat for a snack, and finally exiting the venue and driving away, then good flow has been accomplished. Signage, other communication such as public address announcements, and the physical set-up of the venue all help create good flow.

A second aspect to crowd management is to know the crowd. An event manager that understands the crowd characteristics can greatly reduce the changes of any negative crowd actions. The expected crowd at a 9:00 P.M. televised college football game where tailgating with alcohol is permitted is different from the crowd for a college swimming meet at noon on a Saturday. There are likely to be intoxicated spectators who are very passionate about the game and their team at the football game. The swimming meet will probably be attended mostly by parents and friends of the student-athletes. Thus, crowd management is a nonissue for most swimming meets but a major concern at many football games. Having trained staff is the first step to reducing the chance of negative crowd behavior. Staff who are paying attention to and know the signs of possible disturbances can help diffuse situations before they escalate. There are also some general actions that can be taken to help in reducing crowd issues at events. The following tips can help event managers create a positive crowd environment:

- Create a fan code of conduct. It sets behavioral expectations for everyone that is communicated in a way that encourages good behavior and sportsmanship.
- Prohibit fans from leaving the venue and returning, often known as pass-outs. For events that do not sell alcohol, this prohibits spectators from drinking outside the venue and then returning to the event.

- For intercollegiate athletics events, set aside pregame time for the head coach to speak about sportsmanship and behavior.
- Use existing in-event communication channels such as public address announcement reads, video board productions, and signage to set the tone for behavior.
- Establish family-friendly areas that allow those attending the event with children the ability to separate themselves from other fans that might be a little rowdier (adapted from Niemuth, Duethman, Brown, Griesemer, and Crockett, 2009).

Crowds can be unpredictable, but creating good flow, understanding the spectators, and implementing some strategies to reduce the chance of crowd issues can assist event organizers succeed in crowd management.

Event Wrap-Up. After the final score and statistics are tabulated, the work is not over for the event manager. Event wrap-up can go on for days, weeks, or even months after an event. To ensure wrap-up is as easy as possible, the event manager keeps up with documentation from start to finish—not only once the event has concluded. By this point, the event manager is tired from all the work that went into the event but the wrap-up cannot be ignored because it sets the stage for future events to continue to improve.

The event file combines all the information from the event into one notebook or electronic file that can be used in the future when planning the event again or a similar event. The file should contain copies of all contracts, copies of all event resources (i.e., checklists, phone lists, etc.), financial reports, staffing information, notes from a debriefing meeting, assessments completed, and incident reports (i.e., injuries, customer complaints). Much of the event file is created by simply filing existing documentation. One of the most important legacies an event manger can leave is an event file that is easy for future event managers to use. Finalizing the budget is one of the most challenging components of wrap-up. The revenues and expenses need to be carefully checked to ensure all expenses are paid and that all revenues are accounted for. The event manager cannot control the timing of invoices, so sometimes the event manager ends up waiting for a bill or two to finally close out the budget.

One of the key components to future improvement is holding a debriefing meeting with the key people involved in the event. During this meeting, the group should be open and honest about what went well and what could be improved upon for the future. Notes from this meeting are then included in the event file. The other piece of the file that takes some work is conducting event assessment. Surveying participants, spectators, coaches, and staff can provide information for the event file as well.

The final piece of event wrap-up is showing appreciation to all involved. Thanking sponsors, volunteers and staff, university administrators, and participants takes time and effort, but is valued by all. If a local business has limited funds to sponsor university events and they receive a thank you note and some photos from one event they sponsored and nothing from another event, it is likely that they will choose the event that showed appreciation when selecting events to sponsor in the future. The same rationale might also be true of event volunteers with limited time, as well as other supporting university departments. Saying thank you is often overlooked, and those that take the time to do so will see their events flourish in the future.

Conclusion

Whether intercollegiate athletics, recreation, or intramural, there is much more alike than different for all types of events that occur in a college or university setting. The role of the event manager is one that requires a broad base of knowledge, an understanding of the campus environment, and the ability to get things done while still paying attention to detail. For those who enjoy variety, challenge, and activity; event management can be a great career. For others, running events might be one part of a more comprehensive job description. For everyone in higher education, having an understanding of how to plan and manage events can be a valuable skill to possess.

The three-phase (conceptualization, development, and execution) approach to event management helps provide structure to the entire process of putting on an event of any size. During event conceptualization, the idea of the event is analyzed to ensure success if possible. Then the event manager evaluates who the rights holder is, whether there is a bid process for the event, and if a sanction is needed. The event development phase encompasses the expansion of the ideas generated in the conceptualization phase, together with creating the budget, marketing the event, securing sponsors, and registering participants and/or selling tickets. This sets the stage for the execution of the event, which focuses on the hosting of the event, as well as completing tasks following the completion of the event. During execution, the event manager gets to see all the work pay off with a well-run and smoothly operated event where the participants and spectators all have a great experience. Finally, the event manager completes the final tasks of wrapping up the business aspects of the event and showing appreciation to those involved in making the event a success.

Intercollegiate athletics and recreation events are an integral part of a lively and dynamic campus environment for students, faculty, and the community. Events can bring people together that share a common interest and can be instrumental in promoting the institution. By using the concepts introduced in this chapter, college or university administrators can approach the event management process from start to finish in a strategic way, thus ensuring that the event will be a success.

Chapter Eleven Key Points

1. College athletics and recreation events in colleges and universities can take many forms including competitive intercollegiate athletics, intramurals, student organization fundraising tournaments, and special events such as midnight madness and spring football games. These events can typically be categorized into one of two groups: non–revenue driven or revenue driven.
2. The purpose of the event will determine much of the planning process.
3. Marketing, sales, budgeting, ticketing, contract management, facility operations, parking management, customer service, risk management, and staffing are all important when planning sport and recreation events.
4. The creation of an event can be broken down into three distinct and manageable phases: event conceptualization, event development, and event execution (Lawrence and Wells, 2009).
5. Conceptualization typically entails consideration of rights holders, bidding, sanctioning, and feasibility.
6. During event development, the financial planning, marketing and sponsorship, ticketing and participant registration, and risk assessment takes place.
7. Execution includes event-day resources, staffing, event operations, crowd management, and event wrap-up.

References

Lawrence, H. J., and Wells, M. (Eds.). *Event Management Blueprint: Creating and Managing Successful Sports Events.* Dubuque, IA: Kendall Hunt, 2009.

Lawrence, H. J., Yiamouyiannis, A., and Wells, M. (2009). "Event Concepts." In H. J. Lawrence and M. Wells (Eds.), *Event Management Blueprint: Creating and Managing Successful Sports Events.* Dubuque, IA: Kendall Hunt, 2009.

Miller, D. "Event Management Checklist: Multipurpose." In H. J. Lawrence and M. Wells (Eds.), *Event Management Blueprint: Creating and Managing Successful Sports Events.* Dubuque, IA: Kendall Hunt, 2009.

Niemuth, J. D., Duethman, S. J., Brown, D. L., Griesemer, P. E., and Crockett, W. D. "Event Safety and Security." In H. J. Lawrence and M. Wells (Eds.), *Event Management Blueprint: Creating and Managing Successful Sports Events.* Dubuque, IA: Kendall Hunt, 2009.

Wells, M. "Event Budget." In H. J. Lawrence and M. Wells (Eds.), *Event Management Blueprint: Creating and Managing Successful Sports Events.* Dubuque, IA: Kendall Hunt, 2009.

CHAPTER TWELVE

MANAGING FRIENDS AND RAISING FUNDS

David F. Wolf

Friend-raising and fundraising are critically important in college athletics and recreation administration. While there may be slight variations, the underlying art and science of friend-raising and fundraising is largely the same across various institutional types, sizes, and athletics association affiliations. This chapter provides and introduction to that art and science.

The chapter begins by introducing basic concepts of fundraising–friend-raising and next moves into donor development. It then discusses integration of the university's central development organization into the departmental development operations. Next the chapter provides insight into the realities of campaigns and how a department can integrate and position itself into a university-wide comprehensive fundraising initiative. The chapter concludes with discussion of the unique qualities of intercollegiate athletics and recreation programs, their alumni, and constituents and how these qualities play in the possibilities of resource development.

Basics of Managing Friends and Raising Funds

Universities, including their intercollegiate athletics programs and recreation programs, are dependent on the availability of a variety of resources in order to function. Friends and funds are among the most important of these resources. Friends of the university are individuals who can offer support in any number of ways—donating funds, providing political support on issues of concern to the institution, or facilitating innovative relationships with economic or cultural partners, for example. Managing friends and raising funds within the context of today's universities' financial hardships is increasingly becoming more vital. Whether developing alumni networks, community support, unrestricted gifts, or endowments, building a healthy pipeline of external support is very much a necessity for universities. There are limited avenues to develop new resources for academic, capital, and extracurricular activities. Countless speeches have been made by university presidents and chancellors over the years noting that the only opportunities for new significant revenue increases stem from tuition increases, research grants, and philanthropic support. Of these three sources, philanthropy can be the most rewarding and challenging to develop and maintain.

Developing and managing a friend-raising and fundraising program should have clear objectives and a sense of reality in terms of what can be accomplished both short and long term. The purpose of a friend-raising enterprise should be to develop friends, alumni, and other stakeholders to invest emotionally and financially within a department or program. Friend-raising creates loyalty and stewards long-term relationships.

Fundraising is the mechanism from which we develop our friends into donors. One without the other is limiting and shortsighted. It seems unlikely there could be a quality fundraising enterprise without friend-raising activities and concepts fully integrated into the core philosophy of the academic or athletics department or program. Fundraising is the result of building loyalty and donor passion with friends. This portion of the chapter presents both basic and advanced concepts in developing a friend-raising and fundraising program.

Managing Friends

Managing friends is typically seen as the process by which a department or program develops and maintains a strategic communications or public relations plan directly connected to its important stakeholders and community. The program of building and strengthening relationships with friends is often led by a university's alumni relations program in conjunction with other development operations at the institution.

Friend-raising typically involves both events and communication, such as direct mail, websites, and electronic and social media, by which to engage and inspire alumni and friends of the university to keep connected. Electronic communication through e-mail, websites, blogs, and other social media outlets is increasingly being used to further connect with alumni and friends. These mediums are tempting outlets given that they are an inexpensive way of getting out the message. However, electronic and other social media outlets are passive by design and cannot take the place of personal visits and events. Developing personal relationships is the key to building long-term opportunities of deep engagement and philanthropic support.

Friend-raising is the initial step toward developing meaningful relationships with external constituencies. Friend-raising activities can be illustrated as the large funnel that eventually provides a steady stream or output of loyal and generous patrons and donors. Specifically, within the context of an athletics department, it is important to understand that many friends will be ticket holders. Within the context of a recreation department, friends are patrons of the department itself.

Fundraising

Fundraising programs typically take one of three forms: annual giving, major giving, and planned giving. Each of these categories has unique purposes and requires unique approaches. It takes all three combined correctly to form a fully operable and vibrant fundraising program.

Annual Giving. Annual giving are those gifts that bring in small to modest sized amounts that help fund immediate needs or unrestricted purposes. In a business context, annual giving can be seen as a cash flow enterprise. It creates small to modest sized immediate infusions of cash creating opportunities for academic or program needs. Annual gifts are typically unrestricted and allow immediate investment into programmatic needs by the department. Since annual gifts are typically small to modest in size, a very wide and broad net should be cast when soliciting.

Typically, annual gifts are solicited through direct mail, telemarketing, and e-mail or other electronic communications. The costs associated with annual gift solicitations can be high when correlated with return on investment. Thus, it is important to consider how an annual gift campaign fits into the long-range plan for friend-raising–fundraising.

Most professional fundraisers consider annual giving the foundation for an emerging fundraising program. Specifically, through a healthy annual giving program donor relationships and enthusiasm can begin to be captured and recorded, thus developing long-term relationships for future larger gifts. Healthy annual giving programs develop potential high-end annual gift relationships with individuals. High-end annual donors are those donors who provide larger annual gifts to one's program or department. It is important to recognize who these donors are and research their long-term capacity. Over time, these donors will be prime prospects for major gift investments.

Major Gifts. Major gifts can be of different sizes and scope depending on the type of department or organization. Typically, major gifts start at the $25,000 to $100,000 level, again depending on the fundraising culture of the university and the department. Major gifts can be given immediately with cash or pledged over a specific period of time. Industry best practices (see Council for the Advancement and Support of Education) typically require that pledged gifts be paid over a period not longer than five years. It may be necessary on some occasions to lengthen the amount of time a major gift donor requires to pay a pledge, however, these types of arrangements should be carefully determined with the institution and university's chief development officer so that university policy is followed when accepting pledged or other unique gifts. The longer the payment period for pledged gifts is, the greater is the possibility that changes in a donor's personal and economic factors can affect the pledge fulfillment.

Major gift fundraising is where the art and science of fundraising converge. Good major gift operations include extensive amounts of research and donor visits to determine donor passion and donor capacity. Understanding and analyzing donor capacity is becoming easier through technology and Internet driven information. Research and its impact on fundraising is discussed later in the chapter, but it is important to note here that good research can raise the ability to take a conversation and relationship with a donor to new levels.

Understanding donor motivation is a more artful enterprise. Through cultivation of major gift donor prospects, the art of listening and sharing donor and institutional passion is the opportunity to connect someone of financial means to one's department or program goals. As a major gift program develops it becomes increasingly important to incorporate more complex and sustainable opportunities for major gifts.

Planned Giving. Planned giving or gift planning is the third, and possibly the most important, category for long-term and legacy-generating enterprises. Planned giving is really two fundraising strategies rolled into one category: estate gifts and specialized gifts.

Most people know planned giving as the receiving of estate related gifts. Estate driven fundraising is a vital component for sustained long-term fundraising. Specifically, estate driven gifts are those gifts received through a will, trust, annuity, or life insurance vehicle. It is becoming more common for donors to notify charities of their intent to give through their estate. However, most gifts are received without prior notification.

Specialized giving is the intersection at which major gifts and planned gifts meet. Specialized gifts are those that are negotiated and solicited through the use of financial instruments such as charitable remainder trusts, gift annuities, real estate, gifts of stock or other securities, charitable lead trusts, life insurance, and other complicated instruments. Success in using specialized giving in major gift negotiations typically involves working with a donor's financial planner, accountant, or attorney. Specialized giving is typically incorporated into planned giving due to the unique and more complicated finance structure that it brings. Good development operations will have access to both staff that can consult on these types of gifts and attorneys who specialize in tax, finance, and estate planning (Ashton, 2004).

Planned giving is a vital component to moving donors toward making large gifts. It also allows for a more strategic plan to be created with relation to the donor's interests and ability to pass their wealth to future generations as well as avoid some taxes. Although more complex and creative, more substantial major gift fundraising is accomplished through planned giving by utilizing these more sophisticated gift planning concepts. Specifically, gifts created through trusts, annuities, and testamentary pledge (a gift pledged through one's estate) can create enormous opportunities for both donors and organizations.

Utilizing planned giving is typically best accomplished through the university's central development office. Most universities employ planned giving professionals who either have the expertise or are connected to local experts such as estate and tax attorneys who can assist both the donor and university in utilizing this very impacting strategy. It is also important to partner with the university's planned giving department to begin to develop a marketing and long-term strategies for realizing gifts through estates and other planned giving opportunities.

Art and Science of Fundraising

Fundraising can be as complicated or as simple as one wants to make it. The realities of today's university driven development operations are that they are continually becoming more sophisticated and technologically driven. Yet without a basic philosophy of what the department or institution wants to accomplish, and how much that vision costs, all the technology and research in the world will not aid much in building a quality and sustainable development operation. Intercollegiate athletics and recreation programs need to develop both a vision and goals for their needs.

Both fundraising and friend-raising boil down to one very simple yet seemingly difficult to manage philosophy—to develop lasting and meaningful relationships between the organization and the prospective donor. While on the surface that seems somewhat easy, the difficulty lies within the context of how to effectively communicate and honestly build deep sustained relationships with the constituency.

Constituency

The first step toward understanding a constituency is to know how many people it includes. Most, if not all, modern universities and colleges maintain an alumni base in the thousands. Small liberal arts colleges might have less than 100,000 known alumni, whereas a large public institution will probably have an alumni base several hundred thousands strong. However, the alumni base is only part of one's constituency. Athletics departments, by way of their nature as being the likely most visible department within the university, maintain a large number of non-alumni contacts such as ticket holders, community friends, and others. Recreation departments may (and arguably should) have a database of persons who take part in their programs and services as well.

Donor Expectations

The reality of fundraising is that gifts are made though relationships with a specific cause or organization. Those relationships are created and sustained by individuals representing the organization. Donors want to know that those who represent their institution are honest and understand their intentions for their gift. More and more donors expect continued validation, reporting, and stewardship related to their charitable giving. What this means is that donors want to know that the organization is using their gifts as agreed upon and that there is some articulation of the benefits that their gift is making within the organization and possibly within society. It is increasingly common for donors to treat a gift as if it were a personal investment, wanting to know how the gift will be used, invested, and the overall return on investment. The challenge is to articulate the return on investment in terms of both a financial and social impact.

A department should consider each of the previously discussed forms of fundraising (annual giving, major gifts, planned giving) and develop a friend-raising–fundraising enterprise that captures and explores how relationships will be managed within each of these contexts. Connecting donors to their gifts through high-quality stewardship programming can create continued giving and new support. Consider what the donor's intent is with their gifts and regularly connect them through correspondence or events intended to showcase how their support has made an impact within the department. Scholarship recipients, program outcomes, and capital expenditures or improvements are all excellent ways to showcase for donors how their support makes a difference.

Staff

The professional fundraiser, or development officer, is a key component to any gift program. Finding and retaining a quality development professional to focus on meeting with and engaging donors allows for the organization to have a face and conduit to the leadership of the department.

Development professionals should be measured mostly on activity instead of dollars generated. Development programs take significant time to realize a return on investment. Development professionals are only conduits; unless significant time and energy are devoted by departmental, school, college, and university leaders, development programs cannot be successful. Typically, development officers are measured on such activities as developing active donor prospect lists, making face-to-face visits, and soliciting or making proposals to cultivated persons or entities.

There are no exact industry-determined metrics or standards to gauge quality development officer activity, but it is typical for productive development officers to make anywhere between ten and twenty visits per month. Furthermore, once a healthy donor prospect list of approximately 100 or more individuals is generated, it is reasonable for major gift focused development officers to generate between one and four proposals per month. Annual gift focused officers should generate ten or more gift proposals per month. Furthermore, utilization of school, department, or program leadership is an important part of the friend-raising–fundraising enterprise. Leadership should consider taking a development officer approach to their day-to-day operations, whereby they commit to making personal calls and visits monthly to build relationships with key donors.

The Ask

Much of the work needed to have a successful solicitation, sometimes called *the ask,* is done early in the donor relationship process. There is an old saying in fundraising that to be successful one must have the right person making the solicitation, for the right amount of money, at the right time for the donor (Smith, 2009). This concept alone will help generate successful gifts for a program. The solicitation is the proverbial icing on the cake—the cake itself is the process and work done to build strategic relationships with donors.

Once the relationship is built, the case for support is articulated over time. The person who likely will be doing the solicitation has a good idea if the donor is motivated to give either through loyalty to the program or because they have emotional connectivity or passion for the program.

The solicitation should be conducted in setting quiet enough to have an honest and candid conversation. Donor offices or home settings are always best. Restaurants or other public places can be troublesome due to interruptions and uneasiness of asking in a loud or busy setting.

When the solicitation occurs, allow the donor to process what has been asked. Often there is a period of uncomfortable silence after the solicitation is made. This is not a good time to reengage with small talk or further discussion about the solicitation. Allow the donor to make a decision and provide his or her answer. In short, the solicitation itself is the climax of bringing together the donor and the donor's relationship with the program. Most development professionals like to work donors up the scale of gifts over time, thus a large major gift donor could conceivably have been solicited ten to twenty or more times successfully before making the large notable gift.

The written proposal is a summary case for support that asks a donor for a specific amount to contribute to doing some sort of specific activity. The proposal, which should be left with the potential donor, ought to be concise, organized, and presented in an artful manner. There is no right or wrong way to create a donor proposal. However, there are some basic essential elements that must be included:

- Explanation of how the gift will used, invested, and stewarded over time
- Impact the gift will make over time
- Exact amount that the donor can consider

University Development

A successful fundraising and friend-raising enterprise in collegiate athletics and recreation needs to become familiar with its institution's type of external affairs operations and culture. Most universities use either the term *advancement* or *development* when describing their externally focused engagement operations. Usually advancement is a more holistic approach in which fundraising, marketing, alumni affairs, university communications, and governmental relations all share a common executive line to the president. Development is typically defined as the actual fundraising enterprise.

The university's central development operation is a critical partner in building a quality departmental level fundraising–friend-raising enterprise. The resources and expertise that the university can provide will broadly determine the opportunities the departmental level can achieve. Teaming up with the university's central development operations will allow the department to move quickly into the major gift arena of fundraising. The challenge often is separating major gift prospects and working within the central development's prospect management system.

Prospect management is a key feature to any successful fundraising program. Often there are major gift donors that reach multiple departments on a campus. For example, it is easy to see how a major gift donor could be an alumnus of a specific school on campus, the spouse also an alumnus of a different program, they support the arts, and also hold season tickets to multiple athletics teams. Who do they belong to? Are they prospects for the school or department from which they graduated, are they prospects of the athletics department, or are they defined as arts patrons? The answer is all of these. In reality, sometimes it comes down to a first come first served basis—meaning that whichever of the above entities establish a relationship first try to capture that donor as their own. Yet in a healthy and thriving development operation, the donor has a relationship with the university and in time will give more generously to all of the programs and ideas with which they share passion if all of the departments work together and solicit in an organized, unified manner. The key to good prospect management is not to capture donors, but instead develop them and build a relationship that benefits not only their interests but also the institution's goals.

Prospect management also relies on research and the capturing of good data. Nearly every university development office utilizes some sort of comprehensive database to capture information about donors and their giving interests. The key to a good data system is the information captured within it. Thus, development officer contact reports, giving history, university affiliations, and many other attributes can allow a healthy development operation to build deeper understandings about donor interests and long-term relationships with the university and its programs.

Campaigns

A common occurrence in higher education is the news that one university or another is developing, announcing, and declaring success in some sort of capital or comprehensive campaign. What exactly does the term *campaign* mean? A campaign is a carefully planned, well-articulated, and suitably marketed strategy to connect donors to big ideas and targeted goals on a campus. It used to be that campaigns were special long-term goal-driven enterprises. Today, however, more and more institutions see the campaign as a cyclical necessity to generate or fuel new programs and building projects, and further develop the overall fundraising enterprise. Regardless of the reason for having a campaign, most universities see themselves as needing to be either in the midst of a campaign or planning for the next campaign.

Campaigns are meant to create new levels of funding, bring new generations of donors, and drive new opportunities for excellence. How a university plans, develops, and executes a campaign can be unique to its culture and fundraising sophistication. From a departmental level it is important to develop achievable fundraising priorities and bring those into the framework of the university's campaign objectives. The financial goal for the campaign should be formulated by knowing the donor base, having a defined pipeline of major gift prospects, and articulating a case for support to constituencies.

The success of any campaign rests on the ability to cultivate and achieve major gifts. When planning for a campaign it is widely accepted that 90% or more of the gifts received will be given by 10% or less of the donors.

There are some key concepts for successful campaign planning and implementation. One very important planning strategy is to simply dream big but be realistic. Once the university has determined that it intends to develop a comprehensive campaign, it becomes the work of the department or program to begin to conceptualize its needs and wants. Whereas it seems easy to dream big about where a program or department might want to go and achieve whether programmatically or in capital projects, the tougher issue is what is realistically achievable.

Connecting the program or department to the goals of the university is incredibly important. This concept alone will catapult your big ideas into strategic ideas that can be articulated into the university's case for support. The process the university will take to approve departmental or programmatic strategies that can only be achieved through strategic fundraising can be lengthy and varying depending on the culture of the academy. However, the more a program does to plan and build its own case for support, the more likely the success of moving forward.

A very important concept in moving the strategic fundraising goals forward is to test ideas on the best donors connected to the program. What a best donor is needs to be considered by the program's relationships with its donor base. Relating back the campaign reality that 90% of gifts will be given by only 10% of donors, it is necessary to test ideas, concepts, and goals with the program's best major gift prospects. However, it is folly to test concepts if no prior relationship exists. Thus, the strategic work done in developing relationships with the donor base will pay big dividends when moving forward in a campaign environment.

Suggestions for Start-ups

Starting a friend-raising and fundraising program may seem daunting; however, as with anything it always good to think big and start small. What this means is begin to develop the ideas and strategy for where the program is going and what resources and sustained help will be required to continue its trajectory. Begin to build a donor base through annual giving programs, while also developing and marketing a long-term base through planned giving concepts. Also, target influential and affluent donors through building personal relationships with them on behalf of the department or program. It is important to work closely with the university's central development office in order to utilize their resources and be a team player in helping the university build its more comprehensive development program. Lastly, remember that it takes time to develop friends and donors. Make it a weekly priority to spend time on activities that will bear fruit in time.

Uniqueness of Athletics and Development

Raising friends and funds in the unique paradigm of athletics creates its own challenges and opportunities for success. Specific to athletics programs is the rallying atmosphere and connectivity through sports that helps generate fan, community, and alumni support. Typically, support is measured through ticket sales or attendance at events. These relationships provide incredibly advantageous opportunities to develop more sophisticated friend and fundraising relationships with the program. School spirit and using society's appetite for sports teams are relationships on which any program can capitalize. Obviously, other issues such as team performance, competitive level, and institutional culture will dictate the extent to which a program can capitalize on its own identity and ability to generate further support.

Transactional philanthropy is a term that is common in athletics related fundraising. It refers to the idea that donors make gifts to athletics departments so that they can gain access to things such as high-quality seating, coaches, facilities, special events, and programming offered by the department (Hodge, 2003). Transactional gifts are more prevalent at the National Collegiate Athletic Association (NCAA) Division I level due to the fan support and attendance needs of those programs, but it is interesting that one can find transactional gifts at every level of athletics. The size of gifts may not be the same, but the underlying dynamic is—donors love to feel connected intimately with athletics departments.

Many departments utilize both alumni and friend networks and advisory boards to further develop donor connectivity. Alumni and friend networks are typically grassroots in nature and are organized by professional affiliations or geography. Developing an alumni network can be achieved through a university's alumni relations office; however, most thriving networks are sustained and supported by those departments that choose to invest in such activities. Networks are typically event driven groups that like to engage in opportunities such as tailgate parties, viewing parties, symposiums, and other traditional events.

Advisory boards are much more specific in nature and are invitation-only developed groups. Most advisory boards have a symbolic cache related to their access and special handling they receive from the departments. Boards can be created and maintained in a number of different ways; however, the goal should be to draw together influential and affluent alumni or friends that want to help move the department or program forward.

Conclusion

This chapter has offered information and advice regarding friend-making and fundraising in intercollegiate athletics and recreation. Two final pieces of advice. First, be mindful of the axiom regarding avoiding a gift that eats. An individual that offers to give your son or daughter a horsey is making a thoughtful gesture, but it may not be one you can afford unless you already have a place to stable the horse, the time to properly care for it, and the resources associated with feeding and maintaining a horse. Similarly, gifts with onerous restrictions, significant associated expenses moving forward, or that obligate the university in specific ways over very extended windows of time may best be politely passed by rather than accepted. Second, always showcase programs as worthy rather than needy. People give to excellence and programs that show promise. Be honest about the program or department, but always present its strengths and the vision for it. Doing that and building lasting relationships with friends and alumni will assure necessary and meaningful support.

Chapter Twelve Key Points

1. Universities, including their intercollegiate athletics programs and recreation programs, are dependent on the availability of a variety of resources in order to function. Friends and funds are among the most important of these resources.
2. Friends of the university are individuals who can offer support in any number of ways—donating funds, providing political support on issues of concern to the institution, or facilitating innovative relationships with economic or cultural partners, for example.
3. Friend-raising typically involves both events and communication, such as direct mail, websites, and electronic and social media, by which to engage and inspire alumni and friends of the university to keep connected.
4. Fundraising is the mechanism from which we develop our friends into donors.
5. Fundraising programs typically take one of three forms: annual giving, major giving, and planned giving.
6. Annual giving are those gifts that bring in small to modest sized amounts that help fund immediate needs or unrestricted purposes.
7. Major gifts can be of different sizes and scope depending on the type of department or organization and be given immediately with cash or pledged over a specific period of time.
8. Planned giving is really two fundraising strategies rolled into one category: estate gifts and specialized gifts. Estate gifts are those received

through a will, trust, annuity, or life insurance vehicle. Specialized gifts are those that are negotiated and solicited through the use of financial instruments such as charitable remainder trusts, gift annuities, real estate, gifts of stock or other securities, charitable lead trusts, life insurance, and other complicated instruments.

9. Both fundraising and friend-raising boil down to one very simple yet seemingly difficult to manage philosophy—to develop lasting and meaningful relationships between the organization and the prospective donor.
10. A successful fundraising and friend-raising enterprise in collegiate athletics and recreation needs to become familiar with its institution's type of external affairs operations and culture.
11. A campaign is a carefully planned, well-articulated, and suitably marketed strategy to connect donors to big ideas and targeted goals on a campus. Campaigns are meant to create new levels of funding, bring new generations of donors, and drive new opportunities for excellence.
12. *Transactional philanthropy* is a term that is common in athletics related fundraising. It refers to the idea that donors make gifts to athletics departments so that they can gain access to things such as high-quality seating, coaches, facilities, special events, and programming offered by the department (Hodge, 2003).

References

Ashton, D. *The Complete Guide to Planned Giving: Everything You Need to Know to Compete Successfully for Major Gifts*. Quincy, MA: Aston, 2004.

Council for Advancement and Support of Education (CASE). www.case.org.

Hodge, J. M. "Transforming Philanthropy: Generativity, Philanthropy, and the Reflective Practitioner." *New Directions for Philanthropic Fundraising*, 2003, 42.

Smith, J. F. *Fund Raising: Rules of the Road to Success*. Auburn, AL: JF Smith Group, 2009.

CHAPTER THIRTEEN

MANAGING MARKETING AND PUBLIC RELATIONS

Scott Branvold

Effective management of the complementary functions of marketing and public relations is essential to virtually any organization, and this is certainly true for athletics and recreation departments at any level. The extensive diversity in size, resources, and philosophy across athletics programs will create very different marketing priorities and public relations demands, but there are fundamental principles that shape these activities.

This chapter addresses both the strategic considerations and tactical activities that are the foundation of marketing, as well as the role that public relations plays in building and cultivating relationships with a variety of constituencies so important to sustainable success. It also discusses some of the general challenges that athletics departments confront as they manage their marketing and public relations efforts.

Marketing and Public Relations Defined

Adapting a general definition of marketing, Mullin, Hardy, and Sutton (2007, p. 11) defined sport marketing as "all the activities designed to meet the needs and wants of sports consumers through exchange processes." The authors go on to note the unique nature of sport marketing, which involves both the marketing of sport and marketing of other products through sport. Stoldt, Dittmore, and Branvold (2006, p. 2) define sport public relations as a communication-based function "designed to identify a sport organization's key publics, evaluate its relationship with those publics, and foster desirable relationships." Key publics include media and community, as well as consumers, donors, sponsors, and regulators. The overlap between marketing and public relations has become more pronounced in recent years. While the ultimate goal for marketing is an exchange of value, there is greater recognition that development of ongoing relationships produces more efficient use of marketing resources. This results in sport organizations devoting additional time and attention to activities that may have more of a public relations orientation. As an example, when a college athletics team visits a hospital to sign autographs or an elementary school to help kids learn to read, the primary purpose is to establish a bond with the community rather than to sell tickets. A byproduct of such activity may indeed be increased ticket sales, but the central focus is on building and nurturing relationships and reflecting an awareness of civic responsibility.

Marketing Management

Marketing management involves both strategic and tactical elements. Strategic elements are broader, visionary aspects of marketing that provide general direction and also serve as the foundation for the tactical or operational marketing activities of marketing.

Strategic Marketing Considerations

There are broad marketing management issues that revolve around strategic marketing activities—those long-term conceptual considerations that are generally determined at the higher levels of an organization. In college athletics, such strategic marketing decisions are likely to be made at the athletics director level and above, and will probably include institutional presidents and boards of trustees.

Strategic marketing considerations begin with fundamental issues that address the purpose for athletics and recreation on the campus. For many schools the athletics offerings provided will be more a means to drive enrollment than to drive publicity. Creating participatory opportunities for student-athletes at the varsity, club, and intramural levels may be a far higher priority than attracting spectators and national recognition. These basic concerns then lead to choices such as where to compete (National Collegiate Athletic Association [NCAA], National Association of Intercollegiate Athletics [NAIA]), the level of competition (Division I, II, or III), who to compete against (conference affiliations), what types of facilities to develop, and what sports to sponsor. Such decisions have a strategic quality but also have profound impact on the tactical marketing activities that will follow. These choices are a part of the positioning of the athletics product in the marketplace to both prospective students and the community at large. The decision to move from Division II to Division I, to affiliate with a different conference, or to add a sport are, at least in part, driven by product positioning strategy. Conference shuffling (such as 2010–11 conference moves of schools like Texas Christian University, Nebraska, Colorado, and Utah) provides an excellent example of actions with strategic marketing implications. Institutions are being forced to consider a range of issues (rivalries, travel costs, geography, marketing opportunities, recruiting opportunities, etc.) as they try to position their athletics programs in the best possible situation. Each of the NCAA divisions (particularly Division II and Division III) has devoted considerable attention to creating an identity that establishes important philosophical and operational distinctions that will set them apart and that members can embrace. While the big-time football conference alliances receive the most publicity and have more substantive financial considerations, conference alignments are an important strategic consideration at all levels of athletics.

SWOT Analysis

From a strategic perspective, marketing management often begins with some form of SWOT (Strengths, Weaknesses, Opportunities, Threats) analysis (Kotler and Keller, 2006). Such an analysis typically engages in both internal and external assessments. The internal evaluation will attempt to contrast the organizational vision with organizational strengths and weaknesses. This exercise helps provide insight into how well organizational aspirations coincide with organizational potential. The external analysis will address the operational environment and attempt to identify potential opportunities and threats. This process will help clarify whether the organizational mission is consistent with organizational capacity and operational possibilities, and provide a better sense of how the product should be positioned in the marketplace. This is a particular challenge for schools in crowded and competitive environments where a variety of sport options exists for consumers. In large metropolitan markets, for example, it is common for major professional sports and high-visibility NCAA Division I sports to dominate the landscape as they compete with each other, making it very difficult for smaller programs to carve out a substantive commercial presence or even much public awareness.

Branding

SWOT analysis can lay the foundation for the concept of *branding*, an increasingly popular concept in marketing. Branding as an activity involves the process of creating a distinctive identity in the marketplace using a range of tools that might include trademarks, symbols, names, jingles, slogans, colors, and so forth. However, these tools are just the outward manifestations of branding. Managing a brand really involves managing constituent perceptions and impressions. Such terms as *image* and *reputation* may also be used in the discussion of how an organization wants to be perceived. Often these desired perceptions are framed in mission and vision statements.

Athletics can have a powerful influence on the institutional brand for some schools, and the exposure and notoriety that can come with a good run in the NCAA basketball tournament or a big upset on the football field can be enticing. Gonzaga University is one example of an institution that has used success on the basketball court to establish a national reputation. A small school in eastern Washington from a mid-major conference, they have been in the NCAA Basketball tournament every year from 1999 through 2011 and have won games regularly. However, national notoriety is an elusive outcome. It is far more likely that the effects of branding achieved through athletics will come at the local or regional level rather than on the national stage, and it is important that administrators involved in strategic marketing identify what their branding aspirations are (how they want to be perceived) and direct their efforts at the appropriate audiences using the right tools.

Marketing Research

Another important strategic element in marketing management involves establishing a marketing research plan. One avenue for this research is developing an intimate knowledge of your constituencies. An encompassing approach to this is commonly referred to as customer relationship management (CRM). This is a process of gathering, analyzing, and utilizing information about customers in order to more effectively employ marketing resources to respond to consumer needs. Computer data bases can be built to include customer attributes and behaviors that allow for more refined and sophisticated marketing. Useful information starts with common demographic and contact information about the consumer but should be expanded to include behavioral data on the consumer (e.g., where do they shop, what do they read, are they on Facebook, what is their mobile device of choice) as well as consumer interaction information (e.g., how many games do they attend, what kind of tickets do they buy, do they purchase merchandise, any service complaints). This information should be routinely updated and can often be integrated with other organizational tools such as ticketing software. These information collection efforts need not be reserved exclusively for ticket buyers, however. Other constituencies such as sponsors and donors are important to a successful athletics department, and a thorough understanding of these groups can be developed in much the same way that knowledge is gained about those who buy tickets. Such efforts may even be employed to gain a greater understanding of intramural and club sport participants.

A properly constructed CRM plan will allow athletics programs to identify discrete populations, referred to as segments, to which they can market and target those segments using uniquely designed strategies. Targeting females, specific student groups, donors, website visitors, or merchandise buyers becomes a viable undertaking if the CRM plan is well conceived. The technological capabilities available to marketers today create enormous potential for targeted marketing activity. Websites, e-mail, and social networking sites such as Facebook and Twitter are just a few of the powerful tools that can be used for reaching both large numbers of people and very specific niche groups very rapidly.

Tactical Marketing Applications

Each of the strategic activities mentioned serve as the foundation for the athletics program's marketing plan. A marketing plan is the mechanism for operationalizing the strategic vision of the organization into a tactical reality. There are numerous templates for developing a marketing plan but the underlying premise behind virtually all of them is designing the tactical manipulation of the basic marketing tools—often referred to as the 4 Ps of marketing—product, price, place, and promotion (McCarthy, 1996). The integration of and interaction among these four elements is at the core of the marketing process.

Product. From an institutional perspective, the sport product may include any athletics or recreational offering that may attract spectators. In that context, club sports, intramurals, and wellness centers could be construed as components of the sport product for a higher education institution and marketed to appropriate constituents. The focus here is primarily on sport as a spectator experience. From a marketer's perspective, this aspect of the sport product has some very unique elements that create interesting challenges and opportunities because it involves a product that is intangible, with much of its appeal provided by its emergent quality of having unknown outcome. The dilemma for the marketer is the limited control over the core product—the game itself. While the core product is manipulated on occasion with marketing appeal in mind (e.g., designated hitter in baseball, four-on-four overtime hockey, shot clock in basketball), those decisions are made well above the level of the first-line marketing staff, and there is little immediacy in such core product adaptation. Perhaps the most direct influence colleges have on the core product is through scheduling. The appeal of the contest will certainly have an influence on spectator interest. Conference affiliations determine much of the schedule in most sports but finding attractive non-conference opponents will have an important influence on attendance at some schools. Natural rivals, high-profile opponents, and special events tend to be the best draws, but the balance of commercial and competitive interests make scheduling more complex than it might appear on the surface. Coaches, rankings, status, and politics all influence the scheduling process and often produce matchups that are less than ideal from a marketing standpoint.

Limited access to core product manipulation does not eliminate product marketing opportunities, however. Sport is rich with product extensions associated with the game that can contribute to the appeal of the product and the fan experience. It is myopic in an environment so full of entertainment options to rely on the game itself to have enough appeal to compete effectively for fan attention and loyalty. There are a few schools that have the luxury of excess demand for tickets, so most schools are going to need to consider providing a more complete fan experience. The components of the game (players, coaches, opponents) and the activities surrounding the game are product extensions that will shape the experience for many spectators. Mascots, bands, and scoreboard video displays have little to do with the game itself but a great deal to do with what the fans take from the experience. Merchandising and concessions are two tangible product extensions that may contribute substantially to the bottom line at larger schools. Concessions present some interesting opportunities, as well as some challenging decisions. Program size is likely to dictate the nature of concession operations. For small programs, it is likely that concessions will do little more than provide a minor revenue boost and not be a particular priority. For large programs, however, concessions will be such an important revenue source that contracting with an outside concessionaire may be a consideration. Similarly, merchandising has the potential to be an important source of revenue for the highest profile athletics programs and serves as an identity mechanism for most programs. The legal issues surrounding the licensing of apparel and other souvenirs can require substantial resource commitments, and it is quite common for athletics programs to contract with outside operations such as IMG's Collegiate Licensing Company or Strategic Marketing Affiliates to manage aspects of the merchandising operation. The services provided by these companies often include not only protection against unauthorized usage of logos and marks but brand development and retail support.

Other product extensions involve efforts to create a broader fan experience that may include pregame activities such as tailgating, in-game activities such as music, video entertainment, mascots, cheerleaders, dance teams, and postgame events such as concerts and fireworks. Product extensions provide marketers with an arsenal of tools that they can control and use to appeal to broader target markets and attract casual, as well as hard core, sports fans.

Price. Price is visible and easily manipulated, making it an important tool in the marketing mix. Pricing decisions are linked to a variety of athletics department activities including tickets, concessions, merchandising, and sponsorships. Most of these decisions are predicated on the typical factors that go into price—supply, demand, cost of production, desired profit margin, and competition, but there are some trends in ticket pricing that have given schools the opportunity to find more creative ways to generate additional revenue. Most ticket pricing strategies attempt to lure the ticket buyer into the purchase of season tickets or ticket packages and usually provide some pricing incentive for these multiple purchases. For sports without substantive demand for season tickets, other pricing strategies may be required to spur ticket sales.

Flexible pricing has become a much more common pricing strategy in recent years as athletics programs attempt to maximize revenues and attendance. The flexibility that has commonly been reflected in sports through differential pricing based on seat location now extends to differential pricing based on the attractiveness of particular games. This appeal is generally associated with the opponent (premium price for premium games) but could also be employed based on seasonal issues for a sport like baseball that may play early season games in marginal weather. One other interesting consideration for college athletics programs is the common practice of not charging for many sports. Frequently students are admitted to a variety of events just by presenting a student ID, and many schools do not charge anyone for some events. Such a practice may encourage attendance and, for students, it is perhaps only a reasonable acknowledgment of their contribution to athletics through their student fees. In some cases logistics may make it difficult to control facility access, and there is also the practical matter of small crowds not generating enough revenue to cover the cost of staffing a ticket operation. The counterargument for free events is that it devalues the product and makes it more difficult to charge for the event at some future date. Some women's sports are likely to be confronted with this issue as spectator demand increases to the point where serious revenue potential exists.

One other issue that may confront programs with sports in high demand is providing access to tickets on the secondary (resale) market, both for ticket holders who want to sell their tickets and for those who want to purchase tickets to sold-out events. Some programs have created their own secondary service or partnered with services such as StubHub, RazorGator, or TicketsNow to control the scalper's market and perhaps generate some revenue by serving as a broker for this ticket market. The NCAA partners with RazorGator. Georgia, Stanford, and Wisconsin are among StubHub's partners (Associated Press, 2010).

Place. The manipulation of place has a variety of components as it relates to sport. The most obvious example of place involves sport facilities. College athletics programs have incentives to develop appealing facilities to attract not only spectators but also student-athletes and students. A state-of-the art wellness or recreation center can be a powerful attraction for prospective students, just as a state of the art training facility may be alluring for a prospective football player. A major concern in recent years has been the "arms race" related to increasingly opulent facilities for games and for practice, training, and conditioning. New or renovated spectator facilities often involve more extensive premium seating designed to produce more revenue. There are a variety of concerns that come into play in facility planning from site location to aesthetic considerations that influence architectural choices. One important aspect of this type of place manipulation is that the decisions made are often expensive and somewhat permanent, which should lead to a more careful and extended planning effort. Bad choices are not easily modified. Even the infrastructure choices such as lighting, sound, scoreboard, playing surface, and concession services need to be carefully considered to avoid costly modifications in the future.

A second component of place manipulation includes the idea of *placement.* This probably has most relevance in the conduct of retail activities such as fan stores, although it may have implications for concession operations as well. How a product is organized and presented to the consumer is very important in buyer behavior. The atmosphere of place is influenced by sensory qualities such as light, sound, and smell. The scents of popcorn at the movie theater and background music in stores are examples of manipulating atmosphere. Disney parks are well known for their cleanliness and the mindset of the consumer as a guest. Creating this type of ambience in sports facilities is an important element in creating a complete fan experience.

A third component of place manipulation involves *distribution* of the sport product. Because media consumption is such a crucial part of consuming sport, sport organizations must be attentive to selecting the best options for reaching the passive consumer—those who watch and listen rather than attend. This component has seen dramatic changes in recent years as platforms for product delivery have grown in remarkable ways. Technology improvements have created a virtually limitless set of options for broadcasting events. National and regional sports channels, conference networks, and sports-dedicated radio stations have provided additional outlets for the broadcast of games and other sport related programming such as coaching and highlight shows.

This expansion is really the tip of the iceberg when it comes to distribution capability. The Internet now provides virtually any athletics program, regardless of size, the opportunity to broadcast events through audio and video streaming. Schools that once had little or no opportunity to receive broadcast media exposure now have a viable outlet that has become reasonably affordable. Many schools now provide free or subscription access to many of their sports events by using their website as the platform. Sports that once had little prospect for coverage are now routinely available to fans. While this may be a revenue source for some programs, it is more likely in most cases to be an amenity for fans that helps maintain loyalty while also providing the student-athletes with additional exposure for their efforts. Internet access to games may also provide some recruiting advantages as schools can extend their reach for student-athletes beyond traditional boundaries.

Promotion. Promotion includes four elements: advertising, publicity, personal selling, and sales promotion. The chapter discusses each briefly, but keep in mind that each element is an extensive marketing subdiscipline in its own right. For many, this tool has long been at the heart of marketing, particularly sport marketing. While that is too narrow a view of the scope of marketing, promotion in all its forms still holds an important place in the marketing of sports for a variety of reasons. Perhaps the two most important reasons are that promotions are largely under the direct control of the marketer (unlike product and place) and there is substantial creative freedom in promotion, with plenty of room for imagination and innovation.

Advertising. Mullin, Hardy, and Sutton define advertising as a "paid, nonpersonal, clearly sponsored message conveyed through the media" (2007, p. 237) designed to create awareness, influence perception, and ultimately spur action. Traditional advertising has often involved print information about game schedules and ticket options placed in newspapers, magazines, and direct mail, and audio and video messages for radio and television that may address the same things but perhaps emphasizing more immediate consumer opportunities. The technology-driven new media offers new platforms and approaches for reaching clientele that has blurred the lines among advertising and other promotional tools. Websites, social networking sites, and Twitter are additional avenues for generating exposure for an athletics program, but such outlets give consumers more control over the nature and extent of that exposure. This provides both challenges and opportunities. In the traditional mass communication environment, advertisers could reach large numbers of people and create broad awareness for the product, but the message also fell on the "deaf ears" of many consumers who were either uninterested in the product or tended to ignore this type of advertising. Since new media exposure is essentially consumer driven, creating awareness among the uninitiated becomes more challenging, but the capacity to target the message to those who have some demonstrated interest in the product has improved dramatically as a direct result of this consumer controlled environment. Consumers show they are interested in the product by visiting a website, agreeing to be a Twitter follower, or joining a Facebook community. Athletics programs that can skillfully tap into that aspect of the "new media" will enhance their marketing effectiveness.

Publicity. Publicity is free exposure, and certain spectator sports have long enjoyed the luxury of enormous amounts of publicity. Beyond being free, an advantage of publicity is that it tends to be more believable than an advertising message because it is produced by a third party that the consumer may view as more objective. The biggest disadvantage of publicity is the lack of control of disseminated information. Publicity can be good or bad, and sport organizations and student-athletes must suffer the indignities that go with negative stories that tend to be all too common (e.g., student-athlete and coach misbehaviors, academic difficulties, rule violations). "Lack of control" does not mean "no control," however. Sports information directors (SIDs) work very hard at trying to generate publicity by distributing press releases, developing media guides, and arranging press conferences and other media access that encourage attention and coverage. One of the most important roles for an SID is to build relationships with the media in order to produce an atmosphere of trust that provides mutually beneficial outcomes. The media want good stories, and athletics programs want as much favorable treatment as they can get.

While external media coverage is still an important source of athletics program exposure, electronic media have altered this arrangement to some extent. Programs can now generate a significant amount of this exposure through internally controlled outlets such as websites and social media outlets, thus creating less reliance on the traditional media sources. While this may not be publicity in the purest sense, since the information is internally produced and controlled, it can have many of the same characteristics provided by external media. For smaller programs that are often overshadowed by more prominent schools or professional teams, websites can provide exceptional opportunity to reach audiences with desirable audio and video content that regular media would rarely consider.

Personal Selling. Personal selling, the face-to-face effort to finalize a transaction, is the third component of the promotional mix. Personal selling can occur in many forms and is often done in informal ways. When a coach or a recreation director interacts with a group to encourage them to attend a game or join a league, it is a form of personal selling. The interest here, however, is a more focused and dedicated effort using trained sales personnel. This is a crucial but expensive promotional tool. Historically, most college athletics programs have not employed the type of dedicated sales staff that is a routine part of most professional sport organizations.

The most common personal selling situations in college athletics are the sale of tickets and the sale of sponsorships. The fundamental concern to be addressed in determining the utility of a more refined personal selling effort should be weighing the costs and benefits. For many smaller college athletics programs, personal selling may not have much of a role because the benefits will not justify the costs. Limited facility capacity, a limited number of games, and small markets result in reduced incentive to invest much effort directed at personal selling. Even among larger programs, a professional sales staff is unlikely to be a common occurrence, but there are circumstances in which personal sales efforts will be required even if a full-blown sales staff is not possible. Athletics programs that are in very competitive markets (e.g., University of Pittsburgh, University of Miami, Seton Hall University) must take more assertive measures to create and maintain a fan base. There are also programs transitioning to higher competition levels such as from Division II to Division I (University of Nebraska-Omaha) or from the Football Championship Subdivision (FCS) to Football Bowl Subdivision ([FBS] University of Massachusetts and Texas State University) or struggling to meet NCAA mandated attendance requirements for FBS membership where some type of sales force may be a viable consideration. These efforts are likely to require having at least a trained person to direct such sales efforts, but staff costs can be reduced by using students and interns to constitute or supplement the sales force. Such a strategy clearly needs to include solid sales training to produce the desired results. There are now occasions in which schools are outsourcing their ticket sales to third parties such as IMG and the Aspire Group to try and increase ticket revenue without incurring large additional overhead costs (Eichelberger, 2011).

While the benefits of personal selling for tickets may be very situational, most schools now generate at least some revenue through the sale of sponsorships. (See Chapter Nine for a more extensive discussion of revenue generation.) The revenue produced from sponsorship sales will range from small supplements for specific teams (and often left in the hands of coaches to generate) to multimillion dollar deals with sports apparel and equipment companies. Obviously the more substantial the revenue potential, the more vital the role of the sales personnel involved in crafting the appropriate relationships and approaches to optimize revenue. The importance of this source of revenue at some levels of college athletics has led many schools to contract with third parties to handle many aspects of sponsorship and media rights. IMG College and Learfield Sports are two of the major entities that manage corporate and media relationships for a variety of schools, conferences, and events. Their ability to leverage their clientele within the marketplace can ultimately provide benefits to athletics programs in ways that many individual programs would be unable to produce on their own. In addition, they have specialists and expertise that many athletics departments will have less readily available within their own staffs. As this segment of the industry evolves, there may be even more opportunity for groups of schools of all sizes to capitalize on some of the benefits that come from this approach to managing media and sponsor relationships.

Sales Promotion. The final element of the promotional mix is sales promotion, long an important part of the marketer's battery of tools. Sales promotion includes virtually anything not included in the other parts of the promotional mix and is commonly associated with give-aways and other incentives that attempt to elicit a product trial—that is, result in a transaction. For sport, it is probably legitimate to include many of the activities designed to enhance the consumer experience as well. Appealing aspects of sales promotion are (1) the direct control marketers have over these activities, (2) the extensive freedom and creativity these activities allow, and (3) the likelihood that sponsors may pay for or at least subsidize these activities (Mullin, Hardy, and Sutton, 2007). Many of the fundamental forms of sales promotion are likely to be associated with price incentives connected to tickets or concessions, give-away items, and supplemental activities. Each of these can take many forms and are often linked to other marketing tools, as well as tied to sponsorship activities. As mentioned earlier, promotion frequently involves product extensions that enhance the fan experience. In intercollegiate athletics, the band, cheerleaders, mascot, and the opportunity to tailgate can create an atmosphere of excitement, entertainment, and social interaction that serves to enhance the fan experience in significant ways.

There are important issues to be aware of in the use of sales promotions. If used too frequently, fans begin to expect them all the time. They may not engender any extended loyalty and can result in fans simply redistributing their consumption to coincide with the best promotions. When using giveaways to entice attendance, there should be a sufficient number of items to give to all targeted consumers. The items should be of high-enough quality so that the fans actually want them. There have been many instances in which these articles have ended up back on the field in protest of a bad call or simply left to be cleaned up and thrown away after games. Used properly, such items can produce extended promotional benefit for both the school and the sponsor.

Public Relations

As should be clear even from this chapter's brief overview of marketing management, many of the marketing management activities in today's marketing environment align very closely with the some aspects of public relations. Certainly the lines between marketing and public relations have blurred considerably, and forward thinking organizations continue to look for how to integrate the two functions in ways that benefit both. Relationship building has become an essential focus of marketing and is the centerpiece of the public relations for most organizations. Several theorists (Hutton 1996; Harris 1998) have distinguished between *marketing* public relations and *corporate* public relations, with marketing public relations focused more on consumer relations and marketing oriented communications. Corporate public relations addresses communication and activity more directed toward shaping organizational reputation and image and attends more to managing issues that are important to the organization's key stakeholders. What follows is a discussion of the core activities of public relations with the primary emphasis on the corporate aspect of the public relations process, as well as a few insights into how sound public relations practice can enhance organizational marketing.

Constituent Identification

For marketers, the key constituency is the consumer whereas public relations staff are charged with relationship building across all organizational constituents or stakeholders. The public relations efforts of an athletics department or recreation department should begin with an audit that identifies all the key constituents with which the department must interact and then prioritize those relationships. Mullin, Hardy, and Sutton (2007) characterized public relations as a combination of media relations and community relations, and certainly the media and the community are likely to be at the heart of most athletics department public relations efforts. There are several components to community relations, including consumers, donors, and sponsors, as well as the general community. Following is a brief overview of these key stakeholders.

Media Relations. Media relations for college athletics is typically managed by a sports information office, which may be a one-person operation or require a very large staff, depending on the extent of the perceived demand for information about any particular athletics program or sport. Traditionally, sports information personnel spent much of their time writing press releases and compiling information (often in the form of media guides) that might be of interest to various forms of media with the hope that some of the information might be picked up and disseminated by print and electronic media. Although this is still a desirable outcome, the media landscape has changed, and sports information's role has changed with it. Identifying the key media outlets in the various media (newspapers, radio, television) is an important function, but total reliance on external media to get information to the public has been dramatically reduced due to the Internet.

Community Relations. College athletics programs have become much more cognizant of the role that building relationships with their community has on the image of the program. Community relations encompass a range of stakeholder categories that includes consumers, sponsors, donors, and the general community. Marketing public relations efforts are likely to be the primary activities when focusing on consumers and sponsors. Service quality and support tend to be key elements in producing loyal fans and sponsors and improving retention rates. These stakeholders also need to be prioritized to take into consideration their relative importance to the program. It only makes sense to devote more attention to a fan that purchases eight season tickets or a sponsor that is making a six figure commitment.

Donors are a somewhat unique constituency for athletics, and the relationship has both marketing and corporate elements. (See Chapter Twelve for a more extensive discussion of fundraising.) Understanding what motivates donors to contribute will have an important influence on perpetuating this relationship. In some respects, the process of building relationships with donors is similar to building sponsor relationships. Just as sponsors may be looking for different benefits, donors may have different interests as well. While some may want recognition, others may want influence, some may want to feel like an insider, and others may want a sense that their money is being used effectively. It is essential to communicate with donors on a regular basis so they feel part of the program, thereby also enhancing donor retention.

The general community is also a public relations target, and the emphasis here is often corporate interests such as image. Targets may be children, senior citizens, local schools, and businesses—really any organization that may have some interest or interaction with the athletics department or the institution as a whole. It is now common for student-athletes and coaches to be engaged in activities that foster goodwill in and around the communities in which they operate, and for those efforts to be chronicled and publicized. From orchestrated efforts to raise money for cancer research to individual student-athletes or teams working with kids in after-school programs, the college athletics community has become much more attuned to the need to be socially responsible and perceived as good citizens. Such perception helps combat some of the negative publicity that college athletics receives from time to time, enhances reputation, and creates connections with the general public that may translate into various forms of support.

Communication Platforms and Strategies

There are many ways to reach the various constituencies so important to an athletics program. The vehicles and approaches used will vary depending on the target audience and purpose. In some cases public relations interests will be best served by using external media and mass communication strategies. External media may provide a sense of objectivity that can be useful in circumstances in which an internal source would be viewed as a tool for spinning the message to protect the department. For many public relations purposes, a more personal and interactive communication strategy will be useful. As with all good communication, a feedback loop is a key component that should be a constant object of attention for all marketing and public relations practitioners. Finding ways in which the program can be a receiver of information rather than just a disseminator of information is essential in creating relationships that provide mutual benefits.

Certainly the platforms available for communicating with the various stakeholders have changed dramatically in recent years. As mentioned earlier, the growth of sport-dedicated media outlets has created additional options for exposure. These changes have resulted in more coverage of women's sports and a greater depth of coverage for the major Division I conferences. The conference-developed networks such as the Big 10 Network have also given some schools a mechanism for supplementing the coverage they receive through more traditional vehicles. Some of the programming on these networks serves as a public relations tool for the institution as a whole, not just the athletics department.

A more profound change for some institutions, however, has resulted in the opportunity for programs without the athletics prestige or economic leverage to command traditional media attention to become their own media outlet by using the Internet, thus enjoying exposure that was unimaginable just a few years ago. University-sponsored websites allow for internal control of information and a way to provide coverage while serving external media needs. These websites are also an accessible repository for most of the information traditional media might require, so they serve a media relations function. Athletics programs can use the Internet to go far beyond what the external media would likely be willing to provide. The ability to stream live video, run live statistics, and post video highlight clips, pictures, and interviews gives any athletics program a powerful tool for reaching target constituencies quickly and effectively. The Internet has probably increased the workload of sports information staff because all the teams now expect an increased level of coverage once reserved for a few high-profile sports. Most websites are now portals that provide access to virtually any constituency that might have an interest in the athletics department. Websites can serve as a location for e-commerce, an information storehouse, an entertainment supplier, an educational tool, a link to other sites, a sponsor platform, a social interaction network, a donor information center, and a feedback resource, among other uses (Farkas and Farkas, 2002).

The Internet extensions, including social media sites such as Facebook and Twitter, also provide new opportunities and challenges. Everyone, including student-athletes, now has a platform to disseminate information to the world at large. There have been more than a few embarrassing situations associated with Facebook postings, Twitter messages, or personal blogs that have compromised the reputation of student-athletes and programs. Compromising pictures of student-athletes or inappropriate comments about coaches or opponents can create problematic public relations fallout for both individuals and institutions. It is now common for athletics departments to have social networking policies and to educate student-athletes on the risks associated with using these communications channels irresponsibly.

Crisis Communication

One other important role of public relations involves managing communication during emergencies and crises. Athletics departments are periodically exposed to situations with either short-term (emergency) or long-term (crisis) implications that will have an impact on the program and the institution. These situations are often negative in nature, such as student-athlete ineligibility, personnel misbehavior, or NCAA violations that produce some type of sanction. They may also simply be occurrences such as coaching changes or conference realignment decisions that often are preceded by rumor and public speculation. Managing serious crisis situations will likely involve, and at times be directed by, institutional communications offices. From a public relations perspective, it is important to control the information that is disseminated about many of these types of circumstances, and one key to such control is a singular voice. That may be very difficult to accomplish in some situations. If this is a high-profile incident, the media will be soliciting opinions and input from a variety of sources, a situation that increases the likelihood that conflicting information is released. Although not every contingency can be anticipated, preparing a crisis communication plan that designates a spokesperson and outlines a general process for handling such situations is essential. Although they may not occur regularly, crisis situations often put public relations activities and personnel on center stage. Managing a crisis in a professional manner can minimize the damage and sometimes even enhance departmental and individual reputations.

Conclusion

Marketing and public relations are complementary functions that have become more intertwined as the emphasis on developing and nurturing relationships with various constituencies has become a focal point for athletics departments. Developing a strategic vision for the role that athletics plays at an institution will provide the foundation for the marketing and public relations tactics that will be employed. For some schools, that will result in a more commercial approach and greater emphasis on consumer-oriented marketing activities. Manipulating the traditional marketing tools of product, price, place, and promotion (4 Ps) gives marketers a rich collection of tools for delivering college athletics to the consumer. Not all programs will have the same emphasis on commercial interaction, and often the priority may be on institutional image and reputation. These are times when more traditional public relations activity will take precedence. The Internet has become a powerful platform for both marketing and public relations and is particularly beneficial to those athletics programs that may have limited access to more traditional media. Websites have become an invaluable tool in engaging the full range of athletics program constituencies in countless ways. As athletics programs have become more aware of extending relationships beyond isolated transactions, the integration of marketing and public relations has become a more intentional process. The development of loyal fans, sponsors, and donors has become a more purposeful enterprise that takes many forms and reaps long-lasting benefits.

Chapter Thirteen Key Points

1. Mullin, Hardy, and Sutton (2007, p. 11) defined sport marketing as "all the activities designed to meet the needs and wants of sports consumers through exchange processes." Stoldt, Dittmore, and Branvold (2006, p. 2) defined sport public relations as a communication-based function "designed to identify a sport organization's key publics, evaluate its relationship with those publics, and foster desirable relationships."
2. Marketing management involves both strategic and tactical elements. Strategic elements are broader and visionary aspects of marketing that provide general direction and also serve as the foundation for the tactical or operational marketing activities of marketing.
3. Branding as an activity involves the process of creating a distinctive identity in the marketplace by using a range of tools that might include trademarks, symbols, names, jingles, slogans, colors, and so forth. However, these tools are just the outward manifestations of branding. Managing a brand really involves managing constituent perceptions and impressions.
4. A marketing plan is the mechanism for operationalizing the strategic vision of the organization into a tactical reality. There are numerous templates for developing a marketing plan, but the underlying premise behind virtually all of them is designing the tactical manipulation of the basic marketing tools—often referred to as the 4 Ps of marketing—product, price, place, and promotion (McCarthy, 1996).

References

Associated Press. "UGA Athletics Becomes Newest Partner in Secondary Ticket Game." *Athens Banner-Herald,* June 30, 2010.

Eichelberger, C. "College Athletics Seek Bigger Profits Outsourcing NCAA Ticket Operations." *Bloomberg,* 2011. Accessed on March 31, 2011 at www.bloomberg.com/news/2011-02-11/college-athletics-seek-bigger-profits-outsourcing-ncaa-ticket-operations.html.

Farkas, D. K., and Farkas, J. B. *Principles of Web Design.* New York: Longman, 2002.

Harris, T. *Value-added Public Relations.* Chicago: NTC Business Books, 1998.

Hutton, J. "Integrated Marketing Communication and the Evolution of Marketing Thought." *Journal of Business Research,* 1996, 37, 155–162.

Kotler, P., and Keller, K. L. *Marketing Management* (12th ed.). Upper Saddle River, NJ: Pearson Prentice Hall, 2006.

McCarthy, E. J. *Basic Marketing: A Managerial Approach* (12th ed.). Homewood, IL: Irwin, 1996.

Mullin, B., Hardy, S., and Sutton, W. (2007). *Sport Marketing* (3rd ed.). Champaign, IL: Human Kinetics, 2007.

Stoldt, C., Dittmore, S., and Branvold, S. (2006). *Sport Public Relations.* Champaign, IL: Human Kinetics, 2006.

CHAPTER FOURTEEN

MANAGING POLITICAL ENVIRONMENTS AND RELATIONSHIPS

Jeremy Stringer and Bill Hogan

There may be no other component of a university so capable of galvanizing public reaction to events as the department of athletics. The furor surrounding allegations involving the men's football team at the University of Colorado in 2004 (Whiteside, 2004) or those directed toward members of athletics administration at Penn State in 2011 provide two examples of this phenomenon. Events such as these inevitably generate highly charged campus and community environments.

In addition to headline-grabbing situations, more mundane day-to-day business can also be the source of interactions requiring the balancing of interests and opinions. Some directors of athletics are directly involved in the administration of campus recreational sports. When reviewing the actual position title it may indicate "Director of Athletics and Recreational Sports," and this alone can create a problem in the political environment. The prioritization of facility use can become a major difficulty. With the renewed emphasis on student wellness, for example, when do club sports and basic physical activities take precedence in scheduling over intercollegiate athletics? From a political perspective, the campus culture may insist that intercollegiate sports do not trump recreational needs.

Because athletics and recreation administrators are public figures, they need to understand how to develop and maintain positive relationships with a broad array of people and groups, both on and off the campus.

This chapter discusses the importance of managing relationships within the administrator's sphere of influence, including managing political environments, maintaining positive relationships with individuals and groups, and dealing with relationships in conflict. The chapter ends with a short case study.

Managing Political Environments

Regardless of institutional mission, type, and size, all colleges and universities are political systems. This section delineates what higher education political systems have in common, and also describes some differences that might be expected among various institutions. The commonalities that exist among higher education political environments include the necessity to operate at macro and micro levels, the use of power, and the importance of issue salience.

Macro and Micro Levels

All higher education institutions exist in a broad societal context, which can be referred to as the *macropolitical* environment (the larger political environment surrounding the institution). Colleges and universities are chartered in specific states, each of which has a unique political operating system. This macropolitical environment affects all institutions, but public institutions are more involved with it, since they receive state appropriations through the same political process that other state agencies experience.

The behavior of individuals occurs in the *micropolitical* world. In a university setting, this embraces the interaction of members of the governing board, administrators, faculty, students and others stakeholders with each other in order to accomplish their political objectives. According to Blase (1991), micropolitics "refers to the use of formal and informal power by individuals and groups," and "both cooperative and conflictive actions and processes are part of the realm of micropolitics (p. 11). College athletics directors are among the few people in a given college or university required to operate at both the macro- and micropolitical levels.

Power

Power is present in all political systems. It has been described as "the ability to produce intended change in others, so that they will be more likely to act in accord with one's own preferences" (Birnbaum, 1998, p. 13). Athletics directors have many sources of power available to them, including positional (coercive) power, expert power, associational (referent) power, access to and control of resources, and collegiality. *Positional power* is the legitimate use of power based on one's job in an organization. Athletics directors are assumed to have the power to make decisions about the important matters in their departments, including strategic direction, personnel, and resource allocation. This type of power may be considered as coercive because of the legitimate authority vested in directors to make these key decisions. In reality, because of the high visibility of many departments of athletics, crucial decisions in these areas are often collaborative ones involving other key members of the administration.

Expert power (French and Raven, 1968) accrues to athletics directors as a result of their specialized knowledge. Expert power is enhanced by staying up-to-date on regulations affecting athletics, trends in college athletics, and effective practices as cited in the literature and at professional meetings. Expertise is a respected form of power in higher education institutions.

Associational power is attached to those who can assist people to become associated with those with whom they identify or admire. In the world of college athletics, this referent power (French and Raven, 1968) has its basis in the strong identification that individuals make with athletics teams, their popular coaches and their star players. This is a major form of power for successful coaches, as well as their athletics directors.

Access and Control. Another source of power in many institutions is access to and control of resources (Bolman and Deal, 2008). The resources available to most administrators on college campuses are severely constrained. Those individuals who control vast institutional resources are inherently powerful. Resources should not be seen as only financial, as many other types of resources are important in university settings, including facilities, personnel, and access to external media and those with money and influence. Administrators of college recreation programs may be very powerful gatekeepers for the use of athletics department's fields, swimming pools, and gymnasia. The time that individuals have to spend, or are willing to spend, on issues is also an important resource.

Collegiality. A final source of power in this discussion is collegiality. Hardy (1996) posits that this type of power accrues to those who avoid conflict. Especially in collegial environments, as many higher education institutions purport to be, this is an interesting form of power for directors to keep in mind. Although the culture of athletics is inherently competitive, collegiality is a cherished value in higher education, and collaboration can be a very important means of bringing about a director's desired outcomes.

Issue Salience

An important feature of political environments is issue salience. At any given time there are literally hundreds of potential issues that may become salient in the university's political system. Becoming salient means an issue will demand concerted attention and (possibly) resolution. At the institutional level, only a few major issues can be salient at the same time. Each major issue will take the time and attention of several key institutional leaders to address. Institutional leaders will likely commit staff and resources to studying it and identifying potential solutions.

The way that potential issues become salient is often the result of intentional political activity. Individuals who are willing to spend the time necessary in order to make their issues salient can be a key factor. Committing time should never be underestimated in any political system. It is a source of power available to everyone, and is often very effective in creating public demand that an issue be resolved.

Sometimes a real or perceived crisis makes an issue salient. Intercollegiate athletics often sees issues become salient in this manner, such as when student-athletes receive attention in the media for misconduct or when alumni decide to exert their influence in order to influence a coaching change. Once a salient issue has become resolved, it loses its urgency, so an effort should always be made to get important issues resolved in a satisfactory manner, since it will have to vie with all other potential issues in the system just to become salient again.

Because the political system inside institutions is limited in its ability to handle multiple issues simultaneously, often those borne of crisis will demand the attention of key decision-makers, and those issues that are important, but less urgent, will receive much less attention. This means that athletics directors must always understand what their important latent issues are, and pursue a long-term strategy for resolving them. These issues will vary by institution, but might include staff salaries, deferred maintenance on older facilities, or upgraded recreation equipment. Often perseverance is the key to making issues salient within the system.

Another very effective strategy for creating issue salience is coalition building. Because the power in colleges and universities is dispersed, athletics directors who can unite individuals from other parts of the institution to pursue common goals may be more successful. Successful higher education leaders must be able to build bridges across the institution for the mutual benefit of those concerned.

Mapping the Political Terrain

Because athletics directors exist in highly charged political environments, they must be aware of other political actors in the system and how they all interconnect. A *political actor* is a participant in a political system that may compete with others for resources or be instrumental in determining whether other participants are able to achieve their political goals. One tool for understanding the connections among political actors is a political map. Administrators at all levels are encouraged to create their own political maps to ensure that they have not failed to develop relationships with an important stakeholder or constituency. Political maps should include all of the individuals in positions to influence, or to be influenced by, a person in a given role. Two will be presented here: one for an athletics director and one for an entry-level recreation staff member. Figure 14.1 contains a political map created for an athletics director at a medium-sized National Collegiate Athletic Association (NCAA) Division I institution. Each of the seven major components represents an important constituent group.

Campus governance includes the leaders and leadership groups responsible for the future of the institution as a whole. This group is headed by the chief executive officer (president or chancellor) and the governing board (board of regents or trustees), and also includes other key university officers, such as the vice-presidents. The athletics director's supervisor is almost always a member of the campus governance group. Because of the high-profile nature of the university's athletics program, and the influence that these individuals have on each other on an on-going basis, athletics directors need to spend time with as many of these individuals as possible.

Campus relations includes the other individuals and groups the athletics director should be expected to know and interact with on a regular basis. They include individual faculty and staff, as well as faculty and campus governing groups, such as the faculty senate, staff council, and academic assembly. Athletics directors need to be on good terms with administrators in many key departments, such as admissions, financial aid, residential life, advancement, and news and publications. In addition, they should make every effort to get to know the academic deans and other academic leaders, including faculty opinion-makers. Athletics and recreation are frequently

FIGURE 14.1. ATHLETIC DIRECTOR POLITICAL MAP

very important issues to students, and periodic visits with the student body president and student senate are also propitious uses of time.

Department relations embraces the internal department headed by the athletics director. This department may include a mixture of high profile and lesser known coaches, as well as staff responsible for much of the day-to-day department administration. In programs where revenue sports attract significant attention, and/or where some coaches expect preferential treatment, internal department politics may require a significant amount of the director's time as well as skill.

Media relations will invariably consume a large amount of the director's available time. Technology now allows individuals to publish stories and opinions about athletics programs literally as they are happening. If a picture is worth 1,000 words, what is a YouTube video worth? Athletics directors are expected to maintain regular and positive communication with local newspaper, radio and television professionals, but are also called upon to both monitor and create content for the blogosphere and social networks. Athletics directors always need to spend time on media relations, as media reports will influence campus decisions, community opinions, and also individual decisions, including those being made by recruited students of where they will go to school.

Fans and donors are a large and significant group. This group includes the formal donor group, individual donors and other supporters of the athletics program, alumni of the institution as well as former student-athletes, and season ticket holders and other fans. This group will have much to say about the direction of the athletics program at any point in time, and they will not hesitate to make their opinions known to the campus leadership and to the media.

Another component of the athletics director's political map is the *intercollegiate athletics establishment.* This group includes the NCAA or National Association of Intercollegiate Athletics (NAIA), the conference to which the institution belongs (if any), and colleagues in other comparable institutions. Inside the athletics establishment are staff members, college presidents, and other athletics directors.

The final component of the athletics director's political map is *community leadership.* This group includes individual business and citizen leaders, and the positional leaders in the community, such as the mayor and city council. For public institutions, key people on the political map may include the governor and state legislature (as well as individual legislators), and the legislative appropriations committees. The institution's chief executive officer will advise athletics directors when they should be involved at the state level. The community leadership will vary somewhat in each community, as it includes not only elected officials and other visible leaders, but also influential behind-the-scenes leaders that are sometimes overlooked as wielding power.

Political maps can take many forms. An example of a map demonstrating the political landscape of an entry-level staff member in recreation is presented in Figure 14.2.

Entry-level staff members are usually on the frontline of service delivery. Unlike athletics directors, they are not usually involved in formulating

FIGURE 14.2. RECREATION STAFF MEMBER POLITICAL MAP

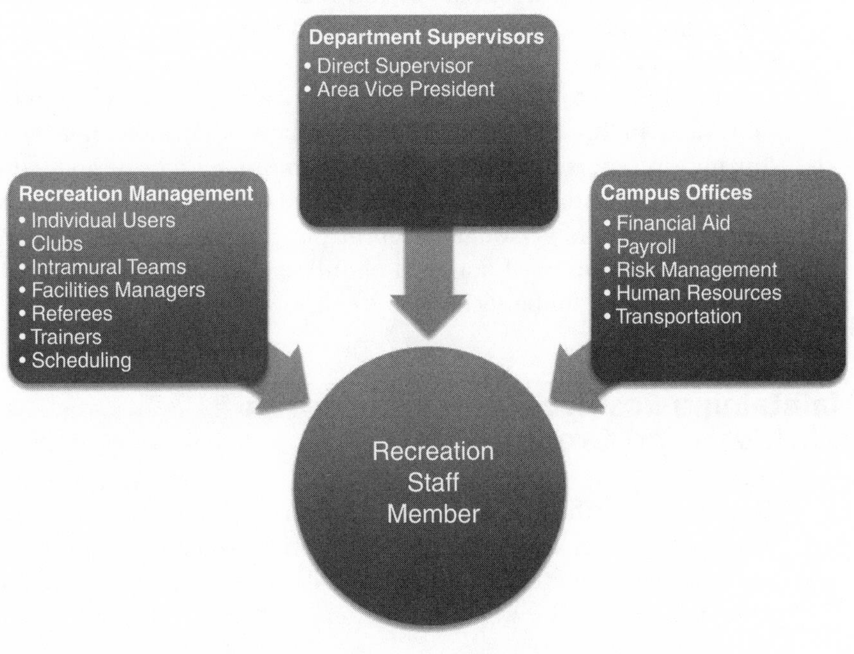

strategy, major personnel decisions or politics outside the institution. However, their need to develop positive relationships inside the institution is just as keen. For simplicity, only three components are shown as part of the recreation staff member's political map: department supervisors, campus offices, and individuals representing the management of the staff member's recreation responsibilities.

Department supervisors not only include the staff member's direct supervisor, but also the department director and the area vice-president to whom recreation reports. All of these individuals are in a position to influence, and be influenced by, recreation staff.

There are many *campus offices* on the staff member's political map. Among these are financial aid, payroll, risk management, human resources, and transportation. The staff in each of these offices is key to helping the recreation staff member be successful.

There are hundreds of people represented in the third part of the staff member's political map, *recreation management.* This category includes the individual and group users of the campus recreation facilities and all of the support personnel necessary to run recreation programs, including individual facility managers, physical plant staff, student staff, trainers, referees, and schedulers.

In addition to the components listed on each of the two political maps illustrated in this chapter, there may be many other individuals or positions on any given person's political map. Even though a position at one institution may seem similar to those at other places, the reality is that positions are shaped by the personalities of the people that inhabit them; therefore, each person's political map will be influenced by the individual qualities that the role incumbents bring to their jobs.

Maintaining Positive Relationships with Individuals and Groups

As indicated by the discussion of the importance of creating a political map, leaders in college athletics and recreation must maintain positive relationships with a large number of individuals and groups, both on and off the campus. This section will describe some of these groups in more detail.

External University Relationships

Successful athletics and recreation administrators should proactively develop positive relationships with several external constituencies. Included among these are alumni, corporate sponsors, centers of influence in the community, the media, individuals looking for an athletics home, and promoters.

Alumni. University relationship building for excellence in athletics and recreation is a difficult undertaking, primarily because of the personalities involved. Developing strong external relationships is necessary because most athletics budgets do not cover operational costs; therefore, the need to generate revenue is basic. The most obvious group to cultivate is the alumni, and there are three general groups:

- Loyal and supportive alumni have low egos and are with their school win or lose. These alumni typically purchase season tickets and provide modest donations to the program. Apart from this, they generally do not need special attention.

- Passionately supportive alumni have a strong affiliation to the program, usually based on a personal relationship with a particular recreation activity, head coach, or athletics director. These alumni are willing to be personally involved in the program, and will attend meetings and make contributions. They also want to see the program moving in what they perceive to be a positive direction.
- Alumni power brokers claim ownership of the program, and will make substantial donations, but they expect their issues to receive immediate attention. They are frequently ego driven and need to be noticed (they will always purchase the most expensive seat or spend the most money at fundraising events). Power brokers may appear to be unreasonable at times, especially when the teams are losing, and positively relating to them may require considerable patience and finesse.

Corporate Sponsors and Trade-Outs. Corporate sponsors play a significant role in the visibility of an athletics or recreation program but do not typically generate high levels of net revenue. Many times the sponsorship provides no net revenue.

An angle that has not traditionally received much emphasis is the trade-out sponsorship. Programs usually prefer cash, but there are times, particularly in a rough economy, when the dollars are just not there. When the traded item is something the department of athletics or recreation would spend money on anyway, it has the clear advantage of reducing expenses. Courtesy cars for coaches, hotel rooms, dinners, pregame meals, airline tickets, or exercise equipment can all have immediate positive impact on the bottom line.

The ability to create the relationships with corporate sponsors and trade-outs is based 100% on likeability. There will be occasions when the corporate sponsors or trade-out will benefit in a directly quantifiable way that substantiates the return on investment, but usually there will be a value added component. Efforts to gain the upper hand in sponsorship agreements may reduce goodwill and limit the retention of sponsors. By establishing a relationship that benefits both the institution and the sponsor, an environment is created whereby corporate sponsorship relationships can last for several years.

Centers of Influence. Centers of influence are respected people in the community who are positioned to positively influence public opinion. Enhancing relationships with centers of influence in the local community can provide major support for building the recreation and athletics programs.

These individuals may have no direct connection with the institution, but somehow are attracted to something or someone, usually a strong personality. The reason for the affiliation may be completely altruistic. One should not underestimate the influence these individuals can have in establishing the credibility necessary for high-level achievement.

Media. Media contacts play an integral role in promoting high profile athletics programs. Strong media relations take time to cultivate, but developing them should be one of an athletics director's top priorities. It is also necessary to face the music when the information from athletics is bad. To attempt to be less revealing for some strategic purpose is always counterproductive and creates suspicion and lack of trust. Directors need to deal with the problem up front, take the hit, and move on. In the high profile sports, the goal should be that when the information is bad, the media impact can be de-emphasized, and when the report is good, it makes the front page (see Chapter Thirteen for a more complete discussion of managing public and media relations).

Home Away from Home. Communities where universities are located always have a large number of people who have relocated there from other geographical regions, or who are from there but attended college elsewhere. In particular, graduates of smaller NCAA Division II, NCAA Division III, or NAIA schools may become sources of season ticket sales and donations for larger NCAA Division I schools. The larger athletics program becomes, in a sense, their home away from home.

Promoters. The number one goal of event promoters is to make money, period. However, building relationships with them can be valuable because of the legwork they have usually already done and the network of external contacts they may have cultivated. They can be especially helpful in enhancing the brand of smaller and emerging programs, and can be expected to build strong relationships with popular teams and coaches.

In summary, strong external relationships are crucial for administrators of successful recreation and athletics programs. Finding common bonds with alumni, corporate sponsors, influential community leaders, those looking for a home away from home, and promoters will help the administrator build a strong foundation for the future. The goal of external networking should always be building positive long-term relationships.

Internal University Relationships

In addition to the many important relationships athletics and recreation administrators need to cultivate outside the institution, positive relationships inside the school are equally crucial. The given in regards to internal university relationships for staff at any level is that unfamiliarity breeds suspicion. Administrators leading recreation and athletics programs need to be visible on campus and proactive about building strong campus relationships. Even the best-intentioned directors may feel a sense of having to prove their integrity over and over again. When internal constituents have a negative experience with recreation or athletics it can shade and possibly disrupt normal professional relationships. Administrators need to be proactive about developing internal relationships so that any negative situations can be quickly resolved. Some of the many internal constituents for administrators to include on their political map include the vice presidents, academic deans, the faculty athletics representative, student affairs professionals, financial aid administrators, admissions officers, facilities staff, academic support staff, and the registrar.

Vice-Presidents. Each vice-presidential area (such as business and finance, advancement, student development, legal, provost, and planning) will provide the administrator with many opportunities to build relationships. It is always best to have developed friendships with the vice-presidents before a problem arises so that individuals who have a solid relationship with each other can approach the problem together. Some vice-presidents may feel threatened by the power of a given director, and this should be taken into consideration because large egos can clash.

Academic Deans. Developing strong relationships with academic deans is important for athletics programs. First, their goodwill is an important resource that may be needed when academic related issues arise. Second, their fundraising often intersects with that of the major sports because they both involve contact with major donors, sometimes the same individuals. Athletics directors should assume that deans want the institution to have a strong athletics program, and every effort should be made to portray a united front to donors.

Faculty Athletics Representative. The faculty athletics representative (FAR) plays a key role in establishing relationships with the faculty, college, or university administration, the NCAA or NAIA, and the conference affiliation.

Typically the FAR is the major decision maker on conference related matters on the NCAA (D II and D III) and NAIA levels and still maintains significant influence at the Division I level.

Student Affairs. The multiple components of student affairs (such as residence life and housing, food service, student conduct, new student programs, and campus safety) are valuable collaborators necessary for the long-term success of a recreation and athletics program. For this reason, administrators need close and collegial working relationships within student affairs.

Admissions. A productive relationship with admissions officers is essential. Athletics administrators must ensure that coaches recruit within the boundaries of admissions acceptability. There is professional judgment involved in college admissions, and coaches will invariably argue that the boundaries be stretched as far as they can be in order to admit stellar student-athletes who might have marginal academic qualifications. If the athletics department staff and the admissions staff have developed a relationship of trust based on integrity, the admissions office is more likely to grant at least provisional admission to these students and the admissions director will be willing to support such decisions in working with academic administrators and faculty. Coaches must be challenged by athletics administrators to ensure that marginally admitted students are given all the support and encouragement they need to succeed in the classroom and to graduate. If most of these admits do well in school as well as in sports, the admissions staff and the coaches will deepen their trust level. Working with students to ensure academic success needs to be a continual priority, as it only takes one bad experience with a marginal admit to completely overshadow dozens of good experiences.

Facilities. Recreation and athletics programs depend heavily on support from the college's facilities staff. Many facilities personnel tend to be enthused about sports programs because they can relate better to them than they can to academia. Therefore, the basis is there for a great working relationship. It is vital that all staff treat facility workers with respect. Taking the time to learn names and something about the members of this important group will be instrumental in getting the little things done.

Academic Support Services. Academic support services deserve the utmost attention because missteps in this area can have a catastrophic impact on an institution. At the University of Minnesota a basketball office manager was paid to write papers for some players, and the head basketball coach tried to convince some faculty to give his players higher grades than they had earned (Sullivan, 1999). These and other violations of NCAA rules, academic integrity and commonly accepted ethical behavior resulted in major sanctions against the university and led to several athletic officials resigning, including the athletics director.

A separate athletics advising department can be problematic. What is considered acceptable editing by NCAA standards may be viewed suspiciously by the university's main academic support center. Because athletics programs exist within an academic institution, supporting the integrity of student-athletes' academic work is essential. Equally, all student-athletes must have the support they need in order to be successful students.

University officials must make a commitment to every student they admit that they will work with them to enable them to be successful. Coaches who advocate for special admissions because of a person's superior athletic talent must be willing to be active partners with academic support services in helping to ensure that student's success in the classroom as well as in the sport.

Registrar. Intercollegiate sports associations commonly require that student-athletes new to an institution, whether as first-year students or as transfer students, be certified as academically eligible prior to their participation in any sports program. Additional certification reports related to the ongoing academic eligibility or graduation rates of student-athletes are required. These processes depend on the ability of the registrar's office to analyze and provide important data that leads to certification. The registrar will be asked to provide highly competent staff to resolve complex eligibility issues. Athletics directors should have a strong relationship with their registrar and be willing to advocate for that person's budget in order to make sure that capable staff are in place.

The variety of internal relationships that must be fostered and maintained by a successful recreation and athletics administrator is one reason why these positions are among the most complex on any campus. It may be unacknowledged, but the typical Division I director of athletics has the budget responsibilities of a dean, the pressures of a vice-president and the visibility of the president. Developing and maintaining strong internal relationships is key to ensuring success in these challenging roles.

Types of Coaches and How to Work with Them

Some of the most critical relationships that directors of athletics and other athletics administrators have are with coaches. Hogan's Coaching Dynamics Theory (2010) states that coaches typically have one of several personality types, which are referred to as The Final Four. The four personality types are the Passionate Driver, the Calculating Professor, the Aggressive Marketer, and the Empathic Empowerer.

Passionate Driver. Passionate Drivers are characterized as confrontational, demanding, decisive, sometimes abrasive, stubborn, and loyal. They seek perfection and can engage in outbursts when it is not achieved. They are not always very political. It is my way or the highway.

Athletics directors should realize that Passionate Drivers will probably upset the university administration and major donors at times. To work effectively with them, emphasize loyalty and the need to have a strong recruiting network. Encourage the appointment of an assistant with a soft touch to handle the inevitable explosive moments from the coach.

Calculating Professor. Calculating Professors are cerebral, courteous, dignified, and meticulous. They believe in a systems approach, and are relatively unemotional, stable, safe, and stoic. John Wooden, the legendary Men's Basketball Coach at UCLA, is the archetype of the Calculating Professor. Coach Wooden stated, "Failure to prepare is preparing to fail" (Wolf, 1995, p. 39).

Calculating Professors need quantifiable data and a supervisor who listens to them. These coaches will create very involved team rules. Athletics directors should see that these coaches always have a personable assistant who can build relationships with many different groups.

Aggressive Marketers. Aggressive Marketers are verbal, creative, positive, and inspirational. They are natural sales people. They can have lots of ideas and also be ruthless at times. Rick Pitino, Men's Basketball Coach at Louisville, an exemplar of this type, said, "The more trying the times the more positive you must be" (Pitino and Reynolds, 1997, p. 89).

To work effectively with Aggressive Marketers, athletics directors should insist on accuracy, and demand that they have full disclosure of what the coach is doing. Athletics directors should be prepared for these coaches to have emotional highs and lows, and insist that the coach's staff includes a meticulous assistant coach who keeps the head coach on task.

Empathic Empowerer. Empathetic Empowerers have low egos, blend in, and attract talented players. Although they are not original, they are very good at reading moods of their teams and what buttons to push. They tend not to be strong disciplinarians, and will give misbehaving student-athletes multiple chances to redeem themselves.

Athletics directors need to prepare for the occasionally loose team discipline of these coaches, and understand that it may be embarrassing at times. They should set up opportunities to take full advantage of the strong recruiting abilities of these coaches, and balance their staff by making sure it includes a driver type of an assistant who is very detail oriented.

None of the four personality types is necessarily better than another; coaches with each have demonstrated the highest level of success. Hogan indicates the importance of understanding each of the four coaching personalities as a means to positively supporting coaches in their work.

Relationships in Conflict

Regardless of how effectively a professional in campus recreation or athletics manages internal and external relationships, conflict is bound to take place. Gareth Morgan (2006) stipulates that

- Conflict will always be present in organizations.
- Conflict may be personal, interpersonal, or between rival groups or coalitions.
- Conflict may be built into organizational structures, roles, attitudes, and stereotypes or arise over a scarcity of resources.
- Conflict may be explicit or covert (p. 163).

This section of the chapter briefly describes differing approaches to conflict and reviews conflict resolution strategies that may be employed by successful administrators. But sometimes relations are irreparably broken, and suggestions about what to do in those situations are also offered.

Approaches to Conflict

Different ways of approaching conflict, according to Kenneth Thomas (1992), include competing, accommodating, avoiding, collaborating, and compromising. Thomas utilizes a schematic that considers conflict situations along the dimensions of assertiveness and cooperativeness.

Individuals who are assertive and uncooperative utilize the *competing* mode. They unabashedly attempt to win arguments or disagreements. Some individuals adopt this mode in both their professional and personal lives; this approach yields clear winners and losers to conflict situations.

The opposite of the competing mode is the *accommodating* individual, who readily accedes to demands made by the other in an attempt to produce harmony. These individuals are unassertive and cooperative. In an environment of highly competitive individuals, such as an athletics department, those who are seen as too accommodating, especially regarding demands from the outside, may have difficulty maintaining the respect of powerful competitors inside the department.

Some may choose to approach conflict by *avoiding* it. Those who choose this mode are unassertive and uncooperative. Athletics directors who choose this mode of dealing with conflict on a regular basis will likely be unsuccessful.

The opposite of this mode is *collaborating*, where individuals are both assertive and cooperative. Individuals choosing this strategy look for alternatives solutions that will satisfy all parties to a disagreement.

Compromising individuals also demonstrate both assertiveness and cooperativeness, yet they may be less invested in looking for creative solutions to difficult dilemmas. Compromise is generally quicker to reach than a true collaborative solution.

Several approaches to conflict may be utilized by the same individual. Rarely will a successful administrator have an unvarying approach to conflict, since different situations and different personalities require variation in approach.

Conflict Resolution Strategies

Although it is useful to understand the preferred approach that individuals have to conflict, it is necessary to understand and employ specific conflict resolution techniques. Four of the most common include facilitation, negotiation, mediation and arbitration. These techniques may be employed by intercollegiate athletics and recreation professionals in certain situations, but will sometimes best be employed by someone outside the organization as a way to ensure fairness and cooperation with the resolution process and outcome. Detailed descriptions of these techniques are found elsewhere (Cheldelin and Lucas, 2004; Fisher, Ury, and Patton, 1991; Nienow and Stringer, 2009; Taylor, 2003).

Occasionally relations between individuals cannot be repaired. When this occurs it is usually true that the most powerful person wins. If an administrator has regular disputes with a departmental employee over philosophy, personality or performance, that employee should probably consider a different position. The same is true if that administrator is having these conversations with his or her supervisor. Frequent unproductive conflicts with your supervisor are clear signs that your résumé should be up-to-date, if not in active circulation.

Case Study

In order to consider the way in which the importance of strong relationships and political considerations play out, consider the following case study.

The new director of athletics has inherited one of the worst baseball programs in NCAA Division I. Last year's team had a horrible record, problems off the field, poor graduation rates and low GPAs. There was no team pride. The head coach is well liked, friendly, and dedicated, but has been under-resourced in scholarships, staffing, and budget for several years compared to competing schools. The baseball stadium is run down, with very little seating, located in the inner city with limited space. The outfield home run fences are short; therefore, because it is a hitter's park, it is difficult to attract quality pitchers, a prerequisite for building a winning program. The program has no history of winning, no outstanding seasons, and nothing to hang one's hat on as a major positive event. The school has never won a conference championship, nor earned an NCAA postseason tournament bid.

Some in the central administration feel the program should be dropped because of all the negatives, but the athletic director successfully argues that the program can be turned around because of an exceptional talent base in the local area. Even though the current head coach has many positives, these are outweighed by the negatives associated with the program and its history, so the coach is released. Many baseball alumni are outraged by the decision because of their loyalty to the head coach. The baseball alumni blame the university for not having supported the baseball program for several years.

The university commits to a plan to try to save the baseball program. The baseball field is changed by extending the home run fences and increasing their height to create a more pitcher-friendly ballpark. New bleachers and a press box are added. A full time assistant coach position is added and additional resources are provided for a graduate assistant and a part-time assistant coach.

The single most important decision is who to hire as the next head coach. The pool of applicants is small because of the program's past failures. It becomes obvious that no "sitting," successful Division I head coach will be interested, so the best candidates will be either Division II head coaches, Division I assistant coaches or junior/community college head coaches.

Of the four types of coaches discussed earlier, which would you recommend for the position? The Passionate Driver, the Calculating Professor, the Aggressive Marketer or the Empathic Empowerer? Why? Why would you not choose the other types of coaches? By choosing a coach with this particular coaching style, what kind of negative situations can you anticipate?

Rebuilding the fractured relationships with the baseball alumni is also a high priority. What strategies come to mind for addressing these conflicts and repairing these important ties?

Conclusion

Successful recreation and athletics administrators are adept at understanding the political dimensions of the job. They know they need to understand and manage a complex network of internal and external relationships, navigate sometimes turbulent political waters, work with widely divergent personalities, and understand and resolve conflict.

Chapter Fourteen Key Points

1. Regardless of institutional mission, type, and size, all colleges and universities are political systems.
2. All higher education institutions exist in a broad societal context, which can be referred to as the *macropolitical* environment (the larger political environment surrounding the institution). The behavior of individuals occurs in the *micropolitical* world. In a university setting, this embraces the interaction of members of the governing board, administrators, faculty, students and others stakeholders with each other in order to accomplish their political objectives.
3. Power is present in all political systems. It has been described as "the ability to produce intended change in others, so that they will be more likely to act in accord with one's own preferences" (Birnbaum, 1998, p. 13). Forms of power include positional (coercive) power, expert power, associational (referent) power, access to and control of resources, and collegiality.
4. A *political actor* is a participant in a political system that may compete with others for resources or be instrumental in determining whether other participants are able to achieve their political goals. One tool

for understanding the connections among political actors is a political map.

5. Leaders in college athletics and recreation must maintain positive relationships with a large number of individuals and groups, both on and off the campus.
6. Some of the most critical relationships that directors of athletics and other athletics administrators have are with coaches. Hogan (2010) identifies four coaching personalities: Passionate Driver, the Calculating Professor, the Aggressive Marketer, and the Empathic Empowerer.
7. According to Morgan (2006), conflict will always be present in organizations; conflict may be personal, interpersonal, or between rival groups or coalitions; conflict may be built into organizational structures, roles, attitudes, and stereotypes or arise over a scarcity of resources; and conflict may be explicit or covert.
8. Kenneth Thomas (1992) describes five ways people approach conflict: competing, accommodating, avoiding, collaborating, and compromising.
9. Four common conflict resolution strategies are: facilitation, negotiation, mediation and arbitration.

References

Birnbaum, R. *How Colleges Work.* San Francisco: Jossey-Bass, 1988.

Blase, J. (Ed.). *The Politics of Life in Schools: Power, Conflict, and Cooperation.* Newbury Park, CA: Sage, 1991.

Bolman, L. G., and Deal, T. L. *Reframing Organizations: Artistry, Choice, and Leadership.* San Francisco: Jossey-Bass, 2008.

Cheldelin, S. I., and Lucas, A. F. *Academic Administrator's Guide to Conflict Resolution.* San Francisco: Jossey-Bass, 2004.

Fisher, R., Ury, W., and Patton, B. *Getting to Yes: Negotiating Agreement Without Giving In* (2nd ed.). New York: Penguin, 1991.

French, J.R.P. Jr., and Raven, B. "The Bases of Social Power." In D. Cartwright and A. Zander (Eds.). *Group Dynamics: Research and Theory* (3rd ed.). New York: Harper and Row, 1968.

Hardy, C. *The Politics of Collegiality: Retrenchment Strategies in Canadian Universities.* Montreal: McGill-Queen's University Press, 1996.

Hogan, W. "Leadership Styles Presentation." *Athletic Administration,* 2010, 45 (7), 35.

Morgan, G. *Images of Organization.* Thousand Oaks, CA: Sage Publications, 2006.

Nienow, D., and Stringer, J. "Understanding and Managing Conflict." In G. S. McClellan and J. Stringer, *The Handbook of Student Affairs Administration* (3rd ed.). San Francisco: Jossey-Bass, 2009.

Pitino, R., and Reynolds, B. *Success Is a Choice.* New York: Broadway Publishers, 1997.

Sullivan, T. "Minnesota Scandal Tests College Sports." The Cincinnati Enquirer, March 11, 1999. Accessed on May 18, 2011 at http://www.enquirer.com/columns/sullivan/1999/03/11/ts_minnesota_scandal.html.

Taylor, S. L. "Conflict Resolution." In S. R. Komives and D. B. Woodard, Jr. (Eds.), *Student Services: A Handbook for the Profession* (4th ed.). San Francisco: Jossey-Bass, 2003.

Thomas, K. W. "Conflict and Negotiation Processes in Organizations." In M. D. Dunnette and L. M. Hough (Eds.), *Handbook of Industrial and Organizational Psychology* (2nd ed.). Palo Alto, CA: Consulting Psychologists Press, 1992.

Whiteside, K. "Another Assault Case Surfaces Against Colorado Player." *USA Today*, February 20, 2004. Accessed on May 18, 2011 at http://www.usatoday.com/sports/college/football/2004–02–19-colorado-accusations_x.htm.

Wolf, A. "Wooden Way: The Bruins Are Back." *Sports Illustrated*, 1995, 39.

CHAPTER FIFTEEN

MANAGING ASSESSMENT AND EVALUATION

George S. McClellan

Colleges and universities have a variety of reasons for having departments of athletics. Those reasons include fostering learning across a number of domains; raising the profile of the institution; meeting the expectations of potential students, staff, and faculty members; promoting a sense of community or pride about the institution; and encouraging healthier lifestyles for students, staff, and faculty. What evidence is there that any of the intended outcomes are being advanced or met through the facilities, programs, and services of these departments? Put another way, how do professional administrators (and others) know that what their departments do makes a difference? How do they use that knowledge? The simple answer is through a program of assessment and evaluation.

This chapter provides an overview of important definitions, principles, and practices of assessment. Throughout, the information presented is related specifically to the work of administrative professionals in intercollegiate athletics and recreation and, I hope, in ways that minimize jargon and alleviate any fears regarding mastery of statistics.

It is important to note here that the chapter focuses on assessment for the purposes of better understanding the impact of facilities, programs, and services. Readers are encouraged to look to other resources for information on the assessment of individual athletic or fitness performance.

Definitions

It is not surprising, given the premium placed on assessment in higher education, that it has been discussed in myriad books, book chapters, journal articles, workshops, conference sessions, and general publications. All of that talk has contributed to the possibility of confusion regarding the definition of some important terms and concepts related to assessment. While not pretending to offer the authoritative final answer, this section offers generally accepted working definitions of several of these terms and concepts. Particular attention is paid to clearly differentiating between definitions while pointing out the ways in which they are interrelated.

Assessment, Evaluation, and Accountability

The terms *assessment, evaluation,* and *accountability* are often used in the same conversation, and in some instances they (particularly the first two) are used almost interchangeably. Although the terms are in fact related, it is helpful to keep in mind the distinctions between them.

According to Upcraft and Schuh (1996, p. 18), *assessment* is "any effort to gather, analyze, and interpret evidence which describes institutional, departmental, divisional, or agency effectiveness." This definition highlights that assessment is a multistep process that takes place at a variety of levels in the college or university with the purpose of better understanding performance at that level. The gathering, analyzing, and interpreting of the gathered evidence leads to the making of meaning—not to any judgment or decision on that meaning.

Evaluation is "any effort to use assessment evidence to improve institutional, departmental, divisional, or agency effectiveness" (Upcraft and Schuh, 1996, p. 19). It is during evaluation that judgments or decisions are made. As Upcraft (2003, p. 555) noted, "Assessment is becoming more important because it can be used to improve the quality of . . . programs and services, guide strategic planning, analyze cost effectiveness, justify . . . programs and services, assist in accreditation, and perhaps most importantly, guide decision making, policies, and practices." In other words, assessment is becoming more important because it can contribute to meaningful evaluation. Evaluation in turn can lead to new, continued, additional, reduced, or eliminated funding and other resources for facilities, services, and programs. Simply put, assessment and evaluation are about maintaining, thriving, or even surviving.

A third term *accountability* is often mentioned in conjunction with assessment and evaluation. Whereas the latter are processes, accountability is both a condition of being and a form of commitment. Accountability, at whatever level of the college or university, includes being responsible stewards of resources, assuring institutional efficiency, and serving public interests (Mallory and Clement, 2009). McClellan and Stringer (2009, p. 627) observe, "There is no doubt that the publics we serve . . . have high expectations for those of us in higher education. Why wouldn't they or shouldn't they? Higher education in the United States has been one of the nation's great success stories and continues to be one of its greatest assets." Mallory and Clement (2009) suggest that assessment and evaluation without a commitment to accountability is insufficient. They advise, "It is no longer enough for institutions to measure the effectiveness of what they do, including the outcomes their students achieve. They must now be purposeful, aligning departmental goals with institutional goals, and institutional goals with state and federal goals. They must also share the information they've collected with a range of constituents, presenting it in ways that are both easy to understand and readily accessible" (p. 105)

Related Concepts

There are a number of concepts related to assessment and evaluation that are important to understand. Several of them will be addressed in this section.

Outcomes

The first of these concepts is *outcomes*. Although not the only type of assessment (examples of others include assessments of organizational culture; campus climate or environment; or student, staff, or faculty needs), when you hear *assessment,* it commonly means outcomes assessment. There are three common types of outcomes: satisfaction, efficiency, and learning and development (Bresciani, 2009).

Most people are familiar with satisfaction outcomes. They focus on the extent to which an individual has been satisfied by their interaction with another individual or with a facility, program, or service. Following a stay in a hotel, it is not uncommon to receive a survey via e-mail asking about perceptions regarding staff friendliness, room cleanliness, other hotel amenities, and the likelihood of a repeat stay or a recommendation to others that they stay at the hotel. Satisfaction outcomes in intercollegiate or campus recreation programs might include the degree to which people are pleased with the offerings and service at concessions or souvenir stands or perceptions of cleanliness in the locker rooms at the aquatic center. An interesting satisfaction outcome for students (and others) is the extent to which they feel that their time involved in a service setting or program was well spent. It is high praise indeed when today's busy and often overbooked students tell you that they feel good about having invested time in something your department has offered them.

As with satisfaction outcomes, professionals in higher education are familiar with efficiency outcomes (sometimes called outputs) in one form or another. The number of season tickets sold for the new premiere seating program or the number of individuals coming into the recently refurbished cardiovascular room in the recreation center are examples of efficiency outcomes. So, too, is rate of return for a new e-mailing to raise funds for new team uniforms or to support club sports. While measuring of efficiency can be helpful and important, it is important to recognize its limitations. "Outputs are simplistic measures of the products of an institution, such as graduation and retention rates ... Outputs can be easily misinterpreted, and they are really only indirect measures of quality. On the other hand, outcomes represent the actual results of education—what students have learned or developed" (Erwin, 1996, p. 417).

The focus on assessment of *learning/developmental* outcomes in administrative units in higher education is a relatively recent phenomenon. The change may reflect both an increased emphasis by accrediting bodies on student learning (Bresciani, 2009) and the heightened need to make the case for relevance in the challenging fiscal environment following the 2009 recession. Learning and developmental outcomes relate to the acquisition of knowledge or skills, as well as to gains in psychosocial development. An example of the former is gaining knowledge about the impact of alcohol, tobacco, and other drugs on success in the classroom, on the court, or in the gym. A related developmental outcome would be developing the maturity to make choices consistent with one's knowledge about the impact of alcohol, tobacco, and other drugs on success. Intercollegiate athletics and campus recreation can be centers of learning and development across an amazing array of dimensions—acquiring skills in outdoor recreation or swimming, deepening a commitment to serving others through philanthropic activity, gaining knowledge of strategies for optimizing physical performance, or understanding and developing commitment to a sense of personal ethics, to name just a few.

Quantitative and Qualitative. The evidence (or data) gathered through assessment typically takes one of two forms—quantitative or qualitative. A common perception is that *quantitative* data is about numbers, and there is some degree of truth to that perception. However, it is an incomplete understanding in that it fails to account for why the gathering of numerical information is helpful. Quantitative data allow for statistical analysis and, given the right set of conditions, the generalizing of findings across settings. If for example a recreation department at a large university has a database of over 10,000 patrons, it can select a representative sample of those patrons and survey them regarding their thoughts on what programs or services ought to be added or cut from existing offerings rather than sending a survey out to all of the patrons. Assuming that a sufficient number of people from the sample respond, it can be possible to make reasonable assumptions about the perceptions of all the patrons. As Erwin (1996) observes, "Measurements and statistical techniques play a central role in quantitative methods. Tried-and-true techniques to ensure reliability, consistency, and validity offer a long-standing tradition for guidance" (p. 423).

Qualitative data draw out the richer details of individual experiences or perceptions. Just as there is a common perception about quantitative data, there is a common misunderstanding of qualitative data as being words. Here again, there is some truth to the statement. Sometimes words are qualitative data. So, too, are the observations of trained professionals regarding behaviors or interactions they are witnessing, and pictures or other graphic representations can also be forms of qualitative data. The director of an aquatics center might ask that students in a course for new swimmers keep a journal about their experiences in the course. The stories they share might include their original fears about being in the water or being in a swimsuit in front of others. They might also address building trust with the instructor or gaining self-confidence as they pick up new swimming skills. These individual stories have a much richer texture than the director would have been able to draw out if they had constructed a survey in which they asked the students to indicate numerically how much they feel they learned in the course. Because qualitative assessment focuses on individual experiences and perceptions, the data cannot be generalized to a wider population. In other words, the director of aquatics should not assume that because the students in that particular course had a set of experiences that students in other sections of the course will have the same experiences.

Much is made in the literature of assessment on when and why to seek quantitative or qualitative data. In the interest of space and sanity of the readers, this chapter will not take a detour through or a position on this question. It should be understood, however, that the best assessment and evaluation plans rely on both quantitative and qualitative data.

Formative and Summative. There are generally understood to be two forms of evaluation—formative and summative. Upcraft and Schuh (1996) offer a clear and distinct definition of both. "Simply put, formative evaluations are those used to improve organizational or institutional effectiveness ... Summative evaluations are used to determine if a particular organizational activity or function should be continued, enhanced, curtailed, or eliminated" (p. 19). College students will immediately recognize the distinction as the difference between the feedback they receive through grades on papers, projects, and quizzes during the course versus the final grade they receive at the end of the course. A member of the marketing staff for campus athletics or recreation will recognize the difference as feedback from pilot versions of a new campaign to promote event bookings in the soon-to-be-built sports and recreation complex versus the feedback that comes with whether or not the final version of the campaign actually leads to event bookings.

Metrics and Rubrics. The concepts of metrics and rubrics can sometimes be difficult for people to understand at first blush. Having identified the desired outcomes for a facility, program, or service, it is important to identify *metrics*—the indicators through which progress toward the outcomes will be measured. Another way of putting it is that metrics are what success will look like. Assume that an intercollegiate athletics program identifies the development of cultural sensitivity as a desired learning and developmental outcome for its staff and institutes a corresponding staff development program in support of this goal. The metrics for assessment and evaluation of the program will be the indicators of success (not how information will be gathered for those indicators). Two possible metrics are that staff are more aware of and feel more confident in working with cultural differences, and satisfaction with interactions with staff will be high across the full diversity of constituent groups.

Rubrics are how distinctions will be made between varying degrees of success for any particular metric. The most elemental and universal form of a rubric is the thinking that underlies the common letter grade scale. An A is excellence, and the instructor has a definition in mind of what excellence for that particular assignment will look like. The same can be said for B (good), C (average), D (unsatisfactory), and F (poor). Referring back to the earlier example of the staff development program and the second metric of satisfaction of constituent groups, the rubric for that particular metric might include a definition of excellence as 80% of all scores from members of historically underrepresented groups as being satisfied or highly satisfied. Note that the assumption here is that quantitative data will be gathered through some form of survey. It is important that purpose and methods be aligned in order to help assure an effective assessment and evaluation program.

Rubrics can take a static form such as the example just offered, or they can be expressed in dynamic terms. Referring back to the staff development example, an example of a dynamic rubric for the confidence metric might be that comments regarding contributions to diversity goals on annual staff self-evaluation reports reflect increased confidence following participation by the staff in the training program. Here the assumption is that qualitative data will be most helpful in assessing and evaluating the particular metric.

Benchmarking is the practice of comparing assessment data for a facility, program, or service with similar data from facilities, programs, or services at other institutions as part of an evaluation. A similar practice is to compare such data against professional standards in the field. The work of the Council for the Advancement of Standards commonly serves for the purposes of such comparisons. The use of benchmarking and standards can also be incorporated into the development of rubrics.

Principles of Practice

There are a number of basic principles that ought to inform any assessment and evaluation program. This section addresses a number of them.

It is important that an intercollegiate athletics or campus recreation department's assessment and evaluation efforts be linked to and nested within those of the division in which they are housed and the institution at which they serve. California State University Stanislaus provides a model of such practice (California State University Stanislaus, 2011).

The work of Upcraft and Schuh (1996) is considered by many to be seminal in the area of assessment and evaluation. They identify a list of principles of good practice that can be particularly helpful in framing assessment and evaluation efforts. They argue that good assessment should

- Begin with educational values
- Reflect an understanding of organizational outcomes as multidimensional, integrated, and revealed in performance over time
- Be clear and have explicitly stated goals
- Pay attention to outcomes and to the processes that lead to them

- Be ongoing, not episodic
- Involve representatives from across the division and institution
- Begin with issues of use and illuminate questions about which people care
- Be part of a larger set of conditions that promote change
- Meet responsibilities to students, institution, and public (Upcraft and Schuh, 1996, pp. 22–24)

Another important principle of good assessment and evaluation programs is that they ought to be conducted ethically. With regard to data collection, this means that ethical, legal, and institutional expectations regarding the collection of data, particularly data from human subjects, must be met. Most institutions have an institutional review board (IRB) that is charged with reviewing proposals for the gathering of data from human subjects. It is often the case that a proposal for assessment need not be submitted for IRB consideration as long as the data are being collected solely for purposes internal to the institution. That being the case, there still are several arguments for obtaining IRB review. First, even though it did not appear to be the case at the time, it may come to pass that interest develops in including the data in future professional presentations or publications. Second, colleagues on the IRB have invaluable experience in the design of assessment and research. Their formative feedback could help strengthen the original plan. It is important to keep in mind that even if an assessment plan is not required or desired to be submitted for IRB review, the ethical obligations to conduct the assessment ethically still exist and must be met.

Models of Practice

In addition to identifying principles of good assessment, Upcraft and Schuh (1996) highlight several important questions that should inform the development of an assessment plan. These include

- Why are we doing this assessment?
- What will we assess?
- How will we assess?
- Who will we assess?
- How will results be analyzed?
- How will results be communicated and to whom? (Upcraft and Schuh, 1996, pp. 25–26)

The University of Montevallo (2010–2011) offers an example of a comprehensive, thoughtful, and thorough assessment plan. In doing so, it addresses the questions posed by Upcraft and Schuh (1996).

The National Intramural-Recreational Sports Association (NIRSA) has two resources that can be helpful to campus recreation departments in conducting assessment and evaluation. The first of these is a framework for good assessment. NIRSA states that such programs should include measures of

- Impact of campus recreation offerings on student recruitment and retention
- Student utilization of different recreational facilities, activities, and programs
- Student satisfaction with facilities, activities, and programs
- Recreational needs and expectations of students and other constituents
- Social, academic, emotional, and health-related outcomes of utilizing campus recreation
- Operational issues such as promotion of recreation activities and accessibility of facilities and programs
- Professional development of staff and student employees
- Cost effectiveness of programs and services (StudentVoice, 2011)

The second resource from NIRSA that provides a model of practice in assessment for campus recreation is a set of standards. Those standards, which are published in association with the Council for the Advancement of Standards, address practice in both general and specialty areas of the field (NIRSA, 2007).

Conclusion

A thorough discussion of assessment and evaluation, particularly in a field as complex and rich as intercollegiate athletics and recreation, would take far more space than allocated to this chapter. Those interested in additional reading in this area are encouraged to explore the work listed in the references in greater depth. There are, however, a number of concluding thoughts and recommendations to share in the final section of this chapter.

First, it is critically important to intercollegiate athletics and campus recreation and to the professional administrators practicing in the field to become better informed and more active in the area of assessment. No doubt there are a number of entirely understandable reasons to be disinclined to do so. These may include lack of commitment at the personal or organizational level, lack of time, lack of resources (including funding or staff), perceived lack of expertise, or fear of the results (Upcraft, 2003). Keep in mind, however, that assessment and evaluation need not be complex, expensive, or fancy. It just has to be good and thorough. Also, an investment now in the time to learn how to engage in assessment and evaluation or in developing an assessment and evaluation program can pay handsome dividends down the road when it comes time to make the case for resources or for the next professional position.

Second, it has been said that all assessment, like all politics, is local. Keep in mind that all assessment is political (Upcraft, 2003). The choices of what to assess, how to assess, who to involve, how to analyze, and what to do with the findings are all political acts that require appropriate reflection, discretion, and diplomacy.

Third, it would be wrong to overlook the potentials for collaboration and partnership in assessment. Faculty colleagues have experience in assessing learning as well as in other forms of assessment as do professionals in institutional research. Administrative colleagues in student affairs may also have significant experience in assessment and evaluation. Developing a program provides the opportunity to engage these colleagues in the activities of the department.

Fourth, and on a similar note, do not think of assessment as a burden that must be carried alone. Assessment and evaluation activities are going on across the institution. Be proactive in finding out about those activities and in exploring whether or not the data from them can be analyzed in ways that help in assessment of facilities, programs, or services in intercollegiate athletics or campus recreation. If not, look for opportunities to work with colleagues to tweak their activities so as to make this additional benefit of analysis possible. Often there are opportunities to add questions to assessment instruments being used in other areas. Here again, look for chances to add questions that help in assessment of facilities, programs, or services in campus recreation or athletics.

Fifth, do not overlook the value of including students in the development and implementation of an assessment and evaluation program (Upcraft, 2003; Upcraft and Schuh, 1996). Their insights and knowledge can be invaluable, and students are at the heart of the work of professional administrators in athletics, recreation, and all other areas of higher education.

Finally, and perhaps most important, remember that collecting, analyzing, and acting on data are not enough. It is critically important to share the information, analysis, and action plan. Higher education, including intercollegiate athletics and campus recreation, can and must do a much better job in telling the story of the ways in which their facilities, programs, and services make a meaningful difference in the lives of students, other members of the campus community, and people in local, state, national, and global communities. The true power of assessment and evaluation cannot be fully realized until the stories of that success are told in the right way, to the right people, at the right time, and for the right reasons.

Chapter Fifteen Key Points

1. According to Upcraft and Schuh (1996, p. 18), *assessment* is "any effort to gather, analyze, and interpret evidence which describes institutional, departmental, divisional, or agency effectiveness." *Evaluation* is "any effort to use assessment evidence to improve institutional, departmental, divisional, or agency effectiveness" (Upcraft and Schuh, 1996, p. 19). Whereas assessment and evaluation are processes, *accountability* is both a condition of being and a form of commitment. Accountability, at whatever level of the college or university, includes being responsible stewards of resources, assuring institutional efficiency, and serving public interests (Mallory and Clement, 2009).
2. Although not the only type of assessment (examples of others include assessments of organizational culture; campus climate or environment; or student, staff, or faculty needs), when you hear *assessment,* it commonly means outcomes assessment. There are three common types of outcomes: satisfaction, efficiency, and learning and development (Bresciani, 2009).
3. Quantitative data allow for statistical analysis and, given the right set of conditions, the generalizing of findings across settings. Qualitative data draw out the richer details of individual experiences or perceptions.
4. There are generally understood to be two forms of evaluation—formative and summative. Formative evaluation is used to inform programs and services as they are in progress. Summative evaluation is used to determine whether a program or service that has run its course ought to be continued, enhanced, or dropped.
5. Metrics are the indicators through which progress toward outcomes is measured. Rubrics are how distinctions will be made between varying degrees of success for any particular metric.

References

Bresciani, M. J. "Implementing Assessment to Improve Student Learning and Development." In G. S. McClellan and J. Stringer (Eds.), *The Handbook of Student Affairs Administration* (3rd ed.). San Francisco: Jossey-Bass, 2009.

California State University Stanislaus. "University Assessment Structure: How Intercollegiate Athletics and Student Affairs Fits Into the Grand Scheme of Assessment and Accreditation." 2011. Accessed on March 10, 2012 at http://www.csustan.edu/studentaffairsassessment/documents/AssessmentStructure/Athletics.pdf.

Erwin, T. D. "Assessment, Evaluation, and Research." In S. R. Komives and D. B. Woodard, Jr. (Eds.), *Student Services: A Handbook for the Profession* (3rd ed.). San Francisco: Jossey-Bass, 1996.

Mallory, S. L., and Clement, L. M. "Accountability." In G. S. McClellan and J. Stringer (Eds.), *The Handbook of Student Affairs Administration* (3rd ed.). San Francisco: Jossey-Bass, 2009.

McClellan, G. S., and Stringer, J. "Epilogue: Continuing the Conversation." In G. S. McClellan and J. Stringer (Eds.), *The Handbook of Student Affairs Administration* (3rd ed.). San Francisco: Jossey-Bass, 2009.

National Intramural-Recreational Sports Association. "NIRSA Consolidates Standards for Recreational Sports." 2007. Accessed on March 10, 2012 at http://www.nirsa.info/know/2008/02/news003.html.

StudentVoice. "National Intramural-Recreational Sports Association Collaborates with NASPA and StudentVoice in NIRSA Campus Recreation Assessment Partnership." 2011. Accessed on May 26, 2011 at http://www.studentvoice.com/app/views/about/partnerships/NIRSA.aspx.

University of Montevallo. "2010–11 Unit Planning and Assessment Report." Accessed on May 25, 2011 at http://www.montevallo.edu/irpa/PlanningAndAssessment/10–11 Unit Plans and Assessment Reports/Unit Plan & Assessment Report 2010–11_Athletics.pdf.

Upcraft, M. L. "Assessment and Evaluation." In S. R. Komives and D. B. Woodard, Jr. (Eds.), *Student Services: A Handbook for the Profession* (4th ed.). San Francisco: Jossey-Bass, 2003.

Upcraft, M. L., and Schuh, J. H. *Assessment in Student Affairs: A Guide for Practitioners.* San Francisco: Jossey-Bass, 1996.

PART TWO CASE STUDIES

The following case studies draw on the information shared in Section Two. They are intended to provide an opportunity to connect the content to professional practice.

Case Study #1

You are the newly hired director of campus recreation at a small college. Like many small schools, all athletics facilities are shared among academics, intercollegiate athletics, and campus recreation. Priority scheduling under this shared facilities plan is academics from 8 A.M. until 3 P.M., intercollegiate athletics from 3 P.M. until 9 P.M., and campus recreation from 9 P.M. until midnight. Prior to the beginning of the spring semester, your intramural supervisor informs you that the head basketball coach, who has been coaching at the college for 20 years, wants to use the gym for basketball practice from 8 P.M. until 10 P.M. on Mondays. The coach says that due to class schedules, the only time that all his players can practice is at that time on Mondays. Although the intramural supervisor has not yet scheduled the intramural basketball leagues, she tells you that traditionally Monday evening is the heaviest evening for participation.

1. What skills might you use in addressing this situation?
2. How would you handle this case based upon the concepts discussed in this section?

Case Study #2

You are the director of athletics and recreation at Small Town College, which has a Division III athletics program offering several men's and women's sports with modest local fan support, as well a growing intramural and outdoor recreation program. Early in the spring term, the president of the college informs you that no new funds will be available for your department in the coming year.

1. What skills might you use in addressing this situation?
2. How would you handle this case based upon the concepts discussed in this section?

Case Study #3

As you read through this case study think about how you, as a leader, would handle this situation. You are the director of campus recreation at State University.

F. Murphy, 19 years old, is currently a facility supervisor (student position) for campus recreation at State University. He has served in this capacity for the past two years. Mr. Murphy has a history of not following agency policies and procedures, but he is a reliable employee who shows up to work and is always on time. Recently his lack of willingness to follow policies and procedures has created issues with cleanliness and safety within the building.

To make matters more challenging, he is well liked by his peers and he is also the son of a highly influential friend of the university who makes large monetary donations. Murphy's father likes to make everyone aware that he is in direct contact with the university president and several members of the board of trustees.

1. What skills might you use in addressing this situation?
2. How would you handle this case based upon the concepts discussed in this section?

PART THREE

ISSUES

Intercollegiate athletics and campus recreation are challenging and rewarding arenas in which to serve as a professional administrator. The chapters in Part Three highlight a number of the issues confronting professionals working in these arenas. In doing so, college recreation and athletics administrators draw on the foundations and skills discussed in the preceding sections.

In Chapter Sixteen, Michael Wartell, chancellor of Indiana University–Purdue University Fort Wayne, shares his perspective on the role of intercollegiate athletics and recreation on a college campus as seen from the office of the chief executive officer. He addresses some of the critiques of intercollegiate athletics and recreation from various sources both within and outside of a university community. Wartell makes an argument for prudent investment in both programs and facilities as a way of meeting the educational and social goals of an institution.

C. Keith Harrison, Scott Bukstein, and Walter Brock address the dimensions of diversity in Chapter Seventeen. The authors review a variety of forms of diversity and the challenges and opportunities that they present to college athletics and recreation programs. In addition to a number of widely recognized dimensions of diversity, the authors put forward the interesting trinity of diversity of privilege, diversity of style, and diversity of life circumstances. Practical examples and recommendations regarding the challenges and opportunities that diversity presents are woven throughout the chapter.

Chapter Eighteen highlights wellness issues in intercollegiate athletics and recreation, particularly as they relate to students and student-athletes. David A. Shor, John H. Dunkle, and Carrie A. Jaworski provide an overview of both physical and mental health issues. The chapter concludes with a review of contemporary ethical and administrative concerns regarding wellness in college athletics and recreation.

Chris King and David Synowka focus on professional development in Chapter Nineteen. Like Chapter Sixteen, this chapter richly draws on the personal experiences and narrative of the authors. King and Synowka frame their discussion in terms of developing a professional brand and discuss a variety of practical pathways through which that brand can be established and enhanced.

The co-editors use Chapter Twenty, the final chapter of the book, to reflect on the themes and highlights from all the preceding chapters. In doing so, they offer a summary of the discussion, an assessment of the contemporary state of college athletics and recreation, and some thoughts about what might lie ahead for those who serve in leadership roles in the field.

CHAPTER SIXTEEN

A CEO'S PERSPECTIVE OF ATHLETICS AND RECREATION

Michael A. Wartell

Before I went to college, I had little use for athletes, athletics, team competitions, or exercise. Of course, I grew up in New Mexico in the 1950s. Football and basketball were in their professional infancy, and major league baseball was an east coast sport dominated by the Brooklyn Dodgers and the New York Yankees. Few women participated in athletics, and high school varsity student-athletes were the only humans allowed to date cheerleaders. Both of those groups held themselves above mere mortals. Athletics contests were attended mostly by parents and friends of the student-athletes. Exercise was reserved for Army recruits in basic training, while high school gym classes were places where students learned the rules of games and arcane aspects of personal hygiene.

Many of those beliefs changed when I went to college. My undergraduate years were spent at the University of New Mexico where Bob King coached the Lobo basketball team. Being a fan was almost a graduation requirement during those years when the "Pit" was built and Texas Western became the Western Athletic Conference and then national champions. Fitness and health were still not high on my list of life's imperatives, but student-athletes were slowly gaining my respect. A charismatic 440 runner named Adolph Plummer caught my attention because, not only was he a great sprinter, but he represented the university in the community.

Attending Yale University as a graduate student, I was introduced to some of the long-standing Ivy League rivalries, beginning with Harvard-Yale Football, continuing with crew, squash, and a variety of other intercollegiate sports. It was at Yale that I began to participate in intramurals, playing on the Branford College squash team and participating in winning the Yale championship.

So as I advanced educationally, I matured in my acceptance of the pervasiveness of athletics in college life at all levels. I also began to understand the importance of the contribution intercollegiate athletics makes to a university and to individual students' lives whether they are intercollegiate student-athletes, participate in intramurals, become fans, or simply attend the institution for an education and ignore athletics. The complexity of administering an intercollegiate athletics program has also become obvious, along with the danger of participating in "big time" athletics and the potential benefit to the institution.

The lessons learned during my undergraduate and graduate careers were reemphasized throughout my professional academic career. Having served at schools having National Collegiate Athletic Association (NCAA) DII and DI programs, both large and small, I have experienced most levels of athletic competition, as well as health and fitness programs.

So my purpose in writing this chapter is to explain in simple terms, the promise and pain of supporting intercollegiate athletics, intramural athletics, and health and fitness programs to university life from the perspective of the chief executive officer. It is also my intent to suggest some best practices, common sense approaches, and just plain appropriate behaviors in dealing with athletics and athletes.

Universities Expand the Mind! Why Bother with the Body?

A mind may be a terrible thing to waste, but so may be a body, and the interrelatedness of the development of mind and body is nontrivial. Even putting aside all of the Greek and Roman arguments about sound minds in sound bodies, world society has become focused on health, fitness, and competitive athletics. Consider, for example, the high percentage of television advertising devoted to muscular development, aerobic fitness, and weight control. Even the advertisements for prescription drugs mention diet and exercise as adjunct to their successful use. In addition, consider the attention paid to World Cup Soccer, professional sports, and even golf, which to everyone's surprise has become a spectator sport. Finally, realize that there is a body of research supporting the idea that learning is facile and more successful when the learner feels good.

All of these observations lead to a conclusion that, since university education prepares students for their place in society, health, fitness, and athletics have a place in university life. In fact, they occupy an important place. Thus, investment in these programs is not only important, but critical.

Given, this three legged stool (health and wellness, intramurals, and intercollegiate athletics), how does a university decide where emphasis, investment, and attention should be applied? Certainly, health and wellness are important. Whether they are a part of the academic program, extracurricular offerings through student affairs, or options through an intercollegiate athletics program, all three legs of the stool definitely have a place in university life.

What about intramural programs? Whether or not a university chooses to support them, students will find ways to compete, physically. Be it flag football, pick-up football, pick-up basketball, casual softball, Frisbee, or any other sport, our students and even our staff will compete. As a result, the university is better served by organizing the activities, lessening the possibility of injury, altercation, and therefore university liability.

Where do intercollegiate athletics fit in? The massive risk and potential reward represented by such programs demands commensurate university attention and investment. If a university opts to participate, initial determination of the level of participation, the investment, and the extent of oversight, becomes a central issue in many administrative discussions. Once a decision is reached, ongoing oversight and support become a continuing part of university administrative life. Depending on the level of participation, that part of university attention can be fairly small or very large. However, whatever the level, the programs demand focused attention.

Continuing the metaphor, the three legged stool requires some strength in all three legs. However, depending on the college or university, one or another of those legs may be stronger or weaker. Some universities are massively invested in intercollegiate athletics programs, to the extent that the stool appears to stand on only one leg. Others are much more evenly distributed. We'll examine these approaches, considering each program individually and then describing an integrated program.

Health, Wellness, and Fitness

Health, wellness, and fitness comprise a broad spectrum of programs and events offering the possibility of long life and happiness to both students and staff. Where students are concerned, most are young enough that they still believe themselves to be both invincible and immortal, causing many to ignore the benefits of participation. Counter balancing that belief is our society's nearly pathological attention to body shape and condition, and the salutary effects of both diet and exercise, and monitoring of body condition.

The result of the weight of such student attitudes is the requirement for the university to provide both programs and facilities commensurate with student demand. Not surprisingly, student demand is geographically dependant, causing requirements for facilities and programs to be greater at institutions located in sun-drenched climates than in cooler ones where student bodies are more often hidden in layers of clothing. However, there are minimum standards to which attention must be paid.

First, exercise facilities are *essential*. It is difficult to imagine constructing new student housing without including both aerobic and weight training devices. Similarly, and depending on the size of the campus, distributing such facilities conveniently to student needs is required. Further, defined running and walking paths often become part of the culture of many institutions, as does the continuous maintenance of both indoor and outdoor exercise areas, as well as the safety of those facilities.

Several issues are worthy of careful consideration:

1. Should faculty, staff, and student indoor exercise facilities be separate? At many institutions, integrating student and faculty-staff experiences is a core value in campus culture, while at others, separation is the norm. Whether or not integration occurs depends on the character of the institution. I am familiar with one institution whose students were banished from the gymnasium steam room when the president wanted to use it. Such behavior, for better or worse, is a defining aspect of the institution.
2. Should intercollegiate athletics facilities be separated from those used by the rest of the community? This is much more difficult question because, for most universities, the funds used to purchase the equipment and facilities consist of comingled general and private resources. Further, the emotional fallout resulting from separation can be

overwhelming; conversely, the intensity of use by intercollegiate student-athletes may be off-putting to many in the rest of the community. An ancillary and potentially controversial issue relates to the quality and quantity of equipment in intercollegiate athletics facilities as opposed to that in facilities available to the general population. Qualitative and quantitative differences can result in controversies that drain leadership time and energy and result in a negative effect on the campus environment.

3. To what extent should leadership be seen using exercise facilities? To a great extent, this question is answered in terms of leadership styles. Use of such facilities by leaders underscores leadership commitment to these programs and promotes a message that the equipment and facilities are "good enough for use by everyone." Furthermore the promotion of fitness is a priority, and leaders must be seen participating.

Health and wellness programs offer an expanded dimension to fitness. Aside from the existence of such programs lessening the cost of health insurance to the university, there are obvious positive benefits to raising awareness of health issues through medical screenings, nutrition training, and general health education. Healthy, fit students are simply more effective learners (Kamijo and Takeda, 2009; Masley, Roetzheim, and Gualtieri, 2009)! Leaders must also participate in these programs to emphasize their support of both the concept and the individual programs.

Aside from the benefits accruing to individuals on a campus resulting from the presence of health, wellness, and fitness programs, the collaboration resulting when different parts of the campus cooperate in developing the programs can be a model in fostering further campus collaboration. This attitude can be nurtured as competitions are created around weight loss, health screening participation, miles or steps taken in walking events, and even cholesterol levels. Staffs throughout the university learn more about each other and, through that knowledge and respect, begin to support students better.

Intramurals and Controlling Intracampus Competition

The natural tendency for college students to play games has been well documented, especially in the conversations of many administrators. However, the extent of the desire for competition is easily seen in the popularity of one-on-one basketball, flag football, and ultimate Frisbee, among other physical contests. Given the liability inherent in having such contests occurring unsupervised on a university campus, it is in the university's best interest to organize these events in environments that might be safer. An intramural program, well supervised, represents just such an environment.

The best intramural programs have several working parts, which include rules instruction, a cadre of trained referees and umpires, venues that are well maintained and therefore safer, safety training for all involved, and a carefully constructed program of competitions and events. While this description might seem a daunting list to institutions expecting to simply "host" games, it is a list that results in the institution's least exposure.

In addition, intramurals can be a means to draining off excess energy through competition and physical exertion. They are also a means to teach sportsmanship, teamwork, communication, and organizational skills. Further, involving students in the administration of these programs emphasizes skill sets that are often ignored in the traditional classroom.

Pitfalls are, of course, numerous. The competition can become so intense that physical confrontations ensue and become uncontrollable. Accusations of cheating can occur (by the way, cheating can occur!). But in spite of these dangers, the investment is worthwhile and possible benefits are enormous!

The investment can be large or small, depending on the sophistication of the program, but it is important to remember that the benefits outweigh all of the negative aspects. And funding, since the program touches so many students, can be gleaned, justifiably from several sources—general fund, private and public funds, student's fees, and even user fees.

On a final note, I don't recommend senior leadership participation in student intramural athletics, unless the sport involved is as benign as golf. There is nothing worse than the regret associated with being physically impaired, temporarily or otherwise, as a result of unnecessary participation. In this case, the possibility of injury outweighs the positives resulting from being seen as a "good guy" (no sexism intended).

Intercollegiate Athletics

Participation in intercollegiate athletics has become the norm for all but a handful of colleges and universities. It's a natural extension of the competitive spirit we all feel as we aspire to work at an institution that one believes is stellar both academically and in every other way. Claiming that an institution is academically outstanding can be a nearly data-free assertion;

the "won-lost" record of its athletics teams directly determines its athletics ranking. Pride in an institution's athletics program should be based not only on its won-lost record, but also on the integrity of its program, its student-athletes' academic performance, and how well its student-athletes represent the institution. The challenge is finding a level of participation that best fits the institution and its values and aspirations and then participating at that level in a manner that best matches the values, integrity, and treasury of the institution, its students, and its faculty.

Levels of Involvement and Commitment: How Deep Is the Quicksand?

Institutional decisions about intercollegiate athletics begin with whether investments of time and money make sense, continue with where the institution fits into existing national athletics organizations, and often end, after much consideration, in a situation that may or may not be good for the institution. The questions that an institution must answer: NCAA, National Association of Intercollegiate Athletics (NAIA), or National Junior College Athletic Association (NJCAA)? Scholarship or non-scholarship? Conference or independent? Number and mix of sports? Staff size? Answers to these questions and others determine how much an institution must invest and to what extent athletics will pervade the life of the institution.

Further, even when an institution is already involved in athletics and is considering changing associations or status within an association, the same questions arise. So for all institutions, it's worth discussing some possible answers.

1. When considering which athletics organization to join, the NJCAA is open only to junior colleges. Both the NCAA and NAIA are open to all four-year institutions. The NAIA is less organized, less well known, and has fewer members than the NCAA. Its rules are less intrusive, enforcement is less rigid, and oversight is less intense. In fact the thickness of the NCAA rulebook is testimony to the high and detailed standards adhered to by the organization and that it grows every year is an indication that coaches are constantly finding ways around the rules, causing new ones to be written and added. All of these organizations are member governed and member driven, but some members have greater influence then others. Many of the colleges in the NAIA are smaller than those in the NCAA and commonly have religious affiliation.

Both the NAIA and the NCAA are divided into divisions. Belonging to the NCAA Division I requires an institution to participate in a minimum of 14 sports (7 men's and 7 women's or 6 men's and 8 women's) and give athletics scholarships and athletics grants-in-aid in excess of 78, whereas membership in NCAA Division II requires no minimum number of athletics scholarships and athletics grants-in-aids but sets upper limits on scholarship numbers and requires participation in 10 (5 men's and 5 women's) varsity sports. Participation in NCAA Division III requires participation in10 (5 men's and 5 women's) sports and that no athletics scholarships or athletics grants-in-aids be allocated. The NAIA has such requirements for divisional participation, but for the sake of simplicity the focus here will be on the NCAA. Imagine, then, the extent of institutional involvement across many university constituencies as changes are made in affiliation, number of sports, and number of student-athletes.

2. Many institutions play football, which is a requirement in the NCAA's Football Bowl Subdivision (FBS, also formerly known as Division I-A) and Football Championship Subdivision (FCS, also formally known as Division I-AA) but not a requirement for participation in Division I-AAA. Playing football is not a requirement for Division II or Division III participation.

3. Once organizational affiliation is determined, an institution must choose a conference in which to play. Sometimes, as was the case with Indiana University–Purdue University Fort Wayne (IPFW), no conference will accept a new institution, and the institution is forced to play as in independent. Playing as an independent makes scheduling difficult and minimizes representation of the institution to parent organizations. This is no longer possible in movement to NCAA Division I, since conference affiliation is required for participation at that level.

Whatever decisions are made, effect on budget becomes of paramount importance, especially to students, faculty, and boards of trustees. Unfortunately, the glitter of athletics prominence often results in cloudy decisions that should be based on the glitter in the institution's budget.

NCAA or NAIA: The Devil or the Deep Blue Sea?

For institutions with four-year programs, there are only two choices for affiliation with athletics organizations, the NCAA and the NAIA. Both organizations espouse a philosophy focused on the student-athlete emphasizing that education is the goal of participating institutions and that the primary goal of the student-athlete and the program ought to be obtaining a high-quality education. Comparing the two organizations, the NCAA is by far the more powerful, the more pervasive, the better organized, organization. It boasts having over 1,000 member institutions divided into three divisions. The NAIA claims approximately 300 member institutions divided into two divisions. Many of the member institutions in Divisions I and II of the NCAA are commonly large (>10,000 students), nationally prominent, or regionally prominent universities. Division III of the NCAA consists primarily of small liberal arts colleges and small regional universities. The entire NAIA comprises small colleges, private and public, many with religious affiliations.

While both are member driven organizations, differences in size between the NCAA and the NAIA are obvious. The other fundamental differences include prominence, oversight and control, and financial commitment and benefit. The NCAA is definitely the more prominent organization exemplified by its ownership of the BCS football championship and the Final Four basketball championship, both national treasures in several senses. This ownership also enhances the financial position of the NCAA allowing it to return resources to member institutions. However, both the size and sophistication of the NCAA have caused the organization (supported by its members) to assert greater control and insist on more thorough oversight of member athletics programs than the NAIA. Although this kind of close control is abhorrent to many academics, the potential for abuse in athletics programs almost demands certification and compliance programs. In general, these programs protect both the student-athlete and the institution. It is important to remember that both organizations can be friend or foe, sometimes simultaneously, depending on the situation. When dealing with them, it is often useful to remind oneself that they believe they have the best interest of the student-athlete in mind.

In general, while some institutional conditions and characteristics might make affiliation with the NAIA the right choice for some colleges and universities, the NCAA offers greater support, organizational gravitas, and service to its members. To further expand on this point, consider the various levels of participation in NCAA sports, exemplified by its divisional structure. Division I is parsed into three levels of participation. FBS comprises very large and/or well-known schools having nationally prominent football programs that will qualify for the BCS. FCS comprises large schools that have slightly less high-profile football programs, but do participate in the sport. Division I-AAA comprises large and small institutions which do not participate in football at all. All Division I schools are required to participate in a minimum of 14 sports and to provide a minimum number of full scholarships which increases from Division I-AAA through FCS and reaching a pinnacle in FBS. Participation in Division I requires large institutional resource commitments to cover the scholarship commitments and large emotional and temporal commitments to cover the level of oversight demanded by the NCAA.

NCAA Division II participation requires fielding fewer teams and providing fewer scholarships than participation in NCAA Division I and rules and oversight are less intrusive and constricting at this level, but the emphasis on academic performance remains. The physical manifestation of this difference is that the rulebook is just plain thinner.

NCAA Division III participation requires offering no scholarship support to student-athletes. As a result, the level of athletic performance may be considerably lower than the other divisions, but the motives and programs are thought to be much purer. Hence, participation at this level includes many liberal arts colleges whose athletics budgets are small, whose athletics motives are pure, and who claim to believe in the "sound body, sound mind" concept.

Considering the NCAA landscape, the financial risks and rewards for participation in NCAA Division I are far greater than those at NCAA Division II or NCAA Division III. However, the excitement, the rivalries, the loyalties generated in athletics can be generated at all levels, so choosing a level of participation might depend on an unexpected set of considerations.

First, Division I is expensive! Not only do the scholarships and number of sports supported result in financial burdens, but the NCAA has imposed an entry fee exceeding $1 million on Division I participation. Further, the infrastructure, which includes locker rooms, weight facilities, personnel, student services, travel, equipment and apparel, compliance officers, sports information directors, and an army of assistant coaches, is formidable. Participation in Division II requires less financial commitment, but much of the infrastructure and many of the scholarships are still required. Division III participation is much less a financial burden. There are no scholarship investments, fewer compliance issues, and less need for legions of athletics personal.

Further, Division I participants are scrutinized to a much greater extent by faculty, governing boards, internal auditors, news media, and the general public than participants in Division II or Division III. If the program is clean and successful, Division I can be a priceless public relations asset. Whether or not a Division II or Division III program is clean and successful or dirty and unsuccessful, unless felonies are committed in the name of the program, seems to be of much less concern to faculty, administrators, and the general public.

This realization lends to an interesting conclusion. If the resources are available for Division I participation and the commitment to carefully construct and oversee the program exist, then the public relations reward can outweigh the risk.

Participation in Division II makes less sense. Fairly large investments must be made in scholarships and infrastructure, and there will be little financial or public relations payoff for the effort.

However, participation in Division III requires little investment, no one will look carefully at the program, and the satisfaction of having intercollegiate athletics will be fulfilled. Put simply, given appropriate resources, participation in Division I or Division III makes sense. Participation in Division II does not.

Many of the same arguments can be made in discussing NCAA versus NAIA, but in terms of prominence, the choice is obvious. However, in many moderate-size communities, publicity within the community is independent of affiliation, so either choice is acceptable. Once that choice is made, the next challenge is joining a conference. Why is it important to be in a conference? Conference membership supports scheduling of athletics events, minimizes team travel (and therefore, student time out-of-class), enhances representation to the NCAA or NAIA, and provides a community of people with like interests who can be called on for advice and counsel.

Attempting to join an athletics conference can be a harrowing experience especially at the Division I level. Conferences should comprise members who fit into a geographical footprint, have similar interests, and are at similar competitive levels. But no matter how much analysis an institution does of its relative position with respect to these criteria, the presidents of the institutions in the existing conference will believe their programs are prettier and more competitive and their academic programs stronger. As a result, the conference commissioner will be coy, the athletics directors will send conflicting messages, and the CEOs will be disingenuous. When it's all over and a decision has been made to accept or reject your institution, you might come away thinking that everyone associated with intercollegiate athletics is dishonest. Of course, that is not accurate.

The important lesson is that you need to be in a conference. In the end, you'll accept all manner of insults and demeaning treatment to get there.

So choosing an athletics association, selecting a level of play, and becoming a member of a conference are necessary parts of developing an athletics program. All of the associated processes have the characteristics of arts rather than sciences. However, once those goals are accomplished, and student welfare, program integrity, and athletics accomplishment can become a focus, the real fun of intercollegiate athletics begins.

Several years ago, we at IPFW made the decision to move from NCAA Division II to NCAA Division I for many of the reasons described above. The combination of public pressure and poor return on investment at NCAA Division II made the choice obvious. We then suffered through all of the problems associated with being an independent, including begging and groveling to become part of a conference. Eventually, we joined the Summit League; but we encountered all of the problems described earlier.

Student Welfare and Institutional Control

Central to the missions of the university and the NCAA and NAIA is the development and welfare of student-athletes. For the university, it is the welfare of all students. For the NCAA and NAIA, the focus is on student-athletes. Unfortunately, because so much resource and energy are invested in athletics programs, the university's obligation can become blurred and student-athletes can be subject to exploitation. University policies and NCAA or NAIA rules work together to minimize that possibility.

Focusing on the NCAA, the rule book governing student-athlete participation is extensive and complicated, containing a broad range of subjects ranging from academic performance to gifts from donors to living accommodations to game and tournament administration. For example, student-athletes are expected to make specific levels of progress toward graduation within specified periods of time. Student-athletes are protected from coaches making undue demands on their time for training, practice, and athletic preparation. Boosters cannot give gifts to student-athletes except under very special, controlled circumstances. Games and matches are run according to a very strict set of rules.

In fact, these rules have become so extensive and the rule book so thick that they must be overseen and executed by a compliance officer. While the general philosophy and attitudes of athletics directors, coaches, athletics staffs, and the central administrations of universities are the primary factors in institutional emphasis on student welfare, the compliance officer is the lynchpin that holds the structure together. If the compliance office continually bends rules in favor of coaches or administrators, student welfare becomes secondary and student-athletes are at greater risk of exploitation. If, on the other hand, the compliance office is completely rigid in enforcing the rules, and actively seeks out rules violations, a chilling effect develops. Coaches and student-athletes become fearful that almost any behavior will result in a rules violation, which, in turn, could result in loss of resource and competitive advantage.

Two structural considerations can help ease potential problems. First, whenever possible, involve multiple parts of the university in athletics decision making. For example, when determining athletics eligibility of student-athletes, appoint a committee which includes at minimum the compliance office, the registrar, and the faculty athletics representative. When dealing with student-athlete transgressions either on or off campus, involve, at minimum, the compliance office, the affirmative action office, faculty athletics representative, and the athletics director. The dean of students should also be involved in transgressions breaching the policies applying to all students. When dealing with significant changes in athletics policy, involve as many faculty committees and administrative committees as time will allow. In general, more involvement results in less extreme behavior.

Second, if the compliance office reports to the athletics director, the athletics director is saddled with a conflict of interest. When a violation occurs, does the athletics director support what's best for the coaches, the student-athletes, the athletics program, or the university? In most situations, it's not hard to figure out what's right since pressures on the athletics director from his or her constituencies are sometimes massive. The simplest solution to this conundrum is for the compliance officer to report to the president or chancellor of the university. While the president or chancellor is fully capable of making an inappropriate decision, it is a less likely occurrence than for the athletics director. Further, such a reporting line better ensures institutional control of the program, which is one of the mantras of the NCAA. The organization expects the CEO to take responsibility for the program and remain in control of the decision-making process. Such control is better ensured by using a direct line to the compliance officer and a separate direct line to the athletics director.

Students as Athletes and Student Recruitment

Recruiting student-athletes is either an art, a science influenced by too many variables, or both. Student-athletes choose to attend an institution based on their feelings about coaching staffs, institutional reputation, housing, facilities, media exposure, and any number of other inputs to a personal algorithm that even they can't describe. So athletics programs structure their recruiting processes to show the program, institution, and community in the best light possible. Since NCAA rules prohibit giving gifts or making attractive promises to recruits, successful recruiting most often rides on the athletics and academic reputation of the institution, the personalities and reputation of coaches, and the quality of university and athletics facilities available.

Presidents and chancellors can influence the process significantly by being involved. At IPFW, I meet with every prospective student-athlete coaches will bring to my office. Not only does my taking the time impress the potential student-athlete, but the parents are even more impressed. Further, I'm able to answer questions from a different perspective than others in the university. But, most important for me and for the prospective student-athlete, I'm able to say to them, "Look at other institutions as well as this one. Think critically! Decide where you're going to be comfortable both athletically and academically. Compare coaching staffs. Decide which ones will bring out the best in you. Because if you're not happy, if you're not comfortable being at our university, you won't perform either academically or in your chosen sport. That is not acceptable, so choose well!"

Beyond that, I'm able to explain that the university expects them to be respected representatives of the institution and that the university appreciates their commitment of time, energy, and effort. As evidence of that appreciation, I commit to being present at as many of their events as possible. Further, I bring donors and other friends of the university, and I expect their behavior to reflect the university's values. I believe that approach gives them a sense of their importance to the success of the university.

In addition, as teams, they are often invited to my home. I show up at their practices for short periods. In general, I make sure that they realize that I believe in the contribution they make to the university. However, I also emphasize that their privilege results from hard work and integrity and that they earn their place in the university. It's not an entitlement, otherwise, they might become just like my perception of the athletes I knew in high school.

A similar philosophy applies to the coaches. Coaching is a tough job. A coach's success and livelihood depends on the hormonal swings of eighteen to twenty-two-year-olds. So the emotional support given coaches directly affects their ability and willingness to support student-athletes. Some coaches, of course, are paid exorbitantly, but most receive fairly ordinary remuneration. They deserve attention, appropriate congratulations, and respect that many universities are unable or unwilling to afford them. In this situation, too, the president or chancellor should fill the gap, because, in the end, both students and the university will benefit.

Students as Employees

Athletics, intramural, and health and wellness programs provide excellent opportunities for student employment within universities. Aside from making funds available to students in support of their education, students employed in the programs become spokespersons, cheerleaders, and advocates for them. Providing such employment becomes a good investment for the institution.

It is important to provide both student-athletes and student employees with advice, mentors, and general support in fulfilling their roles as representatives of the institution. That support is manifested in programs, advice, coaches' attitudes, participation in public service projects, and administrative interaction that teaches and models the importance of that responsibility. Conscious effort by both athletics and general administrators in this regard should be encouraged.

Students as Fans

The fan base for student-athletes is as important to its success, both financially and competitively as any other part of the program. While fans external to the university can be financially supportive, it is the students who become the local supporters of our teams. Further, it is often student fees that provides program financial support, so gaining and maintaining student loyalty must be a goal of the program.

Student fans can be a source of great pride for the program and the university, but they can also be a source of great embarrassment. Excessively exuberant fans cause adverse publicity, expose the institution to unwanted liability, and even cause injury to themselves and student athletes. So, from the beginning, a set of standards for fan behavior, especially on the part of students, must be established. Similarly, public fan groups, if they are formally tied to the athletics program, should adhere to behavioral standards set by the institution.

Fan behavioral issues are problematic for most universities. They simply must be monitored and dealt with sensitively so as not to lose fan support unnecessarily.

Athletes as Students

Whatever the perspectives are concerning the presence or absence of athletics on campus, it is always true that the mission of a college or university is teaching and research. Student-athletes, by and large, come to the university to learn. As the NCAA is quick to point out, student-athletes will become professionals in a broad spectrum of fields beyond athletics. Even for the few that do become professional athletes, it is important to develop the set of skills that will help them invest and expand their considerable earnings wisely.

It is the obligation of the university to ensure that student-athletes have equal access to education that the regular student population enjoys. That obligation includes integrating coaches' demands on their time and energy, helping faculty understand that intercollegiate athletics travel does not occur on a schedule chosen by the student, providing advice and counsel on progress toward degree and meeting NCAA (or NAIA) academic requirements, and an assortment of other support services that help achieve academic success.

Also helpful in developing academic integrity in an athletics program is supporting a culture wherein coaches recruit student-athletes who are academically qualified to succeed at the institution. However, persuading many coaches that athletic ability is not the sole criterion determining an student-athlete's attractiveness is difficult. Maintaining such a culture requires constant attention and expenditure of energy. Further, that approach begins in the attitude of the president or chancellor and must extend throughout the organization.

Finally, there must be constant and consistent reminders to coaches and student-athletes that their goals for education and the university's goals must be coincident. Throughout the university, there must be a common understanding that participants in athletics are student-athletes, and it is not a coincidence that the word *student* comes first.

Conclusion: In the End, Is Athletics Worth the Effort?

For the university, answering the question of whether or not to support intercollegiate athletics does not require "rocket science." It's a "no brainer." Society, students, the general public, even parents demand it. For some, it's the rivalries. For other, it's the excitement of being a fan. For many student-athletes, it's an affordable path to an education. For the media it's a professional feast. For the president or chancellor and many administrators and faculty, it can be either a dream or nightmare.

The nightmare is the risk of scandal, impropriety, breaking NCAA rules, fiscal deficit, and even moral deficiency. Many faculty view athletics as a money pit that consumes funding, which would be otherwise available for academic programs. Often, they forget that athletics scholarship funding is essentially "redeposited" into the general fund and subsistence dollars find their way into auxiliaries. That describes part of the expense side of the ledger.

On the income side, many donors support athletics while supporting nothing else at the university. Further, a significant fraction of athletics donors eventually give to academic pursuits as well. I have almost never heard of an academic donor eventually giving to athletics.

There are also the intangible credits and debits. It is difficult to measure the effects of negative publicity relating to NCAA violations, student-athlete felonies, and coaching excesses. Similarly, it is difficult to assess quantitatively the positive effects of athletic successes. However, private donations and applications have increased immediately following athletics accomplishments at many institutions.

It is also difficult to assess the negative effects of the constant concern that a president or chancellor must deal with in relation to athletics programs. Few care if an academic program becomes obsolete or fails, but everyone cares when the team loses. If there are too many NCAA violations, or a losing coach is retained, the president or chancellor has "lost control" and is blamed.

In an era when few athletics programs are profitable, when the press examines every detail of a program microscopically, and when student-athletes are pathologically intolerant of tough, old-school coaches, athletics programs remain an integral part of university life. Athletics programs are still the best way to develop passion, loyalty, and support for a university. From the presidents' or chancellors' point of view, we're all almost pathologically competitive. Athletics are just one more playing field.

Chapter Sixteen Key Points

1. Health, fitness, and athletics have a place in university life.
2. The massive risk and potential reward represented by intercollegiate athletics demands commensurate university attention and investment.
3. Health, wellness, and fitness comprise a broad spectrum of programs and events offering the possibility of long life and happiness to both students and staff.
4. Exercise facilities are *essential.*
5. Health and wellness programs offer an expanded dimension to fitness. Aside from the existence of such programs lessening the cost of health

insurance to the university, there are obvious positive benefits to raising awareness of health issues through medical screenings, nutrition training, and general health education. Healthy, fit students are simply more effective learners (Kamijo and Takeda, 2009; Masley, Roetzheim, and Gualtieri, 2009)!

6. The best intramural programs have several working parts, which include rules instruction, a cadre of trained referees and umpires, venues that are well maintained and therefore safer, safety training for all involved, and a carefully constructed program of competitions and events.
7. Pride in an institution's athletics program should be based not only on its won-lost record, but also on the integrity of its program, its student-athletes' academic performance, and how well its student-athletes represent the institution.
8. Institutional decisions about intercollegiate athletics begin with whether investments of time and money make sense, continue with where the institution fits into existing national athletics organizations, and often end, after much consideration, in a situation that may or may not be good for the institution.
9. Two structural considerations can help ease potential problems related to student welfare and institutional control. First, whenever possible, involve multiple parts of the university in athletics decision making. Second, if the compliance office reports to the athletics director, the athletics director is saddled with a conflict of interest. The simplest solution to this conundrum is for the compliance officer to report to the president or chancellor of the university.
10. Athletics, intramural, and health and wellness programs provide excellent opportunities for student employment within universities. Aside from making funds available to students in support of their education, students employed in the programs become spokespersons, cheerleaders, and advocates for them.

References

Kamijo, K., and Takeda, Y. "General Physical Activity Levels Influence Positive and Negative Priming Effects in Young Adults." *National Institute of Advanced Industrial Science and Technology*, 2009, 120(3), 511–519.

Masley, S., Roetzheim, R., and Gualtieri, T. "Aerobic Exercise Enhances Cognitive Flexibility." *Journal of Clinical Psychology in Medical Settings*, 2009, 16, 186–193.

CHAPTER SEVENTEEN

DIMENSIONS OF DIVERSITY

C. Keith Harrison, Scott Bukstein, and Walter Brock

This chapter addresses diversity and inclusion issues that impact college sport and recreation. In addition to discussing issues related to race and gender, the chapter emphasizes other dimensions of diversity. A primary focus of this chapter is on issues that current and aspiring college sport and recreation administrators are likely to face with respect to diversity and inclusion. The chapter also provides strategies and recommendations to aid current and future leaders in intercollegiate athletics and recreation in their decision-making process when diversity and inclusion issues arise or when diversity and inclusion initiatives are developed and implemented.

Dimensions of Diversity

A common perception is that diversity is a relatively new phenomenon in higher education, but a review of the history of colleges and universities in the United States quickly reveals that issues of diversity have been a part of campus life from pre-Colonial days. However, the dimensions of diversity, and the challenges and opportunities flowing from diversity, have evolved over time (El-Khawas, 2003).

Many of the current interrelated issues and trends regarding diversity and inclusion in intercollegiate athletics and recreation are thoroughly and thoughtfully examined in Cunningham's *Diversity in Sport Organizations* (2011). The remainder of this initial section of the chapter draws upon Cunningham's work and emphasizes some additional current issues regarding diversity and inclusion in college athletics and recreation programs.

Ethnicity

One of the many positive aspects of intercollegiate athletics and recreation is that they bring together many people from different backgrounds and perspectives with a finite number of common goals. Coaches and administrators have the opportunity to cultivate the interaction of teammates and program participants and to integrate various cultural perspectives throughout the team experience. With respect to ethnic diversity, one of the most pressing issues facing future college sport and recreation administrators is the miseducation of college students and the lack of precollege preparation during the K–12 socialization process for far too many participants in college athletics and recreation programs. Teachers, coaches, and other administrators must be responsive and supportive to the students they serve by understanding the students' ethnic and cultural backgrounds and the academic environments that facilitate or impede critical personal development and meaningful intergroup interaction (Comeaux, 2007).

One of the most controversial and challenging issues in intercollegiate athletics relates to the lack of equality and diversity at institutions of higher learning with respect to leadership roles within college sports (Lapchick, 2009). For instance, although 2009 and 2010 were watershed years for college athletics programs as the total number of African-American coaches at the Football Bowl Subdivision (FBS) and the Football Championship Subdivision (FCS) levels reached an all-time high of 13 African American head football coaches, the data reveal that over 90% of head coaches and administrators in college athletics are White males (Harrison and Yee, 2009; Lapchick, 2009).

Similar statistics exist for other sports (as well as in campus recreation leadership and participation) regarding the overall lack of opportunities for women and people of color at the collegiate level. Why do White males continue to occupy the vast majority of the leadership and decision-making positions within college athletics and recreation departments, and what strategies (if any) can effectively and efficiently facilitate sustainable and meaningful change to the current (unfortunate) realities? As explained by Dr. Richard Lapchick, Director of the Institute for Diversity and Ethics in Sport at the University of Central Florida (TIDES), it is imperative to focus on changing numbers *and* changing attitudes through diversity management training and other diversity initiatives (Lapchick, 2009).

Nationality

As college campus recreation programs and athletics teams continue become more diverse in terms of international student enrolment and sport participation, sport and recreation administrators need to be cognizant of cultural differences and potential language barriers. Colleges and universities should look to international companies such as Disney to learn best practices. For instance, cast members at Disney point with two fingers because it is impolite in some cultures to use one finger to point.

The Drake University Bulldogs football team and the CONADEIP All-Stars, a group of student-athletes from universities in Mexico, have provided a wonderful and innovative example of working toward enhancing national diversity through intercollegiate athletics. These two teams traveled to the country of Tanzania in May 2011 to play in the Global Kilimanjaro Bowl, the first American football game in Africa. After the historic game, players from Drake and the CONADEIP All-Stars participated in community service projects in and around Moshi. According to Sandy Hatfield Clubb, Director of Athletics at Drake University, "Participation in the Global Kilmanjaro Bowl and the accompanying activities in Tanzania are a perfect coming together of Drake University's mission and values. We strive to provide opportunities that will facilitate leadership learning and prepare student-athletes to be responsible global citizens and to become champions of positive change" (Drake University, 2010).

Gender

Gender diversity is an inherently complicated and complex matter. Current important issues and problems include policies concerning how to best handle pregnancies of female student-athletes, the still-prevalent imbalances regarding Title IX compliance (see Chapter Six), the lack of revenue devoted to women's sport teams on university campuses, the divergent media coverage for women's sports, and the overall lack of leadership opportunities for women in college athletics (Cunningham, 2011).

Although Title IX has helped bring gender equality to college campuses, including intercollegiate athletics and recreation programs, efforts must continue not only to create opportunity for women to participate but also to encourage equality through co-ed events, cross-gender collaborations, and other male and female partnerships. One example that Washington State University used during the mid-1990s to bring awareness to women's abilities is a "midnight madness" mutual practice and three-point contest between the top male and female basketball players. The co-ed three-point shooting contests during the NCAA Final Four is a related example that has over the years enabled women to win, compete, and have fun shooting the basketball just as the men do.

One of the rapidly evolving issues in the realm of gender is that of transgender politics in sports. This topic has the potential to challenge the traditional definition of gender, as well as the effects on employees in sport organizations and opportunities for athletic participation. For example, in response to a lawsuit the Ladies Professional Golf Association recently decided to remove the female-at-birth requirement from the tour's constitution, thereby allowing transgender players to compete on the LPGA tour (Thomas, 2010).

Sexual Orientation

Sports, gender, and sexuality have been linked throughout much of the history of mankind (Coad, 2008; Lenskyj, 1987; Pronger, 1992). Changing societal constructions of gender and sexuality are shaped by and in turn shape the world of sports, including intercollegiate athletics and recreation. Recent years have seen significant changes in societal attitudes and opinions regarding homosexuality. College campuses have been centers for this change, but campus athletics and recreation (like sports in the broader society) have not been as quick as other areas to embrace (or even address) this area of diversity.

College students and student-athletes can be the catalysts for changing the culture of intercollegiate athletics and recreation. Hudson Taylor, a former student-athlete at the University of Maryland, serves as an example of this sort of leadership. Hudson founded Athlete Ally as "a resource to encourage athletes, coaches, parents, fans and other members of the sports community to respect all individuals involved in sports, regardless of perceived or actual sexual-orientation or gender identity or expression" (Athlete Ally, 2011). As of March 2011, over 2,000 individuals have signed

Hudson's Athlete Ally pledge, "to lead my athletic community to respecting and welcoming all persons" (Athlete Ally, 2011).

Professionals in college athletics and recreation can also play an important role in better aligning broader societal values regarding sexuality and diversity with the values within their programs and profession. The extent to which they fulfill their potential in this regard will be shaped by their own commitment to diversity, as well as by the challenge and support offered academic preparation programs (see for example the efforts of the graduate program in Sport Management at Ithaca College) and by professional associations (see for example the It Takes a Team Program in the NCAA).

It is important to note that issues of respect and inclusion are not as simple as right and wrong. Like many questions that administrators in intercollegiate athletics and recreation address in their professional practice, these issues are complex. Take for example the decision by Belmont University, a religiously affiliated institution in Tennessee, to part company with a coach who had announced she and her female partner were having a baby (Organ, 2010).

Age

According to Cunningham (2011), "a person's age has the potential to influence various opportunities and experiences encountered in the workplace, including (a) selection; (b) training and development; (c) mentoring; (d) performance and promotion potential; and (e) exiting the organization" (p. 141). Among the coaches, players, participants, administrators, and fans of intercollegiate athletics and recreation, there are the traditionalists, the Baby Boomer generation, Generation X, and the millennial group known as Generation Y (Chamberlin, 2009). Current and future administrators must be able to relate to all of these groups, especially today's students and student-athletes (Sutton, 2010). Colleges and universities must also give thought in their recreation programs to the needs of participants at all stages of life. Adult learners, staff and faculty at mid-life or who are seniors, and children who may be dependents of members of the campus community or part of the public have very different abilities, interests, and needs when it comes to recreational activities.

Varying Ability

There is always a need for role models and mentors who challenge and even alter preconceived notions of how we view and disappointingly categorize individuals and groups based on traditional definitions of ability and disability. It is essential for current and future leaders in intercollegiate athletics and recreation to focus on the mental and physical abilities of students, student-athletes, department staff, and program participants rather than the perceived disabilities. We also need to change the culture in college athletics and campus recreation so that members of the media (for example, sportscasters) do not write articles with titles such as, "Wrestler with One Leg Wins NCAA Title" (2011).

Appearance

With respect to diversity of appearance, it is imperative to consider variables in terms of perceptions about weight, height, and physical attractiveness. In terms of weight, the pressures of body image have traditionally been associated with women in general, as well as women in sport. However, stereotypical notions about weight and body image are also present in how we perceive men.

Religious Beliefs

Although religion and spiritual beliefs are not the same, both may influence people's work behaviors in intercollegiate athletics and recreation departments, as well as directly impact the performance of students who participate in athletics or recreation activities. Future college sport and recreation administrators are encouraged to develop programs that recognize and support the religious convictions and spiritual beliefs of students, staff, and faculty while also recognizing and respecting that some may not hold such convictions or beliefs.

Team prayer at banquets and before athletics competition is a common practice both formally and informally. To respect the spiritual and religious beliefs of others, a moment of silence as a collaboration and team-building strategy attempts to equalize the divergent attitudes of faith inherent in a world with infinite religious practices. A moment of silence (with no religious undertones) can function as a way to unite, rather than divide, teammates and peers.

Social Class

Social class is now receiving greater attention as a critical dimension of diversity on college campuses than it has at any time in the history of higher education. According to Cunningham (2011), social class has the potential to influence "cognitive, interpersonal, and institutional distancing on the maintenance and promotion of classism; impact the effects of classism on people's education, health, and well-being including their sport participation; and the manner in which sport involvement results in social mobility" (p. 237).

Student-athletes come from privileged, middle class, and disadvantaged backgrounds as well as possess international perspectives about the realities of life. One of the first chances for this social class disconnect is during the recruiting process for all college sports—particularly for the revenue sports such as football and basketball. Student-athletes in many instances are recruited to predominantly White institutions that reflect the values, norms, and mores of a middle class lifestyle. Student-athletes at the micro level and institutions at the macro level must become more informed and must be able to code-switch and effectively communicate with mainstream populations as they make the transition from young adult to business professional in the corporate world.

Diversity of Thought

One area not addressed in depth by Cunningham (2011) is that of *diversity of thought.* As explained by Liswood (2010), "Diversity—true diversity—requires changes to unconscious attitudes. To start, it is important to be aware that in all social and work settings there are dominant and nondominant groups" (p. xvii). Dr. Bill Sutton (2006) observes, "You want an individual to come into an organization and get you to think about some things you had not thought about prior to their arrival, but further you want them to challenge you to think about some things differently than you have already thought about." Diversity of thought encompasses three related concepts: *diversity of privilege*, *diversity of style*, and *diversity of life circumstances.*

Diversity of privilege relates to differences associated with privilege-related dynamics such as access to resources and one's personal sense of racial, cultural, and athletic entitlement. Inherent tensions exist with respect to access to financial and educational resources, and the resultant assumed entitlements (for example, tensions between growing up without access to certain resources and material possessions versus the perceived benefits and rights associated with "earning" an athletics scholarship). For example, five Ohio State University football players were suspended in December 2010 by the National Collegiate Athletic Association (NCAA) for the first five games of the following football season and had to repay certain amounts to charity for selling championship rings, jerseys, and other personal awards. Notably, the NCAA did not suspend the players for the team's bowl game because the student-athletes "did not receive adequate rules education during the time period the violations occurred" (Miller, 2010). Miller continues by saying, "as a student-athlete, you're not allowed to use your persona to get discounted services." Gene Smith, director of athletics at Ohio State University, also expressed that he thought the penalty imposed on the student-athletes should have been mitigated and reduced because, "The time this occurred with these young men was a very tough time in our society. It's one of the toughest economic environments in our history ... The decisions that they made they made to help their families" (Miller, 2010). The comments by Gene Smith argue for taking into account *diversity of life circumstances* when developing, implementing, and enforcing policies, rules, and regulations. When Jim Tressel, former head football coach at Ohio State University, was asked to comment on this situation, he responded, "We all have a little sensor within us, 'Well, I'm not sure if I should be doing this' ... And sometimes it gets overrided by what you think your necessity is ... I would have to think that there was no way that they just thought that [selling items] would be common practice" (ESPN, 2010). The former high school football coach of one of the suspended Ohio State University student-athletes explained, "Sometimes when you're young you don't realize the ramifications" (ESPN, 2010).

College sport administrators cannot assume that today's college students and student-athletes (or college coaches for that matter) have the sensor in their brains that Coach Tressel referred to; instead, we need to proactively educate and inform students and student-athletes to shift their mindset and alter problematic behavior patterns before major predicaments surface. It is imperative to understand how students and student-athletes *think* before leaders and administrators in collegiate athletics and directors and campus recreation administrators can effectively impact how student-athletes *act*.

Diversity of style relates to the various ways in which students (including those members of the general student body who participate in campus recreation programs) and student-athletes express their individuality and personality. Examples include the hair style of student-athletes (for example, shaved head versus cornrows), how student-athletes celebrate after making a three-point shot or scoring a touchdown (and the resultant—oftentimes overly critical—response by members of the media), and the manner in which student-athletes express themselves through other material possessions such as clothes and accessories. This concept also relates to how students and student-athletes conceptualize the right way to resolve disputes, which is impacted by their unique value structure and upbringing. College sport administrators must become adept at making judgment calls regarding which expressions of style should be tolerated and embraced (hair style and end-zone celebrations) compared with which expressions of style need to be addressed and altered (teammates fighting and violating NCAA rules to get a tattoo).

The reality is that some of the current decision makers in collegiate athletics and recreation programs struggle in their attempts to relate to and understand the thought and decision-making process of contemporary student-athletes in part due to diversity of life circumstances. Before we can effectively change attitudes on diversity (see, e.g., Lapchick, 2009), we need to continue to work on changing numbers. Dr. Lapchick's research reiterates "how important it is to have a diverse organization involving individuals who happen to be of a different race or gender. This element of diversity can provide a different perspective, and possibly a competitive advantage for a win in the board room as well as on the athletics fields of play" (Lapchick, 2009, p. 2).

Integrating Diversity and Inclusion into College Athletics and Recreation Programs

College students, including student-athletes, possess unique, multidimensional identities with respect to their academic, athletic, and social experiences. Numerous factors contribute to (or impede) cultural inclusiveness and meaningful diversity in college athletics and recreation. Academic research and scholarly literature in this area indicate that some of the key determinants in achieving team cohesion are working cooperatively toward common goals and having a coach (or another authority figure) emphasize his or her support for intergroup interaction (Whit, Edison, Pascarella, Terenzini, and Nora, 2001). Previous research in this area also indicates that working cooperatively toward common goals increasingly requires effectively interacting with racially and culturally diverse peers (Brown, Brown, Jackson, Sellers, and Manuel, 2003).

Two Program Models

This section of the chapter highlights two models/programs that attempt to inform student-athletes about the intersection of leadership and diversity and help increase the substance and quality of interaction among all students on campus. While designed with student-athletes in mind, both programs can be adapted for use in campus recreation departments to promote diversity and inclusion.

NCAA. The NCAA encourages its member institutions and athletics conferences to be "committed to creating and supporting an inclusive culture that fosters equitable participation for student-athletes and career opportunities for coaches and administrators from diverse backgrounds" (NCAA, 2011). The NCAA understands that academic institutions and their corresponding athletics departments must work together to develop creative and practical programs relating to diversity and inclusion. Each year the NCAA conducts diversity education workshops to help student-athletes augment their understanding of and respect for diversity and inclusion in college athletics.

In addition, the NCAA developed the CHAMPS (Challenging Athletes Minds for Personal Success)/Life Skills program in part "to develop and enhance the life of the student-athlete through educational programs and resources focusing on gender equity, student-athlete welfare and life skills" (NCAA CHAMPS/Life Skills Pamphlet, 2005, p. 1). The NCAA recently rebranded the CHAMPS/Life Skills Program when it created the Student-Athlete Affairs unit, which aims to provide "life skills support in the areas of academics, athletics, personal development, career development and service through the distribution of accessible resources, strategic partnerships and customized programming" (NCAA, 2011).

Individual NCAA member institutions have also developed innovative and impactful diversity training workshops and seminars. One example of such an initiative relates to a program hosted at the University of Central Florida in March 2011. Dave Pallone, a former Major League Baseball umpire, delivered a powerful presentation to students, faculty, and members of the local community on sexual orientation issues in sport.

Scholar-Baller Program. The Scholar-Baller® Program, which was established in 1995 to help bridge the gap between education, sport, and popular culture, serves as an example of a culturally relevant program that incentivizes student-athletes to excel academically and that also fosters positive and meaningful interaction between team members. The Scholar-Baller Program focuses on deep-level diversity (Harrison, Price, and Bell, 1998), which relates to meaningful differences that only become apparent through interacting with others who posses dissimilar attitudes, beliefs, values, culture, or preferences (Cunningham, 2011). The Scholar-Baller Program focuses on culture, race, gender, and lifelong learning with a foundational focus on diversity.

The mission of the Scholar-Baller Program is to inspire youth and young adults to develop leadership skills and to excel in education and life by using their cultural interests in sport and entertainment. Scholar-Baller, which is a not-for-profit organization endorsed by the NCAA, has developed an extensive curriculum for NCAA member institutions (Harrison and Boyd, 2007). Student-athletes at schools that have adopted the Scholar-Baller Curriculum have an opportunity to compete in terms of *academic* performance while simultaneously gaining the opportunity to interact with teammates of different races, ethnicities, and social classes—teammates who also have diverse personalities, perspectives, and values. The Scholar-Baller Program requires cooperation and interdependence among all student-athletes on each athletics team, which reduces prejudice toward "out-group" members (Allport, 1954; Cunningham, 2011).

Scholar-Baller has also partnered with the National Consortium for Academics and Sports (NCAS) to establish the Academic Momentum Award to recognize student-athletes who demonstrate significant classroom performance. The Academic Momentum Award highlights various diversity frameworks and constructs, as male and female student-athletes with diverse skill sets and learning abilities all have the opportunity to earn this prestigious annual award. Each year for the past four years, the Academic Momentum Award has proven that many student-athletes overcome the stigmas attached to their potential to perform at the highest level.

Preparing Future Leaders in College Athletics and Recreation

Academic institutions must continue to systematically address issues concerning diversity and inclusion. Intercollegiate athletics and campus recreation programs serve as forums where educators (including coaches, administrative staff, and students) are able to teach one another about the complex nature and meaning of diversity and inclusion.

In the course of developing this chapter, the authors consulted with colleagues regarding advice for administrative professionals in college recreation programs on diversity-related issues. The list provided by Stan Shingles, vice-president of Campus Recreation at Central Michigan University, Jim Wilkening, recreation and wellness director at the University of Central Florida, and Michael Freeman, assistant director in the Office of Diversity Initiatives at the University of Central Florida includes advice for those working in recreation and for those working in intercollegiate athletics:

1. Recruit and hire a diverse staff that is representative of the broader university.
2. Create a welcoming and supportive environment that promotes an all-inclusive atmosphere.
3. Offer nontraditional programs that will attract female and other underrepresented student populations.
4. Develop handicap accessible participatory areas and programs.
5. Provide private family locker rooms that accommodate transgender students.
6. Improve the cultural competency of the entire campus recreation staff (J. Wilkening, personal communication, January 20, 2011).

Conclusion

The preceding strategies and recommendations illustrate that facilitating diversity and inclusion requires dedication, preparation, persistence, and relevance. However, effective initiatives need to move beyond diversity and need not be labeled as diversity workshops. There is clearly a difference between tolerating diversity and celebrating diversity. Stated differently, "when we put different people together—which diversity inherently does—we have to go the next step, move beyond diversity, and be conscious of who we and others are. Only then can we get the true value of that diversity, make the workplace fair, keep the pipelines flowing, and have more effective global companies" (Liswood, 2010, p. 134).

Current and future leaders in intercollegiate athletics and campus recreation are encouraged to continue to develop and implement creative, culturally relevant, practical, and impactful programs that focus on professional development, embrace all forms of diversity, and facilitate meaningful intergroup interaction. In addition, college faculty members are encouraged to design practical courses on diversity and social issues in sport.

Chapter Seventeen Key Points

1. A review of the history of colleges and universities in the United States quickly reveals that issues of diversity have been a part of campus life from pre-Colonial days. However, the dimensions of diversity, and the challenges and opportunities flowing from diversity, have evolved over time (El-Khawas, 2003).
2. One of the many positive aspects of intercollegiate athletics and recreation is that they bring together many people from different backgrounds and perspectives with a finite number of common goals.
3. One of the most controversial and challenging issues in intercollegiate athletics relates to the lack of equality and diversity at institutions of higher learning with respect to leadership roles within college sports (Lapchick, 2009).
4. As college campus recreation programs and athletics teams continue to become more diverse in terms of international student enrolment and sport participation, sport and recreation administrators need to be cognizant of cultural differences and potential language barriers.
5. Changing societal constructions of gender and sexuality are shaped by and in turn shape the world of sports including intercollegiate athletics and recreation.
6. Colleges and universities must also give thought in their recreation programs to the needs of participants at all stages of life.
7. It is essential for current and future leaders in intercollegiate athletics and recreation to focus on the mental and physical abilities of students, student-athletes, department staff, and program participants rather than the perceived disabilities.
8. There is clearly a difference between tolerating diversity and celebrating diversity.

References

Allport, G. W. *The Nature of Prejudice.* Cambridge, MA: Addison-Wesley, 1954.
"Athlete Ally." Accessed March 29, 2011 at www.athleteally.com.

Brown, K. T., Brown, T. N., Jackson, J. S., Sellers, R. M., and Manuel, W. J. "Teammates On and Off the Field? Contact with Black Teammates and the Racial Attitudes of White Student Athletes." *Journal of Applied Social Psychology*, 2003, 33(7), 1379–1403.

Chamberlin, J. "Overgeneralizing the Generations." *Monitor*, 2009. Accessed December 30, 2010 at www.apa.org.

Coad, D. *The Meterosexual: Gender, Sexuality, and Sports*. Albany: State University of New York, 2008.

Comeaux, E. "The Student(less) Athlete: Identifying the Unidentified College Student." *Journal for the Study of Sports and Athletes in Education*, 2007, 1(1), 37–44.

Cunningham, G. B. *Diversity in Sport Organizations*. Scottsdale, AZ: Holcomb Hathaway, 2011.

Drake University. "Drake to Play First American Football Game in Africa." Drake University, 2010. Accessed May 3, 2011 at http://www.drake.edu/magazine/?p=2325.

El-Khawas, E. "The Many Dimensions of Student Diversity." In S. R. Komives and D. B. Woodard, Jr. (Eds.), *Student Services: A Handbook for the Profession* (4th ed.). San Francisco: Jossey-Bass, 2003.

Harrison, C. K., and Boyd, J. "Mainstreaming and Integrating the Substance and Spectacle of Scholar-Baller: A New Game Plan for the NCAA, Higher Education, and Society." In D. Brooks and R. Althouse (Eds.), *Diversity and Social Justice: Sport Management and the Student-Athlete*. Morgantown, WV: Fitness Information Technology, 2007.

Harrison, C. K., and Yee, S. *Protecting Their Turf: The Head Football Coach Hiring Process, and the Practices of FBS & FCS Colleges and Universities*. Report submitted for the Black Coaches & Administrators (BCA), Indianapolis, Indiana, 2009.

Harrison, D. A., Price, K. H., and Bell, M. P. "Beyond Relational Demography: Time and the Effects of Surface- and Deep-level Diversity on Work Group Cohesion." *Academy of Management Journal*, 1998, 41, 96–107.

Lapchick, R. *The 2009 Racial and Gender Report Card: College Sports*. University of Central Florida, Orlando, FL: The Institute for Diversity and Ethics in Sport, 2009.

Lapchick, R. *Protecting Their Turf: The Black Coaches and Administrators (BCA) Hiring Report Card for NCAA FBS and FCS football head coaching positions (2009–10)*. Report submitted for the Black Coaches & Administrators (BCA), Indianapolis, Indiana, 2010.

Lenskyj, H. *Out of Bounds: Women, Sport, and Sexuality*. Toronto: Women's Press, 1987.

Liswood, L. (2010). *The Loudest Duck: Moving Beyond Diversity While Embracing Differences to Achieve Success at Work*. Hoboken, NJ: Wiley.

Miller, R. "5 Buckeyes Banned for 5 Games in 2011." 2010. Associated Press. Accessed February 28, 2012 at http://www.news-herald.com/articles/2010/12/24/news/nh3450797.txt.

NCAA. *NCAA CHAMPS/Life Skills Pamphlet*. Indianapolis, IN: NCAA Publications, 2005.

NCAA. "Diversity and Inclusion." NCAA, 2011. Accessed March 27, 2011 at www.ncaa.org.

ESPN. "Ohio State Football Players Sanctioned," 2010. Accessed December 31, 2010 at www.espn.com.

Organ, M. "Belmont Disputes Gay Coach Was Fired." *The Tennessean*, December 3, 2010. Accessed on May 3, 2011 at http://www.tennessean.com/article/20101203/SPORTS06/12030362/Belmont-disputes-gay-coach-was-fired.

Pronger, B. *The Arena of Masculinity: Sports, Homosexuality, and the Meaning of Sex.* New York. St. Martin's Griffin, 1992.

Sutton, W. A. *Diversity of Thought.* Orlando, FL: University of Central Florida, 2006.

Sutton, W. A. "Leagues, Teams Must Give Fans New Reasons to Give Up the Sofa." *Sports-Business Journal,* 2010, 14.

Thomas, K. L.P.G.A. "Will Allow Transgender Players to Compete." *New York Times,* December 12, 2010. Accessed on May 2, 2011 at http://www.nytimes.com/2010/12/02/sports/golf/02lpga.html.

Whit, E., Edison, M., Pascarella, E., Terenzini, P., and Nora, A. "Influences on Students Openness to Diversity and Challenge in the Second and Third Year of College." *Journal of Higher Education,* 2001, 72(2), 172–204.

"Wrestler with One Leg Wins NCAA Title." *Fox Sports, 2011.* Accessed March 30, 2011 at www.msn.foxsports.com.

CHAPTER EIGHTEEN

HEALTH AND WELLNESS ISSUES

David A. Shor, John H. Dunkle, and Carrie A. Jaworski

All college students require life balance and overall wellness to achieve at the peak of their potential (Dunkle and Presley, 2009). The many models of health and wellness in the literature today all share the central idea that wellness is more than the absence of disease; it is finding an optimal balance in the symbiotic relationships among mind, body, and spirit (Sweeney and Witmer, 1991). For student-athletes, finding this optimal balance includes the extra challenge of seeking excellence athletically in addition to excelling academically.

Many institutions of higher education in the United States today offer some form of recreational services and intercollegiate athletics programs. Recreational opportunities such as intramural and club sports and fitness and aquatic facilities provide students the opportunity to maintain healthy and balanced lifestyles as well as other avenues in which to engage outside the classroom. While they may require a significant financial investment, intercollegiate athletics programs have the potential to give much back to the institution in terms of developing campus pride and community, among many other things. In addition, both recreational and intercollegiate athletics programs offer valuable student learning opportunities that augment the academic mission of the institution.

The purpose of this chapter is to highlight the various health and wellness issues of students who participate in recreation and athletics programs and to discuss how those programs have the potential to enhance students' overall wellness and learning experiences. The chapter begins with a discussion of the health and wellness benefits of student participation in recreation and athletics programs. As suggested above, there are several benefits to students' well-being and development when they participate in these programs. The next section reviews the various physical student health issues to consider both prior to and during student engagement in activities. Following the discussion of the physical health issues, the chapter addresses the equally important student mental health concerns, including a brief overview of student health issues that have both physical and mental health components. Finally, the chapter includes a discussion of various administrative issues, including, ethical, legal, and best practice parameters of student health and wellness concerns.

The various topics discussed in this chapter are relevant to most campuses offering these programs across the country. There are a variety of institutional types and resource availability for recreational and athletics programs and for meeting the health and wellness needs of students. The focus of this chapter, however, is on student health issues only. It is understood that many campuses open their recreational services to faculty, staff, and, at times, the general public. Addressing the specific health and wellness issues of the latter groups would be beyond the scope of this chapter.

Health and Wellness: Benefits of Participation

By providing opportunities for and encouraging participation in recreation and athletics programs, institutions of higher education send a strong message that they understand the importance of overall student health and development and the importance of students finding balance while pursuing their academic pursuits. In an interview with the National Collegiate Athletic Association (NCAA) News, U.S. Secretary of Education, Arne Duncan, a former student-athlete at Harvard University, underscored the importance of students striking a balance among academics, sports, and other life activities (McKindra, 2010). The Center for Disease Control (CDC; Centers for Disease Control, 2008) reported a variety of medical and mental health benefits of physical exercise, including, but not limited to, building and maintaining healthy bones, muscles, and joints, and reducing symptoms of depression and anxiety. The CDC emphasized the essential role of creating opportunities for physical activities, providing access to facilities, offering a range of programs to meet the needs of diverse populations, and encouraging health care providers to educate young adults about the importance of regular exercise. The following sections review some of the health benefits of physical activity as well as opportunities for student learning and character development.

Benefits of Physical Activity

According to the American College Health Association-National College Health Assessment II (ACHA-NCHA II; American College Health Association, 2010), a significant number of students experience depressive symptoms that negatively influence their capacity to maximize their college experience. For example, 30% of students surveyed indicated that they "felt so depressed it was difficult to function" within the past 12 months, while 45% reported feeling "things were hopeless" in the last 12 months. These self-reports, along with the findings of increased usage of counseling center resources (Gallagher, 2010), reflect the tremendous impact of mental health concerns on the college experience. Research findings indicate that physical activity is related to positive mental health and symptom reduction and can be a key component in mediating the impact of mental health concerns on campus (Landers, 2007; Dunn and Jewell, 2010). Furthermore, physical activity need not be of excessive intensity or duration to influence mental health symptoms (Craft and Landers, 1998).

Student Learning

Physical activity and student involvement in intercollegiate athletics also create opportunities for out of classroom learning, such as character development. For example, self-discipline is developed when learning to meet the simultaneous demands of athletics and academics. Though they occur at different levels of intensity, club sports offer similar opportunities for the development of discipline through participation in rule bound physical activity. Team membership also provides the experience of responsibility to others, sharing challenges, subsuming personal desires for the greater good, and working together toward shared goals (Marsh and Kleitman, 2003). Students who participate in athletics and club sports also learn leadership skills, effective ways of dealing with authority, and the opportunity to belong to and interact with a group of diverse people (Bailey, 2006). Finally, participation in athletics nurtures the ability to maintain focus and productivity in the face of fear and anxiety.

Discipline, teamwork, healthy response to leadership, experience with diverse cultures, and anxiety management are aspects of character that enrich the lives of students. However, not all students can reach these aspirational goals easily and may struggle in the process. The following sections focus on how medical and mental health concerns are affected by the challenges and demands of athletic participation.

Physical Health Issues

As mentioned above, partaking in varsity or recreational athletics can be extremely beneficial for students on college campuses. This population is typically healthy and, therefore, few contraindications to participation usually exist. Athletics participation does, however, come with certain physical risks, making it imperative that universities take a proactive approach in educating staff and students alike on who should and should not be participating. This section discusses the main medical issues that college students participating in athletics and recreation programs face and how administrators might address them.

Pre-participation Examination

The pre-participation examination (PPE) is the foundation of sports medicine care. It is particularly important with the college-aged student-athlete, as it may be the only healthcare received in a given year. A well-done PPE can uncover contraindications to participation, identify high-risk behaviors, and provide much needed health education. Many templates exist that outline the necessary topics to cover, with the most widely recognized and accepted being the 4th edition PPE monograph (ppesportsevaluation.org). The PPE can be done on an individual basis in an office setting or for large groups as part of a station-based approach. The benefit of the individual approach is that it provides the student-athlete with privacy and more dedicated time with the physician. Station-based PPEs are more efficient and allow for greater numbers of physicals to be completed.

The most integral part of the PPE is the history, as it serves as the starting point for the examination. Important areas to address are current illness or injury, prior injuries, surgeries, and history of cardiac and respiratory conditions and concussions. Additional issues to review are nutritional habits, use of medications, herbs, and supplements, and abuse of alcohol and/or illicit drugs. Menstrual history in the female student-athlete is essential, as many women are unaware of the risks associated with exercise-induced amenorrhea.

Less than 1% of athletes are excluded from sports participation entirely (Kurowski and Chandran, 2000). More than likely, the medical issue leading to exclusion is something that can be corrected through surgery, medical management, or rehabilitation. These situations require coordination between the student-athlete and the provider to establish a plan for returning to the sport. In the meantime, mental health support (discussed below) can help alleviate associated depression or anxiety that may accompany the student-athlete's hiatus from his or her sport.

A disparity exists on many college campuses where varsity student-athletes are required to have PPEs, but club and recreational student-athletes are not necessarily required to be cleared prior to participation. Recreational programs should, at a minimum, educate their participants on the importance of the PPE and provide information on how to obtain one.

The Immune System and Exercise

For the most part, the saying that "exercise is medicine" is true for athletes. Immunologic research supports the fact that moderate exercise can help to prevent illness and control chronic disease (Mackinnon, 2000). However, the "J curve hypothesis" proposes that moderate exercise is protective from mild illness, while extreme exercise increases susceptibility (Nieman and Nehlsen-Cannarella, 1992). High-level athletes are at risk for over-exercising because of the many hours dedicated to practice and competition. Overtraining syndrome is a true medical condition that may lead to excessive fatigue and more than six to twelve illnesses in a given year where no other explanation is apparent (Mackinnon, 2000). All students participating in sports need to be educated on proper diet, hygiene, recovery, and sleep habits in an attempt to minimize this risk. Resources such as sport nutritionists, sport psychologists, and stress and time management seminars can be highly effective methods to assist in this endeavor.

Infectious Disease

Student-athletes are often in close quarters both on campus and on the athletics fields. The sharing of cups, water bottles, and other equipment makes them even more susceptible to exposure to infection. Commonly seen infections on college campuses include mononucleosis, influenza, and gastroenteritis. All are viral illnesses that can significantly affect both the individual athlete and the entire teams because of the high rate of spread, risk of complications, and lack of effective or timely treatment options. Infectious mononucleosis puts an student-athlete at risk for splenic rupture, while influenza and gastroenteritis may cause significant dehydration. Community acquired methacillen-resistant staphalococcus aureus (CA-MRSA) is a bacterial skin infection that can also affect otherwise healthy individual student-athletes and teams on college campuses. Spread of CA-MRSA is from skin to skin contact or contact with infected surfaces (Hosey and Rodenberg, 2007).

Student health centers, athletics departments, and university administrators should work collaboratively to develop educational initiatives in an effort to prevent spread of such diseases. The recent H1N1 scare of 2009 was an example of how, with the help of the CDC, universities and athletics conferences across the nation were able to successfully plan to limit the spread of the disease. Placement of hand sanitizing stations at athletics and academic facilities, as well as paper and website-based educational information, helped decrease both the spread of disease and the fear of the disease. In addition, athletics teams should receive influenza vaccinations annually, if resources allow, to further minimize the risk of disease. Club and recreational sport student-athletes should be reminded to seek out services at their health centers to do the same (Harper and colleagues, 2009).

Common Illnesses

Other common illnesses, such as the common cold, are seen year-round in student-athletes, and the key question is whether or not a student-athlete should participate. The usual rule is to do a "neck check" popularized by Eichner (1993). The rule is that if the symptoms are above the neck, such as congestion, runny nose, and sore throat, most can participate as tolerated. Student-athletes with symptoms that are below the neck such as fever, vomiting, diarrhea, shortness of breath, or productive cough should be educated to curtail physical activity until symptoms subside. Education on proper hydration during illness is also essential to recovery.

Injury, Surgery, Rehabilitation

Medical staff must address several issues with a student-athlete who is injured. First, the staff must determine what will be required to return safely to participate. Orthopedic injuries often need imaging and rehabilitation initially, but some may warrant immediate surgical intervention. It is critical that clear communication on time frames and expectations occur among the medical team, the student-athletes, and the coaches. While the student-athlete is injured, accommodations for transportation and academic responsibilities may be required.

A concussion will require a great deal of education to the student-athlete on the recovery process and the benefit of brain rest. It is often recommended that the concussed student-athlete avoid excessive reading and computer work in order to speed recovery. A concussed student-athlete may also need ongoing neuropsychological evaluation. Educating academic advisors and professors on the expected duration of academic restrictions that a concussed student-athlete faces will assist greatly.

Any injured student-athlete should be monitored for mental health issues that could potentially arise. Ongoing monitoring should occur as the student-athlete reintegrates with the team and his or her sport. Having a medical staff who can address these issues in an expedient manner is essential to avoid putting student-athletes at risk. Most universities have an athletic training staff and team physicians for their varsity programs, however, the recreational side is often at a disadvantage in this area. Making sure these student-athletes are aware of student health and other resources for care is essential.

Mental Health Issues

Though physical activity (Landers, 2007) and participation in intercollegiate team sports may enhance mental health (Proctor and Boan-Lenzo, 2010), engagement in athletics and recreational competition may create unique challenges that potentially contribute to the development of psychological conditions. The culture of sports contains its own rules, norms, and values; therefore, to understand the issues facing student-athletes, one must take cultural context into consideration. This section focuses on the aspects of athletic and recreational involvement that may contribute to and potentially exacerbate existing mental health concerns.

Depression

Student-athletes are at-risk for developing depressive symptoms when participation does not have a buffering influence that is common for students who participate in athletics and recreation programs. For example, an adverse change in the relationship with one's sport may result in or exacerbate depressive feelings. Also, negative relationships with coaches can affect the mood of a student-athlete; coaches have a significant impact on the lives of student-athletes, including controlling the opportunity to compete. The loss of competition and positive athletic self-regard may threaten important elements of a student's identity.

Dealing with an injury can be a painful and disruptive process for an athlete (Taylor and Taylor, 1997). Within athletics, there is a difference between being hurt and being injured. When one is hurt, the implicit expectation is to play through the pain. However, when injured, one is unable to compete. On the base level, there is dealing with ongoing pain and the potential problems associated with undergoing surgery. If a surgery does not go as planned, it can be career ending. The period of rehabilitation from injury remove student-athletes from the physical outlet to which they are accustomed and isolates them from their community. Rehabilitation itself can be a lonely and painful process, with progress sometimes measured in small or barely noticeable increments. Inevitably, doubt and worry are present for rehabilitating student-athletes. When preparing to return, the conscious awareness of potential re-injury may increase the chances it will occur. Thus student-athletes must be aware enough of their bodies to know they need to stop an activity but not be so focused on the injury that they heighten injury risk.

Stress and Anxiety

According to the ACHA-NCHA II survey data, 76% of all students and 82% of student-athletes reported feeling overwhelmed in the prior twelve months. For many student-athletes, their athletics commitment restricts the opportunity to prepare for class or exams, often leading to stress and anxiety. For intercollegiate student-athletes, maintaining academic eligibility may interact with the opportunity to participate, because poor academic performance may lead to a suspension from their sport. Knowing how much time and energy to put into academics, athletics, or socializing at any given time requires ongoing and complex decision making.

Body Image and Eating Concerns

Athletes' bodies are their instruments, and the desire for increasing control over their instrument—and therefore their performance—may lead to body image distortions and/or eating disordered behaviors. According to Greenleaf and colleagues (2010), body dissatisfaction, increasing control over food intake, and excessive guilt are highly correlated with eating disordered symptoms in student-athletes, particularly in sports where low weight is expected or demanded (for example, wrestling or cross country running). Yeager and colleagues (1993) describe the "female athlete triad" of increased risk for eating disorders, amenorrhea, and osteoporosis. In sports requiring greater bulk or lean muscle mass, student-athletes have increased risk for muscle dysmorphia—a form of body image distortion consisting of a pathological need for muscularity. Muscle dysmorphia may increase the risk of restrictive eating and use of performance enhancing drugs (PEDs) (Pope et al., 2005).

Eating concerns may lead to a "contagion effect" (Crandall, 1988), wherein the presence of an eating concern within a group increases the likelihood of other group members engaging in unhealthy eating. Club and intercollegiate athletics teams frequently spend time eating together. Other team members may be susceptible to emulating others' behaviors (for example, restrictive eating or purging after meals), especially if it is perceived to provide an athletic edge.

Substance Use and Negative Consequences

There is evidence that students involved in athletics in high school or college may abuse alcohol more and engage in more risk-taking behaviors than students who have never been involved in athletics (Hildebrand et al., 2001). One explanation for this finding is the "work hard, party hard" frame. Student-athletes dedicate a great deal of time and energy to required activities and responsibilities, leaving less time for decompression. When the opportunity arises, they may drink more for a cathartic effect. For some male student-athletes, heavy drinking is associated with masculinity (Kimmel, 2008) and has been correlated with competitiveness (Serrao et al., 2010). Thus, binge drinking is an opportunity to prove toughness and tolerance and to continue to feel competitive.

Gaining a competitive edge may also foster the use of PEDs. The drive to do anything and everything to be the best and the fear that others will gain an advantage may lead some to risk their health and eligibility to participate. Similarly, students may misuse prescription medications in the service of trying to gain an edge academically. This is particularly the case for the class of medications prescribed for attention deficit disorder (ADD), such as Adderall, Concerta, or Ritalin. Alcohol, PED, and prescription medication abuse increase student-athletes' risk for negative consequences including, but not limited to, behavioral misconduct, missed classes and practices, sexual assault and violence, and, in the most extreme cases, death.

Another potential negative consequence of substance abuse is the increased risk of sexual violence. The risk of perpetrating sexual violence is greater when substance abuse is combined with an environment of entitlement and lack of knowledge of the definition of consent. Student-athletes may receive special treatment socially if they are campus (or national) celebrities. It is the responsibility of the recipient of special treatment or celebrity to maintain perspective and to remain respectful of others. A culture of entitlement is enhanced by the agreement to remain silent bystanders to sexual violence. The vast majority of student-athletes have never committed an act of sexual violence. However, many have witnessed behavior that made them uncomfortable but believed the social milieu prioritized silence over the opportunity to prevent significant physical and emotional damage to another person.

Adjustment Disorders

Many college students struggle with the initial adjustment to university life; however, student-athletes may face unique challenges in this regard. For example, some student-athletes leave high school early to begin practicing with their college team while others are required to end their summer early for preseason training. Thus, the adjustment to college athletics and academics must occur simultaneously. For most student-athletes, these adjustments include the shift from being a star student-athlete in high school to being the freshman on the team, trying to deal with everything and everyone being bigger, faster, smarter, and stronger than in high school. While appropriate team building activities have been shown to alleviate transition issues by enhancing team cohesion, hazing activities, which are often justified as increasing a sense of belonging, actually exacerbate adjustment issues by decreasing the overall sense of team cohesion (Van Raalte, et al., 2007).

The other side of adjustment for student-athletes is the end of one's athletic career. This can occur at the end of high school, if a student-athlete is not able to participate in intercollegiate sports, or at the end of or college, if there is no opportunity for professional participation. As a popular NCAA commercial states, "98% of student-athletes will be seeking a career outside of sports." After a five to ten year sport career, student-athletes are suddenly "retired" from an activity to which they have dedicated a great deal of time and life energy. Maintaining connection to a career identity, staying physically fit, coping with the loss of structure provided by athletics, and learning to establish social support outside of the culture are some of the challenges faced by graduating student-athletes.

Gambling

The prevalence of gambling on campus has been thoroughly documented, including the impact of sports wagering (Rockey and King, 2006) and the growth in Internet gambling (Brown, 2006). According to the Gamblers' Anonymous website (www.gamblersanonymous.org), one of the primary causes of addictive or compulsive gambling is the need to feel the adrenaline rush of risk to avoid boredom or worry. Student-athletes may be particularly susceptible to the pull of gambling, as they must attempt to fill the void left after the rush of a big game, at the end of a season, or at the end of a career. Student-athletes are also susceptible to outside gamblers who may approach them with the lure of "easy money" in exchange for inside information or game fixing.

Ethical, Legal, and Administrative Issues

The health care industry is replete with ethical, legal, and other administrative and compliance issues. These matters may be further complicated on college campuses where administrators must also abide by rules and regulations of external bodies, such as the NCAA, and institutional policies, and procedures. This chapter section highlights some of these issues and their implications for athletics and recreation programs.

Legal and Ethical Issues

The leading legal and ethical issues for health care professionals are privacy and confidentiality. While all students have the rights of confidentiality, privacy is particularly important in working with student-athletes, as they are often treated as public figures on campus. Confidentiality statutes, which are typically codified in state laws, protect medical records including both physical health and mental health records. There are, however, federal statutes, such as the *Health Insurance Portability and Accountability Act* (HIPAA; Public Law 104–191, 1996) that also affect privacy and confidentiality of medical records/information. Beginning in 2003, institutions of higher education had to assess the degree to which HIPAA influenced their campus health care services. The outcome of this process has led to a variety of interpretations and changes in policies and procedures on campuses nationwide. How the various medical confidentiality and privacy laws interact with the *Family Educational Rights and Privacy Act* (FERPA; 20 U.S.C. § 1232g, 1974) is another key issue with which institutions must grapple. FERPA, also known as the Buckley Amendment, is a federal statute that covers the confidentiality of student educational records, including disciplinary records.

While students should be able to expect health care providers to maintain their confidentiality and privacy, it is important to point out that these ethical and legal hallmarks are not absolute. There are specific circumstances under which health care providers must breach confidentiality, mainly involving danger to self or others. Patients are typically apprised of these specific conditions as part of the informed consent to treatment. FERPA has similar exceptions; however, they are much broader than the narrowly defined ones by the health related confidentiality statutes. In short, there is much more leeway to share information under FERPA on a need-to-know basis than what treatment providers can share, especially mental health providers.

Administrators and other staff of athletics and recreation programs must understand the laws surrounding privacy and confidentiality and their practical implications in working with and coordinating care for students with health care providers. Similarly, health care providers should collaborate with athletics and recreation staff when appropriate. One way to facilitate coordination of efforts among systems would be to create and maintain treatment teams who meet to discuss student-athlete cases. The team could be made up of health and mental health services and key staff from the athletics department (Shor, 2010). This teamwork is especially important given the overlap between mental and medical health in such concerns as substance abuse, eating disorders, injury rehabilitation, and prescription of psychotropic medications.

Proper care for each of these concerns requires ongoing consultation and sharing of information and may include consideration of capacity for continued participation in sports. Eating disorders, for example, may leave student-athletes at higher risk for injury such as stress fractures. Also, mental health providers must be aware that the NCAA does not permit some psychotropic medications, while others are only permitted with specific documentation of need. To ensure that confidential information can flow among team members, release of information forms could be developed for students to allow communication. In consultation with legal counsel, administrators should be aware of what is specified in statute for creating and executing a valid release of information.

Another legal and ethical trend has been the increase of students with mental health issues who may be potentially dangerous toward others. These issues continue to receive heightened attention in higher education in the aftermath of the tragedies that occurred on the campuses of Virginia Tech, Northern Illinois University, and the University of Alabama, Huntsville. In the aftermath of the Virginia Tech shootings, the Governor of the Commonwealth commissioned a review panel to evaluate the response to the incident (Virginia Tech Review Panel Report, 2007). One major recommendation from the report was the clarification of what information could be shared by campus community members about individuals of concern; the rules of FERPA were frequently misunderstood by campus administrators and others, for example. In addition, the panel underscored the importance of having campus threat assessment teams to share information and develop interventions to help prevent potential violence.

One legal outcome from these tragedies has been the legal requirement in Virginia (Va. Code § 23–9.2:10) and Illinois (110 ILSC § 12/20), for institutions of higher education to develop campus threat assessment teams to detect, assess, and monitor individuals of concern to the campus community. Other states will most likely follow the leads of Virginia and Illinois, and many institutions have had or are developing threat assessments teams without a legal mandate.

Dunkle, Silverstein, and Warner (2008) and Deisinger and colleagues (2008) discuss frameworks for developing threat assessment teams and the legal parameters surrounding them. At times, staff from the athletics and recreation departments may be called upon by the team to join discussions about students who they believe are troubled and causing disruption on or around campus. In addition to providing specific observations about students, athletics department staff are able to offer guidance around the impact of potential interventions with a student-athlete on relevant rules and regulations concerning eligibility to participate in sports. The threat assessment team provides a central location for information gathering and for staff support and guidance in dealing with a troubled student. Staff in athletics and recreation services should be aware of the threat assessment teams and how to share information with them.

Leave Policies and Fitness to Participate

At times students' health and wellness may be so compromised that they must take time away from school and, in the case of student-athletes, their sport. Further, campus athletics staff may believe that a student is not fit to participate based on health concerns. Most institutions have student leave policies that allow students to take time away from school to focus on restoring their health. Dunkle and his colleagues (2008) discuss mental health leave policies specifically, however, the issues discussed in the article are just as applicable to leaves due to other medical reasons. In most cases, students will agree to medical leave voluntarily in consultation with their health care providers and perhaps their parents. It is important with student-athletes to involve the athletics department early on, as leaves may have an impact on student eligibility issues with their sport. The athletics staff should also familiarize themselves with the institution's leave policies to understand how to initiate student leave with other systems and what reentry procedures are required to return to the institution. A coordinated effort among all campus systems can lead to the best plan for the student so that he or she can return as quickly and smoothly as possible.

There are times when a medical leave is recommended and the student does not want to take one. In such cases, administrators have to assess whether the student poses a threat to self or others by not taking a leave. Some institutions have implemented involuntary leave policies to manage these types of situations. Involuntary leave policies are controversial in higher education, mainly because there are concerns that institutions may use them in a discriminatory way to remove students with mental health issues. Because of the concerns about potential discrimination, some schools prefer to use summary or interim suspension policies for removing troubled students from campus, basing the intervention decision on the student's behavior only. Disability laws, such as the American with Disabilities Act (ADA) and Section 504 of the Rehabilitation Act of 1973, protect students from discrimination based on real or perceived disabilities, including mental health disabilities. These laws apply to all entities that receive federal funds, including most institutions of higher education. The Office of Civil Rights (OCR), the U.S. Department of Education agency charged with overseeing disability laws and investigating any claims of discrimination, has provided very specific guidance to institutions of higher education for implementation of involuntary withdrawals (OCR, 2005). The OCR has specified that involuntary leaves must include sufficient and documented due process that demonstrates that a direct threat assessment was done.

Dunkle and his colleagues (2008, 2009) discuss this issue more fully, and it is recommended that administrators learn what leave policies are in place on their campuses so that they can be accessed when appropriate.

Treatment and Prevention Issues

Access to adequate and appropriate medical and mental health services is crucial for all students. Many colleges and universities offer some form of these services on campus, including primary care, counseling center, and various prevention services. For those that offer on-campus services, the programs are usually funded by student health fees or fee-for-service and are often limited. Liaison relationships between health and wellness departments and the departments of athletics and recreation may enhance ongoing communication and consultation, prevention efforts, and referral opportunities. Use of mental health and health promotion and wellness professionals, and other community and university resources can be beneficial in providing regular workshops on a variety of topics, including, for example, support groups for injured student-athletes. These resources could also provide education to staff about mental health and wellness concerns, thereby enhancing staff capacity to identify, intervene, and refer. Student team leaders could also be identified and trained to provide peer education and assistance.

Not all institutions, however, have the resources to offer on-campus services, and must rely on off-campus providers instead. Furthermore, student health care needs may call for an off-campus specialist, such as an orthopedic surgeon. When students need to use off-campus services, health insurance coverage becomes a key issue. Insurance plans vary widely in terms of benefits. In February 2009, representatives from college student health, student affairs, and other health care experts met to form a nonpartisan study group, called the Lookout Mountain Group (LMG). The group's main goal was to review the impact of health care reform on the college student population. Significant concern was expressed regarding the large number of uninsured and underinsured college students. Although there are no data available on total number of uninsured college students, estimates from the LMG project the number to be between 2.8 to 3.3 million students out of a current total population of about 17 million (LMG, 2009).

These frightening projections have major implications for a significant number of students being able to access health care. For students involved in athletics and recreation programs, the potential for injuries is always present, and not having health insurance coverage could pose major financial burdens for a family. Coverage for mental health services is another specific concern, as there is not always parity in benefits between physical and mental health issues. Many colleges and universities require students to either purchase a university health insurance option or to present evidence that they have comparable coverage from another plan (for example, parental insurance plans). The bottom line for administrators and for students is to know specifically what the plan covers and what options are available when the student is uninsured or underinsured.

Conclusion

Participation in intercollegiate athletics or in college recreation programs offers potential benefits in terms of both physical and mental health, but such participation also presents potential challenges in both arenas. As a matter of both institutional and professional responsibility, administrators in athletics or recreation on college campuses ought to be aware of these benefits and challenges and ought to develop and assess their programs and the participants in them accordingly. Successfully doing so will likely require close collaboration with trainers, physicians, and mental health professionals among others. Failure to do so may result in diminished outcomes and damaged bodies and minds.

Chapter Eighteen Key Points

1. All college students require life balance and overall wellness to achieve at the peak of their potential (Dunkle and Presley, 2009). Participation in athletics or recreation activities can positively influence health, mental well-being, and learning.
2. Overtraining syndrome is a true medical condition that may lead to excessive fatigue and greater than six to twelve illnesses in a given year where no other explanation is apparent (Mackinnon, 2000). All students participating in sports need to be educated on proper diet, hygiene, recovery, and sleep habits in an attempt to minimize this risk.
3. Student health centers, athletics departments, and university administrators should work collaboratively to develop educational initiatives in an effort to prevent spread of [infectious] diseases.

4. Medical staff must address several issues with an student-athlete who is injured. First, the staff must determine what will be required to return safely to participate. Any injured student-athlete should be monitored for mental health issues that could potentially arise.
5. Student-athletes are at risk for developing depressive symptoms when participation does not have a buffering influence that is common for students who participate in athletics and recreation programs. For example, an adverse change in the relationship with one's sport may result in or exacerbate depressive feelings.
6. According to the ACHA-NCHA II survey data, 76% of all students and 82% of student-athletes reported feeling overwhelmed in the prior 12 months. For many student-athletes, their athletics commitment restricts the opportunity to prepare for class or exams, often leading to stress and anxiety.
7. Student-athletes' bodies are their instruments, and the desire for increasing control over their instrument—and therefore their performance—may lead to body image distortions, eating disordered behaviors, or both.
8. There is evidence that students involved in athletics in high school or college may abuse alcohol more and engage in more risk taking behaviors than students who have never been involved in athletics (Hildebrand et al., 2001).
9. The prevalence of gambling on campus has been thoroughly documented, including the impact of sports wagering (Rockey and King, 2006) and the growth in Internet gambling (Brown, 2006). Student-athletes may be particularly susceptible to the pull of gambling, as they must attempt to fill the void left after the rush of a big game, at the end of a season, or at the end of a career.
10. Among the legal and ethical issues related to health and wellness that may have an impact on the professional administration of intercollegiate athletics or campus recreation are privacy and confidentiality, student behavior indicative of a threat to self or others, leave policies and fitness to participate, and treatment and prevention issues.

References

American College Health Association. *American College Health Association–National College Health Assessment II: Reference Group Data Report Spring 2010*. Linthicum, MD: American College Health Association; 2010.

Bailey, R. "Physical Education and Sport in Schools: A Review of Benefits and Outcomes." *Journal of School Health*, 2006, 76(8), 393–397.

Brown, S. J. "The Surge in Online Gambling on College Campuses." In G. S. McClellan, T. W. Hardy, and J. Creswell (Eds.), *Gambling on Campus*. New Directions for Student Services, no. 113. San Francisco: Jossey-Bass, 2006.

Centers for Disease Control. *Physical Activity and Health: A Report of the Surgeon General*, 2008. Washington, D.C.: CDC.

Craft, L. L., and Landers D. M. "The Effect of Exercise on Clinical Depression and Depression Resulting from Mental Illness: A Meta-Analysis." *Journal Sport and Exercise Psychology*, 1998, 20, 339–346.

Crandall C. S. "Social Contagion of Binge Eating." *Journal of Personality and Social Psychology*, 1988, 55(4), 588–598.

Deisinger, G., Randazzo, M., O'Neill, D., and Savage, J. *The Handbook for Campus Threat Assessment and Management Teams*. Stoneham, MA: Applied Risk Management, 2008.

Dunkle, J. H., and Presley, C. A. "Helping Students with Health and Wellness Issues." In G. S. McClellan and J. Stringer (Eds.), *The Handbook of Student Affairs Administration* (3rd ed.). San Francisco: Jossey-Bass, 2009.

Dunkle, J. H., Silverstein, Z. B., and Warner, S. L. "Managing Violent and Other Troubling Students: The Role of Threat Assessment Teams on Campus." *The Journal of College and University Law*, 2008, 34(3), 586–635.

Dunn, A. L., and Jewell, J. S. "The Effects of Exercise on Mental Health." *Current Sports Medicine Reports*, 2010, 9(4), 202–207.

Eichner, E. R., "Infection, Immunity, and Exercise: What to Tell Your Patients." *Physician Sports Medicine*, 1993, 21, 125.

Gallagher, R. P. *National Survey of Counseling Center Directors 2010*. Alexandria, VA: The International Association of Counseling Services, 2010.

Greenleaf, C., Petrie, T.A., Reel, J., and Carter, J. "Psychosocial Risk Factors of Bulimic Symptomatology Among Female Athletes." *Journal of Clinical Sport Psychology*, 4(3), 2010, 177–190.

Harper, S. A., and colleagues. "Seasonal Influenza in Adults and Children: Diagnosis, Treatment, Chemoprophylaxis, and Institutional Outbreak Management: Clinical Practice Guidelines of the Infectious Diseases Society of America." *Clinical Infectious Diseases*, 2009, 48, 1003–1032.

Hildebrand, K. M., Johnson, D. J., and Bogle, K. "Comparison of Patterns of Alcohol Use Between High School and College Athletes and Non-Athletes." *College Student Journal*, 2001, 35(3), 358–365.

Hosey, R. G., and Rodenberg, R. E. "Infectious Disease and the Collegiate Athlete." *Clinical Sports Medicine*, 2007, 26, 449–471.

Kimmel, M. *Guyland*. New York: Harper Collins, 2008.

Kurowski, K., and Chandran, S. "The Pre-participation Athletic Evaluation." *American Family Physician*, 2000, 61, 2683–2690.

Landers, D. M. "The Influence of Exercise on Mental Health." *Research Digest of the President's Council on Physical Fitness and Sports*, Series 2, No. 12, 2007.

Lookout Mountain Group. Analysis and Policy Recommendations for Providing Health Insurance and Health Care Services for the College Student Population, 2009. Accessed May 14, 2011 at http://www.hbc-slba.com/LMG/LMG_abstract_3.5.pdf.

Mackinnon L. "Chronic Exercise Training Effects on Immune Function." *Medicine & Science in Sports and Exercise*, 2000, 32(7), S369–S376.

Marsh, H. W., and Kleitman, S. "School Athletic Participation: Mostly Gain with Little Pain." *Journal of Sport and Exercise Psychology*, 2003, 25(3), 228–233.

McKindra, L. "Secretary of Education Duncan Urges Student-Athlete Balance.," 2010. Accessed May 14, 2011 at http://www.ncaa.org/wps/portal/ncaahome?WCM_GLOBAL_CONTEXT=/ncaa/ncaa/ncaa+news/ncaa+news+online/2010/association-wide/secretary+of+education+duncan+urges+student-athlete+balance.

Nieman, D. C., and Nehlsen-Cannarella, S. L. "Exercise and Infection." In R. R. Watson and M. Eisinger (Eds.), *Exercise and Disease*. Boca Raton, FL: CRC Press, 1992.

Office of Civil Rights. "Letter to Guilford College." U. S. Department of Education. OCR Complaint 11–02–2003. 2005.

Pope, C. G., Pope, H. G., Menard, W., and Fay, C. "Clinical Features of Muscle Dysmorphia Among Males with Body Dysmorphic Disorder." *Body Image*, 2005, 2(4), 395–400.

Proctor, S. L., and Boan-Lenzo, C. "Prevalence of Depressive Symptoms in Male Intercollegiate Student-Athletes and Nonathletes." *Journal of Clinical Sport Psychology*, 2010, 4(3), 204–220.

Rockey, D. L., and King, C. "Sports Wagering." In G. S. McClellan, T. W. Hardy, and J. Creswell (Eds.), *Gambling on Campus*. New Directions for Student Services, no. 113. San Francisco: Jossey-Bass, 2006.

Serrao H. S., Martens M. P., Martin, J. L., and Rocha, T. L. "Competitiveness and Alcohol Use Among Recreational and Elite Collegiate Athletes." *Journal of Clinical Sport Psychology*, 2010, 2(3), 205–215.

Shor, D. A. "Student-Athletes and the AISP Model: Further Applications and Consultations." In J. H. Dunkle (Ed.), *Dealing with the Behavioral and Psychological Problems of Students: A Contemporary Update*. New Directions for Student Services, no. 128. San Francisco: Jossey-Bass, January, 2010.

Sweeney, T. J., and Witmer, J. M. "Beyond Social Interest: Striving Toward Optimum Health and Wellness." *Individual Psychology*, 1991, 47(4), 527–540.

Taylor, J., and Taylor, S. *Psychological Approaches to Sports Injury Rehabilitation*. Gaithersburg, MD: Aspen Publishers. 1997.

Van Raalte, J. L., Cornelius, A. E., Linder, D. E. and Brewer, B. W. "The Relationship Between Hazing and Team Cohesion." *Journal of Sport Behavior*, 2007, 30(4), 503–507.

Virginia Tech Review Panel Report. "Mass Shootings at Virginia Tech: Report of the Review Panel." Virginia: Office of the Governor of the Commonwealth of Virginia, 2007. Accessed May 14, 2011 at http://www.governor.virginia.gov/tempcontent/techpanelreport.cfm.

Yeager, K. K., Agostini, R., Nattiv, A., and Drinkwater, B. "The Female Athlete Triad: Disordered Eating, Amenorrhea, and Osteoporosis." *Medicine & Science in Sports & Exercise*, 1993, 25(7), 775–777.

CHAPTER NINETEEN

PROFESSIONAL DEVELOPMENT AND ADVANCEMENT

Chris King and David P. Synowka

Two decades ago a young student at Robert Morris College (now Robert Morris University) with a strong passion for the sports industry transferred into the college's sport management program. Although the student had a love for the field, he had little if any significant knowledge about it or skills with which to be involved in it. The curriculum, internships and volunteer opportunities, and faculty mentoring available through the program provided the first critical steps in the professional development of that student. Enrollment in graduate school was yet another step, as were beginning to serve in a series of professional positions and becoming involved in professional association activities. That student eventually advanced to the position of athletics director of a National Collegiate Athletic Association (NCAA) Division I institution and is one of the coauthors of this chapter. His coauthor, who has continued to provide mentorship to him in the intervening years, was one of the faculty members for that student at Robert Morris College.

Drawing on our experiences in athletics and academic administration in higher education, this chapter provides guidance, insights, and strategies for professional development in intercollegiate athletics and recreation administration from entry into an undergraduate program, through graduate school, and throughout all levels of a career.

Defining Professional Development and Brand

Professional development refers to skills and knowledge attained for both personal development and professional career advancement. Professional development encompasses all types of facilitated learning opportunities, including college degree programs, certificate programs, non-degree coursework, conferences, and informal learning opportunities situated in practice. There are a variety of other formal and informal pathways to professional development, including volunteering, mentoring, networking, involvement in professional associations, and life-long learning practices (Speck and Knipe, 2005).

Starting to Build Your Professional Brand

Professional development is an important activity in building a professional brand that helps assure success in searching for a job, building a career, building a lifelong personal and professional network, or fulfilling one's responsibilities to the students and institution they serve. An effective professional brand portrays a positive impression of the future or current intercollegiate athletics or campus recreation administrator to employers, students, or other contacts. It also allows one to differentiate and position oneself from the competition, whether for a professional position or a major donor.

Professional brand is built on one's reputation and the impression that one makes on others. The most important aspect of the brand is demonstration and practice of the values expectation of the professional recreation or sports manager. Values such as credibility, ethics, open-mindedness, honesty, empathy, responsibility, proactive approach, and self-control form the foundation of one's professional brand. Appearance, physical presence, personal style, public speaking skills, and interpersonal communication skills also contribute to professional brand.

The most obvious strategy for building a personal brand is to act in ways that will contribute to being perceived as an exemplary professional administrator. However, as with any brand, a good communication strategy can go a long way in promoting awareness. Maintaining an active professional network, developing an Internet presence, creating attractive and readily available business cards—are all examples of communication strategies that can be helpful in building one's professional brand.

Education and Professional Preparation

The successful university athletics or recreation administrator must have general knowledge and competencies related to the overall field. Earlier chapters have addressed a number of those general areas of knowledge and skill. In addition, professionals require technical knowledge and competencies specifically associated with the particular specialty are in which they practice. Completion of a professional degree program, either at the undergraduate or graduate level, is one way in which mastery of both the general and technical domains can be developed.

In comparing the professional preparation of the athletics management profession to the recreational area, there is a significant difference. With recreation, there is more of a broad base of activities and the technical expertise required with the delivery of services and product to the student consumer. With the athletics management professional, there is more of an emphasis on basic tasks of planning, organizing, control, marketing, and revenue generation related not only to an internal constituency but to a greater diversity of external constituencies environmental factors.

Selecting a Program

Many colleges and universities offer specialized academic degree programs such as exercise science and wellness, physical education, recreation, entertainment, and sport or hospitality-tourism management to provide a structured curriculum and related professional field practicum. The selection of an established quality academic program is important. Program criteria to be considered should include quality and depth of curriculum, number and qualifications of program faculty, number and quality of applied and engaged learning experiences, placement of students within the respective industry, success and support of alumni, and overall quality and environment of the university or college. The reputation of a university's program can lead to many opportunities with networking and placement.

A sport administration or recreation management degree program is specifically designed to prepare the future sports professional or recreation management student for working in higher education. The curriculum provides the necessary structure of college organizations and covers areas such as financial management, strategic planning, public relations, facility and operation management, and fundraising. The curriculum also includes building relationships with professionals in the college athletics world and practical experience with internships and volunteer opportunities.

Value of Professional Curriculum

The core concepts covered in recreational and sport academic programs include event management and activities programming, facility management, small group dynamics, legal issues and risk management strategies, basic budgeting, management and planning concepts, technology, special needs populations, marketing and communications strategies and techniques, and instruction of students about the basic skills and competencies associated with various recreational and sport activities. Additional educational value may be provided with a student's decision for an academic minor or a dual major such as in business, communications, education, or technology.

Engaged Learning Practices

Historically the academic preparation of recreation and sport professionals has incorporated field experiences, internships, and practicums to develop, reinforce, and support the affective, cognitive, and psychomotor aspects of learning. These experiences can be volunteer as well as part-time employment opportunities (Synowka, 1996).

Benefits of engaged learning experiences include the identification and development of a student's academic and professional abilities and skill sets such as creativity, leadership, interpersonal, and group communications. Such experiences also offer the opportunity to develop and enhance one's vita and portfolio. In addition, engaged learning experiences can be an opportunity for students to enrich their professional preparation through working with a diverse array of individuals in a variety of settings. This exposure assists students in their creative and problem solving abilities. Experiential learning experiences can also be venues through which students are introduced to a network of professionals. The creation of a lifelong personal and professional network within an industry helps students identify mentors and a collegial support system and is essential to career success. Table 19.1 illustrates the engaged recreation and sport learning opportunities available to students both inside and outside the campus.

Professional Associations

Students' educational preparation should include exposure to and integration of professional associations within the educational learning

TABLE 19.1. EXAMPLES OF ENGAGED LEARNING OPPORTUNITY SITES

Aquatic facilities and natatoriums	Intercollegiate athletics
Big Brothers and Sisters	Middle school and high school sports—coaches and referees
Boys and Girls Clubs of America	Racquet club facilities
Boy Scouts of America	Resorts
Campus recreation	Senior and retirement centers and communities
Community recreation	Special events—golf, 5K/10K races
Country, urban, and yacht clubs	Special Olympics
Cultural events	Veteran Administration Hospitals
Fundraising and development	YMCAs, YWCAs, Jewish community centers
Governing bodies	Youth Sports—Little League, Pop Warner Football
Greek (fraternity and sorority)	
Health and fitness clubs	
Hotel fitness centers	

environment. These are formal organizations established by volunteer industry professionals, related stakeholders, and faculty within a respective professional field or academic discipline (Chelladurai, 2006). The typical purposes of a professional association include

1. Promotion of a profession or discipline to the public at large
2. Establishment of professional educational objectives and curriculum for the preparation of future professionals (including establishing a formal accreditation process and review of higher education programs)
3. Testing or certification of individuals working in the designated professions to ensure the safety and welfare of the public and further upgrade its professional credibility
4. Establishment and promotion of a code of conduct or ethics to its membership
5. Creation and dissemination of new knowledge and skills through regional and national conferences, research symposia, publications such as periodicals and newsletters, and continuing education programs and requirements
6. Ongoing professional development opportunities
7. Development of relationships with external agencies and related organizations to benefit the profession

Most associations offer a student membership category, which is significantly discounted but will vary regarding benefits and privileges. This category helps socialize future professionals to the industry and ensures the particular association's future growth as an organization. Students should be encouraged to join and participate, as well as starting to network to learn about educational and professional career opportunities and standards. Student membership and involvement can lead to significant professional development opportunities such as contributing to the profession through education, research, and service, as well for one's own personal and career advancement.

Career Opportunities in Intercollegiate Athletics and Campus Recreation

Professional expectations and responsibilities have increased for intercollegiate athletics and campus recreation staff. Not surprisingly, specialization within campus recreation and athletics has also increased. Students in preparation programs may have an interest in or even a love of intercollegiate athletics or campus recreation, but they may not be fully familiar with the many professional roles in the field. Tables 19.2 and 19.3 offer

TABLE 19.2. POSITIONS IN INTERCOLLEGIATE ATHLETICS

Director of athletics	Facility coordinator
Senior woman administrator	Marketing and promotions coordinator
Assistant or associate athletic director	Video services coordinator
Business officer	Media relations director/sports information director
Academic advisor	Sports medicine director
Development officer	Strength and conditioning coach
Life skills coordinator	Equipment manager
Ticket operations officer	Head coach
Academic coordinator	Assistant coach
Compliance coordinator	Director of sport-specific operations
Event management coordinator	

TABLE 19.3. POSITIONS IN CAMPUS RECREATION

Dean of student affairs or student life	Head golf professional
Associate or assistant dean of student affairs or student life	Assistant golf professional
Director of intramurals	Pro shop/outside operations
Associate or assistant director of intramurals	Golf course superintendent
Fitness and wellness director	Assistant golf course superintendent
Facility coordinator/assistant	Food and beverage manager
Aquatics coordinator	Building supervisors, front desk assistants, intramural supervisors
Club sports director	Fitness consultants, group exercise instructors, fitness desk monitors
Coordinator, programs and events management	Program assistants
Coordinator, outdoor recreation	Lifeguards, swim lesson instructors, water aerobics instructors
General manager or director of golf	Ropes and climbing wall facilitators

a sample of professional positions in intercollegiate athletics and campus recreation.

Graduate Education

A key credential required for full-time employment or upward mobility in higher education for the sport and recreational professional is a graduate degree. There is a range of graduate degree areas in business, communications, education, law, recreation, sport, and technology. A quality graduate degree program allows the professional to acquire new skills and knowledge, as well as developing intellectual abilities such as research, analysis, and ideally the process of innovation or synthesis of new knowledge or practices within the area of professional practice. Finally, quality graduate programs provide professionals the opportunity to enlarge new personal and professional relationships with their career network.

Professional Development Outside a Preparation Program

Professional development can and should extend beyond the boundaries of a professional preparation program. The nature of the professional development opportunities that should be explored or pursued will vary depending upon at what point the individual professional is in their career. A professional development program for an entry level manager should be geared toward enhancing on-the-job training, which would include technical skills, team building skills, organizational and time management skills, and customer service skills. A professional development program for a middle level manager should be geared toward enhancing the management skills and abilities, which would include leadership, communication, budget management, and supervision. A professional development program for a top level manager should be geared toward enhancing and integrating all of their experiential skill sets into the operation and strategic functions of the designated organization unit.

Regardless of career status, professional development programs for working administrators can include a variety of strategies. The first and most obvious is increased breadth and complexity of responsibility at work.

Service activities can also serve as a pathway to professional development. Service can be provided internally to the organization by serving on committees and taskforces or by being advisor to a student organization. Internal service activities provide an opportunity to learn more about the

TABLE 19.4. EXAMPLES OF PROFESSIONAL ORGANIZATIONS IN INTERCOLLEGIATE ATHLETICS

Examples of Related Intercollegiate Athletic Professional Organizations	Web sites
1A Athletic Directors' Association	www.d-1a.com
American Baseball Coaches Association (ABCA)	www.abca.com
American Football Coaches Association (AFCA)	www.afca.com
American Volleyball Coaches Association (AVCA)	www.avca.org
Black Coaches Association (BCA)	www.bcasports.cstv .com
College Sports Information Directors of America (CoSIDA)	www.cosida.com
National Association of Basketball Coaches (NABC)	www.nabc.org
National Association of Intercollegiate Athletics (NAIA)	www.naia.cstv.com
National Association of Collegiate Directors of Athletics (NACDA)	www.nacda.com
National Association of Collegiate Women Administrators (NACWAA)	www.nacwaa.org
National Athletic Trainers Association (NATA)	www.nata.org
National Christian College Athletic Association (NCCAA)	www.thenccaa.org
National Collegiate Athletic Association (NCAA)	www.ncaa.org
National Fastpitch Coaches Association (NFCA)	www.nfca.org
National Junior College Athletic Association (NJCAA)	www.njcaa.org
National Soccer Coaches Association (NSCA)	www.nscaa.org
Women's Basketball Coaches Association (WBCA)	www.wbca.org

organization and developing new relationships that can complement and support the recreation or sport program focus.

External service can be to any community based organization or to a professional association, such as serving on a committee or as an officer. Examples of intercollegiate athletics organizations websites are outlined in Table 19.4, and Table 19.5 offers examples of campus recreation associations.

Another pathway to professional development for the campus recreation or sports professional can be through attending conferences or workshops. Here again, these may be specific to one's current role and responsibilities, or they may focus on knowledge or skills closely related to one's role and responsibilities. There can be great benefits to attending professional development programs away from campus, including gaining or refreshing knowledge or skill bases, networking, and identifying ideas for new services or programs. The fiscal challenges facing higher education have led many institutions to eliminate or restrict funding in support of professional travel. As a result, teleconferences and webinars are becoming

TABLE 19.5. EXAMPLES OF PROFESSIONAL ORGANIZATIONS IN CAMPUS RECREATION

Organization	Web sites
American Alliance for Health, Physical Education, Recreation and Dance	www.aahperd.org./
American College of Sports Medicine	www.acsm.org/
American Council on Exercise	www.ace.org/
Club Managers Association of America	www.cmaa.org/
National Intramural and Sports Association	www.nirsa.org/
National Recreation and Park Association	www.nrpa.org/
North American Society for Sport Management	www.nassm.org/
Resort and Commercial Recreation Association	www.rcra.org/
Professional Golfers Association of America	www.pga.com/

TABLE 19.6. EXAMPLES OF CAMPUS ATHLETICS AND RECREATION PERIODICALS

Athletic Business
Athletic Management
Club Industry.com
NCAA News
PGA Magazine
Recreation Management
Recreation Sports Journal
Resort and Recreation
Sports Business Journal
Training and Conditioning

increasingly common options. While not offering the same networking opportunities, they can be valuable and cost-effective.

Keeping current through reading is also a strategy for professional development. Administrators in intercollegiate athletics and recreation should read articles and books directly related to their professional field (see Table 19.6 for a partial list of such periodicals), but they should also review materials relating to other industries such as entertainment, sport, hospitality, and tourism, as well as on history and culture. A goal for any professional would be to learn three new concepts monthly from their reading and to apply or incorporate these into their personal lives or professional practice.

Additional resources exist on the university campus to help the professional development of athletics and campus recreation administrators. Departments such as institutional technology (IT), human resources, and student affairs can be valuable sources for professional development opportunities. IT often provides workshops and seminars that demonstrate and provide instruction on the newest technology. The human resource department offers information and instruction on current strategies regarding affirmative action, hiring, firing, and evaluation as well as changes in the law which deal with these issues. The student affairs department on campus can give information about dealing with students, trends of new generations of students, and financial support for travel for professional development.

Emerging Ideas in Professional Development

The administration of intercollegiate athletics and campus recreation continues to evolve as a field. Not surprisingly, professional development for those in the field is also changing. This section addresses a number of emerging ideas in professional development.

In today's society, professionals have learned to rely on emerging and new technology to perform their day-to-day duties and continue their professional development. Technological advances such as Blackberries and iPads permit professionals to keep up with daily operations whether in the office or on the road, including receiving voice mails, e-mails, daily tasks, and calendar record management. The new technology also has opened the door to online professional branding and networking. While the impact of these technological advances on the pace of life may be debatable, it is difficult to imagine that the future will hold anything other than an increasing array of computing and communication innovations. However, with 24/7 electronic worldwide communication, the need to ensure organizational image enhancement or protection requires a greater practice and vigilance of personal ethical behavior, along with appropriate professional, public relation response strategies with crisis management.

Search consulting firms (headhunters) have long been a part of job searches to fill senior academic and administrative positions in higher education. More recently, the use of such firms in searches for athletics directors and head coaches has become more commonplace. Searches led by search firms remain highly confidential, which with today's media, is important for potential sitting athletics directors and head coaches under contract with an institution. With today's budgets and high dollars within intercollegiate athletics, in particular with football and men's basketball, presidents and athletic directors prefer to use the search firms to cultivate candidates and assist when interviewing head coaches making seven figure salaries with star power. Search firms also assist in the evaluation process and for academic, compliance, and personal and criminal background checks.

With the explosion of revenue within intercollegiate athletics at large Division I institutions, presidents are hiring CEO-type athletics directors and institutions are hiring professional advisory services to provide expertise in the areas of strategic planning and professional development programs. Professional advisory services are designed to provide athletics executives and management teams with professional conduct skills, such as strategic planning, personal branding, meeting skills, communication skills, and even dining and business etiquette skills.

Multimedia and marketing rights have become a big business within intercollegiate athletics, and a majority of major Division I intercollegiate athletics departments outsource the multimedia rights combining sales, public relations, Internet, television, and radio rights to an outside company. This emerging trend has provided additional volunteer and internship opportunities to students who seek to work in intercollegiate athletics, and has led to cross training in both the corporate and higher education fields, including numerous professionals becoming athletics directors directly from the corporate world.

Conclusion

Professional development practices in today's world of intercollegiate athletics and campus recreation include education, real life experiences, networking, and branding. Professional development is a priority for all members of our profession. In our experiences, professional development has defined our careers as students, learners, managers, and leaders in the sport industry. Professional development—it's a marathon, not a sprint.

Chapter Nineteen Key Points

1. Professional development refers to skills and knowledge attained for both personal development and professional career advancement. Professional development encompasses all types of facilitated learning opportunities, including college degree programs, certificate programs, non-degree coursework, conferences, and informal learning

opportunities situated in practice. There are a variety of other formal and informal pathways to professional development, including volunteering, mentoring, networking, involvement in professional associations, and life-long learning practices (Speck and Knipe, 2005).

2. An effective professional brand portrays a positive impression of the future or current intercollegiate athletics or campus recreation administrator to employers, students, and other contacts. Professional brand is built on one's reputation and the impression that one makes on others. The most important aspect of the brand is demonstration and practice of the values expectation of the professional recreation or sports manager.
3. The successful university athletics or recreation administrator must have general knowledge and competencies related to the overall field. In addition, professionals require technical knowledge and competencies specifically associated with the particular specialty in which they practice. Completion of a professional degree program, either at the undergraduate or graduate level, is one way in which mastery of both the general and technical domains can be developed.
4. Students' educational preparation should include exposure to and integration of professional associations within the educational learning environment. These are formal organizations established by volunteer industry professionals, related stakeholders, and faculty within a respective professional field or academic discipline (Chelladurai, 2006).
5. Professional development can and should extend beyond the boundaries of a professional preparation program. Strategies include increased breadth and complexity of responsibility at work, service activities, attending conferences and workshops, and keeping current in the profession through reading.

References

Chelladurai, P, *Human Resource Management in Sport and Recreation* (2nd ed.). Human Kinetics, 2006.

Speck, M., and Knipe, C. *Why Can't We Get It Right? Designing High-Quality Professional Development for Standards-Based Schools* (2nd ed.). Thousand Oaks, CA: Corwin Press, 2005.

Synowka, D. "Develop a Nuts and Bolts Strategy: A Blueprint for Building Your Career." *Sports Careers: The Insider,* March 15, 1996.

CHAPTER TWENTY

SUMMING UP AND LOOKING AHEAD

George S. McClellan, Donald L. Rockey, Jr., and Chris King

The preceding chapters have provided a thorough overview of intercollegiate athletics and recreation from their earliest days in American higher education to their contemporary practice. In doing so, the contributing authors have addressed the foundational framework, essential skills, and important challenges that inform the work of professional administrators serving in campus recreation and college athletics. This concluding chapter serves to highlight themes that occur throughout the earlier chapters. It also presents thoughts on what the future holds for athletics and recreation programs on college campuses and for those who lead them.

Themes

Despite the wide array of topics discussed, there are a number of common themes that emerge throughout the earlier chapters. This section identifies and discusses several of those themes.

Mission

The importance of institutional and departmental missions to an intercollegiate athletics or campus recreation department has been stressed in a variety of ways by the contributing authors. First and foremost, the very existence of such departments and their charge and placement within the institution are, or at least ought to be, a function of the institutional mission. The institutional mission also helps shape campus culture, which in turn plays out in significant ways in recreation and athletics programs on campus. For those institutions with an athletics program, the university mission informs the athletics association affiliation (if any) for that program.

Professional administrators in intercollegiate athletics and campus recreation should assure that staff members in their departments understand the institutional mission statement and how their work contributes to the pursuit of that mission. These administrators must also assure that the mission statement for their program is consistent with the institutional statement. Just as the institution's strategic plan should flow from its mission, the department's plan should flow from its mission. The facilities and events hosted in them, programs, and services of intercollegiate athletics and campus recreation programs must also be consistent with and contribute to the department and institutional strategic plans and mission. Therefore, it is also important to understand that the budget for the department is one of the most important tools for advancing its strategic plan and mission.

Importance

Intercollegiate athletics and campus recreation programs can play an important role in the success of an institution. The extent to which programs fulfill this opportunity rests largely on the degree to which the facilities, programs, and services offered through campus athletics and recreation are aligned with institutional mission.

First and foremost, recreation and athletics can and should be centers of learning on a college campus. Student employees have the opportunity to acquire general knowledge regarding the world of work, and some may learn about a field that may (or may not) become their future profession. Student-athletes can learn about the sport in which they participate, leadership, diversity, teamwork, ethics, responsibility, and philanthropy. Student, staff, faculty, and community participants in programs and services learn about exercise and recreation, teamwork (for those in intramurals or club sports), and the benefits of and strategies for a healthy lifestyle. The administrative, clerical, technical, and coaching staff can learn about student development, problem solving, diversity, teamwork, leadership, and a host of other work-related skills.

Campus recreation and intercollegiate athletics programs are also important to the sense of community on campus. They serve as centers of activity in which students, staff, faculty, alumni, and members of the local community participate together. Similarly, they provide a focal point for common interest and celebration.

These programs also play a significant role in shaping public awareness and perceptions of the college or university. Rightly or wrongly, the public sees the presence of intercollegiate athletics and campus recreations departments, like campus housing, as part of what defines quality in a university. The success of an athletics program, particularly on a national stage, can have a halo effect that extends across the institution, and an active recreation program with recently built, attractive, state-of-the-art facilities can be viewed as evidence of an institution on the move.

Given their potential impact on learning, community, and image, it is not surprising that another reason campus athletics and recreation programs are important is their potential impact on the ability of the institution to recruit students, student-athletes, and staff and faculty. Similarly, these programs can play a critical role in the friend-making and fundraising activities of a college or university.

Diversity

Intercollegiate athletics and campus recreation programs reflect the increasing diversity in higher education. Given their potential as centers of learning and community, these programs can play a pivotal role in an institution's response to the challenges and opportunities that diversity across a variety of dimensions presents. Facilities design, services and programs, and staffing decisions can all be arenas in which these opportunities and challenges play out. Professional administrators in intercollegiate athletics and campus recreation play an essential role in the extent to which their departments are just, inclusive, and multicultural places in which to work, learn, and play.

Complexity

If nothing else, the preceding chapters provide ample evidence of the complexity of campus recreation and college athletics administration. Professionals in the field are responsible for facilities, programs, and services that involve or are impacted by bodies of theory, ethical considerations, legal issues, governance structures, human resources administration, budgets, event management, development activities, marketing, political actors and actions, and contemporary issues. All of this while trying to steer their way through a professional development pathway that advances them toward their career goals.

People and Relationships

The final clear and strong theme throughout this book is that, when all else is said and done, the success of professional administrators in intercollegiate athletics and recreation rests on their ability to interact with others and to develop and sustain meaningful relationships with them. Professionals interact with students, staff, faculty, and alumni of the institution. They also interact with community members and other friends of the university. Professionals engage with the student employees and other staff in their departments, as well as with professional colleagues outside the institution. These administrators are also involved with people in various governance roles and the media. The relationships they build with this broad range of individuals are critically important, and they rest on the perceived integrity of the professional administrator, the respect in which they are held, and the sense of trust that others have for them.

Looking Ahead

Having identified and discussed some of the themes from the earlier chapters as a way of summing up the discussion to this point, it is time to turn attention to the future. This section presents thoughts on some of what lies ahead for those involved in the administration of campus recreation and college athletics.

Fiscal Environment

The recession in 2009 had a severe impact on higher education (Barr and McClellan, 2011), and intercollegiate athletics and college recreation programs were not spared from the financial strains. Looking ahead, it is reasonable to assume that finances in higher education will continue to be severely constrained (Schuh, 2009). Institutions will face difficult decisions regarding the allocation of resources from state allocations, tuition and fees, and other sources—all while probably continuing to experience significant increases in expenses, particularly in the areas of salaries for coaches and athletics directors in large Division I programs, benefits, energy and utilities, and maintenance and renovation of aged and aging facilities (Barr and McClellan, 2011).

Professional administrators will need to be skillful in developing and managing the budgets for their departments. They will also need to be innovative in identifying opportunities to enhance revenues from sources other than state appropriations or student fees. The wise administrator will work with their staff and other constituencies to develop a keen sense of the difference between wants and needs, as the reduction or elimination of growth in expenses will also be required.

Importance

As noted in the opening chapters of this book, there has been critical discussion regarding the appropriate role, if any, of athletics and recreation on college campuses since the earliest days of both. Those discussions have continued throughout the history of higher education, but they have resurfaced with vigor in the past decade or so (see for example Sperber, 2000; Yost, 2009). At the same time, and for some of the same reasons, various public constituencies are beginning to question the value (or at least the cost-benefit ratio) of higher education.

It will be increasingly vital moving forward that administrators in intercollegiate athletics and campus recreation are able to articulate the importance of their services and programs to the mission of the institutions, particularly to the success of students. Particularly promising are arguments that highlight the linkage between learning, community, and healthy lifestyles, as all three continue to be valued by the constituencies of higher education.

Assessment and Accountability

It will not be enough for professionals in campus recreation and intercollegiate athletics to simply assert that their services and programs make an important contribution to the mission and goals of their institution. They will need to provide evidence to support their claims. In other words, administrators in intercollegiate athletics and recreation must articulate measurable learning, efficiency, and satisfaction outcomes (Bresciani, 2009) that are linked to institutional mission and then must develop and maintain an active, ongoing, and thorough program of assessment in order to assure that programs and services are contributing to progress toward those outcomes.

In addition to helping make the case for the value of programs and services, an active and ongoing assessment program is an essential element in meeting the obligation of accountability to those who provide resources to support those programs and services. Public officials, philanthropic entities, individual donors, granting agencies, and contract partners all have expectations of higher education, including college athletics and recreation programs. Administrators have an ethical, legal, and professional responsibility to assure that the programs and services of their department are responsive to those expectations, and to be proactive and transparent in demonstrating accountability for their responsibilities and the resources vested in their control.

Law

The legal framework of professional practice in campus recreation and intercollegiate athletics will continue to evolve moving forward. Administrators will need to be fully informed about changes in law affecting the facilities, services, and programs of their department.

There are a number of areas of the law that will warrant careful attention. Among them are the evolving interpretations related to meeting the requirements of the Americans with Disabilities Act (1990), particularly as it relates to equal access to video and other electronic materials. The changes, which among other things require the closed captioning of such materials, will have an impact on athletics and recreation alike.

Another likely focus of changes in law will be related to issues of the rights of gay, lesbian, bisexual, and transgendered individuals. There has already been a good deal of movement on these issues at both the state and federal levels, but the law is far from settled. Future developments related to marriage or civil unions will affect eligibility for staff benefits and for family memberships in recreation programs. Eligibility for recreation programs and athletics competitions that are gender-based is also in play.

The rights of student-athletes relative to control of the use of their image also constitute an area of evolving case law. The growth in computer-mediated forms of communication and in the popularity of video games is likely to continue to fuel litigation.

Risk Management

Risk management is already an important issue in athletics and recreation on college campuses. It affects these departments in a variety of ways, including design and implementation of programs and services, event management, travel, facilities design and management, budgeting, and staffing.

Looking ahead, there are a number of continuing or emerging trends in risk management that will require attention from professional administrators in intercollegiate athletics and recreation. First, expectations of the public, legislative bodies, and the judiciary regarding foreseeability and prevention of accidental injuries or death are on the rise. Second, juries and judges have increasingly demonstrated a willingness to award substantial punitive damages in liability cases. Third, as a result of the first two trends, the cost of liability insurance for athletics and recreation departments is ever increasing. In addition to the rising cost of liability insurance related to routine events in the course of doing business, some institutions are recognizing the need to add coverage for catastrophic events that will help fund facilities renovation or replacement, make up lost revenues from games or events that have to be rescheduled, relocated, or canceled, and cover costs related to returning to normal operations.

Diversity

As noted earlier, legal changes related to issues of sexual orientation, gender identity, and varying ability constitute one of the ways in which issues of diversity will continue to play out in campus recreation and athletics programs in the future. The growing enrollment of Hispanic students in higher education (Santiago and Brown, 2004), as well as the growing disparity in completion rates for men, particularly men from some underrepresented groups or men who are first generation students (Bensimon, 2005), will require attention from professionals in intercollegiate athletics and campus recreation. Disparities in salaries for women administrators and coaches, as well as in the number of women and members of historically underrepresented groups in administrative and coaching positions, are both also likely to be the subject of scrutiny in the years ahead.

Health Issues

The misuse of alcohol and its negative impact on the lives of students have been a part of higher education since its earliest days and continue to this day. More recently, the misuse of drugs, including performance enhancing and prescription drugs, have become an unfortunate part of society and of campus life. In addition, the problems of obesity and lack of physical fitness are well-documented and growing (Dunkle and Presley, 2009). Among the reasons for increasing rates of obesity and lack of fitness may be the increasingly hectic pace of daily life and the stresses associated with that pace. Intercollegiate athletics and campus recreation programs are uniquely positioned to play an important leadership role in the future on these and other public health issues.

Conclusion

Campus recreation and college athletics are challenging, important, and rewarding areas in which to serve as an administrator. Both the level of responsibility and the pace of change are daunting, but they are not insurmountable. Professionals who enter the field well-prepared as a result of their education and experiences are positioned to provide the leadership necessary to help assure the success of their departments, their institutions, their students, and themselves. In the course of pursuing such success, administrators can be guided through the white water of change (Vaill, 1996) by the stable and sustaining framework of history, theory, ethics, and professionalism.

References

Americans with Disabilities Act, 42 U.S.C.S. §12101, et seq. (1990).

Barr, M. J., and McClellan, G. S. *Budgets and Financial Management in Higher Education.* San Francisco: Jossey-Bass, 2011.

Bensimon, E. M. "Closing the Achievement Gap in Higher Education: An Organizational Learning Perspective." In A. J. Kezar (Ed.), *Organizational Learning in Higher Education.* New Directions for Higher Education, No. 131, 2005.

Bresciani, M. J. "Implementing Assessment to Improve Student Learning and Development." In G. S. McClellan and J. Stringer (Eds.), *The Handbook of Student Affairs Administration* (3rd ed.). San Francisco: Jossey-Bass, 2009.

Dunkle, J. H., and Presley, C. A. "Helping Students with Health and Wellness Issues." In G. S. McClellan and J. Stringer (Eds.), *The Handbook of Student Affairs Administration* (3rd ed.). San Francisco: Jossey-Bass, 2009.

Santiago, D. A., and Brown, S. *Federal Policy and Latinos in Higher Education.* Washington D.C.: Pew Charitable Trust, 2004.

Schuh, J. H. "Fiscal Pressures on Higher Education and Student Affairs." In G. S. McClellan and J. Stringer (Eds.), *The Handbook of Student Affairs Administration* (3rd ed.). San Francisco: Jossey-Bass, 2009.

Sperber, M. *Beer and Circus: How Big-Time College Sports Is Crippling Undergraduate Education.* New York: Henry Holt, 2000.

Vaill, P. *Learning as a Way of Being: Strategies for Survival in a World of Permanent White Water.* San Francisco: Jossey-Bass, 1996.

Yost, M. *Varsity Green.* Stanford, CA: Stanford Economics and Finance, 2009.

APPENDIX

RESOURCES FOR LEADERSHIP, MANAGEMENT, AND SUPERVISION OF STAFF AND VOLUNTEERS

Ayman, R., Chemers, M. M., and Fiedler, F. "The Contingency Model of Leadership Effectiveness: Its Levels of Analysis." In R. P. Vecchio (Ed.), *Leadership: Understanding the Dynamics of Power and Influence in Organizations.* Notre Dame, IN: University of Notre Dame Press, 1997

Cassidy, C., and Kreitner, B. *Supervising: Setting People Up for Success.* Mason, OH: South-Western Cengage Learning, 2010.

Hersey, P., Blanchard, K. H., and Johnson, D. E. *Management of Organizational Behavior: Utilizing Human Resource* (8th ed.). Upper Saddle River, NJ: Prentice-Hall, 2001.

Horine, L., and Stotlar, D. (2004). *Administration of Physical Education and Sport Programs* (5th ed.). Boston: McGraw-Hill, 2004.

House, R. J., and Mitchell, T. R. (1997). "Path-Goal Theory of Leadership." In R. P. Vecchio (Ed.), *Leadership: Understanding the Dynamics of Power and Influence in Organizations.* Notre Dame, IN: University of Notre Dame Press, 1997.

Hurd, A. R., Barcelona, R. J., and Meldrum, J. T. *Leisure Services Management.* Champaign, IL: Human Kinetics, 2008.

Krotee, M. L., and Bucher, C. A. *Management of Physical Education and Sport.* Boston: McGraw-Hill, 2007.

Lussier, R. N., and Kimball, D. C. *Applied Sport Management Skills.* Champaign, IL: Human Kinetics, 2009.

NAME INDEX

SUBJECT INDEX

M

N